S0-BOG-215

THE

GERMAN PIETISTS

OF

PROVINCIAL PENNSYLVANIA

FRONTISPIECE.

THE ANCHORITE CELL OF KELPIUS.

NEGATIVE BY JULIUS F. SACHSE.

THE PIETISTS OF PROVINCIAL PENNSYLVANIA.

THE

German Pietists

OF

Provincial Pennsylvania

BY

JULIUS FRIEDRICH SACHSE

1694–1708.

AMS PRESS
NEW YORK

The Library of Congress cataloged this title as follows:

Sachse, Julius Friedrich, 1842-1919.
The German Pietists of provincial Pennsylvania, 1694-1708. [1st AMS ed.] New York, AMS Press [1970]
xviii, 504 p. illus., coats of arms, facsims., maps, ports. 23 cm.
Reprint of the 1895 ed.

1. Pennsylvania—History—Colonial period, ca. 1600-1775. 2. Pietism—Pennsylvania. 3. Pennsylvania Germans. I. Title.

F152.S12 1970 917.48'06'31 76-135723
ISBN 0-404-07204-6 MARC

Library of Congress 71[74]

Reprinted from the edition of 1895, Philadelphia
First AMS edition published in 1970
Second AMS printing: 1979

Manufactured in the United States of America

AMS PRESS, INC.
NEW YORK, N.Y.

PART I.

THE WOMAN IN THE WILDERNESS.

PART II.

THE HERMITS ON THE WISSAHICKON.

APPENDIX.

FOREWORD.

IN submitting this volume to the public, the writer ventures the opinion that it will prove an acceptable contribution to our local history. The annals of Pennsylvania and Philadelphia have for years past been conspicuous in the chronicles of the nation. There is, however, one particular in which they have been more or less deficient, viz., in the history of the early Germans who came to this country with the firm intent of founding a home in the new world for themselves and posterity, and who took so large a part in the formation of our great commonwealth.

The promise of liberty of conscience caused Pennsylvania, toward the close of the seventeeth century, to become the dream of the various religious sects and enthusiasts then arisen in Germany, and at variance with the established orthodox church of their special divisions of the Fatherland. They longed for the religious freedom offered them in the Province of Penn, and gave shape to their desire in an extended emigration from Germany, fostered, as it were, by Benjamin Furly, the agent of Penn at Rotterdam. Thus arose the peculiar religious condition of the Province, and the establishment of the many different sects in the early period of our history. Some of these congregations, founded upon the tenets of true religion, have maintained their autonomy, and exist even to the present day, having increased with the growth of the country. Others, again, whose foundation was not so stable, or whose system of congregational government proved unsuitable to the changed conditions resulting from an increasing population, exist now only in tradition and history.

Conspicuous among the latter class is the Community of German Pietists, or true Rosicrucian Mystics, who came in a body to these shores in the year of grace 1694, under the leadership of Magister Johannes Kelpius, in the firm belief that the millennium was near.

To this body of religious enthusiasts the present volume is devoted. The influence exercised by them, coming, as it did, at the critical period when the Quaker hierarchy was rent with internal dissension, was of the greatest importance; and to the efforts of individual members is due the honor of holding the first orthodox church services within the Province since it became Penn's domain.

It was through their efforts that the Church Party took heart, and, toward the close of the seventeenth century, perfected organizations which resulted in the establishment of congregations of the various Protestant denominations in Pennsylvania.

How their influence extended into neighboring colonies, and how one of their number was the first person to be ordained to the ministry in America for missionary purposes, is also shown in these pages. The text is amplified by several hundred foot-notes and illustrations. Where rare or unique books are quoted, a fac-simile of the title-page is given wherever possible. Another object has been to preserve every scrap of information bearing upon this interesting episode of Pennsylvania history. At the same time the greatest care has been taken to verify the old legends and traditions and trace them to an authentic source. The search for documentary information has been carried on over both continents, and no time or expense has been spared with pen, pencil and camera to make the volume exhaustive and complete.

Acknowledgements are due to Fredk. D. Stone, Litt. D., the learned librarian of the Historical Society of Pennsylvania, for advice and suggestions; to the Hon. Judge Samuel W. Pennypacker, of Philadelphia, for the use of rare books and documents in his library; to the Sesqui-Centennial Memorial Committee and the authorities of the Moravian Church at Bethlehem, for courtesies extended to the writer in his investigations; to the Reverend J. H. Sieker, pastor of St. Matthew's congregation in New York, for access to the old church records; to the Rev. Roswell Randall Hoes, for the use of his abstracts of S. P. G. Records; and also to Albert Edmunds and the many other friends, at home and abroad, who in various ways have assisted the writer.

JULIUS FRIEDRICH SACHSE.

Philadelphia, November, 1895.

LIST OF PLATES.

CONTENTS.

PART I.

PART II.

APPENDIX.

ILLUSTRATIONS.

D. O. M. A.

INTRODUCTION.

SEAL OF THE PROVINCE 1694.

NO subject of local history offers a greater field for study to the historical student, or is of greater interest to the general public than that of the so-called "Sect" people of provincial Pennsylvania.

By the term "Sect" people, as applied to early emigrants to this State, are to be understood such communities or bodies of German emigrants as left their native land for conscience sake, or were driven out by bigoted persecution, and who, either prior to their departure or shortly after their arrival in this country, for religious or social reasons formed distinct communities or congregations in the New World, keeping themselves distinct and separate from their dissenting countrymen as well as from their English-speaking neighbors.

These people on account of the adherence to their native tongue, unostentatious mode of life, frugality, and peculiar religious ceremonies,—devout and loyal as they were,—

D. O. M. A.—From title page of Theosophical manuscript; abbreviation of *Deo Optimo Maximo Altissimo*.

became from the start more or less objects of suspicion, and later on, after the influx of the more aggressive Irish element, were maligned, and no opportunity was let pass to injure or oppress them. This was especially the case after the outbreak of the French and Indian wars, as nearly all of the so-called "Sect" people of Pennsylvania were, like the original Friends or Quakers, what are known as non-combatants.

Their peaceful and domestic habits, their refusal to meddle with politics or the affairs of State, their tenacious adherence to their mother tongue, together with their subsequent success in nearly all their undertakings, both industrial and agricultural, all tended to excite the envy of their more intemperate and turbulent neighbors, and resulted in ridiculous charges of heresy being brought against some of these distinctive communities, when, as a matter of fact, they were composed of none but God-fearing men and women.

These calumnies have been repeated so often in print that they are now received as truth by the casual reader. It is this state of lamentable ignorance or misrepresentation by writers upon the subject, together with the persistent vilification by a certain class of New England writers, that has given to readers at a distance the impression that even the present generation of Pennsylvania-Germans of certain denominations are but a single remove from the animal creation.

Although all of the early "Sect" people of Pennsylvania were non-combatants, it is not for a moment to be understood that they were deficient in courage, as in cases where they submitted meekly to ruthless oppression it was not caused by any lack of manhood, but was merely putting into practice the religious teachings they professed.

It is a curious fact that the writer, in all of his travels throughout this State and in his historical researches, has yet to find the first specimen of firearms or murderous weapons brought over by the original German emigrant. Yet there is hardly any Pennsylvania-German family which cannot point with pardonable pride to the old German "Bible," "Catechismus," "Gesangbuch" or some devotional book (usually Arndt's "Wahres Christenthum"[1] and "Paradies Gärtlein") still in the possession of the family, and which formed the chief treasure of the original emigrant, as it proved his comfort in times of sorrow and

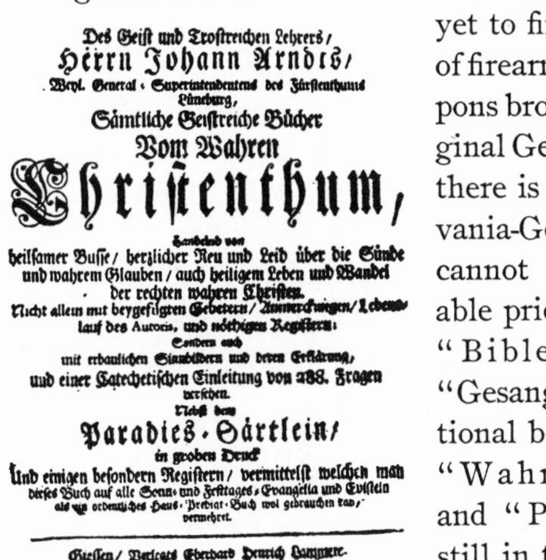

Des Geist und Trostreichen Lehrers /
Herrn Johann Arndts /
Weyl. General-Superintendentens des Fürstenthums Lüneburg,
Sämtliche Geistreiche Bücher
Vom Wahren
Christenthum,
Handelnd von
heilsamer Busse / herzlicher Reu und Leid über die Sünde und wahrem Glauben / auch heiligem Leben und Wandel der rechten wahren Christen.
Nicht allein mit beygefügten Gebetern / Anmerckungen / Lebens-lauf des Autoris, und nöthigen Registern:
Sondern auch
mit erbaulichen Sinnbildern und deren Erklärung,
und einer Catechetischen Einleitung von 288. Fragen
versehen.
Nebst dem
Paradies-Gärtlein /
in groben Druck
Und einigen besondern Registern / vermittelst welchen man dieses Buch auf alle Sonn- und Festtages-Evangelia und Episteln als ein ordentliches Haus-Predigt-Buch wol gebrauchen kan, vermehret.

Giessen / Verlegts Eberhard Henrich Lammers.
1749.

[1] Arndt's "Wahres Christenthum" was originally published in Germany in 1605, and was followed by many subsequent editions. This devotional book was held in great esteem by the early Germans, especially such as adhered to the Orthodox Lutheran faith; it was usually bound together with the "Paradies Gärtlein," making a volume of 1300 pages quarto. The titles reproduced are from the copy which was brought to this country by the ancestors of the writer. As all the various pietistical "Sects" in Pennsylvania took kindly to the writings of Arndt, whom they claimed as one of their members, the demand for the book became so great that Benjamin Franklin, together with Johann Böhm, in 1751, proposed to publish an American edition provided 500 subscribers could be obtained. The preface to this American edition was written by the Lutheran minister, Rev. J. A. Christoph Hartwig, and had the support of both Lutheran and Reformed Churches. This was the largest book printed in Philadelphia during the last century. It contained 32 pages of preface and 1356 pages of text, with 65 imported copper plates. This edition did not contain the "Paradies Gärtlein." Fourteen years later, in 1765, Christopher Saur, of Germantown, published the latter; it was a 16 mo. with 32 pages of preface, and 531 of devotional text and index. Both of these books are now extremely rare.

trial. Where relics of worldly handicraft still exist, precious heirlooms as they are, they are found to be implements of peaceful arts, such as were used in the farm economy or the domestic household.

The Mennonites were the first body of emigrants to come to these shores as a distinctive sect;[2] the original party consisted of thirteen families, who arrived at Germantown, October 6th, 1683.

The next distinctive community, a party of "Labadists" from Friesland, arrived in the fall of 1684, under the leadership of Petrus Sluyter and Jasper Dankers, who settled on a tract of land known as the "Bohemia Manor," a portion of which was in New Castle County, and then formed a part of Pennsylvania.[3]

Ten years later, June 24th, 1694, Kelpius and his chapter of Pietists or true Rosicrucians landed in Philadelphia, walked to Germantown, and finally settled on the rugged banks of the Wissahickon. It is to this community and their successors on the Cocalico the subsequent pages are mainly devoted.

Des Gottseligen
Herrn Johann Arndts/
Weyl. General-Superintendentens des Fürstenthums Lüneburg,
Anmutiges
Paradis-Gärtlein
voller
Christlichen Tugenden/
Solche
Durch andächtige und geistreiche Gebete
in die Seele zu pflantzen.
Deme die wunderbarsten Geschichte dieses Büchleins beygefüget.
Giessen/
Verlegts Eberhard Heinrich Lammers,

The year 1719 marks the advent of the Dunkers or Ger-

---

[2] For a full account of the early Mennonites and their settlement in Germantown, see the exhaustive papers upon the subject by Hon. Samuel W. Pennypacker, viz.—*Mennonite emigration to Pennsylvania*, "Penna. Magazine," vol. ii, pp. 117, et. seq. *The settlement of Germantown, Pa.*, "Penna. Magazine," vol. i, p. 1, et. seq.; also "Historical and Biographical Sketches," Philadelphia, 1883.

[3] The members were under the impression that they were wholly within the bounds of Penn's domain.

man Baptists;[4] twenty families arrived in Philadelphia in the fall of that year. Germantown also became their stronghold, whence emanated all the other congregations of the faith throughout the State.

The "Neu-geborenen," or the "Stillen im Lande,"[5] settled in the vicinity of Germantown about 1725.

The Ephrata Community, on the Cocalico, who were the virtual successors to the Mystics on the Wissahickon, dates from about the same period, and the names of the two leaders, Conrad Beissel (Father Friedsam Gottrecht) and the Rev. Peter Miller (Prior Jabetz) are well recognized in Pennsylvania history.

The Schwenkfelders arrived in Philadelphia from Berthelsdorf and Görlitz in the fall of 1734, and located in Philadelphia and Bucks Counties, where their descendants still religiously celebrate from year to year the anniversary ("Gedächtniss Tag") of their arrival.

The last and the most important body of German religious enthusiasts to come to this Province as a community was the Unitas Fratrum, or Moravian Church, also called the Moravian Brethren. Their first permanent settlement was made on the Lehigh, where Bethlehem now stands, in 1742, though a small colony had arrived in Pennsylvania in 1740, and their first evangelists as early as 1734.[6] Now their influence extends throughout the whole continent, from the

Seal of the Unitas Fratrum.

[4] See "Chronicon Ephretense." Translation by Rev. J. Max Hark, D. D., chapter i.

[5] See "Hallische Nachrichten," orig. edit. p. 226. New edition p. 348, annotations by Rev. J. W. Mann, ibid. p. 417.

frozen wilds of Alaska to the tropical glades of the West Indies. Wherever a mission station is needed there is to be found the Paschal Lamb and cross of the Moravian Church.[7]

The most interesting of these communities, by reason of the air of mystery which has thus far enshrouded their history, was the one led by Johannes Kelpius, the members of which were imbued with the highest religious and purest moral motives.

THAULERI "PREDIGTEN."

These people came to the colony, then in its earliest stages of development, for the purpose of permanently settling within its borders, and at the same time enjoy to

[6] The first Moravian evangelist in America, George Böhnisch, landed at Philadelphia, September 22d, 1734, having been sent by Zinzendorf with Christopher Baus and Christopher Wiegner to accompany the Schwenkfelder exiles to America; Böhnisch engaged in evangelistic activity for several years, and returned to Europe in 1737.

Spangenberg and Bishop David Nitschmann came to Pennsylvania in April, 1736, and labored for awhile among the Schwenkfelders and others, making Wiegner's house their home.

George Neisser arrived in Pennsylvania in February, 1737, from Georgia, and took up his abode temporarily at Wiegner's. So for awhile there were three of them in Pennsylvania, viz., Böhnisch, who returned to Europe, 1737; Spangenberg, who left for the time being in 1739, and Neisser; Nitschmann, the fourth, left in June, 1736, and returned in 1740.

Andrew Eschenbach, sent to the Pennsylvania-Germans by Zinzendorf at Whitfield's suggestion, arrived at Philadelphia in October, 1740.

Christian Henry Rauch and Frederick Martin (afterwards missionary bishop in the West Indies) were also in Pennsylvania before the end of 1740.

[7] A full and exhaustive history of the Moravian Congregation at Bethlehem is now in course of preparation by the Church authorities. This work is intended to be a Sesqui-Centennial Memorial of that Church in America. It will give a full and concise account of the early trials and struggles of the Moravian pioneers in America, whose chief object was to spread the gospel among all persons irrespective of creed, color or nationality.

the fullest extent the promised liberty of conscience and religious freedom.

Another cherished object was to put into practical operation the mystic and occult dogmas taught and studied in secret for many previous ages, looking not only to spiritual but also to physical regeneration and perfection. These dogmas, it was believed, also existed among the aborigines in this continent.

There has always been a veil of mystery about this community; numberless are the traditions which have been handed down from generation to generation; gruesome the tales current in Germantown and believed throughout the country. They have been repeated time and again during the long winter nights while sitting beside the flickering fireside until they have been accepted as facts. Weird were the tales recounted by the naturally superstitious population, of the occult rites and ceremonies which it is said were performed by the adepts, and their followers within the tyled portals of the tabernacle in the forest.

The object of the following pages will be to lift somewhat this veil of mystery which has so long shrouded the history and ceremonial of this community and to set aside the erroneous traditions, so as to place these Theosophical enthusiasts in their proper light before the enlightened community of the present day, now almost on the verge of the Twentieth Century.

Another aim will be to show how, with the decline of the first organization, the scene shifted from the Wissahickon to the Cocalico, at Ephrata, where the Mystic Theosophy Phœnix-like once again rose from its ashes. In that retired valley beside the flowing brook the secret rites and mysteries of the true Rosicrucian Philosophy flourished unmolested for years, until the state of affairs brought about by the American Revolution, together with pernicious Sunday legislation[8] which also discriminated against the keepers of the scriptural Sabbath day[9] gradually caused the incoming generation to assimilate with the secular congregations.

The information used in this narrative is mainly derived from original sources, manuscripts and books used by the different communities, now either in possession of the writer or to which he has had access, together with contemporaneous accounts sent to Europe by trustworthy persons, supplemented with extracts from manuscripts in the archives of the Moravian Church and elsewhere. Little or none of the matter in these pages has ever been published, and then only in a fragmentary form.

EPHRATA RELICS.

In addition to the above authorities, trustworthy traditions have been incorporated, some of which were related to the writer in his boyhood days.

The text has been embellished and amplified with illustrations and fac-simile reproductions of references and originals whenever obtainable. A number of these illustrations consist of the secret symbols of the Rosicrucians, copied direct from an ancient manuscript, an heirloom in the writer's family. It is similar to those used by the

[8] The Sunday law of 1794; for a full account of the causes which led to its passage see paper by J. F. Sachse in "The Outlook" for April, 1890,

[9] The seventh day, or Saturday.

Apocal. 1. 11. 22.

A & Ω

Rom. 11.

PHISICA, METAPHISICA, ET HYPERPHISICA.

D. O. M. A.

Deo Omnipotenti sit Laus, Honos, et Gloria in Seculorum Secula, Amen!

Einfältig A-B-C-Büchel, für junge Schüler, so sich fleissig üben in d. Schule des heiligen Geistes, ganz einfältig Bildnissweise für Augen gemahlet, zum Neuen Jahres Exercitio In dem natürlichen und theologischen LICHT.

TITLE-PAGE OF ROSICRUCIAN MSS. (Original in possession of writer.)

communities on the Wissahickon and on the banks of the Cocalico, and so far as is known, is the only perfect copy extant. The title of this literary treasure is here reproduced in reduced fac-simile, the original folio measuring 12 x 18 inches. The manuscript consists of thirty pages exquisitely written aud embellished with illuminated symbols.

The history of these people forms a most romantic episode in the history of the Commonwealth of Pennsylvania, and the influence they exerted in the early days of our development extends down even to the present time.

ARMS OF THE COMMONWEALTH, 1894.

RELICS OF THE GERMAN PIETISTS.

IN POSSESSION OF THE WRITER.

Deo Omnipotenti sit Laus, Honos, et Gloria in Seculorum Secula, Amen!

THE EXODUS FROM THE FATHERLAND.

ARMS OF THE GERMAN EMPIRE, A. D. 1694.

IT was just two centuries ago, on the thirteenth day of February, in the year of grace 1694 (O. S.), that a number of religious enthusiasts from various parts of the Fatherland embarked in a body on the good ship "Sarah Maria," at London, for a voyage over the trackless ocean to the Province of Penn,—a voyage undertaken not only at the inclement season of the year, and against the advice and counsel of relatives and friends at home, but in face of the war then being waged between European nations on the high seas, a source of danger almost greater than that of the elements.

Sad had been the parting from the loved ones in the Fatherland. The farewells then said were looked upon as the final parting in this world; family ties then severed, in most cases, were never to be re-united. These conditions were well recognized by the determined band of pilgrims.

Deo Omnipotenti, etc. From title page of Theosophical Manuscript: "Unto Almighty God be praise, honor and glory for ever and ever. Amen."

Even the loss of their leader at the very outset of their departure from Holland failed to turn them from their avowed purpose of entering upon a pilgrimage to the unknown wilds of the West with the sole view of extending the Faith in Christ.

It was not until the evening of the twelfth of June, after many vicissitudes and hairbreadth escapes from shipwreck and capture by foreign foes, that the shores of the New World were sighted. Two days later the ship entered Chesapeake Bay, and after a sail of five more days, anchor was finally dropped at the Bohemia Landing.

A Pietistical Emblem of Christ, A. D. 1692.

The first act of the party after landing, according to the devout Magister Johannes Kelpius, was to thank the Almighty upon their bended knees for having carried them "as on eagle's wings such an immense distance through all the gates of death."

They at once reported to the royal commissioners of Maryland, informing them who they were and why they had come to reside in America. After this formality they started overland to the town of New Castle, then the chief port on the Delaware, where they arrived on the twenty-second day of June. Early in the next morning they embarked upon a sloop which was in readiness, and wafted by favorable winds and tide, the party landed safely in Philadelphia on the same day.

THE VOYAGE TO AMERICA.

Arms of Penn.

TWO accounts of this remarkable voyage have come down to us: one is contained in the diary of Magister Johannes Kelpius,[10] the other in a letter or "Sendschreiben," written by Daniel Falkner, dated Germantown, August 7th, 1694, about six weeks after their arrival in America. This letter, sent to friends in Germany and Holland, was published and circulated there shortly after it was received.

A copy of this interesting communication has found a resting place among the treasures of the Pennsylvania His-

J. N. J.—Abbreviation for the Latin *In Nomine Jesu*, *i.e.*, "in the name of Jesus." *Votum* at commencement of Kelpius' Diary.

[10] This journal has been reproduced entire in photographic facsimile by the writer. Copies are to be found in the collection of Hon. S. W. Pennypacker and the Historical Society of Pennsylvania.

I. N. J.

Anno 1694.

Septima Januarii convictus à Deo iter in Americam instituere cum fratribus Henrico Bernhardo Costero, Daniele Falknero, Daniele Lütkio, Johanne Seeligio, Ludovico Bidermanno et comitibus simul 40. circiter quorum recensiti et alii convicti à Deo in Germania praecedente adhuc anno iter istud inivierant.

Conductam igitur navim nomine SARA MARIA BONAE SPEI Capitaneo Johanne Tannero Anglo conducebam ego septima Februarii pro septem argenti libris Anglicanis, quas in navi 14ta ejus exsolvebam, quam 13 ingressus eram, religavi autem 12ma, quae erat 3

Prima haec dies in Tamesi fluvio Anglicano tranquilla transigebatur à nostris à me maxima [illegible] gravi [illegible]: vesperi de ordinandis lectis concertatio oriebatur quae zelum in P. S. accendebat adeo ut exercito solitario [illegible] cordi pacifico dejectus zelum pro lecto, coelum Christi vita [illegible] scelus scelere cumularet; donec Maria solitaria virginem Aethiopicam adsciscerent, quae prius de puritate virginis Europeae informari volebat antequam connubium consentiret. [illegible] vero morbum [illegible] [illegible] [illegible] [illegible] cur [illegible]

Secunda dies 4. 15. Febr. secunda nobis: sed Tertia fatalis erat. Mens praesaga, mala cum eventu felici mihi praesagiebat. Idem Falknerus de se [illegible] mabat. Visitabamur primo à Militum Conscriptoribus Regiis. Dein vento contrario et turbulento [illegible] arenosis admovebamur, quas effugere volentes [illegible] salutem quaerebamus, quae ipsa nos perdidisset, nisi Divina Providentia fecisset ut [illegible] tante moles sub navi navim perforare volens fractum fuisset ipsum. Anchora [illegible] deperdita turbine tandem ferebamur in [illegible]

Fac-simile of First Page of Diary of Magister Johannes Kelpius.

torical Society, from which the title is here reproduced,[11]—(translation) "Copy || of a Missive from || and relating to the New World || The Narration of a dangerous || Sea Voyage, and propitious disembarkation of some || Christian Fellow-travelers || who upon this Pilgrimage set out the || Faith in Jesus Christ even there || to extend. || Tob: xii. 8.[12] Printed in the year 1695."

COPIA
Eines Send-Schreibens auß
der neuen Welt/betreffend
Die Erzehlung einer gefährlichen
Schifffarth/und glücklichen Anländung etlicher
Christlichen Reisegefehrten/welche zu dem Ende diese Wallfahrt angetretten/ den Glauben an JEsum Christum allda außzubreiten

Tob. XII. 8.

Der Könige und Fürsten Rath und Heimlichkeiten soll man verschweigen/ aber GOttes Werck soll man herrlich preisen und offenbaren.

Gedruckt im Jahr 1695.

In the main facts the two accounts agree, the only difference being in some of the detail of minor occurrences. From these accounts it is learned that the start from Germany was made in the summer of the year 1693. They first rallied in Holland.

After remaining in Holland for some time, the party left Rotterdam for London, where they arrived during the month of August. While in London the leaders of the party had considerable intercourse with the so-called "Philadelphists," a society which was formed in England by the celebrated Jane Leade and others, originally for the purpose of studying and explaining the writings of Jacob Boehme. The outcome of this movement was a league of Christians who insisted on depth and inwardness of the spirit. A

---

[11] Translated in full by the late Dr. Oswald Seidensticker, "Penna. Mag. Hist. and Biography," vol. xi., pp. 430 et. seq.

[12] This is a typographical error in the original. It should be Tob. xii, verse 7.—"It is good to keep close the secret of a king, but it is honorable to reveal the works of God. Do that which is good, and no evil shall touch you."

number of pamphlets were published by this society, and afterwards translated into German.

A correspondence between Johann Kelpius and Henry John Deichmann, secretary of the London society, was kept up for several years after the arrival of the party in Pennsylvania.

Der
Philadelphischen Societät
Zustand und Beschaffenheit;
oder
Die Gründe / worauf sie fussen und gehen; betrachtet in einer
Antwort auf ein Schreiben
von
Philalethe, auf Veranlassung der Theosophischen Transactionen &c. an ein Glied der Societät gestellt.
Ezech. XII. v. 23.
Ja / sprich zu ihnen: Die Tage und der Effect und die Erfüllung aller und jeder Gesichten sind vorhanden.
Aus dem Englischen aufs getreuste übergesetzt.

Gedruckt im Jahr Christi 1698.

The party remained in London until February 13th, 1694 (O. S.), when they sailed down the Thames to Gravesend, where they embarked on their ship. This vessel, commanded by Captain Tanner, was armed and carried fourteen large cannon.

The name of the vessel, "Sarah Maria" (according to Kelpius, *Sara Mariabonæ spei*), was taken by the theosophical enthusiasts who composed the party as a propitious omen for the journey. To them the prosaic everyday name of the ship indicated "*Glaube*, *Liebe*, *Hoffnung*" (Faith, Hope and Love or Charity). According to their mystical interpretation they argued,—

1. By Faith (Sarah) we got for our journey the means that were not in sight.

2. By Smyrnean Love [13] (Maria—in Hebrew Mar, bitter, whence Maria) which is not obtained without toil and trouble, but remains faithful unto death. [Rev. ii, 10.]

3. And at last, through "Hope" we will be "Well" (safely) landed. "For so we have been taught by God." [14]

Many were the vicissitudes experienced by these religious

[13] An allusion to the epistle to the church of Smyrna: Rev. ii, 8–10.

[14] "Penna. Mag.," vol. xi, p. 430.

enthusiasts during this eventful voyage. The first mishap came at the very outset when they ran into a furious gale in the channel. The pilot, taking his course close to the English coast for fear of French privateers, was forced to steer between cliffs and sand-banks. As the storm increased in fury, fearing for the safety of the vessel, they cast their largest anchor. When the gale was abating, the ship drifted against the anchor; it broke, knocking a hole in the ship, which, however, caused no leak. Towards night another storm arose, and the vessel was driven by wind and waves against a hard sand-bank.[15] There was a crash as if everything in the ship was turning topsy-turvey, and as two more thumps followed, the cry was raised, "Commend your souls to the Lord; we shall go down."

The passengers and crew now gave themselves up as lost, and all threw themselves on their knees and prayed for about an hour, expecting the vessel to go to pieces every moment; when suddenly Johannes Kelpius, the leader of the party, upon a "third inward prompting," told Captain Tanner that the Lord had promised deliverance, that more dangers were impending but Divine Providence would grant a safe arrival.[16] Falkner in his account writes, "Here Faith, which conquers the world and its elements, proved so strong and heroic in some of the passengers, that they forgot the danger, went to the captain and told him to be of good cheer: the danger was not meant for destruction, but for testing the belief and the love of many. This proved to be true, for when the prayers strove most earnestly against the wind and waves, the most powerful waves came, as it were, to the support of the prayers, and at the behest of the Creator, whom they obeyed, lifted the ship

[15] Probably one of the shoals known as the Goodwin Sands.

[16] Kelpius' MS. Journal.

and carried it over the bank into a safe depth, contrary to all experiences upon sea and to the surprise of the crew."

After a general thanksgiving service led by Magister Kelpius, in which all on board participated, the journey was continued through the channel. Eventually the Downs[17] were reached (February 21st) without further mishap; here a stop was made for over two weeks; a new anchor was obtained in place of the one lost, and the ship thoroughly overhauled, while waiting for the arrival of a good convoy, which was to have been sent from London.[18]

Alluding to this delay at the Downs, Kelpius mentions in his journal—"On the 27th of February we sent letters to London and to Tob. Ad. Lauterbach and others in Germany, from whom we had received most cheering answers.

"On the 4th of March I received a letter from Samuel Waldenfield, in London, at the Lamp in Fennhard[19] Street, with a draft of the pious virgin Catherine Beerens van Bofing on Samuel Standerwick in Deal.[20] This gentleman received me and my friend Selig[21] the next day very kindly. He listened with the greatest pleasure to our account of the Pietists in Germany, and invited us to repeat our visit; we were prevented from doing so by our sailing."

This time while lying at anchor was utilized by the party in edifying discourses and biblical study. The expected convoy not arriving, sail was set on the eighth day of March,

---

[17] "The Downs," a spacious roadstead in the English Channel, affording an excellent anchorage. It is between the shore and the Goodwin Sands and is much used by the British navy.

[18] This was during the universal war then waged against Louis XIV. of France, 1689–1697. In American history it is known as "King William's War."

[19] Query: Fenchurch Street?

[20] Deal, a seaport and market town in Kent, England. It has no harbor.

[21] Johann Selig, one of the members of the party.

in company with eighteen other vessels, three of which were men-of-war.

Under date of the next day (March 9th) the following memorandum in English is inserted in Kelpius' Latin diary in a different handwriting:

"Instructions for the better keeping company with their Maj's ship Sandador Prize under my command.

"If I weigh in the day I will haule home my foretopsail sheets and fire a gunn. If in the night, I will putt a light in the main top mast shrouds and fire a gun, which light you are to answer. If I weigh in a fog I will fire 3 gunns distantly one after another. If I anchor in the night or in a fogg, I will fire 2 guns a small distance of time one from the other and putt abroad a light more than my constant lights, which light you are to answer.

"If I lie by or try in the night, I will fire two guns and keep a light abroad more than my constant light in the Main shrouds and if through extreamity of weather we are forced to lye a Holl or under a Mizen, I will fire three guns and put abroad two lights of equal height more than my constant light; and if I make sail in the night after blowing weather or after lying by or for any other reason I will make the same sing [sign?] as for weighing in the night, which light you are to answer.

"In case of separation if we meet by day the weathermost ship shall lower his Fore top sail and then the leward shall answer by lowering their main top sail.

"He that apprehends any danger in the night shall fire guns and put abroad three lights of equal hight and bear away or tack from it; but if it should happen to be strange ships, then make false fires and endeavor to speak with my; and to better to know each other in the night, he that hails shall ask what ship is that and he that is hailet shall answer *Adventure*, then he that hailet first shall reply *Rupert*.

The "SARA-MARIA," Captain Tanner, Master.
(From an old Dutch print.)

"If I have a desire to speak with you I will hoist a Jack-Flag in my mizen-top mast shrouds and make a weft with my ensign.

"If you have a desire to speak with my; you shall hoist your ensign in your Main-Top-Mast Shrouds.

"If in the night you chance to spring a leak keep firing of Guns and showing of lights."

Dated on Board Their Maj.ts Ship Sandades Prize March ye 9. 169 3/4 Will. Allen

After an uneventful sail of four days anchor was dropped in the harbor of Plymouth on March 12th, a good place for anchorage being secured under the guns of the fort. In this harbor the vessel remained for five weeks waiting for the convoy from London.

It was while here in port that letters were received from Lieut. Schmaltz[22] and others in Erfurth, and friends in Cleves, Konberg[23] and elsewhere in Germany, questioning

---

[22] Lieut. Schmaltz was a leading spirit of the *Collegia Pietatis* in Erfurth. He died in 1702. An entry in the town chronicle states "Lieut. Schmaltz could not be induced during his last illness to make any confession as to the person of Christ or the justification of a sinner before God; he also refused to receive the sacrament."

When his friends attempted to bury his body at night by torchlight, they were set upon by the authorities, who drove back the mourners, the parish beadles (Stadt-Knechte) extinguished the torches, and took the body and buried it in an unconsecrated corner of the *Mercatorum* cemetery.—"Historia Civitatis Erffurtensis," pp. 1069.

[23] This is evidently a typographical error in the original, no such place as Konberg is to be found on any atlas of that period. Königsberg is no doubt intended, the seat of the celebrated Albertine University (Collegium Albertinum) founded in 1544 by the Margrave Albert, and which at that period numbered 2000 students on its roster. In later years it became celebrated as the place where the philosophy of Kant was first propounded.

the expediency of the party emigrating to the unknown shores of America, and urging the enthusiasts to return to home and friends, notwithstanding the edicts and manifestoes which were being issued against all Pietists and religious enthusiasts. Kelpius in reply addressed communications to Lauterbach, De Watteville, Meerkamp and others, declining their advice, and adhering to his determination of going to Pennsylvania.

The expected convoy not arriving, a final start was made on the 18th of April under the protection of several foreign men-of-war, Danish, Spanish and Swedish[24] then in the harbor, and which were to sail from Plymouth to Cadiz. For this purpose an agreement was entered into with the Spanish Admiral, Nicholas De Rudder, for a certain sum of money to convoy the vessel two hundred Dutch miles into the ocean; and on the 25th of April the actual voyage to the new world commenced, in company with another English vessel, the "Providence," carrying 18 guns.

After parting with the armed escort the two vessels followed a southwestern course, and for the rest of the month were favored with good weather and favorable breezes.

Magister Kelpius, in writing about their life on shipboard, states: "Our exercises on board the ship consisted in discourses of various kinds and interpretations of the Scripture, in which those who felt inclined took part. We had also prayer meetings and sang hymns of praise and joy, several of us accompanying on instruments that we had brought from London."

On the 10th of May the two vessels fell in with three French vessels, one a frigate of 24 guns; a lively action took place, lasting four hours, and resulted in the repulse

---

[24] In this war, under the league of Augsburg, almost the whole of Europe was arrayed against France.

of the French frigate and the capture of a prize by the consort "Providence." Falkner has left us the following interesting details of this incident, viz.:

"On the 10th of May our faith was again put on trial. We were only two ships and saw in the morning, when the weather was fair and quiet, three vessels in the distance. (Mark, when at sea a foreign ship comes in sight, immediately alarm is given and everything put in readiness for an encounter.) Many of us became depressed in mind from a presentiment that they were hostile French ships. They steered directly towards us, but on account of the calm could make no headway for 5 or 6 hours. About noon we could see by the telescope that they carried white flags with lilies, enough to show, that this day things would take a French, not a Christian turn. As soon as this was ascertained, every thing was made ready for battle. The passengers were given the choice to fight or not. We, of course, abstained of carnal weapons and taking the shield of faith sat down between decks behind boxes and cases, prayed and invoked the Lord, every one for himself, as on account of the great noise and the report of cannons nothing could have been heard. We had hardly got down, when a French frigate with 24 cannon and a merchant ship with 6 cannon made straight for our ship and opened fire so vigorously, that it was really time to pray for averting great calamity. The merciful Father made the enemies' balls drop into the water before our ship, only one cannon ball struck the ship over our heads without doing harm to anybody, though the ship got a hole two ells above the water line. In the mean time our cannon and ball were not idle, but did great damage to the enemies' ships, which we inferred from their retreat. But half an hour afterwards they resumed the attack. Then a 12 pound ball was sent right through the captain's room, but inflicted no damage; the captain's boy who carried a bottle in his hand came very near being hit; the ball took the bottle so neatly out of his hand that he hardly knew the ball had done it. An hour later the frigate fell back a little and with the third vessel, which carried 12 guns attacked our fellow ship, which, however, made a good defense. Here it happened that a Frenchman on the merchant vessel while aiming with his rifle at our captain, while on the point of shooting, was rent to pieces by a cannon ball, before he could pull the trigger. Whether the shot came from our companion ship or ours nobody knows. The enemy stopped firing, expecting us to capitulate or else, designing to turn to our port, but it pleased the Lord to make an end of the racket that day and to drive the enemy to flight by means no one would have thought of. For the Lord put it into the heart of our captain to call all males on deck, and to make them join his crew in raising a pretended shout of joy. When this was done, and the enemy observed on our ship, contrary to expectation, so many heads, whom, they thought, had been fighting and would continue to fight, it was as if their cannons had at once become dumb and their courage sunk into the sea like a millstone. The Lord struck them with fear, so they suddenly turned their ships about and fled away from us.[25] The large frigate gave the signal of flight; but the others could not follow so swiftly and we might easily have captured both of them. Our captain, however, was satisfied when the merchant ships hoisting a white flag surrendered. Then we also stopped firing. The two other

[25] It was at this point that the "Providence," the companion of the "Sarah Maria," came up and joined in the pursuit. Being the faster of the two, she chased and engaged the hostile frigate. The battle lasted four hours, but only three balls of the enemy struck, doing little damage to the ship and none to the men. (Kelpius' MS. Diary.)

ships got off; the third fell into our hands. There were on board twenty four Frenchmen, among them one of the reformed faith, who had been attending mass under compulsion. Seven were taken aboard our ship, including this Huguenot, who liked our company and was pleased that we could speak his language and assuage in some measure his bruised conscience.[26] The others were taken on board by our fellows. The ship had a cargo of sugar and came from Martinique under the 17th degree of Latitude. At first the prisoners raised a great wail and lamentation; they had expected to land in France as freemen and had now to return to America in captivity. But thus they had meant to serve us. The Lord fulfilled on them what is written Revel. ch. 13, "He that leadeth into captivity shall go into captivity."[27]

NAVAL TROPHIES.

After this episode nothing further of importance occurred, except several false alarms by hostile ships, until June 12th, when, at 10 o'clock A. M., an eclipse of the sun was observed, the craft being in lat. 36° 45′. On the evening of the same day (June 12th) the party had their first glimpse of the western world, the capes of Virginia were sighted, and two days later (June 14th) the "Sarah Maria" entered Chesapeake Bay. It took the travelers five days to sail

[26] Kelpius makes no mention of this incident.

[27] The distribution of the cargo, consisting of sugar and cider, gave rise to dissatisfaction, which the captain finally quelled by allowing to all an equal share in the "unjust Mammon." (Kelpius' MS. Diary.)

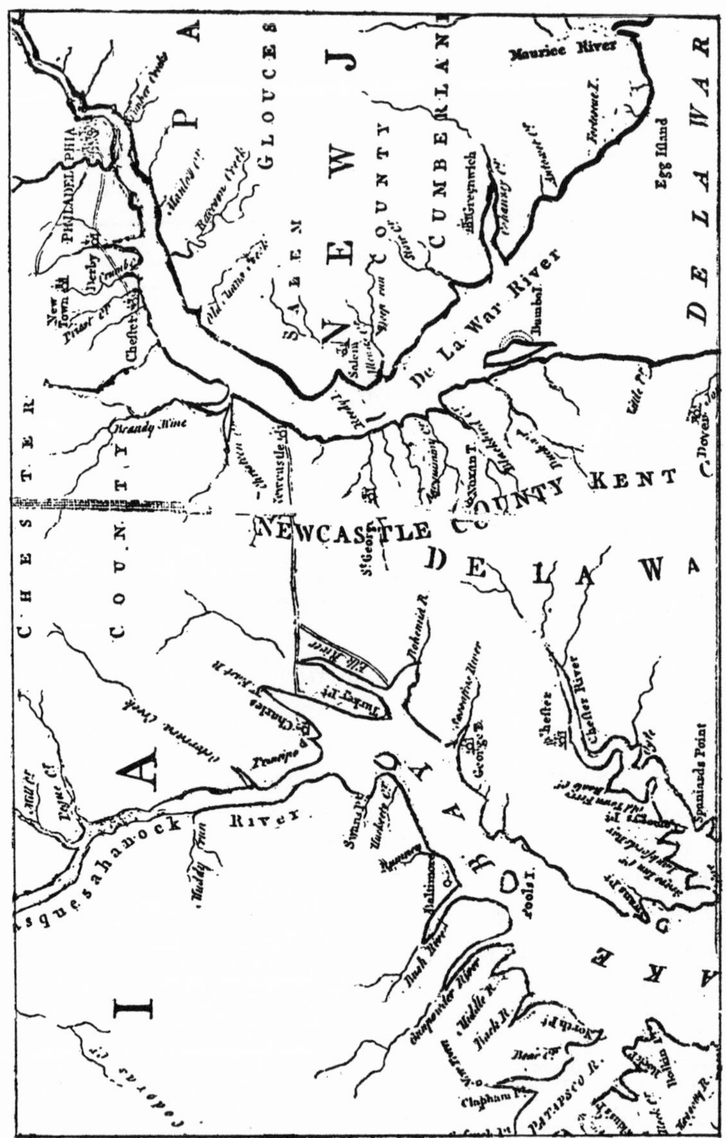

Ancient Map Showing Road Between Chesapeake Bay and Delaware River.

up the Bay of Virginia, during which time occurred one of the strangest and most unaccountable episodes of the voyage. This was a disagreement between some of the party, in which a woman, who was one of the ship's company, was evidently the leading cause, or at least a prominent character. All that is definitely known about the affair is the entry in the Kelpius diary[28]—June 17th, under the sign of the sun—"that Falkner was excommunicated by Köster, as was also Anna Maria Schuchart."[29]

That this estrangement between the leaders of the party was but temporary is shown by the fact that no subsequent mention of the episode appears in either the Kelpius or Falkner papers.

Five days after the vessel had entered the capes of Virginia the anchor was dropped, and the landing made at the Bohemia Landing, as before stated. Daniel Falkner, in his account, at this point notes: "We hope, in this land also, His mercy will not be wasted on us, especially as we are assured that we have come hither by His will."

---

[28] Notabilis illa Falkneri a Cœstere excommunicatio, ut & Annæ Mariæ Schuchartinæ (?) Prophetissæ Erphortianae !

[29] A further account of this person will be found under the chapter devoted to Köster.

THE ARRIVAL IN PENNSYLVANIA.

THE sun was past the meridian on Saturday, June 23, 1694, when a sloop, whose deck was crowded with passengers, made fast to the public wharf of Philadelphia. This landing was built out from the sandy beach at the northwestern shore of the point where Dock Creek emptied its waters into the Delaware; this beach was almost immediately in front of the Blue Anchor Tavern,[30] and was the same point where the Proprietor William Penn had landed just twelve years before.

The passengers, as they left the vessel and gathered upon the sloping beach, at first sight looked like a motley crowd; they numbered forty

[30] The Blue Anchor. This ancient hostelrie stood at what is now the northwest corner of Front and Dock Streets; it was taken down in 1810. For an extended notice of this landing place see "Penna. Magazine," vol. x, p. 61.

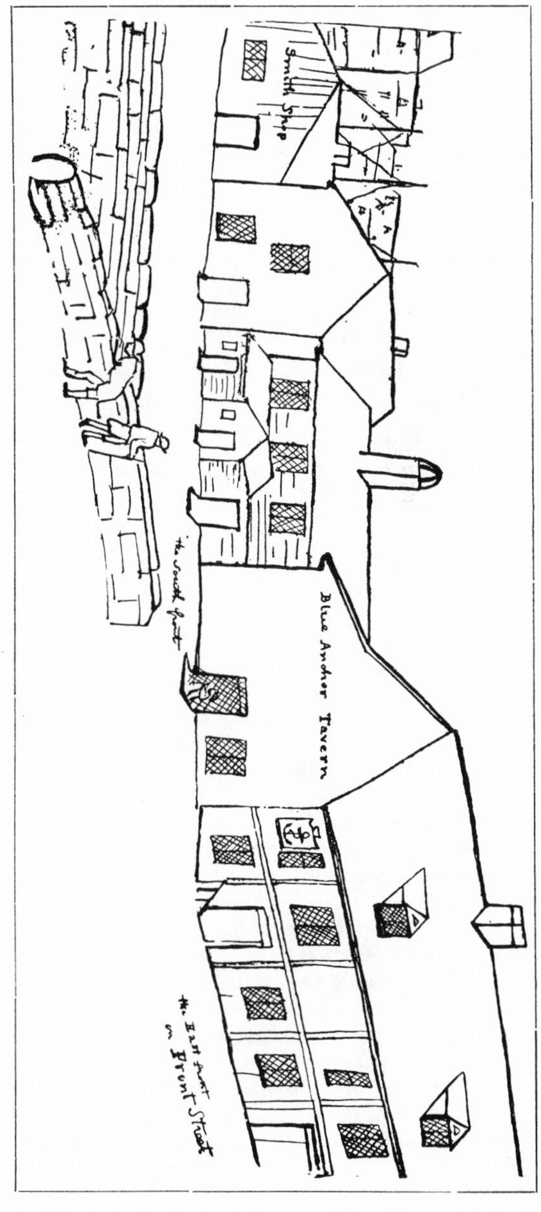

THE BLUE ANCHOR TAVERN.

Fac-simile of the oldest known picture of this ancient landmark. The original is a pencil sketch in "Watson's MS. Annals," in the Ridgway Library, it bears the following endorsement: "View of the Blue Anchor Tavern, at which Wm. Penn first landed at Philada. Drawn as it really stood when viewed from the Drawbridge."

men of various ages, all with intelligent features, and clad in strange attire. Some were in a coarse Pilgrim garb, others in the peculiar dress of the Teutonic university student, while others again wore the distinctive costume of the German interior provinces. It was the same party of religious enthusiasts who had crossed the ocean in the good ship "Sarah Maria."

After a short religious service the party, walking silently two by two, took a survey of Philadelphia, then nothing more than a straggling village of perhaps five hundred houses,[31] as yet undivided into wards or divisions. Great was their surprise when they learned that, notwithstanding the promises of religious liberty that were granted by the charter of Penn, not a single house of worship other than those of the Quakers existed within the bounds of the Province ;[32]

---

[31] In 1700 there were about seven hundred houses; see "Scharff & Westcott," page 145.

[32] Christ Church was not built until 1695. The first Baptist congregation on the Pennepack had no house of worship until the year 1707 (Historical sketch by H. G. Jones, p. 11). The Presbyterians erected their first church in 1704. The Swedish Blockhouse at Wicacoa, although still standing, was then (1694) in a very ruinous condition, so much so that no services could be held in the building. The old Dutch pastor, Jacobus Fabricius, so far back as 1685 petitioned the Provincial Council for permission to keep an ordinary or tavern [for the support of himself and family]. This was refused by Council in the curt sentence that "they don't think fitt to grant ye Petitioners request." [The action of Council was no doubt influenced by the known intemperate habits and life of that pioneer clergyman. "See Doc. Hist. N. Y.," iii, 243 ; "Hallische Nachrichten," new ed., pp. 619–20].

In August, 1693, Magister Jacobus Fabricius again petitioned William Markham, Lieutenant-Governor under Gov. Fletcher, and the Provincial Council. This time the petition was one for relief, and set forth that he had now became totally blind, and was reduced to the direst poverty, and that he had not whereupon to live.

Council "Ordered that the church wardens of their church have notice to appear att Council the ffifteenth instant, to make ansr to the said Complaint." This order was aimed against the Christina (Wilmington) connor could the embryo city as yet boast of town-hall, court-house or prison.[33]

Considerable commotion was caused at first among the staid inhabitants of the Quaker City by the advent of this party of strangely robed foreigners walking in a body through the streets. Naturally the question was asked, "Who were these peculiar people in outlandish attire and of foreign tongue?"

The information vouchsafed was merely that they were German students who had became convinced of the Quaker doctrine, and were going to settle upon a tract some distance out of the city near the German township—a piece of news which allayed the fears of the inhabitants.

The first act of the leaders of this band of emigrants upon their entrance into the city was to call upon Benjamin Fletcher, Captain-General of Pennsylvania, and William Markham, his Deputy Governor, for the purpose, as an old manuscript states, "Of taking the Oath of Allegiance and explaining their reason for coming to the Colony;"[34] Pennsylvania then being a province under the Crown of England, and out of the control of William Penn.[35]

SEAL OF GOV. FLETCHER.

gregation of the lower counties. No notice whatever seems to have been taken of this action of Council. The death of the old clergyman is recorded in the same year.—"Records of Old Swedes' Church," Wilmington, p. 7.

The present church at Wicacoa, "Gloria Dei" or "Old Swedes'," was not built until the year 1700.

[33] When the General Assembly, consisting of fifty-four members, first met in the city of Philadelphia, they hired a room and paid the expense. The country members took lodgings out of the city and walked in to

Unfortunately, we have no positive record where this unique ceremony took place. The probabilities are that it was either at the "great house" built by Robert Whitpain on the lower side of Front Street between Walnut and Spruce, and which is said to have been the official residence of Governor Fletcher when in Philadelphia, or at the Penn Cottage, which formerly stood on Lætitia Court near Second and Market Streets, the residence of Lieutenant-Governor Markham. It was in the latter house,[36] then surrounded by ample grounds, that the Provincial Council

attend the meetings, frequently bringing their dinners with them.—"Hazard's Register," vol. v, 113.

[34] This was then a custom of the country. See "Record of Rev. Ericus Bjork;" "Records of Holy Trinity (old Swedes') Church," Wilmington, Del., pp. 11.

[35] In October, 1692, William and Mary, King and Queen of England, appointed Benjamin Fletcher, Governor of New York, to be also Governor of Pennsylvania and the lower counties on the Delaware. Thus Penn lost the government and jurisdiction over these provinces, without, however, being deprived of his right as proprietary. In making this appointment he was as little thought of as the charter that had been granted to him; in order, however, to strengthen the royal authority, the new governor was invested with the power of negativing all laws, and none was to be in force, unless approved by the King. In April, 1693, Fletcher made his solemn entry into Philadelphia, where Governor Lloyd and his Council gave up the government to him without being thereunto authorized either by the crown or the proprietary.—*Ebeling*.

The government of Pennsylvania remained under the Crown of England from April 26, 1692, to March, 1695.

[36] This building was erected by Governor William Markham prior to the arrival of William Penn. The bricks and finer parts of the framework were brought from England, together with Penn's workmen ("servants") to set them up. A few years ago this old landmark was taken down and re-erected in Fairmount Park. The illustration here given represents it as it appeared about thirty years prior to its removal.

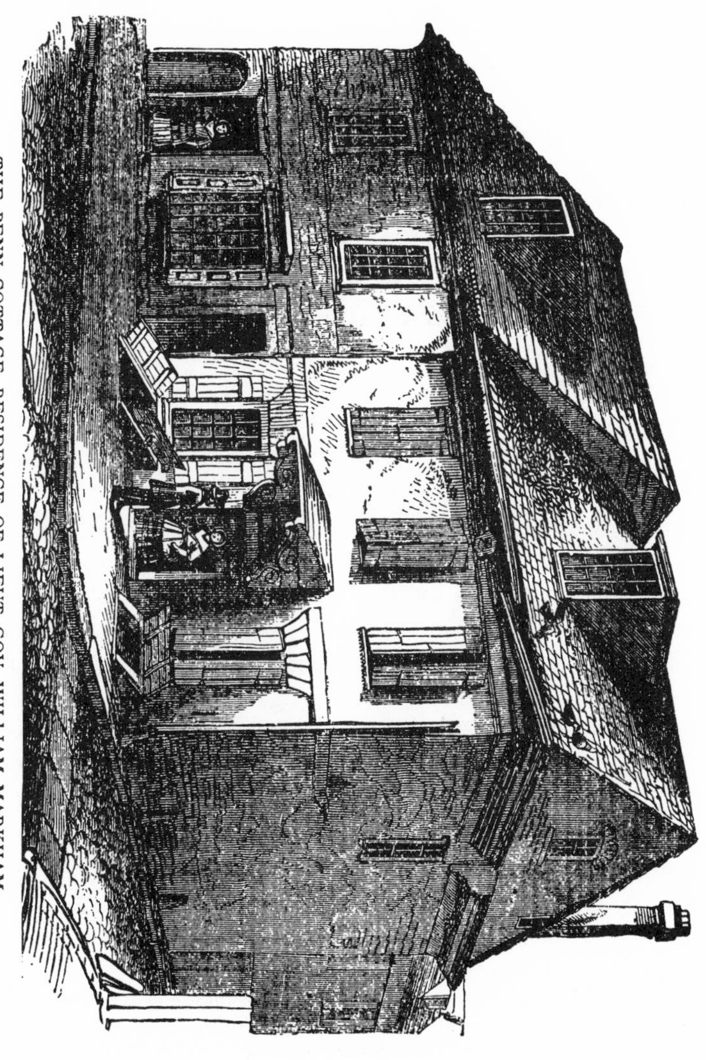

THE PENN COTTAGE, RESIDENCE OF LIEUT.-GOV. WILLIAM MARKHAM.

held its deliberations at that time and for many years afterwards, while the Assembly for some years met in "the large room" of the Whitpain house.

In former years there was a curious tradition current among the older German residents in connection with the short sojourn of this party within the city. After the formality of reporting to the representative of the Crown had been complied with, arrangements were made for shelter and sustenance as best they could be for so large a party, and it was well after nightfall before this was completed.

When night had fairly set in a number of the strangers, tired and weary as they were, wended their way towards one of the highlands that loomed up just northwest of the old city proper, and which are still known as "Bush-hill" and "Fairmount." Arriving at a suitable point, dry leaves and brush-wood were hastily gathered, a tinder-box was produced, and fire struck with flint and steel. After the leaves and fagots were ignited, pine boughs were broken off and heaped upon the fire until a bright flame extended skyward.

Then the mystic rites incident to St. John's eve were performed, after which the burning brands were scattered down the sloping hillsides with considerable ceremony. The party then returned to the sleeping city, after having lit for the first time in America, so far as is known, the "Sanct Johannis" or "Sonnenwend-feuer," a mystic ceremonial and religious rite which dates far back into the most remote period of time when the early Aryans were yet a small colony in northern Europe.[37]

---

[37] The rite of the "Sonnenwend-feuer," held on the eves of June 24th and December 25th, to celebrate the recurrence of the summer and winter solstices, dates back to the dark days of heathen mythology. The rite on the eve of the summer solstice consisted in building a fire on an eminence ;

The party did not tarry long in the city; the early Sabbath morn, even before the sun rose in the east, found them on their way to "Germanopel," as Germantown was then called. Their path led up Second Street, then a mere country lane, due north to Fairhill; thence northwest to the German settlement under Pastorius, where the "town" consisted of a few houses on a single street.

It took the party almost four hours to reach their goal, and the sun was well up on the horizon on that double holiday—"St. Johannis Tag," June 24th, (St. John the Baptist's Day) and Sunday—when the company filed into the village of their countrymen and inquired for the house of one Jacob Isaac Van Bebber,[38] a native of Crefeld on the Rhine, near the borders of Holland.

Here the weary travelers found a haven of rest. Their arrival had been long looked for by their host, and he forthwith secured for them shelter and sustenance.

Much anxiety had been felt by Van Bebber and his friends in Germantown on account of the non-arrival of

---

when brightly blazing, flowers, pine boughs and bones were thrown into the fire, and the esoteric rites and incantations were performed: these were for the purpose of allaying any possible pestilence or disease. The embers were then rolled down the hillside, indicative of the waning of the sun's power. The rites on the eve of the winter solstice consisted mainly in lighting resinous pine boughs giving an upward flame, denoting the growing power of the sun. The custom of the present day of lighted tapers on the Christmas tree is a relic of this ancient rite. The object of this ceremonial was believed to be a sure safeguard against many evils. The practice still survives in some parts of Germany and may occasionally be witnessed in Pennsylvania.

[38] Daniel Falkner, in his "Sendschreiben," notes: "We have here in Germantown a man by the name of Jacob Isaac, a native of Crefeld on the Rhine, near Holland. He was formerly a Mennonite, but he desires to depart with his whole house to acknowledge and abandon the follies, scandals, shortcomings and stains of his former religion."—"Penna. Mag.," vol. xi, p. 440.

this party. The long and uncertain ways of communication at that early day precluded any news reaching them as to the causes of the delay before or after their embarkation. On account of the prevailing war with France, great fears were entertained that the party might have been captured and fallen into the hands of the enemy, or succumbed to the elements. But now all uncertainty was removed. The joyful feeling, however, was not confined to the residents of Germantown. Doubly thankful were these weary pilgrims that they had arrived safely at the end of their long and eventful journey on the natal day[39] of the Saint whose example they strove to follow by words and action.

[39] In the whole calendar there are but two natal days, viz., St. John the Baptist's Day, June 24th, and Christmas Day, December 25th. All other saints' days are memorial days, which mark the day of their supposed martyrdom or death.

SYMBOL FROM THEOSOPHICAL MS.

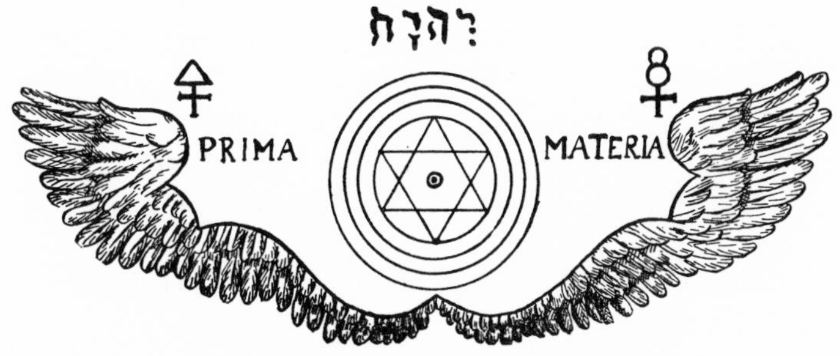

THE CHAPTER OF PERFECTION.

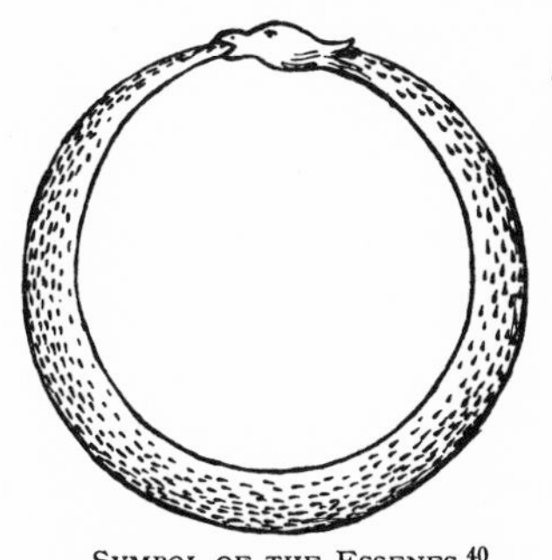

SYMBOL OF THE ESSENES.[40]

THIS party of emigrants—so different from the general mass of settlers who were then flocking from Germany to the Province of Pennsylvania—were not Quakers or Friends, although they are so considered in some of the old records; but they were a company of Theosophical Enthusiasts—call them Pietists, Mystics, Chiliasts,[41] Rosicrucians, Illuminati, Cathari,[42] Puritans,[43] or what you

---

PRIMA MATERIA, a Theosophical symbol from Rosicrucian MS., on folio 12, descriptive of "Eternity and the uncreated inscrutable" PRIMUM MOBILE (Primordial Motion, the first life-impulse).

A Theosophical authority defines Materia Prima (primordial matter) *A' Wasa*, as a universal and invisible principle, the basic substance of which all things are formed. By reducing a thing into its *prima materia* and clothing it with new attributes, it may be transformed into another thing by him who possesses spiritual power and knowledge. There are several states of matter, from primordial down to gross visible matter; some of the early philosophers therefore distinguished between *materia proxima*, *materia remota* and *materia ultima*.—Dr. Franz Hartmann in "Cosmology," Boston, 1888.

may—who in Europe had formed what was known according to their mystical dogmas as a "Chapter of Perfection," and then came to the western world to put into execution the long-cherished plan of founding a true Theosophical (Rosicrucian) community; going out into the wilderness or desert, after the manner of the Essenes[44] of old, as also did

---

[40] The serpent was not at first a personification of evil, but of wisdom and salvation, and was used as a symbol of immortal life. The symbol here reproduced is frequently met with in ancient sculptures, and symbolizes eternity, or a world without end.

[41] Croese's "Quakeriana," p. 551.—(Latin Edition.)

[42] Cathari,—a mystical sect which dates back to the tenth or eleventh century; the name is derived from the Greek, and signifies "the pure." It is from this name whence came *Ketzer*, the German word for heretic. The Cathari regarded the exaltation of the soul over the moral nature, so as to become wholly absorbed in mystical contemplation, as the highest stage in the religious life of man.

Deep devotion of the heart in prayer and a life of purity connected with abstinence from carnal pleasure and from the use of stimulating food, were their exercises of piety.

It is claimed by some writers that the Waldenses were an outcome of the original Cathari.

[43] Puritans is here but another term for Cathari.

[44] The Essenes,—a mystical Jewish sect, not mentioned in the Jewish or Christian scriptures, and concerning whom the only original sources of information are passages in the works of Josephus, who lived about the time when the Essenes had reached their highest point of development. The notices of them ascribed to Philo are of doubtful authenticity. Even Hippolytus appears to have drawn his account of them from Josephus. They lived an austere life in the solitudes on the western side of the Dead Sea, where they held their property in common, wore a white robe, prayed and meditated continually, made frequent ablutions, for the most part renounced marriage, and often practised medicine. According to Bellermann (Berlin, 1821) the creed or chief doctrine of the Essenes was contained in the word "Love" (charity). This was divided into the "Love of God," the "Love of Virtue" and the "Love of their Fellow-man." Especial stress was laid upon obedience to the law or government (*obrigkeit*), as all law emanated from God. Prayer, abstinence and labor were the chief features of their life. St. John the Baptist is said to have been an active member of this Jewish sect of Mystical Theosophists.

Moses, Elijah and other biblical characters, to perfect themselves in holiness, thus preparing themselves for the millenium which they believed to be approaching; or in case that their calculations should have misled them as to the ending of all things terrestial, the community would prove a nucleus from which the individual members would be qualified to come forth among men again as holy men, to convert whole cities and to work signs and miracles.

This party of religious enthusiasts, who were led by the noblest impulses, and whose hearts were filled with the sole desire to live a godly life and serve their fellow countrymen, as well as the aborigines, was under the leadership of Magister Johannes Kelpius, with Heinrich Bernhard Köster as deputy magister, and Johann Seelig, Daniel Falkner, Daniel Lütke and Ludwig Biedermann as wardens or assistants, together with thirty-four brethren, all men of learning, making a total of forty, the symbolic number of "Perfection."

[In the theory of mystic numbers, unity is called the Monad, and is no number. It is the first ring in the chain of existence, and one of the qualifications which the ancient philosophers have given the Deity. Its symbol is the mathematical point. The figure **2** consists of repeated unity, which is no number, and is represented by the mathematically straight line, consequently is not perfect. The figure **4**, however, is known as the equal perfect number,[45] and has been held in high esteem by all schools of mystic philosophers. This is explained by the fact that the simple figure not only represents the square of the repeated unity ($2 \times 2 = 4$), and the product resulting from the

[45] The number **4** derives its sacredness from concrete and material relations, from external perceptions, and has its application in the objective and phenomenal world.—"The Origin of Sacred Numbers."

addition with itself (2+2=4), but also the potential decade 1+2+3+4=10; it also forms the enclosed figure known as a true square, whenever 2 and 2 parallel lines are placed at right angles to each other. It is from these facts—properties which are not found in any other number—that the numeral has for ages past been held in reverence,[46] and been the visible symbol of the Deity, and is constantly recurring in the symbolism of every religious cult. It is also identified with justice, because it is the first square number the product of equals. Thus the name of the Deity is represented by four letters in all languages, the English language being the exception.

Whereas 4 represents the perfect Deity,[47] the mysterious numeral 3, figured as the Triad by the equilateral triangle, is the emblem of the attributes of God only, as it reunites the properties of the first two numbers.

40, the decade of the perfect number, is known as the number of perfection, to which the greatest importance has always been attached both in religious and esoteric lore. This is partly explained in the symbolical chart here reproduced. It forms the seventh folio of the Theosophical MS.]

---

[46] Daniel G. Brinton, M.D., LL.D., in the "American Anthropologist," April, 1894, states that among the aborigines throughout America the tribal mythologies, rites, ceremonies, beliefs are constantly and profoundly governed and moulded by this sacred number.

[47] As a type of Deity, we all know of the famous Hebrew title *Tetragrammaton*, or incommunicable name, Jehovah, IHVH; this name was disclosed by the Kabbalistic Rabbis as a blind to the populace and to hide their secret tenets.

"Almost all the peoples of antiquity possessed a name for Deity consisting of four letters, and many of them considered 4 to be a divine number." —W. Wynn Westcott, in "Numbers, their Occult Power and Mystic Virtue," p. 22.

Von der Wunder-Zahl 4.

Erstlich: Warum GOTT der Herr der ersten Welt dreymahl Viertzig Jahr, das sind 120. Jahr Frist und Zeit zur Busse gegeben? Genesis am 6.

Weiter: Aus dem alten und neuen Testament:

Im alten Testament:

40. Tage und Nächte regnet es, da die Sündfluth auf Erden kam.
40. Tage hernach, da die Sündfluth verlauffen, öffnete Noah den Kasten.
40. Tage und Nächte war Moses auf dem Berg Sinai.
40. Jahr waren die Kinder Israel in der Wüsten.
40. Tage und Nächte hat Elias gefastet.
40. Tage hatte die Stadt Ninive Zeit und Raum zur Busse.

Im neuen Testament:

40. Wochen, Christus, wie alle Menschen, in Mutter Leibe gebildet.
40. Monat der Herr auf Erden gepredigt und Wunder gethan.
40. Tage und Nächte in der Wüsten gefastet und versucht worden.
40. Stunden, der Herr Christus im Grabe gelegen.
40. Tage nach seiner Auferstehung auf Erden gewesen, und sich im verklärten Leibe sehen lassen.
40. Jahr nach Christi Himmelfahrt ist die Stadt Jerusalem zerstöhret worden.

Summa 3. mahl 4. mahl 40. ist die geheimbde Auslegung.

Wehe mir, ich vergehe, denn ich bin unreiner Lippen, die Geheimnissen auszusprechen. Esaia. 6.

Seventh Folio of Rosicrucian MS.

TRANSLATION.

Firstly.—Wherefore the Lord God vouchsafed to the first world 3 times 40 years; that is, 120 years of respite and time for repentance.—Genesis vi, 3.[48]

Further.—From the Old and New Testament.

IN THE OLD TESTAMENT.

40 days and nights it rained, as the deluge spread over the face of the earth.

40 days after the deluge the waters subsided, and Noah opened the Ark.

40 days and nights Moses sojourned upon Mount Sinai.

40 years the Children of Israel wandered in the desert.

40 days and nights were spent by Elias in fasting and prayer.

40 days were granted to the city of Nineveh for penance.

IN THE NEW TESTAMENT.

40 weeks Christ, like unto all men, was formed in his mother's womb.

40 months the Lord preached on earth and performed miracles.

40 days and nights He fasted in the desert and was tempted.

40 hours Christ lay in the grave.

40 days after His resurrection He spent upon earth, and showed Himself in His glorified body.

40 years after Christ's ascension the city of Jerusalem was destroyed.

Result.—3 times 4 times 40 is the secret interpretation.

Woe unto me, I perish, for I am of too unclean tongue to proclaim the mystery.—Isaiah vi, 5.[49]

---

[48] Ich will ihnen noch frist geben hundert und zwanzig Jahr (*i.e.*, "zu leben und busse zu thun," Martin Luther).—Basel Bible, ed. 1753.

[49] An allusion to the sanctification of Isaiah for his prophetic station.—Basel Bible.

A & Ω
Rom. I.

PHISICA, METAPHISICA, ET HYPERPHISICA.

GERARD CROESE.

ARMS OF HOLLAND, 1693.

But little is known from their own writings as to the immediate causes which led these men to take the momentous step, and forsake their home and friends to come to America. A contemporary account in Latin, published at Amsterdam in the year 1696,[50] or two years after their departure, gives us a little information about this Chapter of Pietists. This record is of the greatest importance, as it shows the fact that the party were assisted on their journey by the Friends or Quakers then in Holland,—a fact

---

A & Ω (Alpha and Omega.)—The beginning and end of all things; *i. e.*, the beginning and end of all manifestation of activity and life in the Cosmos.

Phisica, Metaphisica et Hyperphisica, from title page of Theosophical Manuscript.

[50] The first edition of Croese's "Quakeriana" was published in 1695. This edition is exceedingly rare: the only copy met with by the writer is

which was afterwards brought up to the detriment of some of their number at the yearly meeting at Burlington in 1695.[51]

A part of this account was evidently written before the company left England, while the concluding part dates from some time in 1695, shortly after the receipt of the first letter or information from the Theosophical community in America.

The chronicler, Gerard Croese,[52] a Protestant divine of Amsterdam, in his "Historia Quakeriana," Liber iii,[53] states (translation, London, 1697): "Among these new mystical Men there was one *John Jacob Zimmerman*,[54] pastor of the *Lutheran* Church in the *Dutchy* of *Wirtemburg*, a Man skilled in Mathematicks, and, saving that he had contracted of these erroneous opinions, had all other excellent endowments of mind, to which may be added the temperance of his Life, wherein he was inferior to none, and who was of considerable fame in the world; Who, when he saw there was nothing but great danger like to hang over himself and his Friends, he invites and stirs up through his own hope about sixteen or seaventeen Families of these sort of Men, to prefer also an hope

Arms of Würtemberg, A.D. 1693.

in the archives of the German Society in Philadelphia; it bears the imprint "Apud || Henricum & Viduam || Theodore Boom, 1695." Of the second edition (1696) there is a copy in the Historical Society of Pennsylvania, and another in the library of the writer.

51 Pemberton MSS., Smith's "History of the Province," Hazard's Register, vol. vi, No. 23.

52 Gerard Croese, a Protestant divine, born at Amsterdam in 1642. He studied at Leyden, whence he went with a son of the celebrated De Ruyter

of better things, tho it were dubious before the present danger, and forsaking their Country which they through the most percipitous and utmost danger, tho they suffered Death for the same, could not help and relieve as they supposed, and leaving their Inheritance, which they could not carry along with them, to depart and betake themselves into other parts of the world, even to *Pensilvania*, the Quakers Country, and there divide all the good and evil that befell them between themselves, and learn the Languages of that People, and Endeavour to inspire Faith and Piety into the same Inhabitants by their words and examples which they could not do to these Christians here.

GERARDI CROESI
HISTORIA
QUAKERIANA,
Sive
De vulgo dictis QUAKERIS,
Ab ortu illorum usque ad recens
natum schisma,
LIBRI III.
In quibus præsertim agitur de ipsorum præcipuis antecessoribus & dogmatis (ut & similibus placitis aliorum hoc tempore) factisque, ac casibus, memorabilibus
EDITIO SECUNDA
Indice locupletior.

AMSTELODAMI,
ANNO M.DC.IVC.

"These agree to it, at least so far as to try and sound the way, and if things did not go ill, to fortify and fit themselves for the same.

"*Zimmerman*, having yet *N. Koster*[55] for his Colleague,

---

to Smyrna, and on his return home became pastor of Alblasserdam, near Dort, where he died in 1710. He wrote the "History of the Quakers," printed in Dutch, 1694, and translated into English in 1696. It was answered by a Quaker work entitled "Dilucidationes quædam valdé Necessariæ in Gerardi Croesii, Hist.," 8vo. Croese wrote also a singular book, with the title of "Homerus Hebræus, sive Historia Hebræorum ab Homero," 1704, 4to. The intent of this work is to prove that the Odyssey contains the history of the Jews in the patriarchial ages, and that the Iliad is an account of the siege and capture of Jericho. He is chiefly known by his history of the Quakers, which went through several editions in Latin, English and German.

who was also a famous Man, and of such severe manners that few could equal him, writes to a certain Quaker in *Holland* who was a Man of no mean Learning, and very wealthy, very bountiful and liberal towards all the poor, pious and good:

"*That as he and his followers and friends designed*, (They are the very words of the Letter which is now in my Custody). *To depart from these Babilonish Coasts, to those* American Plantations, *being led thereunto by the guidance of the Divine Spirit, and that seeing that all of them wanted worldly substance, that they would not let them want Friends, but assist them herein, that they might have a good Ship well provided for them to carry them into those places, wherein they might mind this one thing, to wit to shew with unanimous consent, their Faith and Love in the Spirit in converting of People, but at the same time to sustain their bodies by their daily Labour.*

"So great was the desire, inclination and affection of this Man towards them, that he forthwith promised them all manner of assistance, and performed it and fitted them with a Ship for their purpose, and did out of that large Portion of Land he had in *Pensilvania*, assign unto them a matter of two thousand and four hundred Acres, for ever of such Land as it was, but such as might be manured, imposing yearly to be paid a very small matter of rent upon every Acre, and gave freely of his own and what he got from his friends, as much as paid their Charge and Passage, amounting to an hundred and thirty pounds sterling; a very great gift, and so much the more strange, that that

---

[53] P. 539, et seq. (English translation, vol. ii., p. 262, seq.).

[54] Zimmermann, p. 563, *ibid*, original edition.

[55] This should be Henry Bernhard Köster.

same Quaker should be so liberal, and yet would not have his name mentioned, or known in the matter.[56]

"But when these Men came into *Holland*, they Sailed from thence directly for *Pensilvania*;[57] Zimmerman seasonably dies, but surely it was unseasonable for them, but yet not so, but that they all did chearfully persue their Voyage, and while I am writing hereof, I receive an account that they arrived at the place they aim at, and that they all lived in the same house, and had a publick Meeting three times every week, and that they took much pains, to teach the blind people to become like unto themselves, and to conform to their examples."

Croese, in explanation, further states (English trans., vol. ii, p. 256): "Moreover, there was in *Germany*, as it were, three sorts of *Pietists* (pardon the expression). One, which I have described, consists of those who sought, and pressed nothing else, but sincere Religion and true Piety; and the greatest part of those are among the Learned and better sort of men, through *Saxony* and all *Germany*.

"[Second.]—Another sort of them was that cryed, That the Church was much Corrupted, and loved Piety; but such, who themselves on the other hand, stagger not a little in the Faith and True Religion, and these same are commonly less moderate and more violent in Celebrating their Assemblies together. . . . . . .

"[Third.]—The third sort of them was that which may be called *Behmists* or *Teutonists*;[58] these called back, as it

---

[56] Everything goes to point to Benjamin Furley as this charitable friend, who was also the agent of Wm. Penn at Rotterdam.

[57] This an error; the party went from Rotterdam to England, thence to America. *Vide*, p. 15, supra.

[58] They were also known as Gichtelians or Gichtelianer, who were conspicuous for their silent, virtuous and benevolent life.

were, *Jacob Behman*,[59] the Shoemaker of Garlingen in Silesia, from the Dead, who was called *Tutonick*, and did both Broach those Opinions, which had been really delivered by him, as also those Errors that had been falsely laid upon him, and ascribed to him, yea, and horrid and hellish Blasphemy, and cried them up as worthy of all Esteem and Glory."

---

[59] Jacob Boehme, or Behmen, was one of the most renowned mystics of modern times. Born in 1575 at Altseidenberg, a village near Görlitz, of poor parents, he remained to his tenth year without instruction and employed in tending cattle. He was then apprenticed to a shoemaker, and in 1594 he became a master shoemaker in Görlitz, married and continued a shoemaker all his days. Several visions and raptures led him to take up the pen. His first work appeared in 1616, and was called "Aurora." It contains his revelations on God, man and nature. Perhaps his most important work is his "Description of the Three Principles of Divine Being." His works contain many profound and lofty ideas. He died, after several prosecutions and acquittals, in 1624.

Several complete sets of Boehme's works (Amsterdam edition, Gichtel, 1682, 10 vols.) were brought over to America by Kelpius and his followers.

ARMS OF THE UNITED NETHERLANDS, FROM AN OLD COPPERPLATE.

Effigy of Johannes Tauler in the former Church of the Dominicans at Strasburg, from a sketch made in 1840.

THE PIETISTS IN GERMANY.

Ancient Episcopal Seal of Erfurth.

IT was in the second half of the seventeenth century, during a marked period of spiritual unrest which pervaded Germany, that an agitation was caused in German theological circles by the well-known divine Philip Jacob Spener,[60] who advocated a system of personal and practical piety, having for its central principle "That Christianity was first of all life, and that the strongest proof of the truth of its doctrine was to be found in the religious experience of the believing."

Organizations were formed which became known as "Collegia Pietatis," and the individual members as "Pie-

---

Greek monogram of Christ and symbol of salvation.

[60] Philip Jacob Spener, born in Alsace, January 13, 1635; died in Berlin, February 5, 1705. As early as 1680 he formulated the dogma that only persons inspired by the Holy Ghost could understand the Scriptures, which produced many enthusiasts. For a time he lived in Dresden, afterwards in Berlin, where he held some ecclesiastical dignities.

PHILIP JACOB SPENER,
FROM AN OLD ENGRAVING IN THE FERD. J. DREER COLLECTION.

tists,"[61] and as Spener obviously based his dogmas upon the writings of Johannes Tauler,[62] these "Collegia" throughout Germany soon became homes for the mystics of all sorts—religious and speculative—with which continental Europe swarmed at the time.

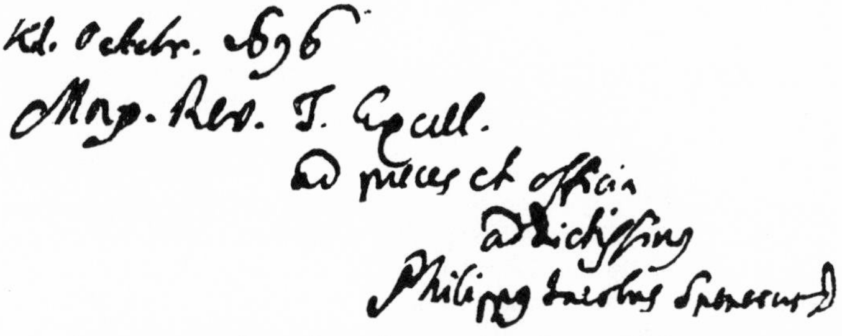

AUTOGRAPH OF PHILIP JACOB SPENER, FROM DREER COLLECTION.

Among the names prominent in this movement are Johann Heinrich Horbius, brother-in-law to Spener, Hochmann von Hochenau,[63] August Hermann Francke,[64] Gottfried Arnold,[65] Dr. Johann Jacob Fabricius[66] of Helmstadt, Dr. J. W. Petersen, Johanna von Merlau and many others of equal prominence.

One of the most important centers of this movement was the ancient city of Erfurth, in Thuringia. At an early period of this agitation it became a rallying-point for students, Mystics and Pietists, from all parts of Germany. Here also was formed the organization a part of which eventually came to America in a body.

ARMS OF ERFURTH, 1693.

The date of the organization of this individual Chapter in Erfurth was in 1690 or 1691, when we find it under the leadership or patronage of Rev. August Hermann Francke,[67] then "Diaconus Augustini" (assistant pastor at the Augustine Church). Under date of January 27, 1691, a commission was appointed by the reigning authority to inquire about the Pietists who held secret meetings by day and

[61] A somewhat similar movement in the Roman Church at the same period was started by one Miguel de Molinos. The members of this sect were known as Quietists. A more extended notice of this order is given in a subsequent chapter.

[62] Johannes Tauler (the name is variously spelled in the old MSS. viz., Tauler, Tauller, Tauweler, Thauler, and even Thaler, *vide*, catalogue libr. MSS., Leipsic, p. 721). This celebrated leader among mystic theosophists was born in 1290 at Strasburg. About the year 1308 he entered the convent of the Dominicans, and became a monk of that order. He acquired great skill in philosophy and scholastic divinity, but applied himself principally to mystical theology, and as it was believed that he was favored with revelations from heaven, he was styled the *Illuminated Divine.*

His great talents for preaching soon made him the most popular preacher of his age. In his great love of truth and the earnestness with which he devoted himself to the instruction of the people, and in his opposition to the abuses of the Roman Church, Tauler was a worthy predecessor of Luther.

His followers were known as *Gottesfreunde*, or the *Friends of God*, a designation derived directly from the words of Christ as recorded in the Gospel of St. John xv, 15. Tauler's followers formed themselves into Chapters and Societies, and after the publication of the ban of the Church continued to meet in secret.

The following extract from a sermon preached by Tauler on the twenty-second Sunday after Trinity (Basel folio MSS., A.D. 1290) gives his reasons for the institution of the new mystical society *der Gottesfreunde.* It also serves as an representative specimen of Tauler's composition and mediæval German,—

„Der fürſte dirre
„welte der hat iezent an allen enden geseget das unkrut
„under den rosen, das die rosen dicke von den dornen
„verdrucket oder sere geſtochen werdent. Kinder, es mûs
„ein flüht oder ein ungelicheit, ein sûnderheit sin, es si
„in den klöſtern oder do uſsen, und das ensint nüt sec-
„ten das sich gottes frünt ungelich üsgebent der welte
„fründen"

A Collegium Pietatis in Session.
(From an old German engraving.)

night, and were harbored by the Diaconus Francke in one of the abandoned cloisters within his parish.[68]

The result of this inquisition was an edict for the suppression of the Chapter, together with a censure and fine imposed upon the Diaconus Francke. Whereupon Francke, as well as his Senior, Dr. Breitenhaupt,[69] preached several sermons against the action of the authorities.[70] This action

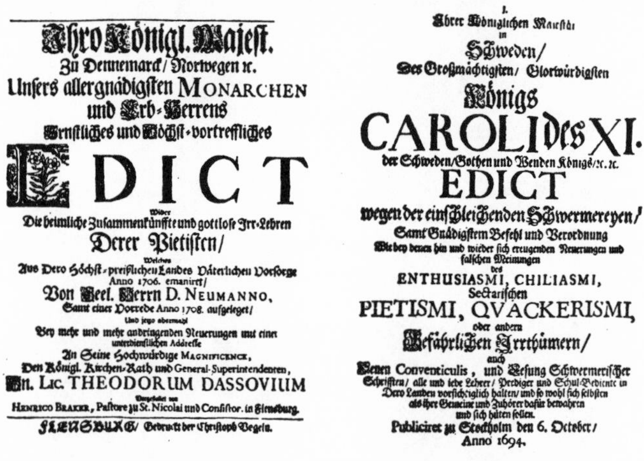

Ihro Königl. Majest.
Zu Dennemarck / Norwegen ꝛc.
Unsers allergnädigsten MONARCHEN
und Erb-Herrens
Ernstliches und Höchst-vortreffliches
EDICT
Wider
Die heimliche Zusammenkünffte und gottlose Irr-Lehren
Derer Pietisten /
Welches
Aus Dero Höchst-preißlichen Landes Väterlichen Vorsorge
Anno 1706. emaniret /
Von Seel. Herrn D. NEUMANNO,
Samt einer Vorrede Anno 1708. aufgeleget /
Und jetzo abermahl
Bey mehr und mehr andringenden Neuerungen mit einer
unterdienstlichen Addresse
An Seine Hochwürdige MAGNIFICENCE,
Den Königl. Kirchen-Rath und General-Superintendenten,
Hn. LIC. THEODORUM DASSOVIUM
Vorgestellet von
HENRICO BRAKER, Pastore zu St. Nicolai und Consistor. in Flensburg.
FLENSBURG / Gedruckt bey Christoph Vogeln.

I.
Ihrer Königlichen Majestät
in
Schweden /
Des Großmächtigsten / Glorwürdigsten
Königs
CAROLI des XI.
der Schweden / Gothen und Wenden Königs / ꝛc. ꝛc.
EDICT
wegen der einschleichenden Schwermereyen /
Samt Gnädigstem Befehl und Verordnung
Wie bey denen hin und wieder sich ereugenden Neuerungen und
falschen Meinungen
des
ENTHUSIASMI, CHILIASMI,
Sectarischen
PIETISMI, QVACKERISMI,
oder andern
Gefährlichen Irrthümern /
auch
Denen Conventiculis, und Lesung Schwermerischer
Schrifften / alle und iede Lehrer / Prediger und Schul-Bediente in
Dero Landen vorsichtiglich halten / und so wohl sich selbsten
als ihre Gemeine und Zuhörer dafür bewahren
und sich hüten sollen.
Publiciret zu Stockholm den 6. October /
Anno 1694.

renewed the trouble and culminated in Diaconus Francke being excommunicated by the Church at Erfurth. This

[63] Ernst Christoph Hochmann von Hochenau, a leading mystic, who while imprisoned in the Castle Detmold, in November, 1702, formulated a Pietistical creed or profession of faith (Glaubensbekentniss). This was republished by Christopher Saur in Germantown, 1743. A fragment of an Ephrata reprint has also been found.

[64] Croese in his account states, p. 545: "The chief whereof (the Pietists) were Augustus H. Francus, the Disciple and Companion for a long time of Spener and John L'Schadeus, Francus' fellow-student, both of them Masters of Art, and Learned and Eloquent."

[65] Gottfried Arnold, a Lutheran clergyman and well-known writer on mystic theology.

[66] The tutor of Johannes Kelpius.

decretum was issued September 18, 1691, and went into force forthwith.[71] Twenty-four hours only were granted him to leave the city; during which time he is said to have composed the beautiful German hymn "Gott Lob ein Schritt zur Ewigkeit." Upon the formulation of this edict Dr. Breitenhaupt, the "Senior Augustini," preached a sermon in justification of Francke, for which he also was dismissed and ordered to leave the city; a body of respectable burghers who attempted to intercede for Francke were summarily imprisoned.

CIVITATIS ERFFURTENSIS
HISTORIA CRITICA
ET DIPLOMATICA,
Oder vollständige
Alt-Mittel- und Neue
Historie von Erffurth,
Worinnen
Von dieser Stadt Ursprung, wahren Anwachs und Aufnahme, denen allda gehaltenen Synodis und Reichs-Tägen, zugestossenen Glücks- und Unglücks-Fällen gehandelt;
Sonst auch viele und größten Theils ungedruckte Diplomata, Verträge, Handlungen, errichtete Recesse und dergleichen Piecen mehr beygebracht, und wo es nöthig mit Anmerckungen erläutert.
Alle Begebenheiten aber
In V. Büchern abgehandelt,
Und mit einem vollständigen Register versehen werden;
Ausgefertiget von
Johann Heinrich von Falckenstein,
Hoch-Fürstl. Brandenburg-Anspachischen Hof-Rathe, und der Königl. Preußischen Societät der Wissenschafften Mitgliede.

ERFFURTH,
Druckts und verlegts Johann Wilhelm Ritschel. 1739.

[AUGUST HERMANN FRANCKE.—This celebrated clergyman was born in Lübeck, March 23, 1663; died June 8, 1727. He is chiefly known for the charitable institution which he founded at Halle for the education of poor children and orphans, and which soon became one of the most celebrated charitable institutions of Germany. It is usually known as "das Hallische Waisenhaus." The usefulness of this institution was soon enlarged by the

---

67 See "Civitatis Erffurtensis," p. 1056, copy in library of writer.

68 "Civitatis Erffurtensis," p. 1055.

69 This was the celebrated Joachim Justus Breitenhaupt, born at Nordheim, February, 1658; died Halle, March 16, 1732. He is chiefly known by his "Thesis credendarum et agendorum fundementalis," 1700, and "De perfectione partium," 1704.

70 Ibid, p. 1056.

71 "Civitatis Effurtensis," p. 1059; "Die Stiftengen Aug. Her. Francke," Halle, 1863, p. 66.

August Hermann Francke.

Theol. Prof. Ord. Past. Ulric. & Scholarch.

PORTRAIT AND AUTOGRAPH FROM COLLECTION OF FERD. J. DREER, ESQ., PHILA.

introduction of a department having for its object the spreading of the Gospel in foreign parts. It was at the instance of this clergyman and under the auspices of the Halle Orphanage that the Rev. Henry Melchior Mühlenberg was sent to America, where he became the patriarch of the Lutheran Church. It is further an interesting fact that the first church built in America by Pastor Mühlenburg, at the "Trappe," in Montgomery County, Penna., was named in honor of August Hermann Francke the "Augustus Church," the congregation of which have just celebrated their sesqui-centennial (September 26, 1893).[72] The church is still in a good condition and is the only provincial church in America which yet retains all of its quaint original features.

Another interesting item in connection with the institution presided over by Dr. Francke is the manner in which he obtained the sustenance for its support. One of the members of the Collegium Pietatis in Erfurth, Burgstaller by name, who was an alchemist and chemist, on his deathbed bequeathed to Francke the receipt for compounding certain medicines,[73] which were sold by the different clergymen in sympathy with the institution.[74] These remedies eventually yielded an annual income of more than $20,000,[75] and

---

[72] See "Sesqui-Centennial Memorial of Trappe Church," by Rev. E. T. Kretschmann, Ph. D., Phila., 1894.

[73] Burgstaller's chief nostrum was the celebrated *Goldtinctur*, or extract of gold. It was also known as the *Essentia dulcis*.

[74] Prior to the Revolution these remedies were sent to America in large quantities, and were disposed of to the Germans and others by the resident Lutheran clergymen. In Philadelphia the main supply was stored in one of the side porches of St. Michael's Church, corner Fifth and Appletree Alley. By many persons these remedies were supposed to have magical or supernatural properties, against which neither Satan nor disease could prevail.

[75] The maximum income from that source was reached in 1761, and amounted to 36,106 thalers.

made the institution financially independent. It combined an orphan asylum, a pædagogium, a Latin school, a German school and a printing press for issuing cheap copies of the Bible.]

Halle. 1693. Jan. 10.

DRAFT OF LETTER BY FRANCKE TO SPENER, FROM AUTOGRAPH COLLECTION OF FERD. J. DREER, ESQ., PHILADELPHIA.

As the Pietistical movement spread and gained foothold in the various governments in Germany, and extended into the neighboring kingdoms, special edicts were issued against it, in which not only public and private[76] assemblages of the Pietists were forbidden, but also their literature.[77]

[76] Edict promulgated at Leipsic, March 25, A.D. 1690.

[77] Edict, Stockholm, October 6, 1694.

In all of these edicts[78] the sale of all Pietistical or suspicious books was prohibited under heavy penalties, while reading and discussing, or even countenancing, such works was interdicted by both Church and secular authorities.

After his expulsion from Erfurth, Francke went to Gotha where his mother then lived. Shortly afterwards he received a call as pastor at Glaucha,[79] a suburb of Halle.

In the year 1694 he was offered and accepted the professorship of oriental languages[80] in the new University at Halle,[81] and four years later (1698) founded the celebrated orphanage in the suburbs of Halle, which exists to the present day.

Notwithstanding the expulsion of Francke from Erfurth, the meetings were continued without intermission, but less openly. Consequently, on July 20, 1693, the authorities issued another edict or "Decretum Senatus," which was publicly read from every pulpit, forbidding under penalty the assemblage of any "Collegia Pietatis" within the jurisdiction.

---

[78] Edict, March 2, 1692; February 28, 1694. Manifesto, February 4, 1697. Edict, January 7, 1698. Edict, Halle, January 25, 1700. A copy of all the edicts above quoted are in possession of the writer.

[79] Glaucha, a village or settlement without the walls of Halle. At that early period Glaucha and Halle were virtually two distinct towns. There was no communication between the two places after sundown, at which time the portals of Halle were closed.—*Stiftungen Francke's*, p. 299.

[80] Francke afterwards filled the chair of theology.

[81] The celebrated Frederick University of Halle—so called after its founder Frederick I, King of Prussia—was opened in the year 1694. The Great Elector of Brandenburg had founded an academy at Halle in 1688, this was known as the "Ritterakademie," and in 1694 was changed into a university, when the celebrated Thomasius came hither from Leipsic, followed by a number of students. A series of distinguished professors and the liberal provisions of government soon raised this university to the rank of one of the first in Europe. The university was twice suppressed by Napoleon (1806–13). In 1815, by a Prussian Edict, the university was united with that of Wittenberg, since which time it bears the official title of the *United Frederick University of Halle-Wittenberg*.

Among the minor clergymen of note who were attracted to the Pietistical movement was the before-mentioned John Jacob Zimmermann, of Bietigheim, in Würtemberg, a man well versed in geometry, geomancy and astrology, as well as theology. He was also a prominent character in the various philosophical and theosophical fraternities in his native country. Upon being deprived of his charge by the church authorities on account of his connection with the Mystics, it appears that he drifted to various places, and while in Hamburgh he became acquainted with Horbius, the brother-in-law of Spener. He finally went to Erfurth, and there perfected the plan of organizing a "Chapter of Perfection," and going in a body to the western world.

Mystical Chart from Merlau's "Glaubens Gespräche mit Gott."

Another of the chief promoters of this scheme of emigration, who never reached these shores, was the celebrated Dr. Johann Wilhelm Petersen, who, together with his wife, Eleonore von Merlau, was a member of the Frankfort Land Company, under whose auspices Pastorius had come to Pennsylvania in 1683. The intercourse between Dr. Petersen and the leaders of this Chapter

Mystical Symbol from Merlau's "Glaubens Gespräche mit Gott."

of Pietists was close and intimate. The former, although a leading figure in the extreme mystical movements of the day, was no mere adventurer. A professor of Poesie in Rostock, pastor in Hanover, and superintendent in Lübeck and Lüneburg he moved in the best society. He was married to the celebrated Eleonore von Merlau, who was subject to ecstatic visions.

The couple conscientiously studied the Apocalypse to ascertain when the millennium of Christ would take place. They were aided in this research by the beautiful Rosamunda von Asseburg, an ecstatical phenomenon of the time, whose piety even Leibnitz and Spener never questioned for a moment. The result of these speculations were published in 1691 simultaneously at Frankfort and Leipsic, under the title of "Glaubens Gespräche mit Gott."

Glaubens-Gespräche
Mit
GOTT
In Drey unterschiedene Theile abgefasset/
Als daß
Der I. Theil/
Das Werck des Glaubens
in der Krafft/
Der II. Theil/
Das Zeugniß/die Macht und
Herrlichkeit des Glaubens/
Der III. Theil/
Das Ende des Glaubens/welches ist der Seelen Seligkeit/
vorstellet/
In dieser letzten Glaublosen Zeit
zur Auffmunterung und Erweckung des
Glaubens auffgesetzt
Von
OHANNA ELEONORA Petersen/
Gebohrne von und zu Merlau.

Franckf. und Leipzig/
Bey Michael Brodthagen/ im Jahr Christi 1691.

The outcome of Zimmermann's efforts, as stated by Croese, was an application made to some prominent Quakers in Holland for aid and sustenance during the proposed voyage. Zimmermann, however, did not live to witness the successful culmination of his hopes, as he died on the eve of the embarkation at Rotterdam, in 1693. His widow with her four children, however, continued on the journey, and came to Pennsylvania with the party that her husband had been instrumental in organizing.[82]

The men who composed this Chapter of Mystics were not only Pietists in the accepted sense of the word, but they were also a true Theosophical (Rosicrucian) Community, a branch of that ancient mystical brotherhood who studied and practised the Kabbala,[83] which, when truly searched for, contemplated and understood, it is believed, "Opens her arms, and from its great height in the unknown essence of the Supreme Deity, the Endless, Boundless One, to its depth in the lowest materialism of evil, gives an opportunity for the reception and acquisition of the grandest and noblest ideas, to the highest and most subtle order of religious spiritual thought.[84]

---

[82] The widow, Mary Margaret Zimmermann, and her three sons and one daughter, viz., Phillip Christian, Mary Margaret, Mathew and Jacob Christopher. *Vide*, will proved in Philadelphia, October 1, 1725, Will Book "D," p. 433, etc.

[83] Various are the opinions of scholars respecting the origin of the Kabbalistic Philosophy. The Rabbis derive the kabbalistic mysteries from the most ancient times of their nation, nay even from Adam himself. But although a secret doctrine existed among the Hebrews in the earliest ages, this had reference merely to religious worship. The origin of the Philosophical Kabbala is to be sought for in Egypt, and dates from the time of Simeon Schetachides, who conveyed it from Egypt to Palestine. [Mansel (Gnostic Heresies) says: Persian influence at the captivity, a much likelier source. The dualism and angelology of Mazdeism suddenly appear in the Old Testament after the captivity.] Thus: 2 Sam. xxiv, 1, Jehovah moves David to number Israel. This is the pre-exilian account. But 1 Chron. xxi, 1, says it was Satan. This is the post-exilian account, after contact with the Zoroastrian doctrine of Ahriman. It is well known that the Asmodeus in the Book of Tobit is a Persian name for a demon. Even such a sober scholar as Bishop Lightfoot admits a connection between Mazdeism and Essenism; while L. H. Mills, one of the translators of the sacred books of the East, is still more pronounced in maintaining a direct historical connection between the late books of the Old Testament and the Zoroastrian cult. While the Kabbala probably arose from the same wave of post-exilian thought as generated Essenism, it is extremely difficult to trace it back as a system beyond the Middle Ages, when its principal writings were composed.

[84] Kabbala.

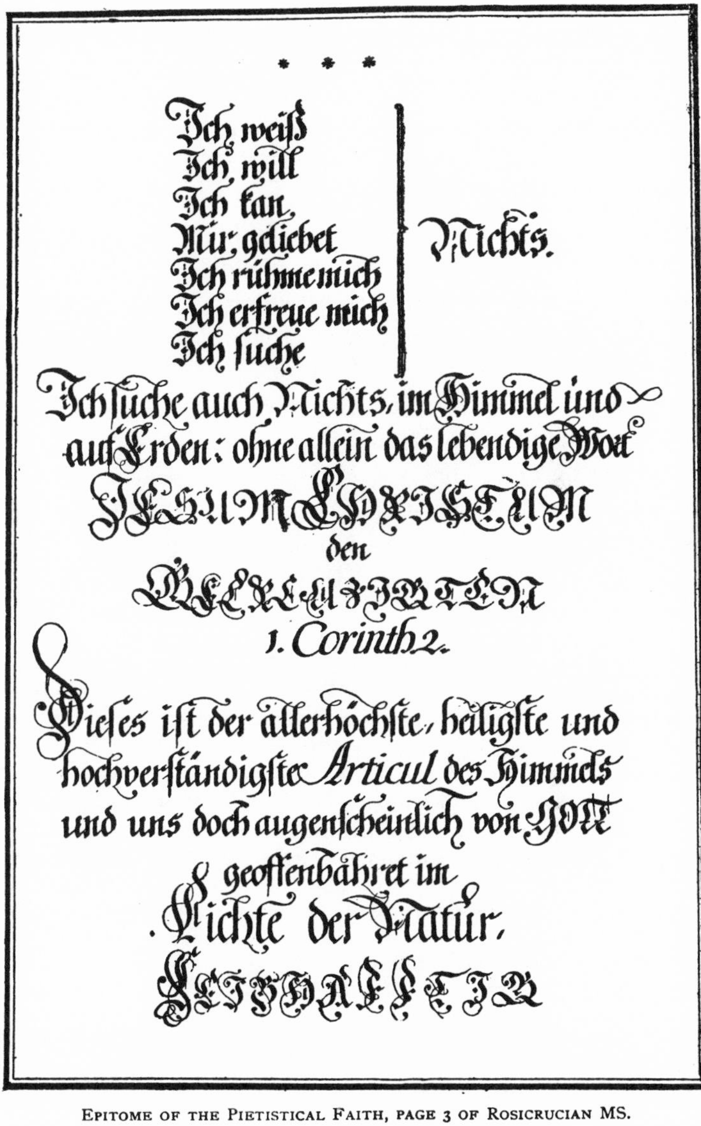

* * *

Ich weiss
Ich will
Ich kan,
Mir geliebet
Ich rühme mich
Ich erfreue mich
Ich suche
| Nichts.

Ich suche auch Nichts, im Himmel und auf Erden: ohne allein das lebendige Wort

JESUM CHRISTUM

den

GECREUTZIGTEN

1. Corinth 2.

Dieses ist der allerhöchste, heiligste und hochverständigste *Articul* des Himmels und uns doch augenscheinlich von GOTT geoffenbahret im

Lichte der Natur.

LEIBHAFFTIG

Epitome of the Pietistical Faith, page 3 of Rosicrucian MS.

The great object of these speculations was to reach the nearest approach that man can make to the unseen, that inner communion which works silently in the soul, but which cannot be expressed in absolute language nor by any words, which is beyond all formulations into word-symbolism, yet is on the confines of the unknown spiritual world. This state, it was held, could only be obtained away from the allurements of the world by entering into silence, meditation and inter-communion with one's self.

"With the absolute negation of all world-matter, thought and world-matter existence; or, in other words, the nearest approach to the Invisible can only be reached by the acknowledgment of the Non Ego."

Translation of epitome,—

"I understand—I purpose—I accomplish—I find pleasure in—I boast of—I delight in—I seek—NOUGHT.

"I also seek nought[85] in Heaven or on Earth, except only the living Word.

"Jesus Christ the crucified.—I Corinth., ii.[86]

"This is the most exalted, holiest and most judicious *Articul*[87] of Heaven, and to us evidently disclosed by God revealed in the Light of Nature."

---

[85] An explanation of the occult term *nothing* is that it is to be taken as the antithesis of something. In occult literature the term *nothing* is sometimes applied to signify something which is inconceivable, and therefore *no thing* to us. In the German, the word is used to denote the Non Ego, or the absolute insignificance of the human being in comparison with the Deity.

[86] "Jesus Christ and Him crucified."

[87] Used in the sense of a point of faith.

IN THE NEW WORLD.

THE first matter to attract the attention of the leaders of the Theosophical community upon their arrival in the German settlement was the pitiful condition of the Germans, who were here entirely without any regularly ordained spiritual advisers, the nearest approach to church worship being the occasional house services of the Mennonite brethren, and the silent meetings like those of the Society of Friends,[88] that were held at the house of Tennis Kundert.[89]

---

[88] Watson, vol. ii, p. 23.

[89] A part of the walls of this old house was standing as late as 1823, a portion of what was then known as Lesher's Inn. At present it is known as No. 5109 Germantown Avenue. Mr. T. H. Shoemaker informs me of a singular fact regarding the old wall used by Lesher in rebuilding, that it would not retain a coat of "dash" or "roughcast," which fell off whenever put on, thus exposing the original stones and pointing.

The early settlers of the German Township, although all were consistent Protestants and persons of exemplary piety, made no attempt whatever after their arrival in America to establish regular orthodox services according to either the Lutheran ritual or the Reformed,—the faiths in which they were all brought up in the Fatherland.[90]

Die Erste/
Vngeenderte/Rechte/wahre
Augspurgische
Confession/
Wie die auff dem Reichstag zu
Augspurg/ Anno 1530. Carolo. V.
vbergeben/ zu Meintz in des Reichs Archiuis beygelegt/ vnd aus dem Original beiden Churfürsten
Sachsen vnd Brandenburg zugeschickt.
II
Confutatio oder Wiederlegung/ von den
Päpstischen wider dieselbige vbergeben/etc.
III.
Die Erste/ Rechte/ Wahre/
Apologia.
Aus Philippi vnd der zeit anwesenden Theologen
Correctur vnd Hand trewlich beschrieben etc.
Allen Christen zur bestendigen gewisheit vnd vngeschewete Bekentnüs auffs new in Druck gegeben.
Cum privilegio Saxonico & Brandeburgico.
Gedruckt bey Friderich Hartman/ Buchführer
in Franckfurt an der Oder/ Im Jahr 1603.

TITLE OF KÖSTER'S PERSONAL COPY OF THE UNALTERED AUGSBURG CONFESSION.

No sooner had the enthusiastic Köster learned of this state of affairs than he immediately commenced to hold religious services in the German language, after the manner of the Lutheran Church, at the house of Van Bebber,[91] wherein he sought to impress his hearers with the importance of remaining steadfast to the dogmas of the Church as founded upon the original Augsburg Confession.[92]

---

[90] Dr. Oswald Seidensticker, in *Cincinnatti Pioneer*, vol. ii, p. 275.

[91] Jacob Isaacs Van Bebber, a baker of Crefeld, was one of the original six Crefeld purchasers who bought 1000 acres of land each from William Penn on June 11, 1683, and whose object was colonization and not speculation. Jacob Isaacs Van Bebber came to America as a Mennonite in 1687, and became one of the most influential persons in the community. He was a man of standing, ability, enterprise, and means. A few years after the arrival of Kelpius in America, Van Bebber moved to Philadelphia, where he is described, in 1698, as "a merchant in High Street." He died in the city prior to 1711. For additional facts concerning the Van Bebber family, see Hon. Samuel W. Pennypacker, in *Pennsylvania Magazine*, vol. iv, pp. 1–41.

[92] The Augsburg Confession, presented by the Protestants at the Diet of Augsburg, 1530, to the Emperor and the Diet, and, being signed by the

These services were public, and from the outset were well attended by the Germans. As they became known throughout the vicinity a number of English hearers presented themselves. On account of their numbers it was at first thought that they were Quakers, who strove to fill the house so as to exclude the regular German worshippers. Such, however, proved not to be the case: they were, in fact, Keithians[93] or Christian Quakers, as the followers of George Keith were then called. Thus it frequently happened that the English outnumbered the Germans.

Impressed with the importance of the situation, Köster informed his German hearers that, as so many of the attendants at the services could not understand German, while nearly all knew English, he would thereafter conduct services in both languages.[94] This course at first caused

---

Protestant States, was adopted as their creed. Luther made the original draught, at the command of John, Elector of Saxony, at Torgau, in seventeen articles; but, as its style appeared to be too violent, it was altered by Melanchthon, at the command of the Elector, and in compliance with the wishes of the body of Protestant princes and theologians. Thus changed, it was presented and read in the Diet, June 25, 1530, and henceforth became the creed of the Orthodox Lutheran Church.

Afterwards Melanchthon arbitrarily altered some of the articles, and a new edition with his changes appeared in 1540. The latter gave rise to the denomination known as "German Reformed."

Köster's copy of the original Confession, the title of which is reproduced in fac-simile, also contains the original seventeen articles as presented by Martin Luther. This book is now in possession of the writer.

[93] George Keith personally disavowed the appellation "Keithian," and objected to its use by his enemies. In a letter written to Rev. Gerard Croese, he states: "As to my part, it is very odious to me that such among the people called Quakers, professing the same *Christian faith* with me, should be called Keithians. For if the name of *Calvinist* be odious to him, why should not the name of Keithian he equally odious to me and to my brethren professing the same faith of Christ with me, which name this author useth in divers places of his history?" See "The General History of the Quakers." (London, 1696; Appendix, p. 1.)

[94] Geschichte jetzt lebender Gelchrten (Zelle, 1743), p. 489.

much dissatisfaction among the Germans. The English services were, however, soon transferred to Philadelphia,[95] where Köster used all his eloquence and learning to lead such of the Quakers as were discontented back to the Church.

The Keithians flocked around his standard, and in the fall of 1694, for the first time since the establishment of the Province under Penn, church services, that approximated orthodoxy, were held at regular intervals in Philadelphia.[96]

One of the first fruits of these services was to show to what a low spiritual state the Province had fallen. As a matter of fact there were few or no English Bibles to be had. As soon as this became known to Köster he wrote to London, and at his own expense had a large number sent over from England[97] to Philadelphia for distribution among his hearers. It is a fact worthy of record that, notwithstanding the theosophical and mystical tendencies of Heinrich Bernhard Köster, the pious and erratic enthusiast, the religious services instituted by him at Germantown and Philadelphia in 1694 were undoubtedly strictly according to the Lutheran ritual, and were also the first of the kind to be held in America in the German and English languages.

Furthermore, it was the influence engendered by these religious meetings, led by the bold and aggressive German, that paved the way for the establishment of the Episcopal Church services as by law ordained in the Province.

---

[95] An account of his later religious services will be found in a subsequent chapter.

[96] Falkner, in his *Sendschreiben aus der neuen welt*, states, "In the house of this man Jacob Isaacs (Van Bebber) there are every week three meetings, at which Köster generally speaks publicly to the great edification of those present. It is also his custom to hold a meeting once a week in Philadelphia in which he speaks English."

[97] Rathelf, Biography, vol. vi, p. 494.

The earliest church services held on the western banks of the Delaware or South River, under both the Swedish and the Dutch *régime*, were also services of the Orthodox Lutheran Church as founded on the Augsburg Confession, but they were held in either the Swedish or the Low Dutch language.[98]

It is true that the Rev. Jacob Fabritius,[99] the last Swedish or Dutch clergyman who served the congregations on the Delaware prior to the arrival of Kelpius and his party, was a German by birth, and had been regularly ordained as a Lutheran pastor at Grosglogau, in Silesia, before coming to America; but there are no records or traditions whatever to show that Fabritius ever held a single service in the German language while in Pennsylvania, or even that he opened communications with the German immigrants who arrived with Pastorius, or subsequently came to the Germanopolis in Penn's Province.

While Köster was looking after the religious needs of the Germans and their English neighbors, Kelpius consummated arrangements looking toward the permanent

---

[98] Acrelius, *New Sweden* (translation), p. 177.

[99] Rev. Jacob Fabritius, before mentioned, see note page 30, was originally sent to America (New Amsterdam) by the Consistory of Amsterdam to serve the Dutch Lutheran churches along the Hudson River. He arrived in New York in 1669, but his conduct there, as is shown by the public documents of the day, was far from bringing honor upon himself or his church. After many quarrels with his congregations and the local magistrates, he finally drifted to the Delaware in 1671, and in the year following he and one Lock divided the Swedish congregations into two parishes. In 1677 we find Fabritius holding services in the old blockhouse at Wicacoa. It also appears that Fabritius lived up the Delaware, somewhere on the river bank near Shackamaxon. He died some time in 1693, about a year before the arrival of the theosophical fraternity. An attempt has been made by a late writer to show that the blind pastor of Wicacoa was the son of the celebrated court preacher of the same name as Gustavus Adolphus.

settlement of his party and the religious and moral education of the neglected youth within the German Township, as one of the best means to promote vital religion, to raise the lukewarm from indifference and excite a spirit of vigor and resolution in those who had been satisfied to lament in silence the progress of impiety.[100]

The individual members of the party who had found refuge among their countrymen in the settlements of Sommerhausen and Crisheim near the Wingohocking,[101] by whom they were most cordially received, and where they shone as peculiar lights, remained in the vicinity of Germantown only until such time as Thomas Fairman the surveyor could locate and survey for them a tract of land some distance[102] from Germantown, containing 175 acres, which was given to them after their arrival by a well-disposed resident of Philadelphia. Evidently this parcel of land had no connection with, nor was it any part of, the 2400 acres given to them previous to their departure from Holland.

This tract was on what is now, after the lapse of two centuries, still known as the "Ridge." It was then supposed to be the highest point of land vacant in the vicinity of Germantown, and was part of the range of hills which formed the rugged dell through which purled a crystal stream, the Wissahickon,[103] over rock and ledge until the waters mingled with the placid Schuylkill.

Here the necessary ground was cleared and a log house built upon the highest point of the tract. This structure

[100] Ephrata MSS.

[101] Fahnestock MSS.

[102] Several old accounts state "three miles."

[103] Then called Whitpaine's Creek. Wissahickon (Wisamekhan), the Indian name, according to Heckewelder, denotes "Catfish Creek."

was forty feet square and true to the cardinal points of the compass. It was for the use of the forty brethern whose number, as before stated, was arrived at according to the esoteric symbolism of the Rosicrucian fraternity.[104]

It was especially designed for their various requirements, and is said to have contained a large room or "saal" for their religious and musical services, in addition to a school-room and the separate "kämmern" or cell-like rooms for the recluse Theosophists.[105]

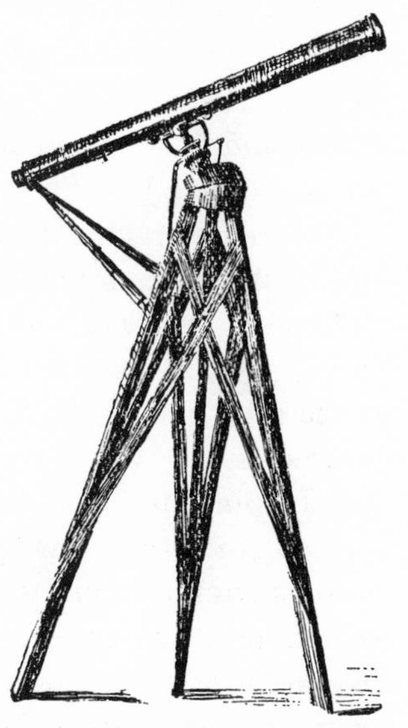
Ancient Telescope now at American Philosophical Society.

Surmounting the roof was a lantern or observatory (sternwarte) for the observation of the heavens. Here some of the scientific members were continually on the watch at night with a telescope and other instruments, being on the lookout for celestial phenomena,—so that in case the Bridegroom came in the middle of the night their lamps would be found to be filled and trimmed.

---

[104] *Vide*, p. 40, ante.

[105] An old legend descriptive of this tabernacle in the forest was incorporated by George Lippard, a novelist of half a century ago, in one of his publications. The writer has heard it stated upon good authority that Lippard's informant had in his youth frequently seen and been about the ruins of the old structure. It may be well to state here that this building is not to be confounded with the massive stone one farther up the stream, which was built in 1738, and is still known as "the monastery on the Wissahickon."

The description given to Lippard says that the building was upon the

This crude observatory, having for its object matters both mystical and astronomical, was without doubt the first astronomical observatory set up within the Province.

Surmounting this structure was raised a peculiar cross or emblem,[106] in such a position that the first rays of the sun as it rose in the east would flood the mystic symbol with a roseate hue.[107]

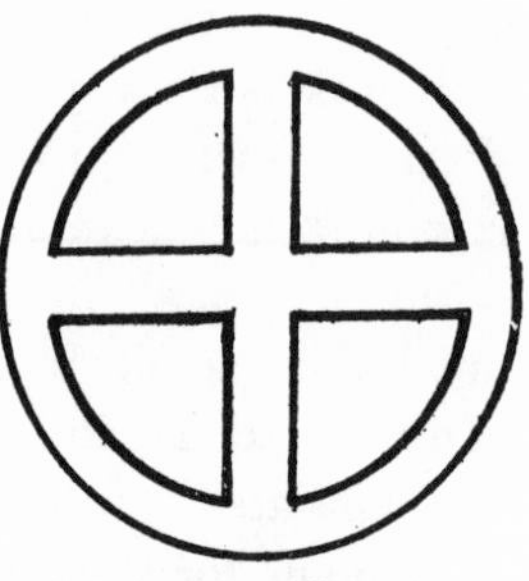

ROSICRUCIAN SYMBOL.

The rugged ravine through which the Wissahickon found its way into the Schuylkill was especially well suited to the uses of the mystic Fraternity and their esoteric studies. Wild, weird, and rugged as it was, shaded by the ghostly hemlock and stately pine, it afforded cool retreats for repose, contemplation, and study during the long summer days. Crystal springs trickled from the rocks; the healing aroma of the balsam-pine and sweet scents from the flowers were wafted in the air, while strains from the throats of scores of feathered songsters added an almost celestial charm to the scene.

---

brow of a hill, a large square edifice built of trunks of giant oaks and pines, and that it rose above the surrounding woods. The roof, in 1770, was crushed in, as though stricken by a hurricane, many of the timbers lying in a shapeless mass. The walls, however, were still intact. Towards the west there were four large square spaces, framed in heavy pieces of timber, while the other sides of the structure were almost blank. In the large lower room, which was circular in form, there were the remnants of an altar and a large iron cross fixed against the wall.

[106] The symbol of the true Rosicrucian Fraternity is a cross within a circle. Its antiquity reaches far behind the Christian era. The symbol, however, is a mere variation of the "Sonnen rad," or solar wheel. The circle denotes the solar year or eternity, while the four arms of the cross typify the four seasons. There are other esoteric meanings connected with this symbol, which are only explained to the initiates.

To complete the enchantment, as it were, a small natural cave existed among the rocks of the hillside, near which flowed a spring. This cave was claimed by Magister Kelpius as his own, and to it, after it was enlarged and made habitable, he was wont to retire for contemplation and prayer until the end of his days.

From an old Ephrata manuscript it is learned that from the outset the plan for seclusion in the forest was strenuously opposed by the residents of the German Township. It seems that various members had made so good an impression upon the people amongst whom they were temporarily quartered that when the time came for them to resume their communal life, considerable opposition arose against it. Arguments were advanced by the citizens that "they were not entrusted with talents to be hid in a napkin, and that the obligations they were under for their valuable inheritance should constrain them to render themselves useful in the promotiou of vital truth for the benefit of mankind."

In vindication of their course the brethren persisted in the "conviction of being impelled by a power to live apart from the vices and temptations of the world, and to be prepared for some immediate and strange revelations which could not be communicated amid scenes of worldly life, strife and dissipation, but would be imparted in the silence and solitude of the wilderness to those who came out from iniquity."

---

[107] "But when the dawning or morning redness shall shine from the east to the west, or from the rising to the setting, then assuredly time will be no more, but the sun of the heart of God rises or springs forth, and RA. RA. R.P. will be pressed in the wine-press without the city, and therewith to R.P.

N.B.—These are hidden mystical words, and are understood only in the language of Nature."—Behmen's Aurora, chap. xxvi, vol. v, pp. 126–27.

The old manuscript further states that against these arguments all persuasion proved futile, and no sooner were the people forced to relinquish the hope of retaining the services and eloquence of the Theosophical students than many branded them as fanatics and self-righteous hypocrites.

However, that in the end they triumphed and obtained the goodwill of the greater portion of the community, is shown by the letter of Daniel Falkner, written to Germany under date of August 7, 1694, wherein he also gives the intentions of the Fraternity,[108] viz.,—

"We are now beginning to build a house there, and the people lend us all possible help. We place this to the public good, and expect not a fool's breadth on our own account. For we are resolved, besides giving public instruction to the little children of this country, to take many of them to ourselves and have them day and night with us, so as to lay in them the foundation of a stable, permanent character. With them beginning must be made, otherwise there will be only mending and patching of the old people."

To these religious enthusiasts in the forest on the banks of the Wissahickon is due the credit of making the earliest attempt to erect and maintain a charitable institution for religious and moral instruction within the bounds of Pennsylvania.[109]

---

[108] Falkner, Sendschreiben, translation, *Pennsylvania Magazine*, vol. xi, p. 441.

[109] It appears from the journals of the Provincial Council that as early as December, 1683, Enoch Flower undertook to teach school in the "town of Philadelphia." His charges, a record of which is still preserved, indicate the simplicity of the period. To learn to read English, four shillings a quarter; to write, six shillings, etc.; boarding a scholar, to wit, lodging, washing, and schooling, £10 for the whole year. It will

A tribute to the educational efforts of this Fraternity will be found in the correspondence of the Rev. Henry Melchior Mühlenberg with the Orphanage at Halle,[110] where, in commenting upon the remarkable incidents that came under his notice during his long pastorate in America, he recites the case of a devout widow who had been a member of the Lutheran Church at Germantown, and to whom he administered spiritual consolation during her last illness. He there states that in her tender youth this devout sister went to school and was instructed by Johannes Seelig, and that it was through his teaching that her mind received such gentle impressions as emanate only from true piety.

A Plain Short

CATECHISM

FOR

Children & Youth,

That may be Serviceable to ſuch Others, who need to be inſtructed in the firſt Principles and Grounds of the

Chriſtian Religion.

To which is added,

A ſhort Paraphraſe or Opening, by way of Meditation on that Prayer which our Lord Jeſus Chriſt taught his Diſciples, commonly call'd, *The Lords Prayer*

By G. K.

Prov. 22.6. *Train up a Child in the way he ſhould go, and when he is Old he will not depart from it*

Heb. 5. 12. *For when for the time ye ought to be Teachers, ye have need that one teach you again, which be the firſt Principles of the Oracles of God, and are become ſuch who have need of Milk, and not of ſtrong Meat.*

Printed and Sold by *William Bradford* at *Philadelphia* in *Pennſilvania*, 1690.

Title of Keith's Cathecism.

In addition to their other labors a piece of ground was cleared and a large garden cultivated for their own support. Considerable attention was also given to growing and acclimating medicinal herbs (kräuter), which was probably the first systematic effort made to raise European medicinal plants for curative purposes in America.

---

be seen from the above that Flower's venture was by no means a charitable institution. The public school system, under the auspices of the Friends, of which George Keith was the first preceptor, was started about 1689; but it was not founded on a firm basis until chartered in 1701. George Keith had printed by William Bradford for use in his school a short catechism. The title-page of this unique book is reproduced in reduced fac-simile. A complete reproduction of the only known copy was made by the writer for the Historical Society of Pennsylvania.

[110] Nachrichten von den Vereinigten Deutschen Evengelisch-Lutherischen Gemeinen in Nord America. Halle, 1787, p. 1265.

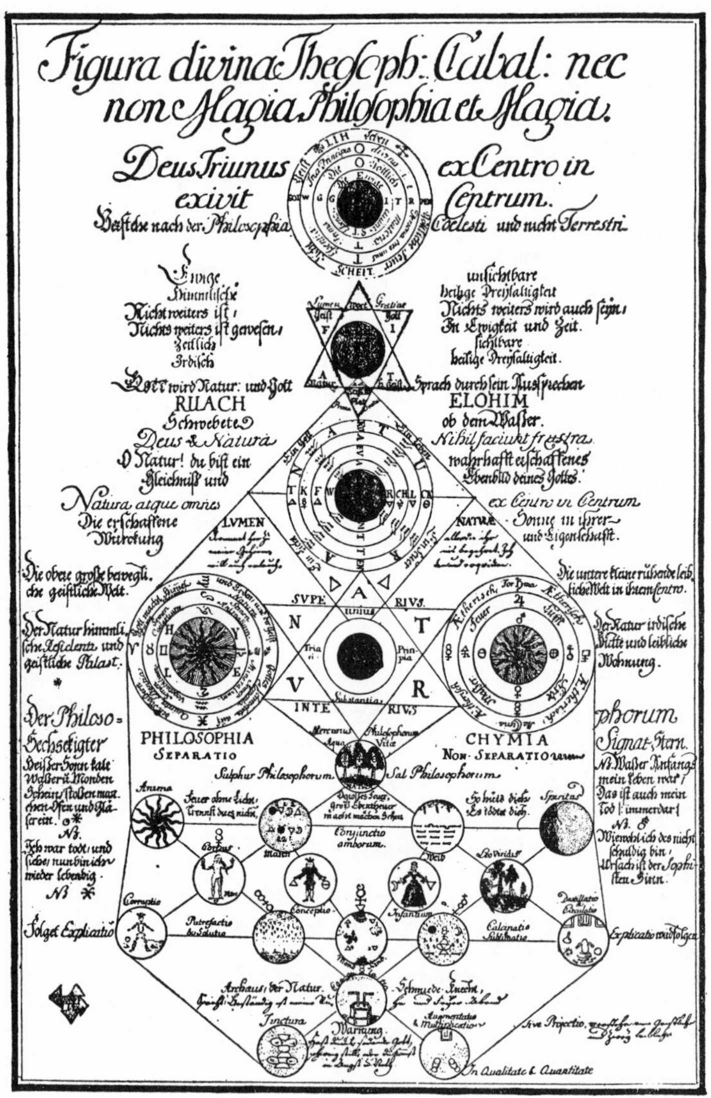

TWENTY-FOURTH FOLIO OF ROSICRUCIAN MS.

Here in the solitude, far away from the bustle and gossip of the village, these Theosophical students when not employed on errands of mercy were free to devote their spare time to their esoteric studies, undisturbed by the temptations of the world or official interference,—seeking Theosophical light, as set forth in their secret and zealously guarded symbolical manuscripts.

SYMBOL OF THE EPHRATA COMMUNITY.

A former writer upon this community[111] well says, "Thus amid the rugged rocks and wild scenery of the Wissahickon, surrounded by the tall forest trees in beautiful groves, God's first temples, these Hermits of the Ridge were wont to commune with their God."

Such as remained true to their original compact, together with the accessions to their number that arrived from various parts of Europe from time to time, lived here in the virgin forest of the New World in almost unbroken harmony for a period of at least ten years, a strictly Theosophical fraternity, whose tenets were founded upon the dogmas of the Cabbala and esoteric philosophy.

---

[111] Hon. Horatio Gates Jones.

Einfältig A-B-C Büchel, für junge Schüler, so sich fleissig üben in d. Schule des heiligen Geistes,

THE WOMAN IN THE WILDERNESS.

AFTER the Community was permanently installed in its new home in the Western World, Johannes Kelpius sought, as one of the chief objects of the Chapter, to bring about a union or combination of all the various sects that existed among the Germans in Pennsylvania and unite them into one universal Christian Church. For this purpose public devotional services, advocating Christian love and unity, were held every morning and evening in the large room or saal of the Tabernacle, to which all were invited.[112]

These services, it is stated, were opened with a prayer and a hymn; then a portion of Scripture was read and critically examined, when any one present could advance his opinion and engage in a dispassionate discussion of any abstruse or unsettled point. Visitors, no matter of what nationality or whence they came, were received with much cordiality by the brethren, and made to feel welcome.

Einfältig A-B-C Büchel, etc.—From title page of Theosophical MS.

[112] Ephrata MSS.

From a small book published over a century and a half ago by Christopher Sauer, it is to be inferred, upon authority of a certain "Doctor Schotte," that some kind of a monastic rule was observed by this band of Pietists, in addition to their esoteric discipline, both before and after their arrival in the New World. According to this somewhat doubtful authority, Kelpius was known as *Philologus*, Seelig as *Pudens*, Falkner as *Gajus*, Rev. A. H. Francke as *Stephanus*, Peterson as *Elias*, etc.[113] A careful search, however, has thus far failed to establish the identity of this "Dr. Schotte," or any corroboration of Sauer's statements.

Ein
Abgenöthigter
Bericht,
Oder:
Zum öfftern begehrte
Antwort,
Denen darnach fragenden dargelegt. In sich haltende; zwey Brieffe und deren
Ursach.

Dem noch angehänget worden eine Historie von Doctor Schotte, und einige Brieffe von demselben zu unseren Zeiten nöthig zu erwegen

Germanton:
Gedruckt bey Christoph Saur 1739.

Frequent religious meetings, exclusive of those conducted by Köster, as before mentioned, were also held at Germantown, and at stated intervals at various places in the vicinity. No request for religious instruction was ever refused, the brethren holding themselves prepared to answer any calls from afar or near at a moment's notice.[114]

It was through these services that the peculiar Theosophical dogmas of the Brotherhood became publicly known, as frequently during the fervent exhortations, Kelpius, Seelig, and other brethren, when shocked at some new evidence of spiritual indifference among their hearers,

---

[113] A reduced fac-simile of the title page of this curious book is here given. It is from the only known copy, in the library of Hon. Samuel W. Pennypacker.

[114] Ephrata MSS.

were apt to call upon the multitude to repent, as the hour of the approaching millennium was drawing near,—fortifying their arguments with well-known quotations from the Apocalypse. It was this feature that led to the Fraternity being called "The Woman in the Wilderness." A contemporary of Kelpius states that this somewhat curious name was given them because they persisted in giving esoteric interpretations to the Scriptures, and indulged in unrestrained mysticism. But the real reason was that the Brotherhood believed and taught in their exhortations, as well as in their explanations of the Apocalypse, that the Woman in the Wilderness mentioned in Revelation xii, 14–17, was prefigurative of the great deliverance that was then soon to be displayed for the Church of Christ.

Emblem of the "Celestial Eve," from Ancient MS.[115]

The appellation, however, was never acknowledged by the Fraternity, as, in accordance with their mystical teachings and precepts, they desired to live in comparative seclusion, without name and, above all, sectarianism, in love and religious harmony with all men, at the same time looking after the spiritual welfare of the general community, while perfecting themselves in their Theosophical and esoteric speculations as to the expected millennium.

A curious entry, corroborative of the above, appears in an old Ephrata manuscript, and states, that "while giving up

[115] In Rosicrucian Theosophy this emblem typifies the "Celestial Eve," representing *Theo-Sophia*, divine wisdom, or nature in her spiritual aspect.

their souls to their Creator, and devoting their whole lives to a preparation of heart for the glorious inheritance prepared for the faithful, they mutually instructed each other, and cemented a bond of brotherly love and holy affection. They professed love and charity toward all denominations, but desired to live without name or sect. 'The Contented of the God-loving Soul' [116] was the only name which they acknowledged."

With the ignorant and rationalistic populace, however, they were almost exclusively known as "The Woman in the Wilderness,"—*Dass Weib in der Wüste.*

The old manuscript goes on to state that the Brotherhood, in using that peculiar part of the Holy writ, showed deep thinking and much ingenuity. As she (the deliverer) was to come up from the wilderness leaning on the Beloved, so [they] the beloved in the wilderness, laying aside all other engagements and trimming their lamps and adorning themselves with holiness that they might be prepared to meet the same with joy, did well to observe the signs and the times and every new phenomenon, whether moral or preternatural, of meteors, stars, and the color of the skies: if peradventure "the Harbinger may appear." They further argued that there was a threefold wilderness state of progression in spiritual holiness, viz., the barren, the fruitful, and the wilderness state of the elect of God. It was this last state after which they were seeking as the highest degree of holiness. To obtain it they believed it very essential to dwell in the solitude or in the wilderness. Hence they were termed by others "The Society of the Woman in the Wilderness."

Another cherished object with the Fraternity was the

---

[116] This fact is not mentioned elsewhere.

Broadside illustrating the Apocalypse.—Berleburg, 1690–93.

conversion of the Indians. In their intercourse with the aborigines they attempted to ascertain to a certainty whether they were actually the descendants of the ten lost tribes of Israel, which at that time was almost universally believed. To settle this much disputed question, special efforts were made to find out whether the different tribes of Indians kept the seventh day (Sabbath or Saturday) holy, and, if so, how they kept it. They also instituted investigations as to whether there were any philosophers or "wise men" among the tribes who practised any system of philosophy, and, if so, how they practised it, what the rites were, and if they observed the course of the heavens; also whether or not the Indians observed and understood any of the extraordinary phenomena, terrestial or celestial; whether any among them ever showed any extraordinary inspiration or inward movements (*motus puta intrinsecus*); and, lastly, whether among the different tribes any extraordinary movements were noticeable indicative of the approaching millennium.

Mithraic Symbol.[117]

A systematic educational movement was also started by Kelpius among the Germans. Thus it will be seen that the mystic Brotherhood by no means passed their time in idle speculation and indolence. The scriptural injunction to labor six days of the week was strictly complied with, as was also the one to keep the Sabbath holy.

To their lasting honor be it said that all services of a spiritual, educational, and medical nature were given free, without price or hope of fee or reward.

---

[117] From ancient Rosicrucian MS.

A RIVAL COMMUNITY.

SYMBOL *Prima Materia.*[118]

LITTLE has thus far been published in relation to the internal affairs or domestic life of the Fraternity after they were established in their new home on the banks of the Wissahickon.

There is ground for belief that in more than one instance internal dissension manifested itself in the Community, in which Kelpius was called upon to act as general peacemaker. The brethren would have been saints indeed, if, under the stress of their peculiar life, jealousies and bickerings had not arisen. But on the whole, the unity seems to have been fairly well maintained, and the Society of the Woman in the Wilderness struck root deeply in the soil.

---

[118] This ancient symbol represents the principle of Nature, the *prima materia* or primordal matter,—the foundation of all things.

Enough, however, is shown in the letter written to Germany by Daniel Falkner, August, 1694,[119] to prove that all did not remain true to their profession, "to remain free according to the better advice of St. Paul."

The first to break his voluntary resolution of celibacy was Ludwig Christian Biedermann, who almost immediately upon his arrival in Germantown married Maria Margaretha, the daughter of the widow of Rev. Johann Jacob Zimmermann. They had been fellow-passengers across the ocean. Their example was followed by several other members during the first year or two. These defections, however, were not serious, nor by any means the greatest trouble that confronted the leaders of this experimental movement in practical theosophy.

The first question to arise after the consecration of the Tabernacle in the Forest was the erratic and dictatorial course pursued by Köster and his few adherents in the Community. Köster, in addition to being a devout, austere enthusiast, was a fearless and impulsive man; and, as before stated, lost no time in extending his ministrations from Germantown to Philadelphia, where he preached and exhorted both in German and English. While in Philadelphia he became more or less involved in the Keithian controversy, which was then agitating the Quakers throughout the Province.

Köster, aggressive and belligerent as he was, without delay took sides with the partisans of George Keith, and whenever preaching to the Keithians lost no opportunity to widen the breach that existed between them and the Orthodox Friends. As an old German manuscript states, "He gradually led them from the ways of the Quakers, farther and farther into the lanes that ended in the true path."

[119] See mention of letter, p. 15.

As the Orthodox Friends, immediately upon the departure of Keith and prior to the arrival of Köster, had commenced a strong effort to heal the schism that then existed in their community and bring back the seceders, Köster's action did not tend to improve the religious situation in Philadelphia. His impassioned and outspoken utterances gave fresh courage to the opposing party, and emboldened them to renew their discussions, which soon undid the efforts that had been made by the Friends in the interest of unity and peace. All the bitterness of the old strife was thereby revived, and dissensions were once more rife in the different meetings throughout the Province.

ESOTERIC SYMBOL.[120]

The stand taken by the German enthusiast in reference to the troubles of the Society of Friends, which also partook somewhat of a political nature, was not only opposed by the latter, but also by his more conservative associates and brother Mystics, who had naught but the best feelings toward the Quakers, and were always in full accord and sympathy with them. Matters went along in this way for over a year, the breach gradually widening between Köster and his old associates as the time passed, and the former became more closely allied with William Davis and several

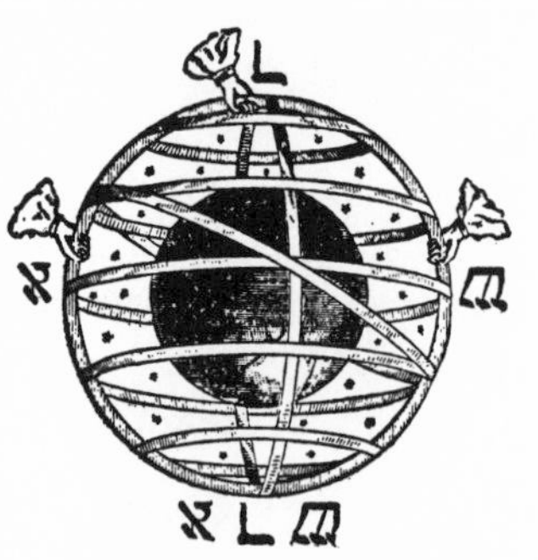

ROSICRUCIAN SYMBOL.[121]

[120] According to the esoteric teachings, this symbol typifies the universal *matrix*, or great invisible storehouse of Nature, wherein the character of all things are contained and preserved.

kindred spirits who had been among the first to foment the Quaker schism. The sequel of the disagreement between Kelpius and Köster was the withdrawal of the latter and a few others from the original Community, who, together with a few of the Keithians, attempted, under the leadership of Köster, to form a new community of religious evangelists. They called themselves "The Brethren in America," and their community was to be known as "The True Church of Philadelphia, or Brotherly Love."

For the purposes of the society a piece of ground was obtained in Plymouth, a short distance north of Germantown. Just how this ground was obtained is not known to a certainty, nor has the location been traced. The old manuscript before quoted states that it was purchased by Köster;[122] another account tells us that it was given to the new community. Be this as it may, a tabernacle or community-house was built on the plot.[123] When finished, the building was consecrated with mystic ritual and called "Irenia,"—that is, "The House of Peace." Thus for a time two separate and distinct religious communities existed in the vicinity of Germantown.

This action of Köster, who, notwithstanding his erratic course, still adhered strictly to the Orthodox Lutheran doctrine in his religious services, had but little effect or influence upon the original Fraternity. Nowhere in the writings of Kelpius, Seelig, or Falkner is this defection of Köster thought worthy of mention.

---

[121] This symbol, representing an armillary sphere sustained by the three forces, viz., Truth, Justice, and Peace, according to the esoteric doctrine portrays the universe.

[122] According to Rathelf, p. 487, the Plymouth lot was bought jointly by Köster and two others.

[123] Ein Bericht an alle Bekenner und Schriftsteller. Von H. B. Köster. New York, 1696; p. 1.

Under the spiritual guidance of Kelpius, and the judicious financial management of Daniel Falkner, the matter proved but a passing episode in the history of the Fraternity, as it soon recovered from whatever setback it had received.

In the subsequent controversy[124] between Köster and the leading Quakers, in which Francis Daniel Pastorius[125] took so active a part, none of the other members of the original community became involved.

The most important incident, from a literary point of view, after the formation of the "True Church of Philadelphia" by Köster was the writing, in the fall or winter of the year 1697, of a Latin thesis, "*De Resurrectione Imperii Æternitatus*," a quarto of forty pages. When the work was finished, as there was no printer in Pennsylvania at that time, he attempted to get it printed by William Bradford in New York. The printer declined the commission, as he could get no one to correct the printed sheets intelligently.[126]

This mystical dissertation is the first theological or theosophical book written or composed in Pennsylvania to be printed in the Latin language, if not within the English

---

[124] This famous controversy will be treated at length later on.

[125] Francis Daniel Pastorius was born at Somerhausen, September 26, 1651. He attended the University of Strasburg in 1672, went to the high school at Basle, and afterwards studied law at Jena. He was thoroughly familiar with the Greek, Latin, German, French, Dutch, English, and Italian tongues, and at the age of twenty-two publicly disputed in different languages upon law and philosophy. After practising law for a short time in Frankfort, he sailed for America from London, June 10, 1683, and arrived in Philadelphia August 20th. His great learning and social position at home made him the most conspicuous person in Germantown. He married, November 26, 1688, Ennecke Klostermann. He died leaving two sons.

[126] Zellische Gelehrten Geschichte.

colonies on the Atlantic coast. The full text of this extremely rare and almost forgotten work reads (translation): "A Directory and Universal View || of the Ashkenaz-Elamite Journals || that is || of the at last triumphant struggles of arising and restoring righteousness || to wit || of the Resurrection || of the Empire of the Eternities || among the Churches exiled yet pressing forward from Jesus to Jesus the Restorer || from the Millennium of the Apostolic Jerusalem unto the Trumpet of Illyricum and to the sixth Vial: || Romans xv. 19; Rev. ix. 13, 14; xvi. 12. || Succinct Axioms || on the arising of the future eternity of the seven Hebrew vials or the || sixth week [or Hebdomad] of the eternities, against the Beast and Babylon the great, to the union of the empire of the || fullness of the nations with the Universal Church of the Israel that is to be saved; || composed || in the City of Philadelphia of America, on the border of great Cymry-Wales || upon the ashes of the Indian husbandman of ancient || Celt-Iberian or Celtic-Hebrew Spain, toward the close of the year 1697; in those days when, in the limits of the City and the whole region of Philadelphia, the first standard and public outcry against every arrogance and enthusiasm || Spanish and Quaker was set up || by the Philadelphian Union of the Unarmed Baptism of the primative churches || of Asia (reviving after the completed ages of Antichrist, in this candlestick[127] [candelabrum] or upon || return of the sixth spiritual day) with the temperate rule of the British Church and Monarchy || being the first Christian [church] thence from Constantius Chlorus under the presidency of the sixth

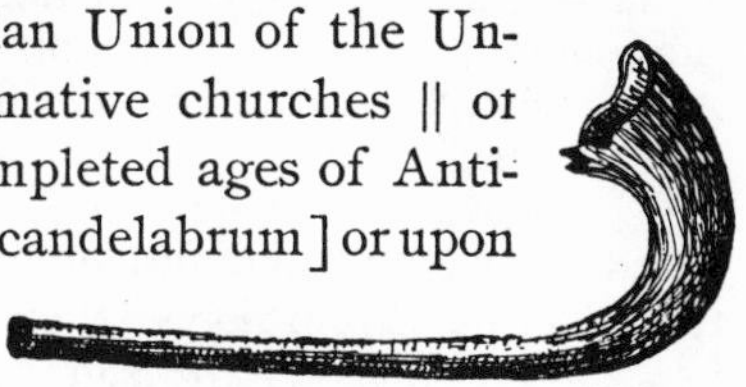

"Sophar," or Sacred Trumpet.

[127] *Candelabrum*, besides its obvious allusion to the Apocalypse, was here used by Köster to designate an evangelist, or one who diffuses light (*Lampenträger*).

DIRECTORIUM ET CONSPECTUS UNIVERSALIS

EPHEMERIDUM ASCHKENAZÆO-ELAMITICARUM,

i. e.

Triumphantium tandem agonum justitiæ exorientis atque reducis,

videlicet

DE RESURRECTIONE IMPERII ÆTERNITATUM

Inter Ecclesias exules & perseverantes à Jesu ad Jesum reducem, à millennio Jerusalem Apostolicæ usque ad Tubam Illyrici & phialam sextam Rom. 15. v. 19. Apoc. 9. v. 13. 14. cap. 16. v. 12.

Axiomata succincta

In exortum Æternitatis futuræ 7 phialarum Hebræarum, Hebdomados sextæ Æternitatum, contra Bestiam & Babylonem magnam, ad unionem Imperii plenitudinis gentium cum salvandi Israelis universi Ecclesiâ,

conscripta

In urbe Philadelphiâ Americæ, Magnæ Cimbro-Cambriæ termino, super cineribus Indianorum colonorum Hispaniæ veteris Celt-ibericæ vel Celt-ebrææ, circa Colophonem Anni 1697. illis diebus, quibus in pomœriis urbis totâque regione Philadelphiæ contra omnem fastum & Enthusiasmum Hispanicum & Quakerianum erigebatur primum vexillum & publicum præconium philadelphicæ unionis baptismi inermis primævarum Ecclesiarum Asiæ (reviviscentium post Antichristi ætates completas, hoc candelabri sive diei sexti spiritualis reditu) cum regimine moderato Ecclesiæ & Monarchiæ Britannicæ, Christianæ primæ inde à Constantio Chloro sub præsidio sigilli sexti completi & redivivi in Christianissimo Heroe & Monarcha Rege Gulielmo III. cumque testimonio vindictarum Sionis Bohemicæ & Waldensis sub reviviscente nunc Tubâ sextâ cum phialâ sextâ, restauratrice justitiæ & sapientiæ Orientalis & civitatis ac gloriæ Hebræorum; demonstrante & publicè nunc promulgante per introitum Hebræo-Waldensem sive Tertium

HENRICO BERNHARDO CÖSTERO,

Prophetiæ Hebræorum reseratæ Studioso.

Lemgoviæ, typis Henr. Wilh. Meyeri, 1702.

THE HOLY LAMP OF THE TABERNACLE.

seal completed || and revived in the most Christian Hero and Monarch King William III. and with the || witness of the liberation of the Bohemian and Waldensian Zion under the now reviving || sixth Trumpet, together with the sixth Vial, the restorer of righteousness and Eastern wisdom and of the state || and glory of the Hebrews. Demonstrated and now publicly promulgated through the Hebrew-Waldensian or third entrance, || by Henry Bernhard Köster || studious of the unlocked Prophecy of the Hebrews. || Lemgo [in Lippe Detmold], printed by Wilhelm Meyer, 1702." A fac-simile of the title is also reproduced from the original. Great was the disappointment of Köster, upon the completion of the thesis, when he found that the work could not be printed in America. Upon his return to Europe he, however, lost no time in having the manuscript put into print. A number of these copies were sent to his friends and late associates in America. The only known copy of this work is now in the library of the writer. This book not only shows the trend of Köster's thoughts and speculations as to the expected millennium, but also furnishes a proof of his great learning and the scope of his researches in both sacred and profane history. His language and ideas, however, are

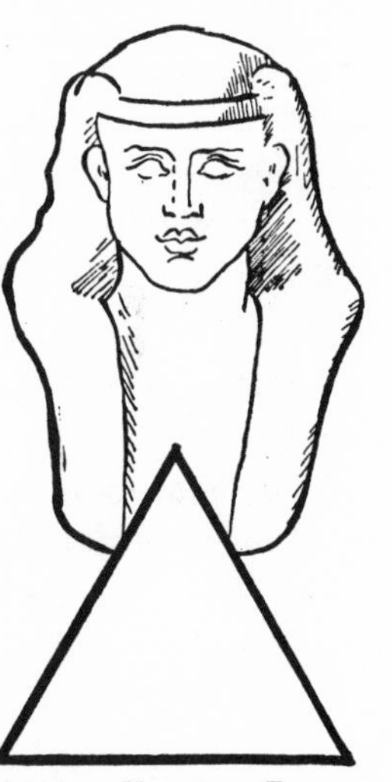

ANCIENT HERMETIC EMBLEM.

frequently presented in an erratic if not somewhat disjointed manner. The following extract will serve as an illustration. His theme here is the coming of the Lord.—(1 Thess., iv 16, 17.)[128]

"Awake! The hour calls to us,—They call unto us with a loud voice,—Awake! thou City of Jerusalem,—Midnight is the Cry,—The watcher is high upon the house-tops,—Awake ye wise Virgins, vel. (or) Awake! the voice calls unto us,—The watcher stands high on the house-tops,—Awake! thou city of Jerusalem,—Midnight is the hour,—They cry unto us with a loud voice,—Wise Virgins, where are you?"

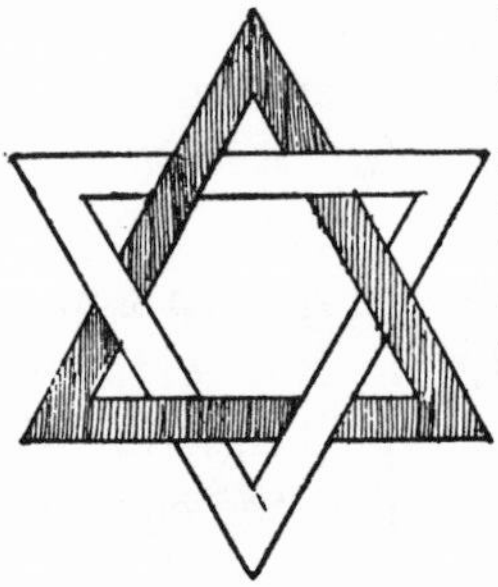

The rival community that Köster attempted to establish at Plymouth never became a success, as the doctrine taught by him at his public services was not conducive to either monastic or communal life. In fact, Köster was more of an Evangelist and Theosophist than a Mystic philosopher. The plain orthodox doctrine preached by him was entirely different from the peculiar mysticism and code of morality promulgated by Kelpius and his followers.

That the former was also versed in occult philosophy, the doctrines of the Cabbala, and believed in an approaching millennium, however, is not denied.

The subsequent career of Köster and his works form the basis of a special chapter.

---

[128] Page 30 of original.

AN EMISSARY TO THE OLD WORLD.

AN EPHRATA SYMBOL.[129]

ON Tuesday, the 29th day of June, 1697, a party of three respectable-looking personages came ashore at the public landing in Philadelphia. They were the missionaries sent to America by Charles XI, King of Sweden, in response to the repeated appeals from the Swedish Lutherans on the Delaware, at the instance of the Rev. Dr. Jesper Svedberg,[130] who was at that time Provost (Domprobst) of the Cathedral at Upsala.

129 From the Blutige Schauplatz, oder Martyræer Spiegel der Tauffs Gesinten. Ephrata, 1745.

130 Dr. Jesper Svedberg (father of Emanuel Svedberg, afterwards called Swedenborg) became an army chaplain in 1682; court preacher in 1689; pastor at Vingaker in 1690; professor of theology at Upsala in 1692; Provost of the Cathedral in the same place in 1695; Bishop of Skara in 1702; died in 1735.

Their first official act after landing was to wait on Lieutenant-Governor William Markham, as did Kelpius and his party three years previous. When he saw their credentials, fortified as they were by a passport, dated at Kensington, November 22, 1696, with the British king's (William III.) own hand and seal, giving liberty of passage from England over to the Delaware, Governor Markham received them with great kindness and welcomed them cordially to Penn's domain, promising them all possible favor and assistance.[131] This trio consisted of Magister Andreas Rudman, master of philosophy, a native of Gevalia, in the Province of Gestrickland; Tobias Eric Biörck, of the Province of Westmanland; and Jonas Auren, of the Province of Wermeland.

On the next day, Wednesday, June 30, 1697, the three clergymen went to Wicaco,[132] then some distance from the embryo city, and held their first service among the Swedes on the Delaware, and, as, Rudman states, "according to the true doctrines contained in the Augsburg Confession of faith, free from all human superstition and tradition."[133] Upon this occasion the three clergymen officiated, clad in robe and suplice. This service, in the Swedish tongue, which the records fail to tell us whether held within an humble dwelling house, or in a barn, or the ruins of the old block-house, or perhaps under the shade of the majestic trees that then lined the banks of the Delaware, was the first in America in which the Lutheran ritual was rendered in its fulness according to the custom of the Mother Country.

---

[131] From diary of Rev. T. E. Biörck. See records of Trinity Church.

[132] Wicacoa is an Indian word, derived from *wicking*, dwelling, and *chao*, a fir-tree. Probably there was in former times a thicket of fir-trees where the Indians had their abode. Acrelius' New Sweden.

[133] Rudman's Memoirs of Wicaco.

The following day the three ministers went to Germantown and visited the Fraternity on the Wissahickon, where they were received with great consideration by Kelpius and his associates. The friendship begun at this time was continued with mutual benefit to both parties without interruption until the death of Kelpius removed the leading spirit of the Community.

The Brethren learned from their visitors, among other things, that the crusade in Germany against the Pietists had not ceased, but, on the contrary, had extended into Sweden and other Protestant countries; also that a poem had lately been printed and circulated praising such princes and rulers as had issued mandates against them. This was called "A Poetical Thanksgiving" by "a lover of truth." [134] One stanza, that is especially aimed at our Community, reads (translation),—

> "Carl, who the fanatic spirit cannot endure,
> Holds God's honor in esteem, commands all Chiliasts
> To Ben-Sylvania, to their Brethren to go,—
> There, according to their teachings, the thousand years to rest,
> And without constraint in constraint to stand.
> A common pebble knows no diamond;
> Egyptian darkness knows no Jacob's sun;
> No prince, no true Christian, loves fanatic kinsfolk,
> Therefore slinks the dreamer away before the blaze of light."

How close the intercourse became between the three Swedish pastors and Kelpius is shown by the correspondence of the latter, addressed to Rev. Tob. Biörck, *pastorem ad Christenam.*[135]

Toward the close of the year 1697 it became evident that

---

[134] Original in possession of writer.

[135] A draught of a twelve-page Latin letter is in Kelpius's diary. See fac-simile reproductions at Pennsylvania Historical Society, pp. 48–60.

the influences exercised and the truths taught both by the Community and the ministrations of Köster had made themselves felt among the settlers and were bringing about good results, notwithstanding such active opposition as that of Pastorius and others of equal prominence, which, however, was aimed chiefly against the enthusiastic Köster and his "Brethren in America."

In view of this greatly improved condition of the religious situation, which, early in 1698, was strengthened still more by the arrival of Rev. Thomas Clayton, the first min-

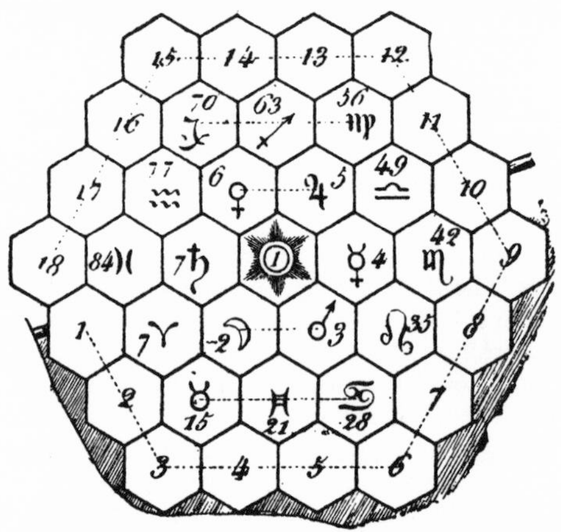

MYSTIC SYMBOL FROM A PHILADELPHIC MANUSCRIPT.

ister of the Church of England who came to the Province, it was concluded by the leaders of the original Fraternity, partly at the suggestion of the Swedish pastors, to send an emissary from among their number to Europe to make public the true state and spiritual condition of the Germans who had emigrated to Pennsylvania; set forth the labors of the Pietistical Brethren among their countrymen in America, and solicit aid and additional recruits, so that the

PHOTOGRAPHED FROM THE ORIGINAL CANVAS IN SWEDEN.

Ericus Tob. Biörck

mystical number of forty could be kept intact, and at the same time could extend their usefulness in educating and ministering to their neglected countrymen in Pennsylvania.

Another important scheme then under consideration was the emigration of the members of "the Philadelphic Society" in a body from England and the Continent to settle in Pennsylvania, and there found a colony where their peculiar teachings should be their only law. Considerable correspondence had taken place upon the subject, and it was thought by Kelpius and others that the time had arrived for a consummation of the scheme. It was therefore desirable that a thoroughly competent person should be sent on the mission at that time. For this important service Daniel Falkner was selected. He was a man of strong character and practical piety, as well as the executive head of the Community affairs, and, in addition to his religious duties, took considerable interest in secular things.

Daniel Falkner, persuant to the above arrangement, returned to Europe toward the close of the year 1698. After a short sojourn in Holland, he went to Germany to visit his old associates. Upon his arrival in Saxony, he found that time had wrought many changes in the condition of his former companions,—some had been banished, others lived in obscurity, while the former leader of the local Pietistical movement, Hermann August Francke, now posed as professor of Oriental languages at the newly established University of Halle,[136] pastor of the suburb Glaucha, and superintendent of an orphanage of his own projection.

[136] The bi-centennial of the Halle (Frederick-Wittenberg) University was celebrated with great *éclat*, August 2, 3, 5, 1894, the Emperor of Germany being represented upon the occasion by Prince Albrecht of Prussia. The present writer attended as a delegate from the Old Augustus (Trappe) Church. For a full description of this Jubilee, see "The Lutheran," Philadelphia, September 6, 1894.

Curieuse Nachricht
Von
PENSYLVANIA
in
Norden-America
Welche/
Auf Begehren guter Freunde/
Uber vorgelegte 103. Fra-
gen/ bey seiner Abreiß aus Teutsch-
land nach obigem Lande Anno 1700.
ertheilet/ und nun Anno 1702 in den Druck
gegeben worden.
Von
Daniel Falknern/ Professore,
Burgern und Pilgrim allda.

Franckfurt und Leipzig/
Zu finden bey Andreas Otto/ Buchhändlern.
Im Jahr Christi 1702.

Falkner during his sojourn in the Old World made a visit to Holland and England in the interests of the Philadelphic Society, without, however, inducing that body to emigrate to Penn's Province. While in Germany, he also made arrangements to issue a book in the colloquial style of the period, containing answers to a number of queries relative to the religious and social conditions in Pennsylvania. This book, before quoted, is entitled "Curieufe Nachricht || Von || Pensylvania || in || Norden America || Welche || Auf Begehren guter Freunde, || Uber vorgelegte 103. Fra- || gen, bey seiner Abreiss aus Teutsch- || land nach obigem Lande Anno 1700. || ertheilet, und nun Anno 1702 in den Druck || gegeben worden. || Von || Daniel Falknern, Professore, || Burgern und Pilgrim allda.||Franckfurt und Leipzig, Zu finden bey Andreas Otto, Buchhändlern, || Im Jahr Christi, 1702." It was published under the auspices of the Frankfort Land Company, and issued simultaneously in Frankfort and Leipzig. It will be noticed that the compiler here signs himself "Citizen and Pilgrim in Pennsylvania." Falkner's visit to Europe also partook somewhat of a political nature, which was destined to work radical changes in the civil affairs of the German settlement.

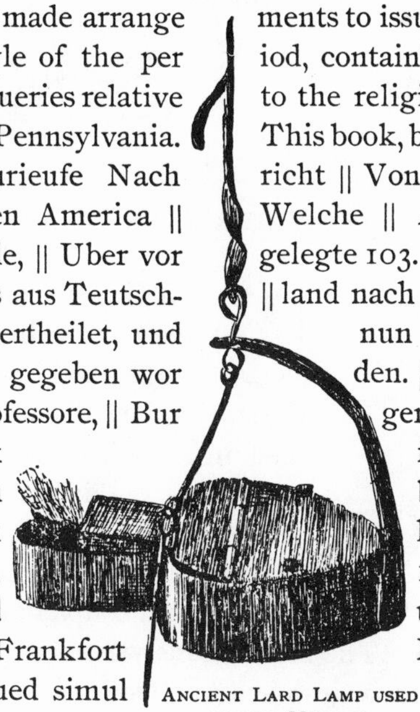

Ancient Lard Lamp used by the Mystics.

REYNIER JANSEN.

EPHRATA HAND PRESS.

KELPIUS, the pious enthusiast, was exceedingly anxious to improve the moral as well as the spiritual condition of his countrymen in America. He therefore had printed, or obtained from Germany, sets of small cards or slips of paper upon each of which there was a different moral couplet or verse (*spruch*) from the Bible. The set of cards was then put in a box or card-case, called a jewel-casket (*schatzkästlein*), and was carried by the members of the Brotherhood for distribution among the worshipers at the Tabernacle and the heads of families, with the request that whenever a curse, oath, or blasphemous expression was uttered in their presence the offending person should be handed one of the slips of paper, which he was to read carefully and then place it upon his tongue. The same rule was to apply to the person who carried the *schatzkästlein:* whenever he did or said anything wrong, or was even tempted to do so, or was led to anger, recourse was to be had immediately to a jewel from the *schatzkästlein;* and so strong was the popular belief,

Eine Sünderin weinete zu den Füssen JEsu;
JEsus sprach: Ihr sind viel Sünde vergeben,
denn sie hat viel geliebet; welchem aber wenig ver-
geben wird, der liebet wenig. Luc. 7 38-47.
Weinen und Lieben.
JESUS höret all dein Sehnen,
JESUS schauet deine Thränen:
Weine frey, doch liebe mit,
So erhört Er deine Bitt.

that nothing could shake their faith in the efficacy of a card, taken out at random, to be pertinent to the individual case in which it was invoked.[137]

The members of the Fraternity in making use of the slips invariably placed them in their mouth. From this peculiar custom arose the ridiculous charge that the Pietists ate their religion.[138]

Alle die Gottseelig leben wollen in Christo JEsu
müssen Verfolgung leyden. 2 Tim. 3 12.
Das erste Looß.
Von aussen Spott und Schmach der Leuten,
Von innen Furcht und Traurigkeiten.
Dis pflegt das Erste Looß zu seyn,
Das hier den Frommen wird gemein.

[137] Kästlein mit zetteln, darauf waren viele schöne Sprüche aus der Bibel und andere Reimen gedruckt die sich auf vielerey Zustande der Menschen schicken. Wann dan in der Companie jemand war der etwas eiteles zu reden anfing, so kam einer mit dem Schatz-Kästgen und ein jeder zog ein Briefgen heraus, dass wurde gelesen und hat sich gemeinlich getroffen dass ein spruch auf dem Zettel stund wie es um des Menschen Hertz beschaffen war, und so wurden die leichtsinnige reden unterbrochen, und davon kam auch die lüge vom Zettel fressen. Christopher Sauer in Almanack, 1751.

A "SCHATZKÄSTLEIN" COMPLETE WITH "SPRÜCHE," SEE NOTE 138.

In order to promote the spiritual welfare of the Germans in Pennsylvania, Kelpius had printed at an early day a small book or pamphlet for distribution among the German settlers, urging them to public and private devotion. The title of this work was "Eine kurtze und begreiflige Anleitung zum stillen Gebet." This book, as well as the moral text-slips, was in all probability a specimen of the Jansen (father or son) imprints, which are now so rare and valuable.[139] Watson, in his MS. Annals of Philadelphia, mentions Kelpius as the author and Dr. Christopher Witt as the translator.[140] Later investigations go to show that

[138] This custom continued in use among the Germans in Pennsylvania for many years. Subsequent editions of these sets of moral cards were printed on both the Sauer and Ephrata presses. The Sauer edition, printed in 1744, was known as "Der Frommen Lotterie." The only complete set of this edition, 381 in number, is in the collection of Hon. S. W. Pennypacker, of Philadelphia. See illustration above.

[139] This devotional work was translated into English and printed at an early day.

[140] See "The First Century of German Printing in America," by the late Dr. Oswald Seidensticker, p. 62.

this unique work was based upon a somewhat similar book published in Germany,[141] as early as 1695, by Hermann August Francke,[142] under the title "Schrifftmässige Anweisung, recht und Gottwohlgefällig zu Beten," and that a number of these books were brought from Halle by the Falkner brothers upon their return to America.[143] No copy of the original Kelpius pamphlet, which was in the German language, is known to the writer. However, as a copy of the Henry Miller reprint of the English translation has been lately found,[144] there is a possibility that a specimen of the earlier editions may also be found at some future day.

Aug. Herm. Francke
S.S.Theol. P Ord Past. Vlric. & Sch
Schriftmäßige
Anweisung
Recht und GOtt wohlgefäll
zu
Beten
Nebst hinzugefügten
Morgen- u. Abend-Gebetl
Und einem
Kielischen RESPONSO
Die
Gewißheit und Versicherung d
Erhörung des Gebets betreffend.
Achte Auflage.

HALLE,
In Verlegung des Wäysenhauses, 1

There is an interesting tradition connecting the Mystic Brotherhood with the Jansen press. It is said that during Daniel Falkner's absence in Europe, Kelpius and

[141] Sachsse, ursprung und wesen der Pietisten, p. 268.

[142] See p. 55 seq.

[143] This work was printed many times on the press of the Halle institution. The copy in the writer's library was printed in 1732.

A

SHORT, EASY

AND

COMPREHENSIVE

METHOD

OF

PRAYER.

Tranſlated from the GERMAN:

And publiſhed for a farther *Promotion, Knowledge* and *Benefit* of INWARD PRAYER.

By a *Lover of Internal Devotion.*

The Second Edition with Addition.

GERMANTOWN,
Printed by *Chriſtopher Sower.*
M DCC LXIII.

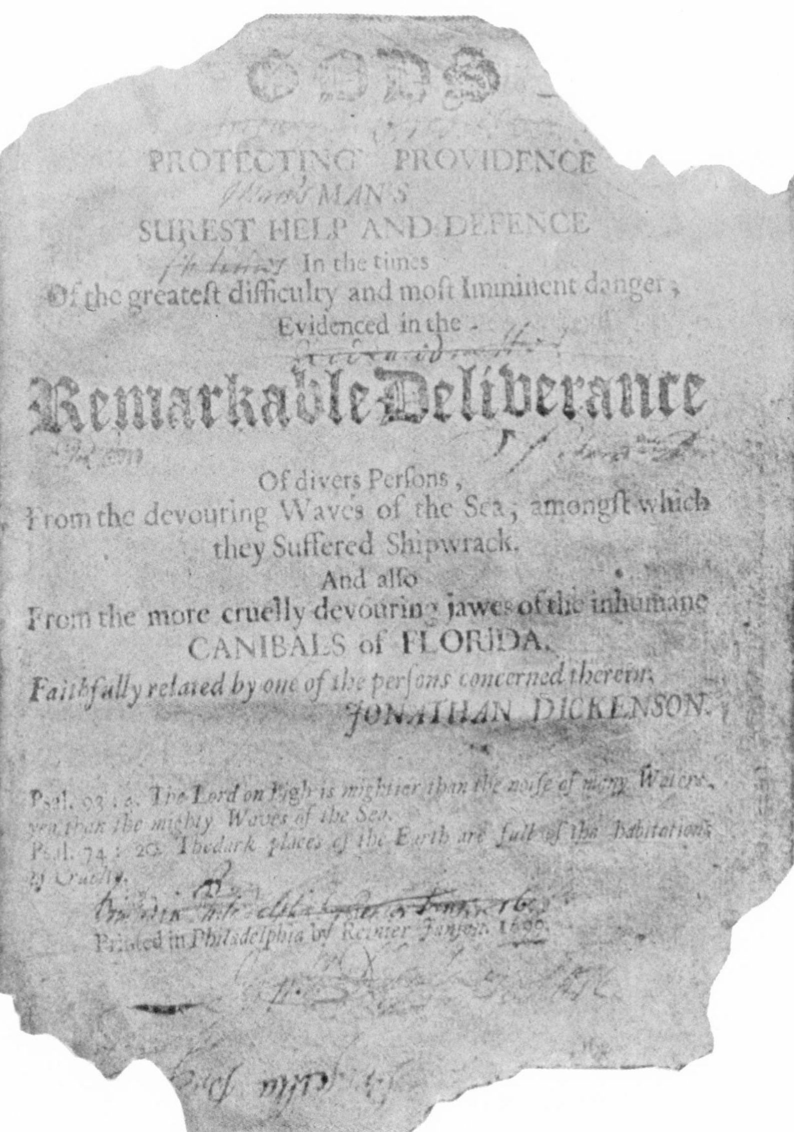
GODS
PROTECTING PROVIDENCE
MAN'S
SUREST HELP AND DEFENCE
In the times
Of the greateſt difficulty and moſt Imminent danger;
Evidenced in the
Remarkable Deliverance
Of divers Perſons,
From the devouring Waves of the Sea, amongſt which
they Suffered Shipwrack.
And alſo
From the more cruelly devouring jawes of the inhumane
CANIBALS of FLORIDA.
Faithfully related by one of the perſons concerned therein;
JONATHAN DICKENSON.

Pſal. 93. 4. The Lord on high is mightier than the noiſe of many Waters, yea, than the mighty Waves of the Sea.
Pſal. 74. 20. The dark places of the Earth are full of the habitations of Cruelty.

Printed in Philadelphia by Reinier Janſen. 1699.

"GOD'S PROTECTING PROVIDENCE."

TITLE PAGE OF THE FIRST BOOK KNOWN TO HAVE BEEN PRINTED ON THE JANSEN PRESS IN PHILADELPHIA.

others were instrumental in inducing Reynier Jansen, a Hollander, to take charge of the printing press which had been ordered from London by the Friends' Yearly Meeting[145] after the removal of William Bradford's press to New York; and this new press was received in Philadelphia 10 mo. 30th, 1698. It is also said that some of the printing was done in Germantown. This latter claim is partly borne out by the statement in a New England Sabbatarian record, that they went to Germantown to get their printing done.[146]

Further, it is a matter of record that on the 29th of November Jansen bought twenty acres of Liberty lands in Germantown, and upon the 7th of February, 1698–99, the right of citizenship was conferred upon him by the Germantown court.[147]

Reynier Jansen was a member of the celebrated family of that name in Holland, the most prominent member of which was Cornelius Jansen the younger (1585–1638), Bishop of Ypres, who was the founder of the peculiar sect known as "the Disciples of St. Augustine," or Jansenists. Another branch of the family was noted as printers and publishers at Amsterdam, and was intimately connected with many of the leading religious enthusiasts and mystics

---

[144] This new English edition was printed by Heinrich Miller, Philadelphia, 1761. (12mo., 36 pages.) The only known copy is among the John Pemberton papers in the Friends' Library of Philadelphia. Christopher Sauer, the Germantown printer, also reprinted the book two years later: the title says "Second Edition."

[145] "Agreed that a press be bought for printing and necessary letters and stamps, either from Boston or England, and be paid for out of the Yearly Meeting stock, the care of which is left to Philadelphia Monthly Meeting. Burlington, 31st day of the 7mo., 1697."—(Extract MSS. Minutes Yearly Meeting.)

[146] MS. records of Newport, R. I., Seventh-Day Baptist Church.

[147] "Penna. Mag.," vol. iv, p. 37.

of whom the seventeenth century was so prolific. It was upon the Jansen press at Amsterdam that many of the peculiar theological and proscribed works of that day were printed.[148] The Philadelphia printer was evidently of this latter branch, and was not so entirely ignorant of the black art as has been generally supposed.[149] He was a close friend of Benjamin Furley and other Separatists who then made their abode in Holland; consequently, it was but natural that after his arrival in America he should gravitate toward his fellow Separatists at Germantown, and, on account of his previous knowledge of the printer's art, assume the charge and responsibility of the new press that had been procured by the Society of Friends. Jansen upon his arrival in the Province had but an imperfect knowledge of the English language, and this, together with the fact that he had for some years previous changed his occupation from printer to lace-maker, accounts for many of the imperfections and crudities of his earliest work. According to the Ephrata manuscripts and traditions, it was in reality such of the Mystic Brethren as had some knowledge of the art, and were conversant with the English tongue, who actually did the type-setting and proof-reading, if not the press-work, of the early Jansen imprints. These traditions are strengthened by the evidence that Johann Seelig was a practical bookbinder,[150] who bound the Jansen books, and

---

[148] Adelung, iv, p. 392.

[149] It was Caleb Pusey, and not Reynier Jansen, who, in the preface to "Satan's Harbinger Encountered," apologizes for misprints thus: "The chief occasion of there being so many errours was the Printer being a man of another nation and language, as also not bred to that employment, consequently something unexpert both in language and calling, and the corrector's [*sic*] not being so frequently at hand as the case required, all which I desire thou wouldst favourably consider."

[150] Levering family, pp. 18, 19.

BY THE HONOURABLE COLLONEL John Evans LIEUTENANT GOVERNOUR of the PROVINCE OF PENSILVANIA AND COUNTIES ANNEXED.

A PROCLAMATION,

AGAINST IMMORALITY and PROPHANENESS

WHereas it hath pleased ALMIGHTY GOD, from the Treasures of His Infinite Goodness [illegible] his favours in an eminent degree, and pour down his peculiar Blessings upon this Colony ~~from the~~ first Erecting thereof; as well by the bestowing a happy success on the Endeavours of its Inhabitants and crowning what so lately was a Wilderness with a large Affluence of all the Necessaries and Comforts of Life; as by supporting it in an undisturbed Peace and Tranquillity during the Commotions that have deeply afflicted other parts of the Christian World and continuing to us, the Enjoyment of those manifold Mercies which, rightly used, tend to make a People truly happy. All which divine Bounties, as they loudly call for the most humble and hearty acknowledgments; so they ought more deeply to impress a just sense of the great Obligations upon Us, so to regulate our Lives with care and circumspection, in a true Obedience and Conformity to GODS holy Laws, that we may not instead of making grateful Returns by Impiety or Negligence, provoke the just Anger of the ALMIGHTY to withdraw His divine Protection, and inflict on us the severe Chastisements of his just Displeasure. Notwithstanding all which, I cannot but be sensible, that too many, forgetting all those Obligations, that as persons professing the Holy Christian Religion they indispensably lye under, have given themselves a *Loose* in their Lives and Conversations, and manifestly trampled on their positive known Duties in many vicious Practices and Immoralities to the great Offence of ALMIGHTY GOD, in the Breach of his Divine Laws as well as of our civil Institutions and to the Scandal of sober Men, and great Discredit of this Government: Which Practice if not timely prevented, may terminate in an utter Depravation of Manners, through the Encouragement taken from those fatal and pernicious Examples, by persons whose better Education and Inclinations might otherwise have restrained them within the Bounds of Sobriety and Virtue; but from those many Instances, sett before their Eyes, are in danger of being hurried on, not only to their own Ruine, but of becoming Accessary to the, Incensing, and drawing down upon us the Vengeance of Heaven.

In a deep Consideration of which, and to the end that all possible Discouragements may be given to the Growth of these Enormities; I have through a sense of the Duty I owe to GOD, and the care of the People committed to my Charge, [illegible] and with the Advice and Consent of the Council of this *Province* and *Territories* [illegible] and Declare That I will Discountenance and severely Punish [illegible] Vice, [illegible] and Prophaneness, in all persons whatsoever, within this Government, that shall be guilty of the same. And I doe hereby strictly forbid all manner of Debauchery, Lewdness, Drunkenness, [illegible] Swearing, C[illegible]ing, Rioting or [illegible]ing of the Sabbath, Night-walking at unseasonable hours without lawful Business & all other Disorders Whatsoever that are contrary to the Duties of a Christian Life & the Rules of true Virtue. And I do strictly Command & Require all Magistrates, Justices, Sheriffs, Constables and all Officers whatsoever, and others her Majesties good Subjects that they not only be regular and circumspect in their own Lives that by their good Examples, they may incite others that behold them to the Practice of virtue, but also that they be very Diligent in the Discovery and Effectual Prosecution of all Offenders and that they rigorously put in Execution all the good and wholesome Laws and Ordinances provided against the aforesaid and such other Immoralities without favour [illegible] to any person whatsoever as they will answer it to Almighty *God* and incur my utmost Displeasure.

And for the more effectual Publication hereof I do require and Command the Justices of Quarter Sessions [illegible] Counties [illegible] and the Mayor and Recorder of the City *Philadelphia*, that they cause this my Proclamation to be publickly read in open Court, immediately after their Charge is given to the grand-Jury.

And that the Ministers of [illegible] Churches, and several Congregations within this *Province* and *Territories*, cause the same to be Read in the time of Divine Service, att their respective places of Worship at least six times in every Year. And that they be very Diligent, in Discouraging all manner of Vice, and Immorality in their Auditors [illegible] Exhorting them to the Exercise of piety and virtue.

Given at Philadelphia [illegible] *October* [illegible] *Reign* of our *Sovereign Lady* ANN by the Grace of GOD of *Eng-land Scot-land, France* and *Ire-land Queen* Defender of the Faith &c. And the twenty fourth of the *Proprietaries Government* Annoq: Domini 1704.

JOHN EVANS.

God Save the Queen.

Printed at Philadelphia by Reinier Jansen 1704.

for years continued in that profession in the vicinity of Germantown.

However, be that as it may, in the main it matters little whether these cards or pamphlets were printed in Europe or America. Kelpius's scheme to raise the moral standard of the Germans by their use had an effect that extended far beyond the bounds of the German Township, and, being seconded by the Society of Friends, culminated in the issuing by Governor John Evans of a proclamation against immorality and profanity. This edict was printed by Reynier Jansen in 1704. A reduced fac-simile of the original broadside is reproduced on another page.

According to Hon. S. W. Pennypacker, in his "Settlement of Germantown,"[151] Jansen, almost a year after citizenship was conferred upon him in Germantown, bought, December 23, 1699, seventy-five acres of land from Peter Klever, in the deed of which he is described as a "merchant" of Philadelphia. This land he, "as printer," sold to Daniel Geissler, October 20, 1701.

His career as printer was very brief.[152] He died about March 1, 1706, leaving personal property valued at £226. 1*s.* 8*d.*, among which was included "a p'cell of Books from Wm. Bradford, £4. 2*s.* 0*d.*" He left a son, Stephen, in business in Amsterdam, whom he had apportioned there, and brought with him to this country two sons Tiberius and Joseph, and two daughters, Imitry and Alice. The sons, after the father's death, seem to have made some attempt to continue in the printing business, as imprints are still in existence bearing the names of both Tiberius and Joseph, respectively.[152]

---

151 "Penna. Mag.," vol. iv, 37.

152 Early Printing in Philadelphia, "Penna. Mag.," vol. iv, p. 432, *et seq.*

THE DIVINING ROD AND HOROSCOPE.

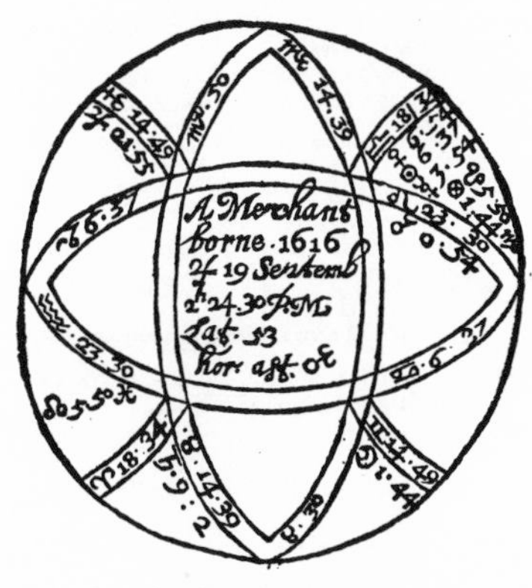

AN OLD HOROSCOPE.

BESIDES the religious and educational work fostered by the Community on the Wissahickon and the speculations as to the expected millennium, Kelpius and the more advanced members indulged in the study of the Hermetic arts, as well as astronomy. Nightly vigils were maintained in the rude observatory that surmounted the Tabernacle. There, high above the tree-tops of the surrounding forest, one or more of the brethren was always on the look-out for celestial phenomena. These astronomical studies and speculations were calculated according to the manuscripts and publications of Johann Jacob Zimmermann, the Magister of the Fraternity, under whose leadership the scheme for emigration to the New World was consummated, but who unfortunately died on the eve of the embarkation at Rotterdam.

Zimmermann was an astronomer of no mean order, who in his deductions combined theology and astronomy, according to the custom of the middle ages. The last work published by him, but a few months prior to his death, is entitled, "Scriptura S. Copernizans seu potius Astronomia Copernico Scripturaria bipartita." That is, An entirely new and very curious astronomical proof of the Copernican system of the universe from the Holy Writ.[153]

SCRIPTURA S. COPERNIZANS
seu potius
ASTRONOMIA COPERNICO SCRIPTURARIA
BIPARTITA
Das ist:
Ein gantz neu und sehr curioser
Astronomischer
Beweißthum,
Des
Copernicanischen Welt-Gebäudes
aus Heil. Schrifft,
Worinnen
I. Beydes der Sonnen samt andern Fixsternen räumlicher Stillstand, als auch der Erdkugel samt anderer Planeten natürlicher Umlauff buchstäblich angewiesen;
II. Die vermeintlich widersprechende Gegen-Sprüche aus dem Hebräischen und Griechischen Text deutlich erörtert werden,
Um, sowohl die Hoheit, Fürtreflichkeit und Autorität des H. Prophetischen Worts, wider die heutigige Verkleinerung der Spinosisten, Naturalisten, Atheisten, als auch (bey gleichwohl nothwendiger Handhabung des Natur-mäßigen Copernicanischen Welt-Gebäudes,) der hochheiligen THEOLOGIÆ zur Veneration, den buchstäblichen Verstand der H. Schrifft, wider den von bißherigen Copernicanern angeschmützten Lügen-Verstand, best-müglichst zu verwahren;
Nebens untermengter Erläuterug einiger Carthesianischen und Chymischen Geheimnissen, auch etlicher durch des Lichts Natur poëticè und sonsten illustrirten Glaubens-Articuln,
In zweyen Theilen einfältig entworffen,
Von
JOHANN JACOB Zimmermann, Philo-Mathematico.
HAMBURG, bey Christ. Wilh. Brandt.

The astronomical feature of the Tabernacle led to frequent visits from Daniel Leeds, who, for some years prior to the arrival of Kelpius and his party, had published an Almanack.[154] Evidences are apparent in subsequent issues of the Almanack that he profited by his visits, and that the intercourse between him and the Community on the Wissahickon was of an intimate nature.

While some of the Fraternity kept the vigils in the *sternwarte*, others busied themselves with the study of

---

[153] The only known copy of this work is in the Royal Library of Würtemberg. The photograph of the title was furnished by Professor D. Th. Schott, librarian. A second edition was published in Hamburg, 1726.

what is known as the Hermetic art. These researches were not made for the transmutation of metals, as many supposed; for in their ambitions they soared to a higher plane than the laying up of this world's riches. Their object was to provide remedies and preparations for the alleviation of human suffering.[155]

In these chemical and pharmaceutical studies, which were mainly based upon the literature of the preceding century, the discovery of the *Lapis Philosophorum*, or the Elixir of Life, naturally entered largely into their speculations. It was believed that if the *menstrum universale* could be discovered, it would be by chemical means, and then it would be possible by its application to remove all seeds of disease from the human body, thereby renewing youth and lessening the infimities of age, if not repelling death.

---

[154] Daniel Leeds was a resident of New Jersey as early as 1676. He lived in Burlington in 1680, and was married at the Friends' Meeting of that place, 2 mo. 21, 1681. His occupation was then given as a cooper. In 1682 he was a member of the Assembly and Surveyor-General of West Jersey. His first quarrel with his co-religionists was about the almanac of 1688; but he did not withdraw from the Society of Friends until the Keithian schism. (Hildeburn, vol. i, p. 7.)

Jacob Taylor, in his almanac for 1707, calls him "That unparalleled Plagiary and unreasonable Transcriber D. Leeds, who hath now for 19 years, with a very large stock of impudence, filched matter out of other men's works, to furnish his spurious almanacks." (*An Almanack* for 1707. *By Jacob Taylor. Philadelphia: Tiberius Johnson.* Am. Philo. Soc., xix, 291.)

[155] Mention has been made in a preceeding chapter (p. 57), of a prescription of a universal remedy, bequeathed, upon his death-bed, by a former member of this Fraternity to Magister Francke, and made under the latter's supervision, from the sale of which and the revenue derived therefrom the large cluster of buildings known as the "Francke Institutions at Halle" chiefly owe their existence.

This remedy, known as the "Gold Tincture" or "Elixir Dulcis," is made and sold to the present day by the *Apotheke* connected with the

In these hermetic studies, that were practised only upon nights when the moon and planets were in a certain position, the brethren were often assisted by several highly respected English Quakers and a learned Scotchman, who were wont to make visits from the city.

Upon the subject of an indefinite prolongation of human life, the members were not unanimous. While all agreed that this was possible under certain circumstances or conditions, some of their number, notably Köster, were incredulous of an elixir of life, but advanced the theory of the use of mystical communications with the unseen world, as founded upon the Cabbala and the Apocalypse.[156]

As a matter of fact, all the leaders of the Brotherhood, which included Kelpius, Köster, Falkner, Seelig, and Matthaï, scouted the idea of physical death, and firmly believed in bodily translation to the realms beyond, if they adhered to their Theosophical faith.

Another favorite occupation of these Theosophical students was the casting of horoscopes and the use of the divining-rod. The latter implement was a forked, slender stick of witch-hazel, that was cut at a certain time in the year under peculiar conditions, at which time a mystic

---

Orphanage. No more than a single person at one time was ever cognizant of its composition. The writer, during his visit to the Orphanage, obtained a vial of this remedy, and was informed by Hugo Hornemann, Ph. D., that he had been the custodian of the secret since June 1, 1863 it having been imparted to him by his father and predecessor who served from 1826 to 1863, and had in turn received it from Prof. Stoltze, who compounded it 1811–26. Prior to this time the secret formula was in possession of the Richters and Madais, who were the successive heads of the *Apotheke.*

Prior to the Revolution, this nostrum had a large sale in Pennsylvania, and to the writer's personal knowledge was used here as late as the early fifties of the present century.

[156] Strodtmann, v. p. 255.

HOROLOGIUM ACHAZ.

CHRISTOPHORUS SCHISSLER, GEOMETRICUS AC ASTRONOMICUS ARTIFEX, AUGUSTÆ, VINDELICORUM, FACIEBAT, 1578.

NOW IN THE CABINET OF THE AMERICAN PHILOSOPHICAL SOCIETY.

incantation and ceremony was used. This rod or "*hexen-stab*" was used to find subterranean springs of water, and to locate veins of precious metal beneath the surface of the ground. To find the hidden spring, a branch of the twig or rod was taken in each hand between the thumb and the forefinger, the two ends pointing down. The rod was held in this position, the palms toward the face: the incantation was then said, the diviner walking slowly over the ground, and when a spring or subterranean water-course was passed the rod would bend downward. When it was desired to locate special metals, small nails made of the metals sought for were introduced into the long end of the rod. For general prospecting, the rod frequently contained nails of the seven metals,—viz., gold, silver, iron, copper, lead, tin, and an amalgam; and it was firmly believed that in passing over a metallic vein the rod would be attracted downward.[157]

The casting of nativities by aid of the horoscope was a far more difficult and important matter than the use of the divining-rod. Two centuries ago the horoscope was firmly believed in by many intelligent persons of all nations and faiths. The calculations in individual cases required considerable mathematical as well as astronomical knowledge. By its use not only the life and fortune of an infant were foretold, but it was pressed into service to find the right position of the heavens for the undertaking of almost all important ventures, such as voyages, marriages, business speculations, and building operations.

Among the treasures of the American Philosophical Society in Philadelphia there are two brass plates, finely

[157] The writer in his youth was shown a bed of iron ore near Flowertown, a small village a short distance above Germantown, which was said to have been located by one of these identical rods.

wrought, engraved, and gilded. They are parts of an instrument once used for calculating nativities, and in other occult studies wherein the hour of the day or night and the position of the planetary system of the heavens took a prominent part. This instrument, when in its original condition, was known as an "*horologium Achaz hydrographicum.*" The smaller of the two plates measures 5¾ inches in diameter, and was the base of the instrument. In a raised centre it contained a compass one inch in diameter. The larger piece is a basin-shaped plate, with a flat, moveable rim one inch wide. Upon this are engraved the signs of the zodiac. The centre or concave part is ten inches in diameter, and is geometrically divided into the different planetary houses. The depth of the basin is 1¾ inches, and the whole forms the dial of the instrument. The rim is surrounded by a brass figure representing an ancient astrologer; it measures 3¾ inches in height, with the left hand raised so as to hold the *gnomon* used to cast the shadow, or whereby a fine ray of light was thrown upon the dial in place of the shadow (photo-sciaterica). The dial and base were formerly connected with a mythological figure; the latter, however, as well as the gnomon and other parts are now missing.

By the aid of this instrument it was possible to see not only the true time of day by sunlight and at night by moonlight, but other solar phenomena, such as the true time of sunrise and sunset,—the orb's place in the twelve houses of the zodiac, its perigee, and apogee, the height above the horizon, the relative length of the day and night, and many other phenomena. The most curious feature about this apparatus is the fact that when the basin is filled with clear water the time marked is advanced or retarded so many degrees as equal the angle of refraction.[158]

On the reverse of the rim that surrounds the large basin is engraved, "Christophorvs Shissler, Geometricvs ac Astronomicvs Artifex Avgvstae Vindelicorvm, Faciebat Anno 1578."

The records of the venerable Society fail to show from whom these relics were received, or even when they came into possession of the Society. Tradition, however, connects this instrument directly with Dr. Christopher Witt, the last surviving member of the Theosophical Community that once occupied the Tabernacle on the Wissahickon, and who, prior to his death in 1765, gave some of his philosophical and scientific apparatus to the Philosophical Society, then presided over by Benjamin Franklin.[159]. It is known that after the death of Kelpius, in 1708, and the virtual disbanding of the Community, all of the philosophical instruments, as well as Zimmermann's astronomical apparatus, passed into the possession of Daniel Geissler and Dr. Witt. It may be assumed without a shadow of doubt that the above relics once formed a part of Zimmermann's scientific outfit.[160]

As an illustration how the horoscope entered into local affairs, there was formerly a tradition current, and which is recorded in one of the Ephrata manuscripts, that prior to the laying of the foundation-stone (*grund-stein*) of the

---

[158] This instrument was known to and its peculiarity mentioned by Zacharias Von Uffenbach, a classmate of Justus Falkner at Halle, in his published travels, Ulm, 1753.

[159] There were at that time two scientific societies in Philadelphia,—viz., The American Philosophical Society and the American Society, held at Philadelphia, for Promoting Useful Knowledge. These two bodies united, January 2, 1769, and formed the present American Philosophical Society.

[160] *Vide* paper read upon this instrument by the present writer before the American Philosophical Society, "Proceedings," February 1, 1895.

Swedish church at Wicacoa, Seelig, at the request of the Swedish pastor, first cast a horoscope to find a proper day for the commencement of the building, so that its completion should be assured. The interesting service took place upon the appointed day in the fall of the year 1698, and was made an occasion of both joy and profit.

The site finally decided upon, after some controversy as to the location, was within the Swedish graveyard at Wicaco, on the banks of the Delaware. The ceremony of laying the first or foundation-stone was performed by the three ministers under the direction of the Master Mason, while the Fraternity, led by Kelpius, intoned the Psalms and responses.

Whether the old tradition that the day and site were selected by the occult calculations of the Mystic Brotherhood on the Wissahickon be founded upon fact or not, the day certainly was an auspicious one, as the old church, after a lapse of two centuries, is still in constant use, and is now the oldest and most venerable sanctuary within the Commonwealth of Pennsylvania. It has stood to be immortalized by the prince of New England poets:—

> "Distant and soft on her ear fell the chimes from the belfry of Christ Church,
> While, intermingled with these, across the meadows were wafted
> Sounds of psalms that were sung by the Swedes in their church at Wicaco."

Among the universal remedies in which the Germans of that period placed great faith was phlebotomy, or blood-letting, which it was believed would prevent sickness as well as effect a cure. Some persons were in the habit of undergoing the operation at regular seasons of the year, no matter whether sick or well. Owing to the belief in astrology, care was taken to perform it under favorable lunar and planetary influences. For this more than any other purpose the different Hermits on the Ridge were consulted by the residents of the surrounding country. The phases of the moon could be gotten from the almanac, either by the patient or the barber-chirurgeon,[161] and even the good and bad days easily calculated;[162] but to find the correct position of the planets and foretell their influence in an individual case, this was another matter, and one of prime importance, as the operation would affect the person for a lunar year to come.

Then, again, it was believed that the disposition of the drawn blood was a matter of great moment to the patient, and the art of the astrologer was once more invoked as to when and how the lost blood should be disposed of.[163]

Every vein or artery had also its own name, and came under the influence of a peculiar sign or planet. Thus there was the cephalic vein which was ruled by Aries; the

---

[161] The barber-chirurgeon was then quite an important personage. His specialties were bleeding, cupping, and leeching.

[162] When the phase of the moon changed before noon the day was counted as the first day. If, however, the change occurred after high noon the day was not counted. From a fragment of an old manuscript, dating from that period, it is seen that according to the accepted theory the first five days of the new moon were all bad for blood-letting: the first caused a bad countenance; the second, a bad fever; the third, lameness; the fourth, a slow death; the fifth, giddiness; while the sixth was marked "good," as it purifies the blood. The seventh, eighth, ninth, and tenth were all bad; then came twelve days all good, with a special reference to the twenty-first, that this was the best day in the year.

[163] The early Moravians in Pennsylvania had a positive rule, that the lost blood should either be buried in fresh earth at once or thrown into running water. This was to prevent any possible spread of disease. (Bethlehem MS. Diaries.)

hepatic, the splenetic, arthritic, quinsy vein, etc.,[164] each with a different sign. The astrologer had therefore to indicate according to the celestial signs what particular vein was to be tapped, as well as when the other conditions would be favorable.

It is not to be assumed from the above that Kelpius and his brother Mystics practised astrology for profit, after the manner of the charlatans of that day. A moderate use of the art was believed in by most intelligent people and the signs were consulted and studied for scientific as well as personal purposes. Though the Mystics on the Wissahickon made use of astrological signs and calculations, and believed in the influence of heavenly bodies upon human affairs, yet that they were free from all charlatanism may be safely assumed from the following interesting extract, which appeared in Vol. xii, p. 270, of the Philosophical Transactions of the Royal Society of London, July 10, 1683.[165] Here, in the review of Johann

PortenDens graVIa eX aqVILone
fVtVra CoMetes.
Das ist:
Neuer
Comet-Stern,
Welcher
In diesem 1682. Jahr/im
Monat Augusto sich anfänglich
von Mitternacht her sehen
lassen.
Kürtzlich und auf das einfältigste erörtert
Durch
M. Johann-Jacob Zimmermann/von Vayhingen an der Entz/ jetzmahligen Diaconum
zu Bietigheim.
Im Jahr
C BLeib bey Vns HErr/ Dann es VVILL nVn AbenD VVerDen
In Verlegung Johann Gottfrid Zubrodten/
Buchhändlern in Stuttgart
Gedruckt bey Paulus Treuen. In disem 1682. Jahr

[164] Hauptader, Leber, Miltz, Gicht, Braun, etc.

[165] Copy in library of American Philosophical Society, Philadelphia.

Jacob Zimmermann's "Cometo-Scopia; or, Three Astronomical Relations concerning the Comets that have been seen in the years 1680, 1681, 1682,"[166] the editor states: "Though as he [Zimmermann] saith he doth not like the common *Astrological Juggling Purse* (so he calls it) [*beutelschneider*] where, according to the Division of the Heaven in twelve Houses, and the Distribution of the Countries to the signs of the *Zodiack*, the Superstitious Fortune-Tellers do Prognosticate things, which have no reasons nor grounds, neither in Nature or experience, yet it seems he [Zimmermann] cannot forbear himself to make use of the same trifles, when he says that *Virgo* being the sign of Sterilty; *Libra*, a sign of *Justice* and *Death;* *Scorpio*, a house of *Mars* and sign of *Poysons*,—the *Comet* must signify *War*, *Famine*, *Sickness*, or a great *Plague*."

[166] No copy of this work is known to exist. The title reproduced is from a similar work relating merely to the comet of 1682. The original is in the Royal Library of Würtemberg at Stuttgart. The writer is indebted to Prof. D. H. Schott, chief librarian, for the photographic copy.

LOCAL SUPERSTITIONS.

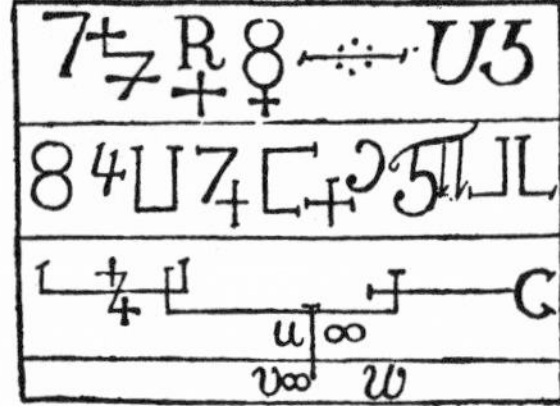

FIG. A.

ANOTHER custom then in vogue among the Germans in Pennsylvania was the wearing of *anhängsel*, a kind of astrological amulet or talisman. They consisted chiefly of small charts upon parchment or paper, formed by astrological signs, together with hieroglyphic figures. In rare cases a thin stone or sheet of metal was used in place of the parchment. These *anhängsel*, or *zauber-zettel* as they were called, were prepared by the Mystics of the Community with certain occult ceremonies at such times as the culmination of a particular star or the conjunction of certain planets. One of the *anhängsel* most in demand (Fig. A.) was prepared at midnight on St. John's eve, and buried for a time in the place where the *sonnen-wend* fire had been. This special one was supposed to abjure all evil spirits. The *anhängsel*, when properly prepared by a com-

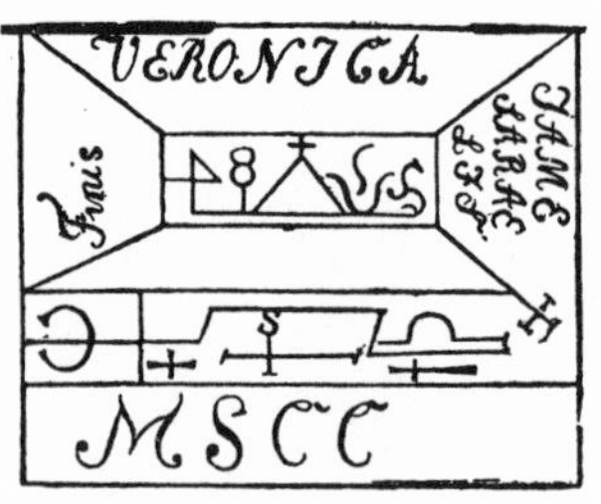

FIG. B.

SEEKING THE LAPIS PHILOSOPHORUM (PP. 111-112).

ORIGINAL BY DAVID TENIERS, 1610-1690, IN ROYAL GALLERY AT DRESDEN.

petent magus (the *hexenmeister* of the ignorant), was supposed to exercise an extraordinary influence over the destiny of the bearer, particularly in averting disease, checking the power of evil spirits, and defending the wearer from malice and all harm.

Various mineral and animal substances, such as bones and teeth, were also used with the same import, after they had been subjected to a certain mystic incantation. Vegetable substances were rarely used, as it was believed that their efficacy only lasted while the plant or tree was in a state of growth or activity.

So universal was the belief among the Germans in the

Fig. C.

efficacy of the *anhängsel* that hardly an adult or child was to be found without one. Frequently a charm of this kind would be placed upon an infant immediately upon its birth, as well as upon a corpse prior to interment. Then, again, some were prepared for special diseases, and worn or applied when the occasion presented itself; and it was firmly believed where a cure was effected that the result was due more to the mystic charm written upon a triangular parchment, and then folded thrice and placed upon the body of the patient, than to the remedies used by the practitioner of physic. Several of these *anhängsel* are here reproduced. Fig. B was supposed to banish all evil spirits, being a secret protection against which no demon could prevail. Fig. C was known as the *wunder-sigel;* it was believed to be a sure protection against any and all kinds of mechanical injuries, as well as against gun-shot or stab wounds of any sort. Fig. D, known as an *artabel anhängsel*, consisted of a thin plate of metal, usually copper, but in rare cases gold or silver. It was worn around the neck by a plaited three-strand cord made of hair taken from the tail of a horse at midnight upon Christmas eve. This charm was believed to insure to its fortunate owner a long life of wealth, power, strength, and cheerfulness, prolonged youth and an easy death. Fig. E: this peculiar chart was called a *Tritheim zettel*, and was supposed to banish all harm from the house in which it was used. The derivation of the characters or their symbolism, however, has not been traced by the writer.

Fig. D.

Independent of the above described charms or talismans, there was another kind of superstition common to the general populace. This was known as *besprechen*, a kind of conjuration for the cure of wounds or minor diseases in both man and beast. The ceremony was nearly always performed by an old man or woman, usually the latter; and in some cases, such as burns, scalds, erysipelas, wounds, and hemorrhages, it was believed to be of greater efficacy than any medical treatment.

A curious matter in connection with the transmission of

the formulæ for these conjurations was, that to maintain their efficiency they had to be handed down by an alternation of the sexes. As an illustration, a woman who could *besprech* fire, as burns and scalds were called, in transmitting her secret formula would have to communicate it to one of the opposite sex, and he in turn to another woman; otherwise the charm would not work.

Another strange belief, one in which the Mystic Brethren figured, was the use of the *wunder-sigel*, or mystic signet. This was nothing more than an ordinary brass seal, one of

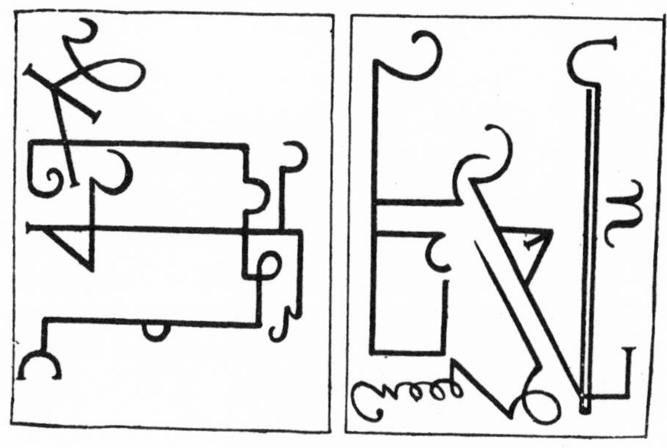

FIG. E.

which is now in possession of the writer, whereon were cut certain astrological figures and signs. It was used not only upon documents and articles of writing, but was impressed upon various parts of the body, whether of human beings or of animals. This was done to prevent or cure certain ailments. For this purpose the signet or *petschaft* was smoked by aid of a fatty flame and then impressed upon the spot where the trouble existed. The application was generally made with an incantation, in which the names of the Trinity bore the leading part. When used upon cattle it was believed, among other things, that it would prevent them from straying away, and would cause them to return home at the regular time; also that no vermin of any kind would come near them. A horse so sealed could not be stolen, but if taken would at once return to its owner. An impression of an electrotype made from one of these identical signets used by the Theosophical Brotherhood is here given, also a drawing of the same seal, showing the size of the original.

Watson, in commenting upon this peculiar phase of German character in days gone by, writes, "Germantown was certainly very fruitful in credulity, and gave support to some three regular professors in the mysterious arts of divination. Besides Dr. Witt, there was his disciple, Mr. Frailey, sometimes dubbed doctor also, though not possessed of learning.[167] The other person alluded to by Watson was an old man known as "Old Shrunk." When cows and horses, and even persons, got strange diseases, such as baffled ordinary medicines, it was customary to consult these persons for relief, and their prescriptions, without seeing the patients, were often given under the idea of witchcraft somehow, and the cure was effected."

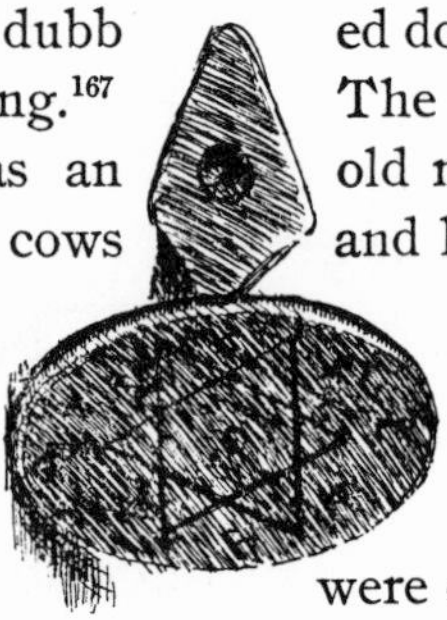

[167] No reference to Dr. Frailey could be found in support of his connection with Dr. Witt.

THE MYSTIC ON THE WISSAHICKON.

Macrocosm, or Seal of King Solomon.

WHEN the Brotherhood on the Wissahickon began to be better known they attracted considerable attention among the Dissenters and Separatists scattered throughout the other colonies, as well as in Pennsylvania. Among the first to communicate with Kelpius and his associates were the leaders of the Sabbatarian movement in Pennsylvania and New Jersey. Abel Noble,[168] the Sabbatarian apostle, who was then active in the Province among the Keithians in Philadelphia and Chester

---

[168] Abel Noble was the son of William Noble, a wealthy Friend of Bristol, England, and arrived in this country in 1684, coming to Philadelphia shortly afterwards. He was a nephew of Richard Noble, who came from England in the "Joseph and Mary," Captain Mathew Payne, the first vessel that landed passengers at Salem, New Jersey, May 13, 1675, and who held some office under the Duke of York, and will be remembered as the surveyor of the Jerseys who laid out Burlington ; he was also active in the early settlement of Pennsylvania after the grant to Penn.

Counties, was a frequent visitor at the Tabernacle in the forest, where the question of the true Sabbath received the earnest consideration of the Theosophists. In these discussions they were frequently joined by the Swedish pastors Rudman and Aurén.

According to the Ephrata manuscripts and traditions, it is to be inferred that not only the rival band under Köster, but the original Community, as well as one of the Swedish pastors, became convinced of the Sabbatarian doctrine and kept the Sabbath or Seventh-day holy. So far as the Keithian congregation under Köster is concerned, as well as in the case of Rev. Jonas Aurén, we have ample documentary evidence to substantiate this claim. The former eventually became a distinct Church, known as the Seventh-day Baptist Church of Philadelphia, with Thomas Rutter as the first pastor; while the Rev. Jonas Aurén embraced the doctrine of the Seventh-day without letting it interfere with his Lutheran pastorship.[169] He also went as a mis-

---

Abel Noble soon after his arrival became possessed of a large tract of land in what is now known as Warminister Township, Bucks County.

The claim of his having been a Seventh-Day Baptist preacher prior to his arrival in this country is a matter of doubt, as he had not yet arrived to the years of manhood when he landed on these shores. Further, from the start he professed Quakerism, and soon became a prominent member among the Society of Friends in the infant colony. However, when the Keithian troubles commenced we find him a staunch upholder of Keith, and his name, together with William Davis, is prominent among the forty-eight who signed the reasons for the Keithian separation. But at the same time he continued in accord with the society and remained in good standing among them, as is shown by his marriage in 1692 at Darby Meeting to Mary Garrett.

After his final separation from the parent society the transition to the Baptists was an easy matter, and the tradition that Noble, during a business trip through the Jerseys, came in contact with Killingsworth and was baptised by him, is probably correct; but how, and through whom he was convinced of the Sabbatrian doctrine is an unsolved question.

[169] Acrelius.

sionary among the Indians, and by a curious coincidence preached the Gospel of Christ and taught the doctrine of the Sabbath to the Indians upon almost the identical spot where thirty years later the Ephrata Community was settled.

[The Rev. Jonas Aurén, of Wermeland in Sweden, accompanied Rev. Rudman and Biörck to America at the king's command. He had been ordained along with Biörck at Upsala, and was under the special patronage of King Charles XI. His special mission was to make a map of the Swedish possessions, with a description of their character and the condition of the inhabitants, all of which he was to bring or send to his Majesty without delay.

The party sailed from Dalarön August 4, 1696, arriving in London October 10th. It was, however, not until February 4, 1697, that they left London for America. Their voyage to the capes of Virginia lasted ten weeks. They first went to Maryland, and remained for several weeks as guests of Governor Francis Nicholson, when they continued their journey on a yacht to Elk River, and reached Pennsylvania by way of New Castle, June 24, 1697. Rudman and Aurén remained in Philadelphia, while Biörck went down the river to the Christiana congregation. Shortly afterwards word was received of the death of King Charles XI, when Aurén concluded to remain in America, and subsequently became pastor of the Racoon Church in New Jersey.

Aurén's intercourse with the Sabbatarians at Providence and Philadelphia, as well as with the Mystics on the Wissakickon, was of an intimate nature, and resulted in his becoming convinced that the seventh day, or Saturday, was the true Sabbath.

He published his reasons for the above in English in Leeds' Almanac for 1700, under the title of "Noah's Dove."

This caused considerable trouble between the three clergymen and in the congregations. It was answered by a counter pamphlet from Biörck, also in English, entitled, "A little Olive Leaf put in the Mouth of Noah's Dove."[170]

In addition to his other labors, Aurén actually engaged in missionary work among the Indians in Chester County (now Lancaster), preaching to them the gospel together with the doctrine of the Sabbath, upon the identical ground on which the Ephrata Community of Mystic Sabbatarians was subsequently established.

A communication from Aurén appears in Biörck's *Dissertatio Gradualis, de Plantatione Ecc. Sued.*, dated January 13, 1699–1700, which gives some account of his labors in this missionary field.

It is further an interesting fact that Aurén laid the corner-stone of Holy Trinity (Old Swedes) Church of Christiana (Wilmington), on the Seventh day, Saturday, May 28, 1698.

Notwithstanding his outspoken Sabbatarianism, Aurén was called as pastor to the Rattcong (Racoon) Church in New Jersey, and as he continued to preach the doctrine of Sabbath, he was cited by Biörck to appear before the Governor of New York; but so ably did Aurén defend his position, that he was permitted to return as pastor, with the understanding that he was to preach the Orthodox Lutheran doctrine on Sunday to his congregation, while he and his family were at liberty to keep the seventh day.

Aurén died February 16, 1713, and was buried in New

---

[170] "A Little Olive Branch put in the Mouth of the (so-called) Noah's Dove, Printed and sold by William Bradford at the Sign of the Bible in New York, 1704," sm. 4to. Title from catalogue of "The Bradford Exhibition" by the Grolier Club, New York, 1893. The copy on exhibition is the only one known. The owner of the specimen refused to leave his name be known to the public.

Jersey. The funeral sermon was preached, February 24, 1713, by Rev. Abraham Lidenius; and on the next day, February 25, he was buried in the Racoon Church, the service being read by Dr. Andreas Sandel.[171] He left a widow[172] and two sons, the youngest only five weeks old.]

As to the Sabbatarian tendencies of the Kelpius party, the evidence is not quite so clear. It is known, however, that at an early day communications were opened between Kelpius and others on the Wissahickon and the leaders of the Sabbatarians in Rhode Island and Connecticut.

This fact is shown by the following letter, the draft of which is in the Journal of Kelpius in his own handwriting, which gives perhaps the fullest and most exact account of the peculiar theosophy of the original Community which it was possible to reveal to any one who had not made the subject an especial study. It is addressed to Steven Mumford, to whom is accorded the honor of establishing the first Sabbatarian congregation in America.

"To Mr. Steven Momfort in Long Island,[173] in America, concerning the Pietists in Germany.

"1699, 11 December.

"Dear Friend and Brother:

"In fellow-fighting in that Free and Royal Spirit which strives for the Prize of the first Resurrection when in this Midnight the Cry of the Bridegroom's coming is sounded forth among the Virgin waiters for the Preparation of the Temple Body, wherein the King of Glory and Father of the coming Eternity is to enter.

---

171 February 16, 1713, Aurén died at Ratkungs Hook, and was buried by me, February 25, in the Ratkungs Church.—*Diary Andreas Sandel.*

172 Aurén was married in November, 1710, by Rev. Biörch to Lydia, daughter of Hans Giostason. He was then living near the Susquehanna River.—*Diary Andreas Sandel.*

173 This should be Rhode Island.

"Your great desire for to be a little further informed of the Principles and Practizes of those People that go under the Name of Pietists,[174] what they hold as Doctrin differing from others, what their Discipline is and what Methods they use in their own Country; this desire I will hope, doth not arise from the Root of that Athenian Curiosity to hear some new thing; But rather you being one among thousands in Juda, who sees how since that glorious Primitive Church of Christ Jesus the Apostacy hath run in a continual current till this very day, and though this Stream hath divided itself in many smaller Rivulets, under several Names of more reformed Purity, yet you are not ignorant how they derive their Emanation from one Spring and ten to the same End, Viz. that the Woman in the Wilderness might be carried away by the Flood. Therefore you, as a Remnant of her seed, long for to see your Mother and groan for the Manifestation of her children. No wonder then, if your continual Gazing upon this Supercaelestial Orb and Sphier from whence with her Children, causeth you to observe every new Phoenomena, Meteors, Stars and various Colours of the Skei, if peradventure you may behold at last an Harbinger as an Evidence of that great Jubelee or Restitation of all things and glorious Sabbathismos or the continual days of Rest without intervening or succeeding Nights, whereof God hath spoken by the mouth of all his Prophets since the world began (Acts 3, 21) and whereof both the Testaments prophesie in evey Title and Iota. If now this late Revolution in Europe (not to speak of that in other parts) which in the Roman Church

---

[174] Christopher Sauer states that the name first arose from an expression used by a Prof. Veller, who, in a funeral sermon on one of the students, said "He was a Pietist," meaning that he was a God-fearing person.—*Sauer's Almanac*, 1751.

goes under the Name of Quietism,[175] in the Protestane Church under the Name of Pietism, Chiliasm, and Philadelphianism, If I say this together or one in Special purtends any thing to this effect. I do not question, but it will be your as well as my desire, who would rejoyce not only to give you full satisfaction as to this, but to see with you, yet in our days, that happy day, which when its new Earth swallows all that forementioned Floud and where its glorious Sun causeth all other Stars and Phoenomena to disappear, no Night succeeds it, but that the Night is swallowed up in ye Day, Darkness into Light, Death into Life, Judgment into Victory, Justice into Mercy, all imperfect Metals into Gold, and Gold itself is refined seven times, and all Churches and Virgins comprised into the one Dove (Cant. 6, 9), then all the Sons of God will shout for joy as they did in the Beginning, when God was all in all, as he will be all in all, when again the End hath found its Beginning. Amen! Halleluiah!

"Dear and worthy friend, though unknown to the Flesh but known in that better, yea in the best Line and highest descent in the Life of our Immanuel, whose Day we rejoyce to hear of and more to see, as well within us as without us, in its Depth, Hight, Breadth and Length, through the whole palsed and groaning Creation, as well as in our Mother Jerusalem above and Beneath! How can I

---

[175] The Quietists were the followers of Miguel de Molinos, a Spanish Mystic. The chief object of this sect was the attainment of spiritual and physical perfection. The founder taught that little value was to be placed upon ceremonial observances, but spiritual perfection consisted in the perfect repose of all the faculties of the soul in God and indifference to all the actions of the body. For those who obtained this "fixed" or "continuous" state there was no sin and no occasion for anxiety. "Mystical theology," said Molinos, "is not a science of the intellect, but of sentiment; it is not learned by study, but received from heaven."

write the particulars of the Quietists or Pietists, Chiliasts[176] or Philadelphians,[177] whose Fame is spread in all the 4 quarters of the now Christianity. They first sprang in Italy, in Rome itself (and are increased now through the whole Roman Church in many Millions, though they was and are still depressed) 15 or 20 years before the Pietists or Chiliasts in Germany and Switzerland (where the first Reformation) in the year '89 and '90, with a swift increase through the whole Nation, so that their Branches also did break forth into other Nations, as in England under the name of Philadelphians. This Penn is too dull to express the extraordinary Power the Pietists and Chiliasts among the Protestants in Germany (and especially in Saxony) and Switzerland was endued with in their Infancy. This only I say, as one who hath read the Histories, that since the days of the Apostels, such Miraculous Powers and operations have not been manifested as in a matter of 3½ years among these. And like as the Miracles wrought by God through the Hand of Moyses was for the main part in the outward Creation or Macrocosm, the Miracles of Jesus the Messia on the Bodys of Man or Macrocosm,[178] so these in our days was wrought (much like unto them in the days of the Apostels) on the Soul and more interiour parts by Ectases, Revelations, Inspirations, Illuminations, Inspeakings, Prophesies, Apparitions, Changings of Minds, Transfigurations, Translations of their Bodys, wonderful Fastings

---

[176] *Vide*, p. 37, 38, *Ibid.*

[177] *Vide*, p. 16, *Ibid.*

[178] Macrocosm, used in a figurative sense to denote the universe or visible system of worlds, literally the great world. The opposite, microcosm, the little world, was a name given to man in the times when astrology flourished, as it was supposed that his organization accurately corresponded to the organization of the universe. The above conception dates back to Democritus (b. 460 B.C.).

for 11, 14, 27, 37 days, Paradysical Representations by Voices, Melodies, and Sensations to the very perceptibility of the Spectators who was about such persons, whose condition as to the inward condition of their Souls, as well as their outward Transactions, yea their very thoughts they could tell during the time of their Exstacies, though they had never seen nor heard of the Persons before.

MACROCOSM APPEARING TO DR. FAUSTUS.

"These and many other Gifts continued as is said, for a matter of three years and a half among all sorts of Persons, Noble, and ignoble, Learned and unlearned, Male and female, young and old, very conspiciously and generally Protestants chiefly, and some Papists, and with some though more refined such and like Gifts last till this very day.

"Thus partly I have declared how they was baptized with such energical drops out of that supercaleistial Pillar of Cloud by Gifts and miraculous Manifestations of the Powers from on high.

"Now will I tell in short in what a craggy, uneven yea dark wilderness they have been led since, when hitherto they have been baptized with the fiery Pillar of many inward and outward Tribulations, Sorrows, Temptations, Refinings, Purifications (but nevertheless this Fiere casts such a Light befor'm that securs'm from the persuing Might and dark influence of Egypt and guides'm in that beloved land and City.) This must be through many Tribulations as the Apostels have witnessed, so they felt it and feel it still very smartly. For when these things begun to ferment every where, 1. The Students in the Universities forsake their former way of Learning and applied themselves wholly to Piety and Godliness, (from whence their name was derived) leaving and some burning their heathenish Logiks, Rhetoriks, Metaphysiks. 2. The Laymen or Auditors begun to find fault with the Sermons and Lifes of their Ministers, seeing there was nothing of Ye Power of the Holy Ghost, nor of the Life of Christ and his Apostels. 3. The children under the Information and Tuition of Pietists, (for the Students applied themselves chiefly to the Education of Children, as they do till this day with great, yea extraordinary success) begun to reproof their Parents if they was working and Lye or unrighteousness! yea some in their tender years came to witness strange things of the Invisible worlds. Till at last Demetrius with his Craftsmen begun to see and hear that not only in Lipzig, (from which University this Motion first begun to spread abroad) but almost throughout all Germany and adjacent Contrys these Pietists did persuade and turn away much People, saying that the Form of Godliness without the Power thereof is meer Idolatry and superstition; Yea they saw, how that not only this their craft was endangered by these and set at nought, but also the Temple or Universities of the great Goddess Dianoria or Reason and Ratiocination (which is quite different from that Dionoria or Understanding or Unction whereof John witnesses

1 Joh. 5. 19. c. 2, 27.) should be despised and her Magnificence (thus the Rectors in the Universities are titled) should be destroyed, if in the place of Dianoria, the Sophia from on high should be adored and instead of Temples or Universities, the Hearts of men should be consecrated. (Excuse me, dear Heart, that I thus run into an Allegoricall Application, for the very same Comedy was played as you read in the Acts of the Apostels, only the time and persons changed.) Thus the Battel and Insurrection begun, which lasteth till this day.

"The Anti-Pietists (so their Adversaries are pleased to call themselves) betook themselves to the secular Arm. But several Princes being partly inclined to the Principles of the Pietists, partly convinced of a superior Agent in these things, took them in their Protection, especially the Elector of Brandeb. In the Principality of Brunswick and Lunebourg, the course was otherwise, for in the very beginning 3 Bishops or Supirts was removed their offices; the same happened in other Countries and Cities, as Erford, Lipzik, Quedlinbourg, Halberstad, Hambourg, Hassen Cassel, where and in Switzerland lately several Ministers are removed and some banished the Country. Thus they increased under the Cross. As for any peculiar Badge or Mark, they have none being above these trifling affections) or any peculiar Church Ceremony or Discipline which should cause a Shism or branch a new sect. For they are not ignorant of the wilderness wherein the Church is and hath been hitherto, and in what a glory she will appear when she comes up from the Wilderness leaning on her beloved. Cant. 8. 5. They see will enough how all the Reformations and Revolutions in this last Age as well as theirs are but Apparitions of the fair colours of the Aurora or Break of the day, mixed with many uncleanness wherein there is no stay (as my beloved Brother and faithful Fellow-Pilgrim in this Wilderness state Seelig hath written) for they are not the substance or sun itself through the various beautiful Apparitions of the Skie, should entice one allmost enamoured in them and to mistake the Harbinger for the King! whom to meet they prepare themselves earnestly, some of'm laying aside all other engagements whatever, trimming their Lamps and adorning themselves with white silky Holiness and golden Righteousness, that they may be found worthy, when the Bridegroom comes; to receive him with confidence and joy and to bring him in the House of their Mother, where He will drink with'm that new spicy wine of the Kingdom in all everlasting Progresses. That we also may prepare ourselves with our whole endeavours continually I wish heartily, who do recommend you in the Clifts of the Foundation-Rock of our Salvation, Jesus Christ. Remaining your fellow Traveller in this blessed work and best engagement.

"JOHANNES KELPIUS."

Dated in the Wilderness.

[Stephen Mumford (born 1639; died July, 1701) is accredited with being the founder of the Seventh-day Baptist Church in America. He was a native of England, and prior to his emigration to America had been a member of the "Bell Lane Church of Christ" (Seventh-day Baptist), London.

He arrived in New England in 1664, and at once joined with Dr. Clarke's First-day Baptist Church at Newport, though his views favored the observance of the seventh day, as Backus states in his "History of New England,"[179] "bringing with him the opinion that the whole of the Ten

[179] Vol. iii, p. 232.

Commandments, as they were delivered from Mount Sinai, were moral and immutable; and that it was the anti-christian power which thought to change times and laws that changed the Sabbath from the seventh to the first day of the week.

Several members of the First Baptist Church in Newport embraced his sentiments, and yet continued with the church for some years. They kept up a correspondence with their brethren in England, by which they were much strengthened in their resolution to lead a Christian life.

These persons were wont to meet together for worship on the seventh day with Stephen Mumford and others, in a very primitive manner, at their own houses.[180] Finally, five of these members withdrew from the First-day Baptist Church, and on December 23, 1671, together with two other persons, entered into a church covenant and formed a Seventh-day Baptist Church upon the model of the one in London.[181]

From this small beginning originated the Seventh-day Baptist Church in America, which now numbers about 9000 members, about 100 churches, three colleges, and maintains missionary stations in Shanghai, China; Harlem and Rotterdam, Holland; together with thirty-four home missionaries operating in twenty-five States and Territories.

But little is known of the personal history of this Sabbatarian pioneer, as many of the records of the church prior to 1700 have been lost. In the year 1671 he became a freeman of the Community. Three years after the formation of the Newport Church, Mumford went to England

---

180 Seventh-day Baptist Memorial, Vol. i, p. 70–71.

181 The members who withdrew were Stephen Mumford, Samuel Hubbard, Roger Baster, William Hiscox, and Mrs. Tacy Hubbard; to these were added Rachel Longworthy, and a sister whose name is now forgotten.

in the interests of the faith and for the purpose of obtaining aid for the struggling Church in America. Upon his arrival in London he writes, under date of March 14, 1675: "I took my journey to London in the Waggon, where I was received by the brethren with much joy, in some of them, who had a great desire to hear of our place and people; some talk of coming with me." He returned to New England shortly afterwards, arriving in Boston in October of the same year.[182] In the year 1687 we find him living in Jamestown. However, November 29, 1687, he and his wife Ann conveyed some of their property at that place to William Phipps, Kt., of Boston, and returned to Newport, after which we have no record of him, except the memorandum in the diary of Magister Kelpius in 1699.][183]

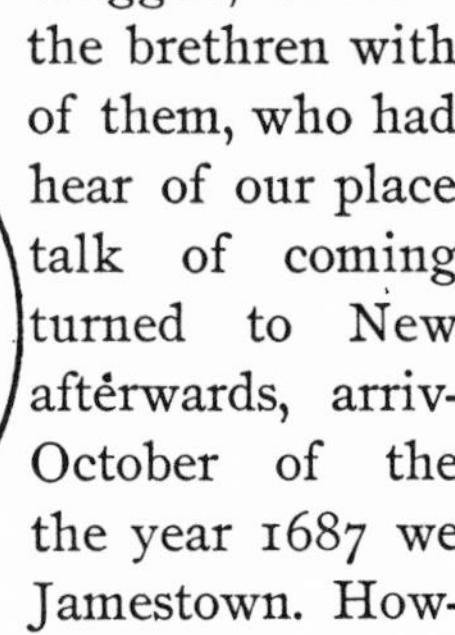

A late writer, in commenting upon the Mumford letter, states: "In such contemplations did Kelpius dream away his young life. Doubtless to him all was a brilliant reality to be enjoyed at some future day; and with a heart full of faith in his doctrines, and sustained by holy aspirations for the higher life, he went forth to meet the heavenly Bridegroom. Far better for him thus to live and die, visionary though he was, than to live and die without hope and without God in the world."

---

182 Austin's Genealogical Dictionary of Rhode Island.

183 Stephen Mumford and his wife are both buried in the old cemetery of the Sabbath-keepers at Newport, R. I.

THE RETURN OF DANIEL FALKNER.

A Mithraic Symbol.

AS the close of the seventeenth century drew near, the leaders of the Community looked forward to the coming of the millennium with greater faith than ever. The terrible scourge of the Barbadoes plague (yellow fever) that had swept the Province during the summer of 1699 was looked upon as but another forerunner of the expected deliverer. It is true their mystic number was far from complete; reports from their emissary in Europe were not encouraging; enemies at home were casting ridicule at their religious teachings, while in Germany their brethren were proscribed and scattered. Still the religious enthusiasts in both hemi-

---

"Gloria Dei," A.D. 1700.

spheres who clung together and adhered to their precepts felt far from discouraged as the sun arose upon the March day which, according to them, ushered in the first day of the seventeenth century. (They made the popular mistake of supposing that 1700 began the new century.) In looking over the situation the American Community felt that their labors had not been altogether in vain. The religious condition of both Germans and English in the Province had been greatly changed for the better by the services which they had instituted and maintained since their arrival. In Philadelphia there were now two churches,—an Episcopal church, solidly built of brick;[184] a Seventh-day Baptist meeting-house,[185] within a stone's throw of the other; while the Swedish Lutheran church at Wicacoa, humble as it was, was nearing completion. Presbyterian and Baptist services had also been held, but as yet no regular organizations had been established. In Germantown such as were followers of Simon Menno were already casting about for a piece of ground upon which to build a regular meeting-house.

Then, again, the educational labors of Kelpius were beginning to bear fruit in the children who received moral instruction at the Tabernacle, and who had there been taught to pray and sing. Many of these children were now growing up into men and women, through whom the religious training would soon make itself felt among the townsfolk.

---

[184] Christ Church, on Second Street above Market.

[185] This house of worship was on Second Street north of Christ Church. It came into the possession of the Baptists in 1707, and became known as the "First Baptist Church of Philadelphia." In 1762 a new church 61 feet by 42 was built. It was enlarged during the present century, and finally sold and abandoned for a more fashionable neighborhood (Broad and Arch Streets). The burying-ground was in the rear of the church.

Toward the close of the old century the Community was reinforced by several Pietists from Halle in Germany, the most important among whom was one Peter Schäffer,[186] a native of Finland and master of arts of the University of Abo. When this party arrived they were cordially received by the brethren and domiciled at the Tabernacle.

Schäffer, who was a learned but somewhat eccentric character, soon differed with Kelpius and the other Mystics as to the sacraments, which were not insisted upon by them. Consequently he offered to withdraw from the Community, and proposed to live a life of seclusion and contemplation.

Kelpius thereupon submitted to him the names of four or five devout families who would give him his living, provided that he would instruct the children of the household for several hours in each day, the remaining time to be passed in his esoteric studies. Schäffer, however, rejected these offers, and concluded to labor as an evangelist among his countrymen along the Delaware and Schuylkill, and when the opportunity offered to act as a missionary among the Indians. He soon left the Tabernacle and came direct to the city. He presented himself to Edward Shippen, one of the magistrates and leading Friends of the Province, and informed him and his wife Rebecca that he had a call to stay under their roof for forty days and nights, during which time he was to subsist on bread and water. He was permitted to remain there during his pleasure; and during this visit, it is stated, he became more and more involved in his mystical speculations.

---

[186] Peter Schäffer, together with Ulstadius, a priest, and Ulhegius, a student of theology, some years prior to the former's arrival in America, had given the courts and consistory of Sweden great trouble. Finally, Ulstadius was condemned to death, and Schäffer recanted and drifted to Halle, whence he went to England and America

Early in the year 1700 he appears to have been chosen as schoolmaster at Wicacoa, where he, according to Pastor Biörck, at first must have given satisfaction, as the latter writes that at last a school has been established at Wicacoa "with an able teacher at the head of it, who also serves as parish clerk." It is not known how long this eccentric visionary remained in charge as schoolmaster at Wicacoa. From there he went to Pennsneck to open a school, but, according to the Swedish records, he effected but little. Soon after he came to New Jersey he entered upon what he termed a "death-fast," and received a revelation that he should arise and wander about at random.[187] From Pennsneck he returned for a short time to the Tabernacle on the Wissahickon. While there he received a call from the Swedes at Pennsneck to return to them and act as their pastor, with the assurance that £24 was ready for his support. This offer he saw fit to refuse, and the next that is learned about him is that he accompanied Jonas Aurén upon one of his missionary tours to the Indians on the Conestoga. Returning from this mission, he had another vision commanding him to return to Europe, which he did forthwith.

After his arrival at Plymouth he subjected himself to an enforced fast of fifty days, at the end of which time he received another revelation that he should return to his old home in Finland and there reprimand his former judges for their course against him. He obeyed, and was imprisoned in the fortress of Gefle, where he became insane and died.

Kelpius, in a letter written to Deichmann in 1699, referring to Peter Schäffer, writes: "His heart yearned toward his own nationality,—the Swedes and Finns, as well as toward the Indians. All three had an interest for him, and he felt that he could do good among them. We parted in

[187] Acrelius, New Sweden, p. 316.

love, and left the doors open so that he could return to us at any time in case that he did not receive the reception he anticipated among his own kindred."[188]

Another interesting incident toward the close of the century was the final parting of Henry Bernhard Köster from his former associates prior to his return to the Fatherland in the winter of 1699. Although he had been separated from his former friends for over five years, and had

"GLORIA DEI," A.D. 1895.

run a somewhat eccentric course, a certain bond of sympathy and friendship had always been maintained between the leaders. So when Köster finally determined to embark for the Fatherland the parting between the men was sad for all, and he went on his way not only with the good wishes of every one of his former companions, but was followed by their blessings and prayers for his safe journey.

The first year of the new century (according to their

[188] Kelpius MS. Journal, p. 29–30.

reckoning) was crowned by two happy events, both bright spots in the history of the Community. One was the consecration of the Swedish Lutheran Church at Wicacoa; the other the arrival of Daniel Falkner and a number of accessions to their number from Europe. Among the number was Justus Falkner, a brother of Daniel, and who was destined to become an important figure in the religious history of Pennsylvania.

The consecration of the Swedish Lutheran Church at Wicacoa took place on the first Sunday after Trinity, July 2, 1700. The building, 60 x 30 feet and 20 feet to the square, had been completed far enough to warrant its use for public worship. The event was made the occasion for a festival that extended over three days. It was opened on Saturday, July 1, with a jollification or *kirchweih*, held after the manner of the Fatherland. On Sunday the consecration services took place. Pastor Biörck preached the sermon from the text 2 Sam., viii, 29,[189] and christened the church "Gloria Dei" (*Gud's Ahra's Huus or Gottes Ehre*). Upon this festive occasion a great crowd was present, not only of Swedes and Germans, but English as well. The latter were so numerous that Pastor Biörck was forced to repeat his Swedish sermon in English at the close of the services.

Prominent among the great assemblage were the Theosophical brethren from the Wissahickon, who not only furnished instrumental music for the occasion, but acted as choristers as well, chanting the dedicatory Psalms and responses; while the three resident pastors, Rudmann as Vice-Bishop or Provost, Biörck as Celebrant, and Aurén as

---

189 "Therefore now let it please thee to bless the house of thy servant, that it may continue forever before thee: for thou, O Lord God, hast spoken it: and with thy blessing let the house of thy servant be blessed for ever."

assistant, all robed in surplice and chasuble, conducted the consecration services. A *nach kirchweih* on Monday concluded the festival.

The other event referred to was the return of the emissary who had been sent to Europe, and had remained there in the interest of the Community for over two years. Great was the joy of the brethren and the rejoicing at the Tabernacle on the August day which marked the return of Daniel Falkner and his companions from the Fatherland who had accompanied him to the New World so that the mystic number of perfection would once more be complete and the circle unbroken. Manuscript and tradition are both silent as to the exact date of Falkner's return: even the names of his companions remain unknown, with the exception of his brother Justus, a *candidat theologiæ* who had studied at Halle, Johann Jawert, Johann Hendrick Sprogel, and Arnold Storch.

When Daniel Falkner returned to America he came fortified with documents from the Frankfort Land Company, dated at Frankfort-on-Mayn, January 24, 1700, which supplanted Pastorius as their agent, and named himself with Jawert and Kelpius in his place, thereby making him virtually the dictator of the German Township. He also had a power of attorney, dated April 23, 1700 (n. s.), from Benjamin Furley, who was William Penn's trusted agent in Rotterdam, to act for him in Pennsylvania. This was subsequently reinforced by an autograph order from Penn to his secretary,[190] ordering him to prepare land warrants for Falkner and his brother.

A certified copy of the power of attorney from the Frankfort Company has lately been discovered among a number of old Pastorius papers in Germantown.

[190] Minute book "G," Penna. Archives, 2 Series, Vol. xix, p. 244.

In addition to the above, Falkner brought a deed of gift for 4000 acres of land, being a part of the 25000 acres belonging to the original German purchasers.[191] This indenture was executed by Catherine Elizabeth Schutz, widow of Johann Jacob Schutz, and was intended for charitable uses, to be administered by the Theosophical Fraternity.

A PHALLIC EMBLEM.

A result of the change in attorneyship became apparent at the next town election (1701), when Daniel Falkner was elected vogt or bailiff; Johann Jawert, recorder; and Justus Falkner, one of three burgesses.[192]

The return of Falkner to the Community and the addition to their number infused fresh courage into the hearts of the leaders, who now felt more sanguine than ever of the ultimate success of their experimental enterprise in the "Wilderness" of the Western World.

---

[191] The original purchasers were Jacob Van de Walle, Daniel Behagel, Johann William Peterson, John Jacob Schutz, and Caspar Menan, who acquired 14,000 acres of land from William Penn, and on April 2, 1683, gave a letter of attorney to Francis Daniel Pastorius to administer the same.

[192] *Gerichtsbuch von Germantown.* See also Collections of the Historical Society of Pennsylvania, November, 1852.

The German township was erected into a borough by virtue of a patent granted by William Penn, dated London, August 12, 1689. This document was recorded at Philadelphia 13th 3d month, 1691. It gave to the corporation the right to have and use a common seal and hold a court of record every six weeks for hearing all civil causes according to the laws of the Province. The separate government of Germantown began August, 1691, and terminated in December, 1706, being fifteen years.

THE CLOSE OF THE FIRST DECADE.

GREAT SEAL OF THE PROVINCE (REVERSE.)

WITH the advent of the new century the Fraternity on the Ridge received numerous accessions from different parts of the Old World, independent of such as accompanied Daniel Falkner upon his return. Prominent among the number was Conrad Matthäi, from Switzerland, and Dr. Christopher Witt, from Wiltshire, England.[193] Another interesting incident that belongs to this period is the intercourse between William Penn and the Theosophical Brotherhood during the former's second visit to the Province. There can be but little doubt that during the proprietary's stay in

---

LUX E TENEBRIS,—from an old Pietistical book.

193 Another account connects Dr. Witt with the celebrated Dutch family of that name. According to the Ephrata MSS., Gottlieb Van der Looft and Frederick Casselberg joined the Community about the same time.

America, from November 28, 1699, to October 2, 1701, there must have been frequent visits to Germantown to attend the meetings held by both German and English Friends, and that upon such occasions the peculiar institution on the Wissahickon was not overlooked by him. This argument is strengthened by the fact that long before Penn returned to America Kelpius had been accused of Quakerism, and his followers had been publicly charged with having embraced the tenets of the Society of Friends,—a charge which was apparently justified by the fact that they refused to administer either baptism or the eucharist,[194] except in rare cases.

A direct evidence of this peculiar feature of the Kelpius party is to be found in the reports made to Halle by Rev. Heinrich Melchoir Mühlenberg. In reply to a communication from Halle respecting the survivors, if there were any, of the original party of Pietists and the particulars of their sojourn here, he states: "So far as I could gather from acquaintances and old residents, it seems to me that most of these former candidates (theological students) cared little or nothing for the holy sacraments of baptism and the eucharist as instituted by the Holy Spirit and recorded by the prophets, evangelists, and apostles. So much of the Holy Writ was a dead letter to them; but, on the contrary, they busied themselves greatly with the Theosophical Sophia, speculations, etc., and at the same time practised alchemy."[195]

---

[194] In Germany they were, on account of this peculiarity, called *sacraments-verächter*, or despisers of the sacrament. See *Civitatis Erffurtensis*, pp. 1065–1069.

The non-observance of the sacrament became one of the chief causes for contention between Köster and Kelpius after their arrival in America, and did much to widen the breach that was formed by the course Köster pursued during the Keithian controversy.

[195] Halle Reports, original edition, p. 1265.

It is not to be supposed from the above statement that the Theosophical students, pious and ascetic as they were, and who had left home, friends, and plenty to banish themselves here in the wilderness, were opposed to the two sacred ordinances. The fact was they merely objected to their abuse by too frequent and unauthorized administration.

Unfortunately, thus far the writer's researches have failed to find any documentary mention of an intercourse between William Penn and the Germans in the Province during his second visit, except the statement in Watson's Annals (Vol. ii, p. 23) that Penn preached in Germantown upon two occasions,—once in a low house, built of framework and filled in with bricks, which formerly stood upon the site of Dr. George Bensell's house (now 5458 Germantown Avenue); and another time in the original Schumacher house, built in 1686, which was still standing in Watson's day. A picture of this interesting landmark has fortunately been preserved.[196]

However, by a tradition which has been current in an old Pennsylvania family for generations, we learn that there

---

[196] Mr. T. H. Shoemaker kindly furnishes the following particulars respecting this old landmark:

"The Shoemaker house was located on Lot No. 8. Gerhardt Hendrick Isaac Shoemaker married his daughter; hence it became known as the Shoemaker house. The house was situated in the meadow, about where Wingohocking station is on the Reading Road. Shoemaker's Lane ran back to it, say a half mile from Germantown Avenue. According to a letter written by Watson to S. M. Shoemaker, it was built in 1682. But I think this an error of memory: the date was more probably a year or two later. The house was taken down in 1846; but close to the railroad at Shoemaker's Lane stands an old stone house known as the 'Rock House,' because it is built on a large rock which stands some twelve or fifteen feet above the meadow. This house was most likely a tenant-house, and tradition says it was from this rock that Penn preached to the people who assembled below in the meadow. I do not know of any other places Penn preached in. It has been said he was present when one of the houses was raised: I think Johnson's old one, but am not sure."

was an estrangement between Penn and Kelpius, as the latter is said to have questioned the religious sincerity of the proprietary on the ground of his being a slaveholder, who persisted not only in holding human beings in bondage, but also sanctioned the traffic in their bodies.[197]

Kelpius in a subsequent letter to Professor Fabritius, his old preceptor at Altdorf and who was now at the University of Helmstadt, intimates rather strongly that Penn and the leading Quakers at that time were mere Christians by word of mouth, *Maul-Christen.*[198] An allusion is also made to Penn's second visit to the Province, and relates an incident where he was refuted by the Indians, at which meeting Kelpius seems to have been present. He states that during Penn's visit in 1701 he went to an Indian festivity or *kintika*,[199] and there took occasion to preach to the Indians about belief in the God of the heavens and the earth. The Indians, after listening to him with great patience, answered him: "You ask us to believe on the great Creator and Ruler of heaven and earth, and yet you yourself do not believe nor trust Him, for you have taken the land unto yourself which we and our friends occupied in common. You scheme night and day how you may preserve it so that none can take it from you. Yea, you even scheme beyond your life and parcel it out between your children,—this manor for one child, that manor for another. We believe on God the Creator and Ruler of heaven and earth. He maintains the sun; He maintained our fathers for so many, many moons. He maintains us, and we believe

197 "William Penn in America," by W. J. Buck, p. 379 *et seq.*

198 MS. Journal, p. 84. See photographic facsimile, Historical Society of Pennsylvania.

199 Probably at Pennsbury, Penn's country residence in Bucks County. John Richardson, in his Journal, makes mention of such an assemblage in 1701.

and are sure that He will also protect our children as well as ourselves. And so long as we have this faith we trust in Him, and never bequeath a foot of ground." Our manuscript unfortunately fails to record Penn's reply to the astute Indian, or even to hint at the outcome of the discussion.

William Penn's second visit to the Province was evidently not a welcome one either to his own partisans or to the so-called "hot church party." But little mention of Penn or his actions is made in any of the literature or private journals of the day. Thomas Story's Journal, which is so full as to the year 1699, is almost silent for the next two years, or the period when Penn lived in Pennsylvania. During this sojourn he spent his time, when not travelling in the Province, between his mansion, known as the "Slate-roof house" in Philadelphia, and his country place at Pennsbury on the Delaware. It was in the "Slate-roof house" that Penn's son John was born a month after his arrival. The founder's life in America during this visit, according to an old Friend's journal, must have been anything but enviable on account of the political dissensions, as well as the objections made by his wife and daughter to taking up a permanent residence in the Province, to which must be added his impecuniosity and the pressing demands of his creditors.

One of the most curious legends in connection with the Tabernacle in the forest is the following tale, recorded in the Ephrata manuscripts, which partakes somewhat of the supernatural: It was the seventh anniversary of the landing in Philadelphia,—a day which was always kept in remembrance, as it not only marked the date of the Mystics' arrival in Pennsylvania, but it was St. John's eve as well. Greater preparations than usual had been made for its celebration, because it was the *seventh*,—the number of the seals on the book, the vials of wrath, the trumpets of the Apocalypse, and the union of the Square and the Triad. The old legend tells us that all preparations for lighting the mystic fires upon the hills at nightfall were completed, when just about twilight, "whilst engaged in their accustomed services or ceremonies in commemoration of their arrival, which they observed with solemnity, a white, obscure, moving body in the air attracted their attention, which, as it approached, assumed the form and mien of an angel. It receded into the shadows of the forest, and appeared again immediately before them as the fairest of the lovely."

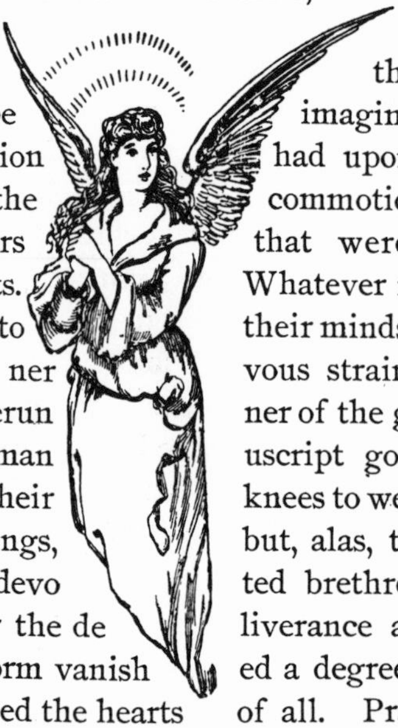

It may easily be imagined what effect this aërial apparition had upon the Theosophical ascetics, the commotion it raised, and the hopes and fears that were engendered within their hearts. Whatever may have been the cause of it, to their minds, which had so long been upon a nervous strain, it seemed as if at last the forerunner of the great Deliverer had come. The manuscript goes on to say: "They fell upon their knees to welcome the harbinger of good tidings, but, alas, the spirit vanished while the devoted brethren were praising their God for the deliverance at hand." As the mysterious form vanished a degree of consternation and alarm filled the hearts of all. Prayer and invocation, however, were continued without intermission until the hour near midnight, when the mystic fires were lighted. High rose the bright flame, until its reflection illuminated the symbol that surmounted the Tabernacle. Weird was the scene as the incantations were chanted, and the blazing embers scattered down the rugged hillsides, sparkling in the dark shadows of the hemlock and the pine.

After the ceremony was over the whole party returned to the *saal*, where they "continued wakeful in prayer and fervent supplication during the whole night without any further disclosures."

The legend further states that when at last the morning dawned "the luminary of the skies appeared above the hills and shed her cheerful rays to renovate the energies of the laboring man; but the gloom of darkness hung upon the waiting hermits."

The next night was anxiously awaited by the watchers, who confidently expected the reappearance of the fair missionary to mankind, but it brought no intelligence.

On the third evening, while all were assembled at prayer in the *saal*, the apparition again appeared. All at once fell upon their knees; but their prayers, instead of availing, always repelled the fair delieverer. After this the apparition did not reappear.[200] The manuscript further mentions that after this episode "Kelpius and his brethren remained at the 'Laurea,'[201] wearing out the thread of life in retirement and patient waiting for the final drama they were to enact in the wilderness."

That the belief in the supernatural in the early days of our Commonwealth was not confined alone to the Germans in the Province is shown by the following interesting story in the diary of Pastor Andreas Sandel. The family was an English one and were members of the Church of England:

"January 12.—A dreadful thing happened in Phila-

---

[200] It is further stated that the probable reason for the non-return of the apparition was a confession made to Kelpius by one of the hermits that he had committed some crime in Europe prior to coming to America.

[201] "Laurea." This term appears only in the Ephrata MS. It evidently has some reference to "Laurentium," a classic grove in the Aventine Hills.

delphia to the wife of a butcher. She and her husband quarreled in the evening. He asked her to make the bed. She said she would not. When she had refused for a while, he said he would turn her out of the house. She said, did he do it she would break the window-panes, invoking the devil to come for her if she did not. The husband led her out. Then she became at her wit's end because of her invocation. Finally, she broke some of the window-panes, and through the kitchen made her way up into the attic, bringing with her a candle, and lay down on the bed greatly disturbed on account of her promise. She then heard somebody coming up the stairs, but saw no one. Shortly afterwards she again heard a noise as if a person were coming up stairs, but could not see any one. This lasted for about half an hour. Becoming more and more agitated, fearing that her awful invocation was about to be realized, she went down to her husband, telling him of her anguish, and asking him to aid her. In lying down on a bench near the hearth she perceived a darkish human face looking at her with its mouth wide open and making horrid grimaces with gnashing teeth. Then she became thoroughly terrified, and asked her husband to read to her. Turning to the 21st Psalm, he read it to her, and then the face was not seen by her any more.

"Soon afterwards she perceived at the window, the one where she had broken the panes, that someone was standing there with both arms extended through the window. By this her fright was increased. At last she saw merely a head coming nearer to her. She could not see where it came through. Her husband then clasped his arms about her, when suddenly such a smell of brimstone was felt that they scarcely could stay in doors. The smell was also perceived by others coming in later. The husband saw nothing, but smelled the brimstone odor.

"At one o'clock she sent for the minister,[202] who came and prayed with her. Upon the next day a great many persons came to her, and in telling it over she was all of a tremble, and had to fold her hands across her knees, so violent was she shaking. But see what were the devil's further doings. On the third evening thereafter there came a godless man, and, in passing her house, he sung the most wicked ditties, repeatedly invoking the evil one to take him, and saying he wanted to drink to him, etc. This doubtless was to cause her and others to continue in the sin of blasphemy or in the belief that no devil is in existence, etc. This was a few days afterwards told me by that same woman herself and by two other English ministers,—Mr. Ross and Mr. Smith." [203]

Reference has already been made of the intercourse between the Mystical Brotherhood and the Swedish Lutheran pastors on the Delaware. This interesting fact is further illustrated by a Swedish account of a farewell service or reception given at the Tabernacle on June 15, 1702, to Dominie Andreas Rudman, prior to his leaving the Province to take charge of the Lutheran congregations in the Valley of the Hudson.[204]

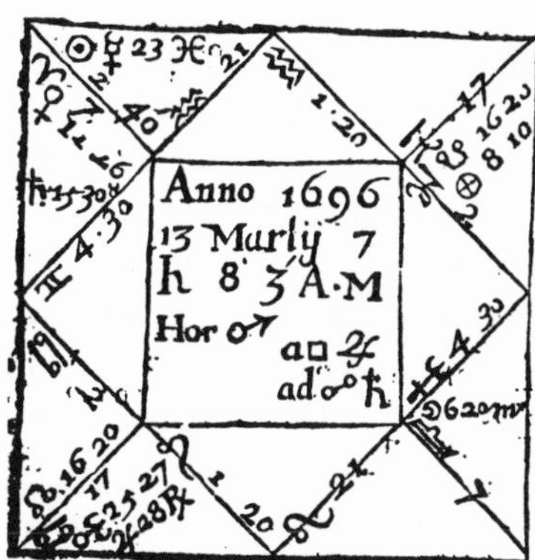

AN OLD GERMANTOWN HOROSCOPE.

[202] Rev. George Ross, then temporarily serving at Christ Church.

[203] The identity of this Mr. Smith has not been established. No record can be found of a minister of that name in the colonies at that period.

[204] *Vide*, chapter Justus Falkner, *supra ibid.*

Upon this occasion a poem was presented to the retiring pastor, or, as the Swedish account states, "a testimonial as a recognition of his faithful work.[205]

Rudman der Armen Sweden Hirte
  Kahm hier ins land zu rechter zeit,
Das Irthum auch noch dass Verwirrte,
  Was allbereit unwissenheit
Von Luther's wahrer lehr bey nahe entfernet,
Das hat Rudmannus nun auch wieder neu gelernet.
  Ein jedes werk preist seinen meister,
    Und wie der Haus herr, so sein lohn:
      Rudmannus hast die flatter-geister
    Und predikt Christum Gottes Sohn;
Sein leben, lehr und ambt, kan selbst vielmehr erweisen
Als meine feder ihn den leser kann an preisen."

With the approach of Midsummer Day, 1704, the first decade of the Theosophic experiment was drawing to a close. Time had made the usual inroads. Notwithstanding the example and teachings of the leading spirits, many of the original members, in view of the conditions under which they lived, had fallen in with the allurements of the world. Some followed the example of Biedermann, and married; others left the Community to gather riches or honors for themselves, while perhaps a few succumbed to the temptations of the wicked world. History and tradition, however, are both silent as to the last.

Then, again, the Community attracted the attention of various adventurers and religious enthusiasts who drifted into the Province, and thought to enter the society and use it for their own sinister purposes. A prominent example was the case of Tolstadius, a Swedish adventurer, who for

---

[205] (Vi, Meddela för egendomlighetens skull ett testimonium, som tyskarne i Germantown gifvit honom den 15 juni, 1702, sasom ett erkönnande of hans trogna arbete. Engeströmska-Samlung.)

a time not only deceived Kelpius, but the Swedish pastors at Wicacoa and Christiania as well. It frequently took all of Kelpius's firmness to discourage and eliminate such undesirable aspirants. But these drawbacks had only a temporary effect, for, owing to the numerous accessions from Europe within the last two years of the decade, the mystic number was once again complete or nearly so.

Yet notwithstanding its apparent flourishing condition, the Community as a distinct organization was rapidly approaching its end. This was no fault of the leaders or of the truths they taught. Their faith, courage, and sincerity were as strong as ever; their belief as firm in the approaching millennium and the coming of the Deliverer as when they left the sand dunes of Holland.

The great increase of the population, the encroachments upon their beloved solitude in the wilderness, the formation of new settlements in the vicinity, and the political changes all tended to have an adverse effect upon a society whose chief aim was to live in seclusion. Another matter that tended somewhat to weaken the influence of the Brotherhood with their German neighbors and countrymen at large, was the bitter strife that had been engendered between Pastorius and Daniel Falkner since the latter's return from Europe, and his active interest in the political and civil affairs of the German township, ending in the final displacement of Pastorius by virtue of the authority Falkner had brought from Europe. This feud was used by the partisans of Pastorius as another argument against the Community on the Wissahickon. Some went even so far as to demand their expulsion. The better judgment of Pastorius, however, prevailed; and, so far as he was concerned, the whole matter was held in abeyance. From some of the Pastorius manuscripts that have come down to us it is to be inferred that the feeling between the two men and their partisans must have been exceedingly bitter. But neither Kelpius nor Seelig were in any way involved in this controversy.

Among the important events in the life of the Community, one that shines out even to the present day, is the ordination of one of their number to the ministry and the sending of him to an adjoining province as a missionary. This was Justus Falkner. He was ordained November 24, 1703, in the Swedish Lutheran Church at Wicacoa, in the German language, by the resident Lutheran pastors, Rudman, Biörck, and Sandel, assisted by Kelpius and the Brotherhood.

This was the first regular ordination of an orthodox Lutheran clergyman in the Western Hemisphere. The full record of his unselfish labors, godly life and unexampled piety still exists and bears witness to the character of his associates.

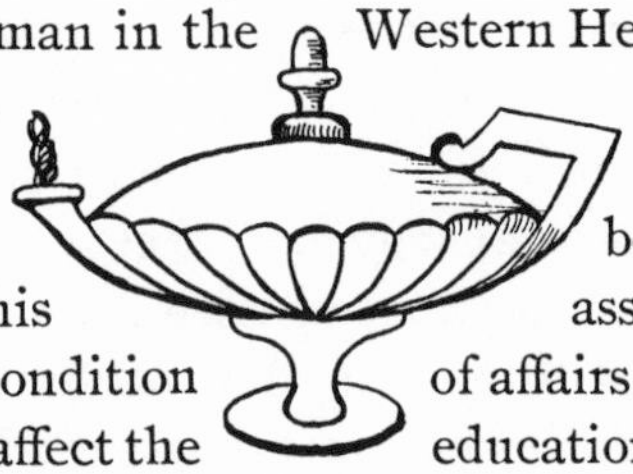

The changed condition of affairs in the Province, however, did not affect the educational efforts that had been originally introduced by Kelpius, but increased their scope and usefulness among the Germans, who were now flocking thither in great numbers. But these efforts were not enough to counteract the general conditions, both civil and religious, as they affected the peculiar institution on the Wissahickon. From month to month it became more apparent that the state of affairs since the Church party became more dominant was inimical to the permanent growth of such a Community.

Great were the changes within the decade since Kelpius' arrival. Where ten years ago the southeastern part of Pennsylvania was but sparsely settled, the settlers were now numbered by thousands; whereas formerly there were no houses of worship, except those of the Friends, there were now a number of fine churches and different congregations in Philadelphia, while throughout the rural districts were scattered churches with organized congregations of various denominations,—Episcopal, Baptist, Sabbatarian, German Lutheran, Mennonite, and Dunker. Stranger than all, George Keith, who had fomented the great schism in the Province among the Quakers from 1690 to 1694, now, in 1702,[206] returned to Pennsylvania as a full-fledged missionary of the English Church.[207] He had but little sympathy with his former adherents who had gone out with him from the Society of Friends a decade before, except with such as had renewed their fealty to the Established Church.

The only record of intercourse between Keith and the Sabbatarian congregations that Heinrich Bernhard Köster had been partly instrumental in establishing in the Province is an occasional notice of the Philadelphia Church, under Thomas Rutter, and the feud that broke out between Keith and William Davis of the Pennepack Church. This ended in a victory for the former, and the Sabbatarians lost their church, which henceforth was known as Trinity Church, Oxford.[208] The latter during his

Great Seal of the Province (obverse).

---

[206] Keith landed at Boston, June 11, 1702,

[207] See "The Sabbath-Keepers," a series of papers by the writer, published in the *Village Record*, West Chester, Pa., March, 1888. No record whatever is known to exist of any meeting or even acquaintance between Kelpius and Keith.

[208] *Ibid.*

sojourn in Pennsylvania was accompanied by Rev. John Talbot and supported by the local minister, Rev. Evan Evans. He paid most attention to the Welsh, as it was thought that they, who were restive under the Quaker supremacy, were ready to throw off the religious as well as civil yoke and return within the fold of the Church of England.

In this supposition the three churchmen were not mistaken, as their efforts resulted in the establishment of a congregation within the Welsh tract at Radnor. This was strictly a Welsh Church, the services being held in that tongue for many years.

It is an interesting fact that both congregations at Oxford and Radnor were served by the Lutheran minister at Wicacoa. Further, at the laying of the corner-stone and dedication of both churches, in 1711 and 1714 respectively, the Swedish Lutheran pastors were prominent actors.

The quaint stone church, subsequently built by the Welsh congregation at Radnor in 1714, and commonly known as "Old St. David's," is now the oldest Episcopal church in Pennsylvania, and has become historic.

An Old Germantown Relic in Possession of the Writer.

VISITS OF THE SABBATARIANS.

SEAL OF THE COLONY OF CONNECTICUT, A.D. 1700.

HOW great the esteem was in which Kelpius and his fellow mystics were held by the various religious separatists throughout the country is further shown by the fact that when the so-called "Rodgerines" sprang into existence in New England an attempt was made forthwith to establish a regular communication with Kelpius and his companions for the purpose of receiving advice and instruction.

Several visits were made from New England to the Wissahickon at an early day by the new Separatists, but without results, as the extravagant religious notions of Rodgers and his followers were foreign to the Theosophy of Kelpius, which was based upon the fundamental doctrines of the Christian faith. In fact, it has been stated that the only point in which they approached agreement was with regard to the keeping of the seventh day.

Toward the close of the year 1700 John Rodgers personally visited the Tabernacle, upon which occasion he arranged with Reynier Jansen, the (Germantown?) printer, for the publication of his differences with Saltonstall. This curious work appeared in the following year (1701) under the title, "An Impartial relation of || An Open and Publick Dispute || Agreed upon || Between Gurdon Saltonstall, Minister of the || Town of New London || and || John Rodgers of the Same place || With the Circumstances leading thereto, and the Consequences thereof || as also a Relation of the said Gurdon Saltonstall's Recovering a || Judgment of Court of Six hundred Pounds, and Cost of Court || against said John Rodgers, for saying, the said Saltonstall went to wave, shun, or shift the said Dispute agreed upon. || The Truth of || which waving, shunning or shifting is here also evidently demonstrated. || By John Rodgers. || Printed [by Reynier Jansen] for the author in the year 1701."

This work is a small 4to, and consists of twenty pages, of which the title forms one; "To the reader," four; and the "Relation" proper, fifteen.[208]

There still exists in Connecticut a traditional, if not documentary, account of another visit made by the same religious enthusiasts to Kelpius in the year 1702, and, further, that upon his return Rodgers stopped at New York to consult with a public Friend, then suffering imprisonment there for conscience sake.

This account the writer has been unable to secure in the original; but there is, nevertheless, a strong probability of its authenticity, as Samuel Bownas, the public Friend in

208 "Issues of the American Press in Pennsylvania," by Charles R. Hildeburn, No. 86. Original in library of Devonshire House Meeting, London, England.

question, was imprisoned in New York at that time, and mentions a visit from John Rodgers in his journal.

"An || account || of the || Life, Travels || and Christian Experiences || in the || work of the Ministry || of Samuel Bownas || Stanford || reprinted by Daniel Lawrence || MDCCC, Page 135 *et seq.*"

Another evidence of the great esteem in which Kelpius and his companions were held throughout the provinces is shown by the action of the Rhode Island Sabbatarian Churches, which, in 1703, appointed two brethren, William Hiscox and Joseph Crandall, as a committee to journey to Wissahickon, and then, with the aid of Kelpius, to adjust if possible the differences which had been fomented by William Davis between the Philadelphia and Pennepack churches (Seventh-day Baptist). The records of these interviews and negotiations, as well as the resulting correspondence, the writer has good reason to believe is still in existence among the musty records of the Sabbatarian brethren in Rhode Island or Connecticut.

The following interesting extracts from the old Westerly, R. I., church records bear upon this intercourse, viz.,—

"The church met at Newport the 3d Sabbath in June, 1703, being the 19th day; and the day before, on which some considerations were proposed, upon the request of our friends in Pennsylvania, relating to some differences between them, and the matter deferred until the First-day following.

"And on the First-day, accordingly, the church met, and appointed Bro. Hiscox and Bro. Clarke, Sen., if Providence should so order, to go to Pennsylvania soon after the first Sabbath in the 7th month.

"The church met the 1st of the 7th month, at Westerly, and Bro. Clark, judging himself incapable to perform the journey to Pennsylvania, Bro. Joseph Crandall was appointed to go with Bro. Hiscox [on the] said journey.

"At a church meeting at Westerly the last Sabbath in the 8th month, 1703, the letters sent to the church from Bro. William Davis were read and acted upon.

"Westerly, the 20th of the 8th month, 1704, the church met at Bro. Maxson's, Sen., to confer with the Pennsylvania Brethren, William Davis and Abraham ——"[209]

[William Davis was a native of Wales. He was sent to Oxford, but, becoming a Quaker, was forced to leave that institution. He came to Philadelphia in 1684, being then in his twenty-first year. He was at once recognized as a preacher of the Society. When Keith separated he became one of his staunch supporters, and was one of the forty-eight signers to the reasons for separation.

After the decline of the Keithian meetings, when their leaders returned to England, Davis became an attendant of the services held by Köster, and soon became one of his most active supporters. He was baptized by the German evangelist, as related in a subsequent chapter,[210] and became pastor of the Sabbatarian congregation on the Pennepack, in Oxford township, a short distance from Germantown.

It was while stationed here that he published a book in vindication of his peculiar doctrine, viz.,—"Jesus || The Crucified Man, || the || Eternal Son of God, || or, an || Answer || to || An Anathema or Paper of || Excommunication, of John Wats, en || tituled, Points of Doctrine preached & || asserted by William Davis. || Wherein the Mystry of Christs Descen- || tion, Incarnation and Crucifixion is || Unfolded. || By William Davis. Philadelphia Printed for the Author [by Reynier Jansen] in the Year 1700."[211]

---

[209] Name illegible.

[210] It appears that William Davis was also baptized by the Rev. Thomas Killingsworth, a First-day Baptist preacher, in 1697.

[211] No. 72 Hildeburn, 16mo. The title of this unique book is reproduced in facsimile.

JESUS
The Crucifyed Man,
THE
Eternal Son of God,

OR, AN
ANSWER
TO

An *Anathema* or Paper of Excommunication, of *John Wats* entituled, *Points of Doctrine preached & asserted by* William Davis.

Wherein the Mystry of Christs Descention, Incarnation and Crucifixion is Unfolded.

By *William Davis.*

[Printed by Reynier Jansen. Philadelphia, 1700.]

Davis was naturally an agitator and disturber, and, by airing his own doctrinal views, he subsequently became involved not only with the regular Baptists and the Revs. Keith, Evans, and Talbot, of the Established Church, but with the members of his own congregation as well.

It was to heal these internal differences in the Sabbatarian congregation at Oxford that the New England churches took the above-recited action.

The differences between Davis, on the one hand, and Keith and Evans on the other, also produced pamphlet and counter-pamphlet.

After the loss of their meeting-house they met for services in the different houses, under the leadership of Davis, until 1710, when he left to take charge of a church at Westerly, Rhode Island. Here he remained until 1727, when he returned to Pennsylvania. In 1734 he again went to Rhode Island, whence ten years later he led a party of Seventh-day Baptists to establish a settlement at Squan, New Jersey, of which he became pastor. He died there in 1745, at the advanced age of eighty-two years, honored and respected as a Christian clergyman.][212]

The fame of Johann Kelpius's piety and learning also extended to other parts of the country, and his correspondence must, for that day, have been quite extensive, and it included various conditions of people. An instance of this is shown by his letter written, "10 8ber 1704," to Maria Elizabeth Gerber, in Virginia. It was in reply to a communication from her in which she asks Kelpius's opinion of the Quakers. His reply is quite lengthy, and he takes the occasion to give his opinions rather fully, and emphasizes that he belongs to no special denomination, but to the elect of Jerusalem. (Gal. iv, 9, 10.[213])

---

[212] *Vide* Sabbath-keepers before quoted.

[213] He might also have added verse 26: "The Jerusalem that is above is free, which is our mother."

ATTORNEY AND BAILIFF.

Arms of Frankfort on the Mayn.

IF the papers of the old Frankfort Land Company were still in existence and accessible, the correspondence would no doubt show that for some reasons there was great dissatisfaction upon their part with Pastorius and his administration of the company's affairs in Pennsylvania. This feeling may have been augmented by Daniel Falkner during his visits to Frankfort in 1699–1700. Whatever the true cause may have been, it is certain that Daniel Falker had the entire confidence of all members of the Land Company, as well as of William Penn and Benjamin Furley, his Rotterdam agent.

It will be seen that the original power of attorney granted to Kelpius, Falkner and Jawert was signed and sealed by all members of the company, viz.:

"We subscribed do manifest & confess herewith, Whereas we joiningly have bought five & twenty thousand acres of unseparated land in Pennsilvania, according to the documents & indentures thereof, with peculiar Privileges & Rights, And therefore in virtue thereof the 12th of November, 1686, by a peculiar writing having formed a Society, & for the cultivation & administration of the sd land have Impowred Mr. Francis Daniel Pastorius, J. U. L. according to the letter of attorney bearing date the 12th of April 1683. And yet because of the death of some heads of the sd Company, & the between Irruption of the French War, as also chiefly because of the absence of the Governor, & the unableness of the sd our Factor, these our affairs in the sd Province are come to a Stop, the more mentioned Mr. Pastorius having also desired by & in several of his Letters to be discharged of his administration, That we for such end do Conferr full Power & special Authority on Mr. Daniel Falkner & Johanes Kelpius as Inhabitants for the present in Pensilvania, And also on Mr. Johanes Jawert the Son of one of our Principals, nominally Mr. Balthasar Jawert of Lubeck, who hath resolved to transport himself thither, thus and in such wise that these our three Plenipotentiaries Joiningly or in case of death of one or the Other, they or he who remains shall have in the best form the Administration of all our goods we have there of the lands in the former where they are joiningly or separately assigned unto us, or shall be assigned, surveyed & set out, and of the City-Lots by reason of the five & twenty thousand acres being Competent to us, viz., the 4 or 6 Places in the City of Philadelphia, and of the 300 acres situated in the Right & Liberty of the City before & about Philadelphia, And of the land bought by the Scullkill for a Brick-kiln, And of all & every erected Building & other meliorations, and of what hath been sent thither or bought there or otherwise got of Victuals, Comodities, Cattels, houshold-stuff, tools, Servants, Tenants & of other Persons, &c., and therefore to call to an account in Our name the sd Mr. Pastorius, who hitherto hath been our Plenipotentiary, and to take of him herewith all such Our Estates & effects, and in Case any of them should be alienated without our knowledge, above all things to vindicate them. So then in general or Special, as it can be done best, to dispose, exchange, sell & receive the money for them, and hereupon to quit, transact, make indentures & documents, assurances, & in sum to do & leave everything what we Ourselves could or might do or leave if we were then & there personally present, Cum potestate, Substituendi, et Substitutionem toties quoties revocandi cumq clausulis rati grati, omnibusq, alijs illius loci & fori necessarijs et consuetis. And in Case our aforementioned Plenipotentiaries should want any larger Power then [*sic*] herein is contained, the same we advisedly do grant herewith unto them, & do decently Implore the Governour in Chief and Magistrates of the sd Province to regard them as such, and to grant them upon their request their magisterial aid, in case they should want the same. On the other hand our Plenipotentiaries Joinedly & Separately are directed to the two Principals in Francfort on the river of Main, viz., the heirs of Jacob van de Walle & Daniel Behagel both deceased, to acquaint & give an acccunt unto them timely of every one of their transactions, and to address unto them moneys or Comodities, to Correspond within and to expect, if need, further Orders & Instructions of them in the name of the whole Company, wherewith they shall further in this Case Communicate and get their Consent. Lastly we grant unto them herewith special Power to appropriate fifty acres of Our land in Germantown for the benefit of a Schoolmaster, that the Youth in reading, writing & in good manners & education, without partial admonition to God & Christ may be brought up and Instructed. All faithfully and without Fraud, In true witness whereof we have with our own hands Subscribed & Sealed this Letter of Attorney, and caused the same to be made under & by publick Authority. Done in Frankfort on the River of Mayn, the 24th day of January 1700.

[L.S.] "Catharina Elizabetha Schutzin, Widow.
[L.S.] "the Widow of Jacob van de Wallen, deceased.
[L.S.] "the heirs of Daniel Behagel, deceased.
[L.S.] "Johannes Kemler.
[L.S.] "Bathasar Jawert.
[L.S.] "Johan Wilhelm Petersen, d.
[L.S.] "Gerhard van Mastricht.
[L.S.] "Johanes Le Brun.
[L.S.] "Maria van de Walle, widow of Doctor Thomas van Willigh with her Copartners."

When, upon Falkner's return, Pastorius was informed of the new state of affairs he did not take kindly to the situation: the recollection of the virulent attack upon him by Köster and his adherents was yet fresh in his memory. Therefore, it excites but little wonder that Pastorius, as well as his friends and followers, protested vigorously against Falkner's action in demanding an immediate account from him as to the company's property. The new agent, however, was firm in his demands, and, having the support of both Council and Proprietary, was well able to enforce his position.

That Daniel Falkner was by far the abler politician of the two is shown at the next general election at Germantown in the fall of the year 1700, when Daniel Falkner was chosen bailiff; his brother, Justus Falkner, a burgess;

Johann Jawert, recorder; and Daniel Geissler, crier of the court.

History is silent as to how this result was brought about: whether there was a general dissatisfaction with the old officials among the German residents, or whether Falkner anticipated the tactics of modern local politicians by voting the Community of Mystics "solid," and thus securing a victory, is a question hard to decide at this late day. Indications, however, are that the election of Falkner's party to civil office was due rather to sharp tactics than to any personal animosity against Pastorius on the part of the older settlers.

Magister Kelpius was entirely innocent of any collusion or sympathy with this movement on the part of Falkner and others to obtain a hold upon the civil power. So far as the Community property was involved, he naturally seconded Daniel Falkner's efforts to maintain their rights. When he first learned that, together with Falkner and Jawert, he had been made joint-attorney of the Frankfort Land Company, he was perhaps even more surprised than Pastorius was of his deposition.

Kelpius refused to act as attorney or take any part whatever in civil or political matters, and eventually renounced all claim to the appointment. To do this in a legal manner he executed the following renunciation:

"Whereas, upon recommendation of Mr. Daniel Falkner, the Frankfort Society hath made me ye subscribed their Plenipotentiary, together with the said Mr. Falkner & John Jewart, But my Circumstances not permiting to entangle myself in the like affairs I do confess herewith that I do deliver all the authority, which is given unto me in the Letter of Attorney, to the said Society & him who did recomend me to the same, towit, Mr. Daniel Falkner, for to act and prosecute the Case of the said Society without me with Johann Jewart upon their account according to the letter of Attorney who attributes to one or two as much power as to three in case of a natural or civil death."

This unique document was witnessed by Johann Gottfried, Seelig, and Johann Hendrick Sprogel.[214]

That there was evidently some understanding and intercourse between William Penn and the Falkner brothers during the former's second visit to the Province, is shown by several entries in Minute-book G of the Board of Property of the Province of Pennsylvania, where, in a dispute about some land, the Proprietary steps in and issues an order in favor of Daniel Falkner.[215] The next entry in the same book, made 12th of 11th Month, 1701, shows that Penn's interest in Falkner continued during the former's stay in the Province. One of Penn's last official acts prior to his departure was the letter quoted in these proceedings before the Land Commission:

"James

"Prepare a War't for 4,000 acres for Benjamin Furley, out of which 3 Wart's for 500 acres Each for Falkner and Brother and Dorthy and Brother and Sister, which recommend to the Commiss'rs of Propriety if not done before I goe. 25th 8ber., 1701.

"WILL'M PENN."

The following interesting entries appear in the old Germantown Court Records, now deposited with the Historical

---

[214] No date is appended to the transcript by Pastorius, from which this copy is made. Johann Heinrich Sprogel came to America either with Falkner, in August, 1700, or else shortly after. His name appears upon the official records as early as 18th 11 mo., 1702. See *Pennsylvania Archives*, Second Series, vol. xix, p. 351.

[215] *Pennsylvania Archives*, Second Series, vol. xix, p. 219.

Society of Pennsylvania. Unfortunately, being fragmentary, they give but little insight into the official doings of the few Mystics who temporarily preferred the excitement of political life to the quiet of the cloister on the Wissahickon.

The first entry after the election held subsequent to Falkner's return sets forth,—

"At a court of record held at Germantown the 7th day of the 9th month, 1700–1, before Daniel Falkner, Bailiff, Cornelius Swert, Justus Falkner, and Dennis Kunders, 3 eldest Burgesses, and Johannes J. Jawert, Recorder.

"F. D. Pastorius being Clerk and Jones Potts, Sheriff, it was ordered that the overseers of the fences in every quarter of the town shall go round some days before the next following Courts of Record, and thereupon acquaint the said Courts how they find the fences in their respective quarters and those who neglect to make them good. May be fined according to their circumstances and the harm done. Abraham op de Graef and Peter Keurlis were sent for to answer the complaints made against their children by Daniel Falkner and Johann Jawert. But the Sd Abraham not being well, and Peter Keurlis gone to Philadelphia, this matter was left to the next session. Daniel Geissler refused to be Crier of the Court, which is likewise left to the general Court.

"28th 4th Mo. 1701. Johann Henry Mehls was chosen (Recorder) in place of J. Jawert."

At the next general election, held a year later, it appears from the entry that none of the old officials, except Pastorius and the sheriff, were re-elected,—

"9th of December 1701, Aret Klinken Bailiff. Paul Wulff, Peter Schumacher and William Strepers three Burgesses. John Conrad Cotweis Recorder, D. F. Pastorius Clerk. Jones Potts Sheriff."

Evidently one of the causes for Falkner's defeat for re-election was the determined effort made by him as attorney to obtain the lands and rights due the Frankfort Land Company, the affairs of which had been either neglected or overlooked by Pastorius. The first effort in this direction appears in an entry in the before-quoted Minute-book G, under date 17th of the 10th month, 1701. He did not confine his efforts to the land office. Again referring to the court record, we find,—

"4th day of the 6th month 1702. Daniel Falkner and Johann Jawert, as attorneys for the Frankfort Land Company, requested in writing the consent of this Court for to call or summon this companies tennants in the companies houses, there to make up their accounts and pay. But this Court thought it needless to give such consent."

Successive appearances before both local courts and land commissioners attest Falkner's activity in fostering the trusts, with which he was charged by the principals in Europe, as well as by his own Community.

In the court records, under date of 16th of 12th month, 1702|3, it appears,—

"By order of this Court the letter of Attorney[216] from Catherina Elizabeth Schultzin to Daniel Falkner and Arnold Stork was compared with the copy which Hans Henry Meels hath delivered to the said Daniel Falkner and were both found agreeing word for word. In witness whereof the said Copy by the said Courts order was signed by D. F. Pastorius."

On 5th of 2nd month, 1703, Daniel and Justus went before the land commissioners, and produced a return of a warrant for fifty acres of Liberty Lands surveyed to Benjamin Furley. They also pressed a claim for a High Street lot of 132-foot front.

---

[216] This was evidently the deed of gift recited on page 146.

24th of 3d month, 1703, both brothers again appear and ask for patents for sundry tracts of 1000, 1900, and 50 acres respectively.

On the 30th of 6th month, 1703, Justus Falkner appears as attorney for Benjamin Furley in reference to a tract of 1000 acres of land in Chester County, which either joined or overlapped the Welsh tract. This claim led to some complication with David Lloyd and Isaac Norris.

On the 3d of October, 1704, Daniel Falkner came into court and "desired that an explanation of a certain letter of attorney from Catherina Elizabeth Schultzin to him the said Daniel Falkner and Arnold Storchen should be read in this Court, which being done, He further desired that the Sd explanation should be recorded. Which the Court consented to."

28th 10th month, 1703. The case of Mathew Smith *vs.* Daniel Falkner being called, the plaintiff by reason of conscience, viz.,—"That this was the day wherein Herod slew the Innocents, as also that his witnesses were and would for the same reason not be here, desired a continuance to the next term of court of Record. To be held for this Corporation, which is allowed to, provided the Sd Daniel Falkner do then appear and stand Tryal."

8th 12 mo., 1703|4. "Proclamation being made the action of Matthew Smith against Daniel Falkner was brought before the Court, and being wrong laid was quasht."

"d 3Mo. 1704 Daniel Falkner request to this Court, was read and answered to the first of his desires, that Mathew Smith hath paid the Court's fees already and departed out of this County (Township). To the second, that Johannes Umstadt hath all the money which he is to receive for the land in the hands of Humphry Edwards where it may be attached."

In the year 1704 there appear three entries that concern the elder Falkner. According to one dated 13th of 4mo., 1704, he was chosen as a burgess in place of Peter Keyser. October 14, 1704, he was fined six shillings for having bad fences. The next entry does not appear in the remaining part of the original manuscript record-book. It is taken from the "Collections of the Historical Society" for 1853, p. 256.

"The 28th day of November, 1704. Daniel Falkner coming into this Court behaved himself very ill, like one that was last night drunk, and not yet having recovered his witts. He railed most greviously on the Recorder, Simon Andrews, and the Bailiff, Aret Klincken, as persons not fit to sit in a Court; he challenged Peter Shoemaker one of the Judges on the bench, to come forth, and more the like enormities. The Sheriff, William de Wees, telling him that he would not do so at Philadelphia, the said Falkner himself, answered no, not for a hundred pounds; and after abundance of foul language, when the Court bid the said Sheriff and the Constable bring him out, he went himself, crying you are all fools! But afterwards coming again, the Court ordered him to pay his fine for having of late been extreme drunk, and convicted before Hans Gerry Meels, a Magistrate or Justice of the Peace, as also to find security for his appearance and answering for the many abuses offered to this Court. He said he would pay the said fine before going out of the house, but concerning security, the Frankfort Company was security enough for him, offering also paper of his to this Court, which the Clerk begun to read, but the Court having heard a few lines of it was not willing to hear it all over, and committed him, the said Daniel Falkner, to appear at the next Court of Record to be held for this corporation and answer for the abuses above expressed."

THE DECLINE OF THE COMMUNITY.

Arms of Sweden, A.D. 1700.

THE gleam of encouragement that enlivened the hopes of the leaders of the Community toward the close of the first decade of the Theosophical experiment on the Wissahickon, when the mystic number, owing to the accessions from Europe, was once more complete, was but like the burst of light that often precedes the dying flame. While to all outward appearances, in the minds of the leading spirits, stability was now assured, it was in reality the turning-point where disintegration began. Many of the new members were imbued with entirely different motives from those that had instigated the original party; and as soon as they commenced to feel the yoke of restraint, resulting from a communal life and discipline, they were the first to return to the freedom of the world. Another matter that hastened the final dismemberment of the Community was the marriage of Daniel Falkner[217] and the course pursued by him and others in taking an active part in the civil and political affairs of the German township.

[217] Frankfort, Pastorius papers, Pennsylvania Historical Society.

While Kelpius and a few others refused all honors and riches, the majority, owing to the continual increase in the population and the demand for men of their capabilities, again entered the world and assumed their previous occupations or other congenial employment.

In consequence of this internal condition of the Fraternity, the vigils in the *sternwarte* were abandoned, and the watch that had been kept so faithfully during so many nights to announce the first sign of the appearance of the harbinger of the Deliverer was kept no more. Then, as the new century increased in years, the expectation of an immediate millennium gradually grew less and less in the minds of many. The strict devotional exercises in the Tabernacle also became fewer in number, while the general discipline relaxed, and the mystical researches and Theosophical speculations were either altogether neglected or left to the leaders and such of the older or more enthusiastic members as proved to be above the allurements of the surrounding temptations.

Daniel Falkner soon found that, by virtue of his new duties as agent for the Frankfort Company and his family cares, he could not give the same attention as formerly to these recondite things. Then, in addition, the landed interests of the Community, as well as those of Benjamin Furley, required his personal attention and occupied much of his time. When the Manatawany tract was finally located and patented, a settlement was projected under his auspices upon the fertile stretch of well-watered meadow-land that is still known as "Falkner's Swamp." Coincident with the earliest settlement of this tract, Daniel Falkner, and not his brother Justus, as has been erroneously stated, organized an orthodox Lutheran congregation, of which he became the first pastor. This congregation, the oldest German Lutheran one in Pennsylvania, is still in existence and in a flourishing condition.

The departure of Justus Falkner for New York immediately upon his ordination at Wicacoa, November 24, 1703, to take charge of the German and Dutch Lutheran congregations scattered along the Hudson and in East Jersey, in connection with the Dutch Lutheran Church of New York City, was another severe blow to the permanency of the Fraternity as originally constituted.

The explanation of the withdrawal of these two brothers, both prominent members of the Fraternity, is that they were men of strong character, and, in view of the changed condition of the German residents of the Province, brought about by the constantly increasing population, felt that the proper field for their activity lay among the populace, who needed spiritual guidance: they could no longer waste their talents and learning in seclusion in the expectation of an immediate approach of the millennium.

To make the situation even more precarious, Kelpius, who was of a somewhat frail constitution, broke down physically under the great mental strain and the rigors of our climate. He, however, kept up his educational labors, as well as his Theosophical studies. He also continued in touch with his former associates in Europe. Letters are still in existence written by him during the summer of 1705 to Heinrich Johann Deichmann, leader of the Philadelphiac movement in Europe, and to his former tutor, Magister Johann Jacob Fabricius of Helmstadt. It is in writing to the latter that Kelpius again refutes the reports that he had turned Quaker or had assimilated to any special denomination. In the winter of 1705 he became so ill and feeble that his companions removed him to the house of Christian Warmer, one of the original Brethren who had come over in the "Sara Maria," and had since married and settled in Germantown, where he was a tailor. Hither, to the humble abode of his former follower, the Magister of the Theosophists in the New World was brought during his illness, so that he might have better care and attention than could be given him at the Tabernacle.

It was while recovering from this attack, in the following spring, that Kelpius wrote the hymn, "A Loving Moan of the Disconsolate Soul in the Morning Dawn," to which he adds: "As I lay in Christian Warmer's house, very weak, in a small bed not unlike a coffin, in May, 1706."

The first and last verses of this hymn will show the state of his mind at that time,—

1

"Here lye I submissive
And weak, in a shrine
O'er Come and made passive
With the sweetest pain
I think on the blooming of that lovely May
Where I my Beloved shall ever enjoy
And the little hut for a new do away.

25

"So will I them set me
Yet better to stand
And over me let thee
Have thy own free hand.
Therefore kiss, or correct, come to me or go,
Give presents, or take them, bring joy, or bring woe:
If I can but have thee, thy will may be so."

This was followed soon after by a peculiar epistle to Hester Palmer,[218] a public Friend[219] from Long Island, who,

[218] Hester Palmer was the daughter of one Joseph Palmer and his wife Sarah. The family is enumerated in the "Exact list of all Ye inhabitants names Wth In Yè towne of fflushing and p'cincts of old and young ffreemen & Servants, white & blacke. &C 1698."

[219] Benezet MSS.

it appears, had had a personal interview with Kelpius previously. On account of its peculiarity this letter is reproduced entire. It treats of the Threefold Wilderness state:

(1) The Barren; (2) the fruitfull; and (3) the wilderness of the Elect of God.

"A. 1706 d. 25, MAYI.

"*My dearly beloved in our Immanuel Jesus the Messiah:*
"*The Son of God our Saviour.*

"Being presented lately with a letter of yours, directed to our beloved Friend M——— B———, I found in the P.S. that the remembrance of mine was not yet slipt out of your Minde, insomuch that you desired to see a few lines from my hand, which Desire is an evident sign to me that the said remembrance is in Love & in the Truth.

"Assure yourself that it is with no less Fervency on my Side, but I finde as yet a double wall between us, which indeed seems to stop the current of this firey love-dream of which no more at present, least we should embolden ourselves to break through before the time appointed by Him, who nourisheth the Woman in the Wilderness (Rev. 12, 14). And since our Discourse broke just as we was about this matter, Viz:—THE THREEFOLD WILDERNESS STATE, I'll venture upon your Patience a few lines Concerning this subject, adding the Third State in the Wilderness, also having Confidence in your good Acceptance since you have in a manner bidden me to write & I finding no better Subject than to begin where we left it.

"Of the first we did discourse somewhat, viz:—Of the Barren Wilderness, & as we was beginning the second, viz:—Of the Fruitfull Wilderness, we was interrupted.

"The first hath a respect upon the Old Birth, like as Ye second upon the *New*. These two run parallel until the

First dieth, & then the Second is set at Liberty. The first is begotten in Egypt, & then arriveth to its manhood, & being led out of Egypt falls and Dieth in the Wilderness. The Second is also begotten in Egypt but is educated, and arriveth to its manhood in the Wilderness, and after the death of the First enters Caanan. The First seeth indeed the stretched out Arm of God in Egypt as well as in the Wilderness, but murmurs, provokes & tempts God & limiteth the Holy one in Israel, alwais turning back with its Heart lusting after Egypt. The Second seeth God & its life is preserved, its face alwais turned Caananwarts & its Heart with Joshua & Caleb (Joshua signifieth Aid, Salvation, Conservation; Caleb, full of heart, courageous, undaunted, faithfull) stands faithfull & seeth Ye salvation of God, being filled with the fervent & only desire of attaining the same. The first is in continual fear of Death, & what he feareth cometh upon him (Num. 14, 28; Prov. 10, 24). The Second is undaunted & liveth (Num. 14, 30, 31) & puts his feet upon the necks of his enemies (Jos. 10, 24; Psal. 94, 13). The Second deriveth its origen from the First, & dying to this riseth & liveth in God: The First when He dyeth, liveth in the Second (This is a great Mystery & wants an Explanation else it may be misconstrued, but I hope you are no Stranger to it). The Second liveth under Moses as well as the First as long as Moses liveth (Gal. 4, 1; Rom. 7), but is hidd inward; by chance he is called the inward Man in the Tabernacle, from which He never departeth (Exod. 33, 11). But when Moses Dyeth the New Man, being arrived now to his Manhood, appears from his inward state outwardly to the Terror of his enemies (see of this coming forth Cant. 3, 6; & 8, 5) of Whose Land he taketh Possession (Num. 27, 15; Deut. 3, 21-end). I will not draw the Parallism further, since a word to the Wise is

Allegorical Representation of all Faiths.

enough. And since we have orally conferred of the First state, viz:—of Ye Barren Wilderness, let us insist a little upon the Mystery of the Second. In which Fruitfull Wilderness we enjoy the leading Cloud by day, out of which so many drops of the heavenly Dew (Psal. 33, 3) as a Baptism of Grace upon us do fall. This is a Day of Joy & triumph, when the Holy Ghost moves & stirreth the waters in our Hearts so that this living spring diffuseth it self through the Eyes in a sweet & Joyfull Gush of Tears: O Thou blessed water-baptism, who would not desire to be Baptized with thee every day. But there followeth a night also upon this Day, wherein nevertheless the Pillar of Fire is our Guide, refining us as Gold in the Furnace, which is the Baptism of Fire of Ye Son, & is indeed terrible to the old Birth, but bright & light to the New; for she learneth by this to be resigned & say 'Not my will, O Father! but Thine be done.' Thus our Tears are our Meat, yea, our Manna, not only by Day but also in the darkest Night (Psal. 42, 3; 80, 5). The most bitter Myrrh (which conditeth the old man in his Grave) hath the most sweetest Sweet hid in herself. For the Tree of the Cross & the Yoak of the Beloved doth but sweeten the bitter water of Affliction & sufferings in Mara (Exod. 15; Matt. 11). The darkest sorrow contains in herself the most inward Joy & Gladness (2 Cor. 6, 10). Darkness is like the Light (Psal. 139, 12). To dye is in this pleasan Wilderness to grow lively. Poverty maketh rich. Hunger is the most desirable Meat, & Thirst the most refreshing Nectar (Math. 5, 6). To be nothing is to be Deified (2 Pet. 1, 4). To have nothing is to enjoy all (2 Cor. 12, 10). To become weak is the greatest strength.

"Disquietness is the surest Peace (2 Cor. 7, 10). No work no Pain doth tire, for the more we work the stronger we grow (Gen. 32, 24), & yet we do experimentally find that the greatest weakness hath the greatest strength hid in herself (Cant. 2, 5). Oh everblessed Wilderness thou rejoyceth & blossometh as a Rose! yea, thou blossometh abundantly & rejoyceth even with Joy and Singing. The glory of Libanon is given unto thee, the Excellency of Carmel & Sharon! In thee we see the Glory of our Lord, & the Excellency of our God! In thee our weak Hands are Strengthened & our feeble Knees confirmed (Esa. 35, 1). Who would not desire to be a Denizon in Thee? Who would not delight to trace thy Solitary and lonesom walks? O! ye Inhabitants of this happy desolation, bless & kiss that gentle hand of that Divine Sophia who at the first did so wittily allure you, when she intended to bring you into this Wilderness, for to speak to your Heart, in order to search & trie the same! Do not forsake her, untill she hath given you from hence your Possessions, & the hindermost Valley for the opening of your understanding (Hos. 2, 14, 15, according to the LXX Achor signifying hindermost, furthest, comp. Exod. 3, 1, Syrach 4, 17–28).

"This Valley of Achor, or hindermost Cavity, leads me to the consideration of a Wilderness yet of a higher (further) degree than the Second, which it exceeds by so much as the second does the First. We may call it the WILDERNESS OF THE ELECT OF GOD, as being traced but by few, & none but peculiarly chosen Vessels of Honour & Glory.

"I shall bring but four Instances for this, Two out of Ye Old & Two out of the New Test. The first is Moses, that great Prophet & mediator between God & the Israel, according to the Flesh, who, as the Acts 2, 7, give us to understand, had a Revelation that He should deliver Israel out of Egypt, whilst He was yet in the court of Pharao; which,

HERMIT'S GLEN ON THE WISSAHICKON.

VIDE, PAGE 214.

as he would put in Execution, miscarried of the Enterprise through the fault of the People, whereupon he fled into the Wilderness, where he remained 40 years. What He did there is nowhere described, only that towards the end of the 40 years He led his Flock to the Backside (or rather to the hindermost or furthest) Desert. And there the Angel of the L(ord) appeared unto him out of a burning Bush, in order to send him in embassage to King Pharao. But so forward as Moses was at the first to go, when he had got only an Intimation or Manifestation or Revelation or Inspiration or Motion (or what we may call it) of what He now was to do, without any express Commission & Credentials (Viz. Miricales & Signs). So backward was he now to go, when he got express orders & extraordinary Credentials, so that we may easily find what he had done during the 40 years in the Wilderness having the two extremes, viz., his Presumption & fervent Zeal at first in which he killed the Egyptian, & his great Humility & meekness at last when God would send him, which last is Symbolically typified by his leading his Sheep by Ye Backside or deepest of the Wilderness. Whereas formerly when his firy Quality was not yet thoroughly tinctured and Metamorphosed into the Lamlike nature, He led his flock, but, as it were, on the Brim & foreside of the Wilderness, of which I had more to say, but lest the Letter should exceed its bounds, I must hasten to the next Instance, which is Fleyah & runs into many things paralell to the first Witness. Read the history 1 Kings 6, 29. He was a very zealous & had slain the Priests of Baal, as Moses had the Egyptian. They did seek his life, as the Egyptians did Moses his. He made his escape & fled into the Wilderness as Moses did. Moses his 40 years was turned to him in 40 days, He came at last into the Hindermost Wilderness to the Mount of God Horeb, the very same where Moses saw the Vision, And here God appeared unto him, & gave him a gentle Reprimende as touching his Zeal & Presumtious. Shewing him withal, that the great and strong winde & the Earthquake & the Fire (wherein Elijah's his Ministry had consisted) did indeed go before the L(ord), but that the Lord did not dwell therein, but in the still aethereall creating voice & that there were yet 7000 left besides him that had not bowed unto nor kissed Baal; though they were hid & unknown to him, & had not ministered publiquily with storming & quaking & burning Jealousy as he had done. Thereupon being Condemned to substitute another in his Room (viz: to edifie, whereas hitherto he had but destroyed), he was soon after taken up into Paradise, by the same element wherein he had ministered. This Eleijah leads to Ye first Wilderness in the New Testament, the Claus of the old John, the Precursor of the Messiah, who after his education was also in the Wilderness, till the day of his Shewing unto Israel in the Spirit & Power of Eleijah, baptizing with water to Repentance, as the first Eleijah had baptized with Fier for Destruction. What he did in the Wilderness is not described, but by that what hath been said we may safely conclude that he was gratified there for his so great a Ministry. That God appeared also unto him there appeareth out of what he saith himself (Joh. 1, 33). He that sent me to Baptize the same said unto me. I will not draw the Parallelism any further, lest I should prove tedious at least. That like as the accorded of him who succeeded Eleijah, raised the dead man (2 Reg. 13, 21), so He who succeeded John, by his death became the Head, the Spring, the Principle & cause of Life & Resurrection unto all that believed in Him, both for Soul & Body. This is the last & greatest Witness I am to produce JESUS the Messiah of

God, our God & Saviour, the centre of all, who also in likeness of the first Lawgiver Moses was 40 days (the 40 years of Moses being thus abridged) in the Wilderness & tempted there with all manner of Temptations (though without sin, wherein He hath the only Preogative above all, Heb. 4,. 15; 2, 28). The Scripture indeed maketh mention of his firey trials (1 Pet. 4, 12). But nowhere saith what they was or are. They cannot be described; it is only experience which can teach them best. The three temptations that happened at the End of the 40 days (Matt. 4) centre in this: *If He was the Son of God or Not!* which indeed hath more to say than is commonly supposed. The very Ground of the Christian Religion circling therein & is founded thereupon, as appears from Matt. 16, 16; Joh. 11, 27; 1 Joh. 4, 15; 5, 5; & is the greatest Stumbling block to the Jews (Joh. 19, 7) & to the Turks, the Latter believing that Jesus the Son of Mary (as they style him) is the word of God incarnate, & that he is anointed to the Holy Ghost above all the Prophets & above Mahomed, & that he is to be the Judge of the Quick & Dead & of Mahomed himself; but that He is the Son of God they cannot believe, for, say they, God is a Spirit & cannot beget a man for his Son, &c. And no wonder, this being a Mystery surpassing all humane & Angeelicall understanding; nor is it to be found out by the same, it depending solely from the Revelation of the Father, like as that of the Father depends from the Reception of the Son & M. K., is yet to answer the ? Why Jesus being God of very God, became to be Man & died? The Prophets & Patriarchs have been tempted indeed with great Temptations, but non like this, none of the Nature of this, they being not cabable of the same, as being the Sons of God through Faith in Him, who being God, was to be made Man (Exod.

3, 14, where it should have been interpeted: I Schall be, what I shall be, viz:—Man) as we through Faith in Him who was God and is made Man. But Jesus having past this firy ordeal, He received the Almightiness from his Father, whereof he made no bragging Ostentation, as Robbers make of their Pray, but humbled himself unto the death even the death of the Cross, styling himself at this side of the Grave only the son of Man (or mankind, the Greek word denoting both the Sexes) though He was the son of God: Wherefore God also by the Ressurection from the Dead powerfully declared him to be his Son (Rom. 1, 4; Psal. 2. Act.) exalting him above all, Lord over all worlds, visible & invisible, this & that which is to come (Eph. 1, 2; Phil. 2, 6–11).

"To these four I will add two more out of the Scripture, passing by the rest (Heb. 11, 38). This first is *David*, that man after God's own Heart, who was 10 years in the Wilderness & exercised in continual Sufferings & Sorrows (as his Psalms bear witness) before He was installed in the Kingdom, to which He was chosen & annointed so many years before. The second is that great Apostle of the Gentiles *Paul*, who abided seven years in the Deserts of Arabia (Gal. 1, 17, & at the antient Church Records bear witness), before he went out for the Conversion of the Gentiles. I could produce a whole Cloud of such chosen Vessels out of the antient Records of the first Christians, who beeing prepared in the Wild's some for 10, some for 20, some for 40 years, after their coming forth converted whole Cities, wrought signs & Miracles, was to their Diciples as living Oracles, as the mouth of God through whom he fed & guided them, but having exceeded the limits of a letter allready, I must stop the Vein which so liberally would diffuse it self; I hope what hath been said manifested to the full, that God hath prepared alwais his most eminent Instruments in the Wilderness.

"When we consider now with a serious introversion of our minds those Three states of the Wild's, we shall find That there is no entring into the first Wild's without a going out of Spiritual Egypt; and so consequently no entring into the second without passing the first; And so on, no entring into the Third without passing the second state.

"We shall find in the next place, that like as there is a long Strugling & Groaning under the Egyptian Burdens before the delivery from the same ensueth, So there is a long contest between the first & second Birth in their Wilderness-Station before the Second is set at perfect Liberty & made ready to enter & possess Caanan: But how long the Parallelism of the second & third state may run together, & where the Borders of each meet together or if there be any Borders at all, I'll leave to higher graduated Souls than mine is to enquire; by it to speak my mind: me thinks the Childhood & Manhood may both well consist with the second state, & one may arrive to the manhood in Christ without ever entering the Third Station, this being only for some chosen Vessels for a peculiar administration which requires also peculiar & extraordinary Qualifications & Endowments, which they are to acquire & make trial of in this Third Station before they appear & show themselves to the Israel of God. So that every one that is to enter the Third must of necessity be acquainted with the second & first. But not every one that hath entered the Second & after he is even with the first must also enter the Third Station.

"By the consideration of the Third State we shall find what a wighty thing it is to appear & to show oneself to the Israel of God, as immediately called chosen & sent by the Lord. Such a being made, as Paul saith (1 Cor. 4, 9) a Spectacle to the World & to Angels & to Men. And what good reason Moses had to resist so hard when he was sent, whom God having heard the crey & Prayers of his People, did force as it were & thrust or cast forth (see Matt. 11, 38) where it should have been rendered thurst or ——— forth instead of sent forth). And what a great presumption it is, on the other Hand, to go forth without being thus duly prepared beforehand. For though such may have inspirations, Revelations, Motions & the like Extraordinary Favours; yea, may have arrived at the very Manhood in Christ (which truly is a high attainment), yet they will effect & build nothing, but only (if they do any thing at all) destroy, as we see in the instances of Moses & Elias, before they had been in that Wild's. Yea, there is no small Danger of loosing themselves & to bruise & grind that good seed, which was not designed for Meat but for increase, not for to be sent forth but to be kept in an honest & Good Heart. (Luc. ———). Such are indeed with Child, they are in pain, but (as the common Translation saith, Esa. 26, 28, and as the common experience wittnesseth to be so) they bring forth as it were but Winde, they make no deliverance in the earth, neither do the Inhabitants of the World fall; Whereas if they was duly prepared & had stood the firey ordeal it would fare with them, not as with the common, but as the Translation the first Christians made use of hath it: Through thy Tears Lord we have conceived & have been in Pain of Birth, & have brought forth the Spirit of Salvation, which Salvation we have wrough on Earth; we shall not fall, but all that dwell on Earth shall fall.

"I had many Considerations more to add, as also what

the Wilderness it self is in each of these States, having spoken only of some of the Inhabitants thereof & of some of their Qualities & Circumstances, & this rather under a veil &, as it were, but glancing at the Marrow & Substance. Nor have I counted the number of the Wilderness-Time, but touched only the root thereof, which is 40 Sun-Days for the New Birth & 42 Moons or Nights for the Old (which last I have not so much as mentioned). Neither have I measured from the Red-Sea of the Old Birth to the Jordan of the New, and a hundred such things more. But my beloved & esteemed Friend! this was to write a Volume & not a Letter, And I begin allmost to fear that I have ventured too much upon your Patience this first time, not considering also the wall between us. Oh! that we may behold our Beloved alwais, standing behind our Wall, looking forth att the Window, shewing himself thorow the Lattesse, saying Rise up my Love, my fair one & come away (Cant. 29, 10). To whose Love-embraces leaving you, I remain,

"Your sincere, though unworthy Friend,

"J. K.

"ROCKSBORROW, 1706, d. 25, Maji.
"For Hesther Pallmer,
"in Long-Island in Flushing."

When the bright warm weather returned Kelpius again rallied, and Midsummer eve (1706) found him once more at the Tabernacle in his beloved solitude in the forest.

That his physical improvement was only of a temporary nature is shown by his next poem, "*A Comfortable and Incouraging Song, made intentionally for two lonesome Widows,*" where he adds, by way of explanation, "By occasion of a great cold which seized me in July, 1706."

Consumption had fastened its clutches upon the frail

form of the Transylvanian Theosophist, and after lingering for almost two years longer, he succumbed, having labored for fourteen years in the Community in the wilds of the New World; as a late writer[220] aptly states, "working, preaching, prophesying, and, we almost may say, ruling by the right of moral and mental preëminence."

The exact date of his death is unknown. All that we know to a certainty is the mention of the fact in Jawert's petition to the Provincial Council held March 1, 1708 | 9, where the words occur: "*Johannes Kelpius now deceased.*"

[220] F. H. Williams, in "The New World," June, 1894.

THE HERMITS ON THE RIDGE.

A Seal of the Ephrata Community.

PERHAPS one of the strangest facts in connection with this peculiar Community on the Wissahickon is that no complete list of the membership is known. Diligent search among the official records in both Europe and America failed to bring to light any additional information as to who composed the original Chapter. The old shipping-lists of Rotterdam could not be found; and, if not destroyed, are supposed to be stored at either The Hague or Flushing.

Another curious fact is that all communications with Europe ceased soon after the death of Kelpius (except possibly the official communications that passed between Falkner and the Frankfort Company), and, on the other hand, the emigrants seem to have been forgotten by most of their former associates; the exception being the inquiry sent from

Halle and mentioned by Mühlenberg in his reports for the year 1769.[221]

All trace has long since been lost of the astronomical and philosophical apparatus, brought over at various times and used by the Mystical Brethren in their studies and speculations; the only possible exception being the Horologium Achaz, mentioned in a previous chapter.[223] As to their books, at least such as were of a theological character, we are more fortunate. After the disbanding of the Community and the departure of Daniel Falkner from the Province, the bulk of the books, consisting of a number of folios, quartos and octavos, mostly bound in parchment, came into the possession of John Henry Sprogel, and later into that of his brother, Ludovic Christian Sprogel, who kept them until the year 1728, when he gave such as were theological and orthodox to the Rector[224] and Vestry of Christ Church in Philadelphia. After the completion of the tower they were placed in one of the lower rooms, where they still remain.

Here these musty tomes, in Latin, Greek, Hebrew and German, representing the profoundest religious thought of the XVI and XVII Centuries, have found a resting-place for the last century and a half forgotten by all. The few of late years who must now and then have noticed a volume or two but little imagined whence they came, and wondered at the import of the book-plate, which vouchsafed the information that they were the gift of one Sprogel: "*Ex dono LUDOVICI CHRISTIANI SPROGELL, ad Bibliothecam Ecclesiæ Anglicanæ, in Philadelphia, Die Decembris 24, 1728.*"

---

[221] Original ed., p. 1265.

[223] Page 114.

[224] Rev. Archibald Cummings.

The writer in his youth frequently heard the legend that all the books and MSS. of the Mystics had been given to Christ Church, as the intercourse between the founders of both organizations in the earliest days was of an intimate nature.

Fortunate, indeed, was the day when it was found that the legend was a true one, and that a large number of these old tomes were yet in existence and in a good state of preservation, though yellowed by age and covered with dust. They had escaped alike the search for cartridge-paper by both Patriot and British foraging parties during the Revolution,[225] and the fate of being discarded as worthless and sold during the several alterations to the church.

Another interesting legend in connection with this bequest is that the books were given to the corporation as a nucleus for a free library. If this be true it would antedate Franklin's efforts in the same direction by fully three years.

The first of these books opened by the writer was a quarto, and bore the above-quoted legend, "*Ex dono*," etc., on the inside cover, while the title read: "*Gasparis Scioppii || Cæsarii & Regii Conselearii-Astrologia Ecclesiastica || Ex officina Sangeorgiana || Anno M.DC. XXXIV.*[226]

Among this rare and valuable collection were the following:

Homiliarum in Evangelia quæ diebus festis tam Jesu Christi quam aliquorum sanctorum ejus, pro concione proponuntur et explicantur. Authore Rodolpho Gualthero. (*Leyden, 1585, 2 vols., fol.*).

Homilies of Lanuza, translated from Spanish into Latin. (*Cologne, 1686, 3 vols., fol.*).

---

[225] So scarce was paper for cartridge-making during the Revolution that almost all the books in the Ephrata Cloister were confiscated and used for military purposes. Many of the Sauer Bibles were so used.

[226] The Ecclesiastical Astrology of Gaspar Sciopo, Imperial and Royal Councillor.

Walton's Polyglott. (*London, 1657, 6 vols., fol.*).

Lexicon Heptaglotton; Hebraicum, Chaldaicum, Syriacum, Samaritanum, Æthiopicum, Arabicum, et Persicum. Authore Edmundo Castello. (*London, 1686, 2 vols., fol.*)

Greek and Latin Lexicon of Sæc. xvi. (*No date.*)

Osiander's Latin Bible. (*Tübingen, 1590?–1592, 3 vols., fol.*)

Examinis Concilii Tridentini, per Mart. Chemnicium scripti, Opus integrum. (*Geneva, 1641, fol.*)

Erasmus' Parallel Greek and Latin New Testament. (*1518, 2 vols. in one, fol.*)

Huet's Origen. (*Cologne, 1685, fol.*)

Conciliorum Quatuor Generalium: Niceni, Constantinopolitani, Ephesini et Calcedonensis: Que divus Gregorius magnus tanqz quatuor Evangelia colit ac veneratur. (*Cologne, 1530, 2 vols., folio.*)

In Mosis Genesim plenissimi Commentarii. Wolfgango Musculo Dusano autore. (*Basle, 1554, fol.*)

Quatuor Unum: hoc est, Concordia Evangelica. Auctore Guidone de Perpiniano Episcopo. (*Cologne, 1631, fol.*)

Johannes Seelig succeeded Kelpius as Magister, but for a short time only. He soon renounced the honor, and, donning his pilgrim garb once more, retired to a hermit cell or cabin, where he spent his days in teaching and studying, while he supported himself by cultivating his garden, and, when the opportunity offered, working at his trade of bookbinder.

Doctor Christopher Witt and Daniel Geissler also left the Tabernacle in the forest and took up their abode in Germantown, where the former for many years practiced as a physician.

After Seelig's retirement, Conrad Matthai became the leading spirit of the Theosophists who still remained at or about the Tabernacle; a Community in the original sense no longer, but merely a number of devout ascetics who lived in retirement on the banks of the romantic Wissahickon under his leadership. Even this reduced number became less and less as the years rolled by, and settlers continued to encroach on their favorite solitude.

According to the *Chronicon Ephratense*, "after their leader (Kelpius) died the tempter found occasion to scatter them, as those who had been most zealous against marrying now betook themselves to women again, which brought much shame on the solitary state that the few who still held to it dared not open their mouths for shame."[227]

Notwithstanding the radical changes which were continually taking place in the vicinity, incident to the growing population, some show of an organization was kept up for many years, without, however, making any claim to communal life. Such as remained upon the original tract lived as did Conrad Matthai, in small houses or cabins, after the manner of the hermits of old, or the Separatists of later days. It was by the latter name that they afterwards became known.

This remnant on "the Ridge" became a nucleus or rallying-point for the many religious enthusiasts, visionaries and separatists who, during the first half of last century, flocked to the Province noted for liberty of conscience; to whom must be added such of the older settlers as were "awakened," or felt inspired to withdraw from the world and its allurements, and live henceforth a life of seclusion.

About a decade after Kelpius' death, quite an emigration of religious separatists set in from Europe. Some of these pilgrims, such as the Mennonites and Schwartzenauer Dunkers or Baptists, came over in a body, and forthwith opened communications with the remnant on the Ridge, some of their number even adopting the solitary mode of life. Several of these new acquisitions remained steadfast and ended their days as recluses; Andreas Bone and Hermann Drost being prominent examples.

---

[227] Chron. Eph., original ed., p. 12; trans., p. 152.

In the autumn of the year following this emigration (1720), a number of men arrived in Germantown with the avowed intention of devoting the rest of their lives to religious study in the wilds of the New World far away from civilized habitations. The names of Johann Conrad Beissel, the Eckerling brothers, Michael Wohlfarth,[228] Simon König, Johann George Stiefel, Jacob Stuntz and Isaac Van Bebber[229] are all prominent in the movement which revived Esoteric Theosophy and Rosicrucian Mysticism in Pennsylvania.

The most trustworthy information we have regarding the subsequent career of the survivors of the original Community who remained in the vicinity of Germantown is to be found among the Moravian records at Herrnhut and Bethlehem.

From these old musty documents we learn that George Böhnish, the first Moravian evangelist, who labored in Pennsylvania from 1734 to 1737, was a frequent visitor among the recluses in the vicinity of Germantown. The

---

[228] Michael Wohlfarth (Michael Welfare). This remarkable man had been an active Pietist in Germany, and occupied later so prominent a position in the Ephrata Community, wherein he was known as Brother "Agonius." He was born in the fortress of Memel, on the Baltic Sea, in the year 1687. Just when he came to America is not known, nor is it known how long he sojourned among the Hermits on the Wissahickon.

He was an active exhorter and evangelist, and first came prominently into public notice by exhorting the Quakers from the old court-house steps at Second and Market Streets, as well as in their meeting-houses.

He became one of the staunchest supporters of Conrad Beissel. Wohlfarth was also a hymnologist of no mean order, and a number of his hymns are found in the Ephrata hymn-books. He died May 1, 1741. His remains rest in the old "God's Acre" at Ephrata, where his tomb formerly bore this epitaph :—

"Hier ruhet der Gottselige Kamfer AGONIUS, Starb Anno 1741.
"Seines alters 54 Jähre 4 Monate 28 Tage."

No trace whatever is to be found of this grave at the present day.

Rev. August Spangenberg, upon his first visit to Pennsylvania in 1736 for the purpose of ascertaining the religious condition of its German population, sought out the survivors of the Theosophical emigrants who almost half a century before had located on the banks of the Wissahickon. His visits to Seelig and Matthai during his stay in the Province were frequent, and the intercourse between them, it is stated, was cordial and edifying to all parties.

From Spangenberg's report to Herrnhut it appears that the survivors were then living as "Separatists." In a subsequent letter he gives us an insight into their daily life and austere habits; he there states that they slept on hard beds, using neither feathers, after the manner of the Germans, nor straw. Their garb was of a coarse homespun material. They would neither barter, trade, nor engage in any occupation for profit or gain.

In another communication Spangenberg, referring to the above, states that "where individuals had a true desire for their salvation and for the cause of Christ, he knew of no fairer land than Pennsylvania." [229]

When, five years later, Count Ludwig Zinzendorf landed upon these shores,[230] his earliest movements were directed towards the forks of the Lehigh, by way of Germantown; and it was during this journey that the Count made the acquaintance of the surviving Separatists of the Kelpius Community.

That friendly relations were established between Zinzendorf and Matthai at the outset is shown from the fact that the latter's name was conspicuous on the call issued for the first Pennsylvania Synod, December 26, 1741.

---

[229] Leben Spangenbergs, Barby, 1794, p. 135.

[230] Arrived at New York, December 2, 1741; Philadelphia, December 10th.

It was at this meeting, which was held at the house of Theobaldt Endt in Germantown, on New Year's day, 1742 (January 12, 1742, N. S.), that the first attempt was made in America, since the unsuccessful efforts of Johannes Kelpius, toward an evangelical alliance and unification of the German Protestants. At this meeting Conrad Matthai was prominent and active, and championed the cause of such as were adverse to being circumscribed by denominational bounds.

A contemporaneous account of this meeting states that certain remarks made by Count Zinzendorf were construed as reflecting against the Mennonites and Schwenkfelders, who were not represented at the Synod. This caused Matthai to resent what he thought was an unwarranted reflection by Zinzendorf, and raised considerable discussion, resulting in a series of resolutions being adopted.

Before the adjournment of the meeting a set of resolutions was agreed to, it is said at the instance of Matthai. The paper was signed by the representatives of nine different religious interests.

The next trustworthy notice of the later period of the old Community is recorded by Fresenius (vol. iii, page 221), who there states: "Towards the end of this month [December, 1742] came Brother Ludwig [Count Ludwig Zinzendorf] again towards Philadelphia; he had secured a Lodgment at Rocksbury, two hours from Philadelphia, where he expected to hold a Conference. According to the testimony of his own followers [Unitas Fratum] the object was to gather in [to their fold] the remaining Solitary.[231] But with two they were not able to accomplish anything."[232]

[231] The survivors of the old Community on the Wissahickon.

[232] The two Separatists here alluded to were undoubtedly Seelig and Matthai.

THE OLD MONASTERY ON THE WISSAHICKON.

BUILT BY THE ZIONITIC BROTHERHOOD, A.D., 1737.

Turing once more to the Moravian records, we find that one of the last official acts of Count Zinzendorf, prior to his departure from America on January 7, 1743, was to hold a deliberative meeting with the Separatists who remained on the banks of the Wissahickon, at which he had a long and earnest interview with Conrad Matthai.

In a future chapter it will be shown how upon Conrad Matthai's advice Beissel journeyed to the wilds of Conestoga. The same was the case with the Eckerling brothers in 1727. It was upon the advice of the old recluse that Israel Eckerling left the vicinity of Germantown for the Conestoga country, whither he was soon followed by his widowed mother and her three remaining sons, all destined to become important factors in the history of the settlement on the Cocalico.

When finally Conrad Matthai was left almost alone on the old Community tract, an unbroken forest no longer, events transpired which led to a renewal of the spirit of mysticism in Pennsylvania, and subsequently took shape in a new Community, "*Das Lager der Einsamen*," the Camp of the Solitary, known in history as Ephrata, a settlement on the banks of the Cocalico in Lancaster County, and which eventually became the most successful Theosophical community of which we have any record.

A branch of this new society for a time flourished in Germantown and vicinity. For the purposes of the new community a massive stone building was erected in 1738 on the Wissahickon, a short distance above the spot where the original Tabernacle was located.

This structure, about which there were formerly so many gruesome tales and vague traditions current among the superstitious residents of the vicinity, is still standing, and although it is now serving the prosaic uses of a farmhouse, it is still known as "the Monastery."

All vestiges of the original "Hermits of the Ridge" have long since passed away. A portion of their domain is now included within the bounds of Fairmount Park, the largest natural pleasure ground in the world.

The straggling town of Philadelphia, as it was at the landing of Kelpius and his fellow-mystics, has extended in all directions, until it now joins and includes the whole of the German Township within its corporate limits. Palatial residences cover a part of the ground once cultivated by these Esoteric students. Over the very spot where rest the remains of some of this Theosophical Community is now reared a Christian church, with pealing organ and white-robed choristers, a fitting monument to their virtue and piety.

Great have been the changes wrought by time during the last two centuries. The metropolis of Pennsylvania is indeed no longer a churchless city. Hundreds of churches, with their tens of thousands of communicants, are now found within its corporate bounds.

In approaching the great metropolis from the sea, one of the first landmarks to greet the eye of the mariner as he nears the end of his journey is the old Swedish church at Wicacoa; and as the city proper is approached, the symmetrical spire of Christ Church becomes a prominent feature.

Both of these churches, the early history of which is cotemporary with that of our band of German Pietists, are now among the most venerable historic landmarks of the great city of Philadelphia with its million of inhabitants.

To return once more to the scene of the early labors of Kelpius and his followers. Of the tens of thousands of pleasure seekers who annually pass along the Wissahickon, from the purse-proud aristocrat who rides behind prancing steeds and liveried servants down to the weary and foot-sore toiler who on a Sunday seeks after a breath of fresh air, how few of this vast number know the derivation of the names "Hermit Spring" and "Hermit Lane," or have even heard the name of Johannes Kelpius, the pious and learned Magister of the Theosophical Fraternity, who settled there two centuries ago in the unbroken wilderness to commune with the Diety according to the dictates of his conscience and benefit the spiritual condition of his fellowmen.

The old Ephrata MS., in referring to the closing period of the original Community, and to such as remained steadfast, states: "Dispensing religious instruction and charitable attentions to their neighbors who came to cultivate the adjoining wilds, they rendered their habitation the seat of piety and usefulness. Thus while years rolled on in rapid succession the few remained steadfast in their faith and patiently watched for the revelations they so fondly anticipated. These faithful ones, however, followed each other to the shades of death and a happy eternity without accomplishing the work of their devotion and self-denial. They were laid side by side in what was once their garden, and their requiems were sung by the remaining brethren. Their history may be closed in the language of the Apostle,—

"'These all died in faith, not having received the promises, but having seem them afar off, and were persuaded of them, and embraced them, and confessed that they were strangers and pilgrims on the earth."'[233]

Notwithstanding that every vestige of these early religious pioneers has passed away, the effects of the truths they taught is yet felt, not only among the German element in Eastern Pennsylvania, but throughout the whole State and country wherever the slightest trace of the Pennsylvania-German is to be found.

---

[233] Heb. xi, 13.

The benign influence exercised by the various Pietistic sects of Provincial Pennsylvania upon the rude pioneers of various nations and races that were attracted to the Province in the early days of our existence will endure for ages to come. Though the personality of the actors themselves may be lost in oblivion, and even their names be forgotten in the modern struggle for wealth and power, yet in our annals the story of these self-sacrificing enthusiasts, with their legends and traditions, will ever remain one of the brightest and most romantic episodes.

THE TABERNACLE IN THE FOREST, ACCORDING TO AN OLD MANUSCRIPT.

THE LOCATION OF THE TABERNACLE.

THE CAVE OF KELPIUS, 1894.

MORE or less uncertainity has thus far existed among writers upon Kelpius and the Hermits on the Ridge as regards the actual location of the original settlement and the tenure by which they held their land. There are no documents whatever on record to show that this or any other land in the vicinity was ever held in fee-simple by either Kelpius or the Fraternity. All accounts that have come down to us agree to the fact that 175 acres were given them, shortly after their arrival, by Thomas Fairman, who was then deputy surveyor general.[234] If any title was passed it does not appear to have been placed on record.

It has, however, been proven beyond all reasonable doubt that the portion of the tract, once the site of the Tabernacle of the Mystic Brotherhood, is identical with the estate now known as "the Hermitage," owned by the Prowattain family.

---

[234] Fairman was not commissioned-surveyor general until 1702.

This is situated on the east side of Hermit Lane, in Roxborough, in the Twenty-first Ward of Philadelphia, and extends down to the Wissahickon. The strip of land along the banks of the creek is now included within the bounds of Fairmount Park, having been acquired by the city under the Act of April 14th, 1868.

Now the question naturally arises: How happens it that here are 175 acres of land without any record of having been either bought or sold, until about fifty years after the gift of Fairman? Nor does this identical plantation ever appear to have been in the name of the person who is accredited with having given it to the German Theosophists.

A careful search reveals to us the fact that at least a part of the land in question was contained in a grant of 200 acres made in 1689 by William Penn to Thomas B. Vicaris,[235] and that Thomas Fairman was in charge of the property, as well as the adjoining one to the eastward, which extended to the Schuylkill, and was also supposed to contain "200 acres," granted by William Penn to John Jennett, by patent dated January 20, 1685.[236]

Jennett, on March 18, 1698, sold to Mathew Houlgate eighty acres of this land, which adjoined the Vicaris tract. Mathew Houlgate the elder, who was for some time either a member of the Community or else intimately connected with the same, erected the first fulling-mill on the Wissahickon. This was in 1720, and was an undertaking in which he does not seem to have prospered.

Vicaris, according to the records, under date of August 4, 1741,[237] sold to Michael Righter seventy-one acres of land

[235] The patent is not on record. Another account names Richard and Robert Vicaris as the original patentees.

[236] Patent Book A, p. 104. Exemplication Book No. 1, p. 86.

[237] Deed Book F T W 103, p. 365.

adjoining the Houlgate or Jennett tract, which one Peter Righter had bought at sheriff's sale, December 6, 1728.[238] This grant included all the improvements erected or made by the Theosophical Community, viz., the Tabernacle, several small log cabins or houses used by the Hermits after disbanding, the cave of Kelpius, a large orchard planted by the Mystics, and other improvements, such as fencing and cleared ground.

Two months after the above conveyance, October 27, 1741, Peter Richter transferred his seventy-one acres to Michael Richter.[239] This gave the latter a plantation of 151 acres, which, without doubt, included all the land once occupied both by the Community and the Hermits who succeeded them.

The Righters or Richters, it is said, were originally connected in some manner with the Brotherhood. A legend, which appears trustworthy, states that Peter Righter, the first of the family in America, came over with Daniel Falkner in 1700, but soon after left the Community and built a stone house on the banks of the Schuylkill a short distance above the mouth of the Wissahickon, where he also established a ferry. This was some years prior to the death of Kelpius.

This ferry was kept by successive generations of the Righter families, until the building of the Manayunk bridge removed any necessity for its maintainance.

The above 151 acres of land remained in possession of Michael Righter until his death, which occurred some time in 1783. His will is dated January 29, 1783, and under its provision three commissioners were appointed by the heirs to effect a division of the real estate. They apportioned

---

238 Record Book A D B 142, p. 485.

239 Deed Book H 9, p. 367.

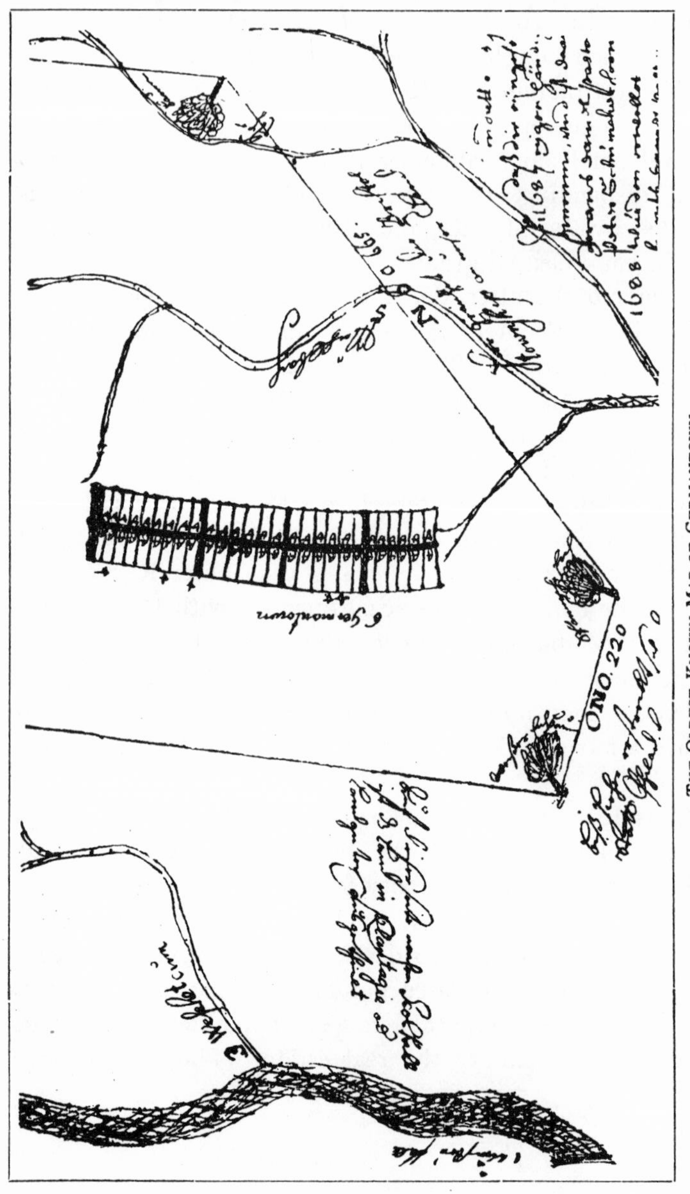

The Oldest Known Map of Germantown.
(Original in library of Hon. S. W. Pennypacker.)

Contour Map, showing the tract formerly occupied by the Theosophical Community, after a lapse of two centuries, and now included within the corporate limits of the city. By George S. Webster, Esq., Chief Bureau of Surveys.

the above 151 acres to Peter Righter (2),[240] March 13, 1787, and from him it passed to Daniel Righter about the year 1818.

It was from Phoebe Righter, the widow of the last named, that the direct proof was obtained of the former tenure of this land by the Mystic Brotherhood.

The tract remained in the Righter family until the year 1848, when a part of it, containing sixteen acres and sixteen perches, which included the site of the Tabernacle and the Kelpius cave and spring, together with one of the Hermit's cabins, was sold by the heirs of Daniel Righter to Evan Prowattain, a merchant of Philadelphia.

The new owner at once commenced a series of improvements so as to make the place suitable for a suburban residence. A large mansion house was built near the former site of the Tabernacle, and upon its completion was called "The Hermitage."

Shortly after this mansion was finished and the grounds laid out, the whole estate was leased to Col. Benjamin Chew, of Germantown, who made the place his home for a number of years. The old log cabin in which Phoebe Righter had passed so many years of her life was at that time in a dilapidated condition.

A gentleman with antiquated taste, who visited the Hermitage during the first year of Col. Chew's occupancy, writes: "On the picturesque grounds of Evan Prowattain, the residence of Col. Benjamin Chew, are the old hut and the spring of Kelpius. About the hut there is some controversy. The settled opinion seems to be, however, that it was either the dwelling or the site of the dwelling of Kelpius. It is built of logs, pointed or mortised at the ends,

[240] Deed Book D 18, p. 632, deed of Daniel Thomas, Mathew Holgate and Anthony Cook to Peter Righter.

and now rotted under the exposure of years. A rickity door and front window gave it the appearance of a tenement, and the chances are that a few more years will witness the demolition of the old landmark.

"It stands on the side of an acclivity, and in the days of Kelpius the foxes burrowed in the cellar. It is now used as a tool-house and a chicken-coop. A few rods from this, farther down the hill, is the spring. It lies at the foot of an old cedar tree. The water is black and cold. Just below the spring is a stone cave, which looks like an old spring-dairy or milk-house. It is said that Kelpius hollowed this out and built it with his own hands.

"Below the hill the glen lies still and always shadowy. Here in [time past] these Magi and Hermits wandered with thoughts of another world. From the Hermitage, as far up the creek as the red bridge, a deep glen or gorge follows the north side of the Wissahickon. This was of old a favorite spot with the Hermits, the scene of their wanderings."

A visit to the Hermitage grounds by the present writer, in June, 1894, just two hundred years after the arrival of the German Theosophists in Pennsylvania, reveals the fact that a few salient features of interest are still in almost the same primitive condition as they were when Kelpius and his associates first trod upon its virgin soil. Other features may still be traced by vestiges and traditions.

The object of this visit was to go over the ground carefully, make a critical examination of whatever was thought to bear upon the former occupancy of the Mystics, and sift as far as possible such of the legends and traditions as hover about the place. Arrangements were also made to photograph such relics as should prove of historic value or interest as illustrations to this work.

The most important relic found was the ruin of the subterranean cell or cave once occupied by Magister Kelpius. This anchorite cell, as before stated, is not a natural formation, but was built against the hillside with an arched roof, which was covered with about three feet of soil and then sodded. Upon it there is now quite a growth of timber of considerable girth.

This cell or "*Einsiedler-hütte*" has now caved in, and is partially filled in with stones and soil. Originally it formed a room sixteen feet long by nine feet wide in the clear, and eight feet high. Entrance to the cave was had by an arched doorway, which faced towards the south. This entrance is now partly choked up with dirt and *débris.*

Reared on either side of the old doorway are two jambstones, which were placed against the cave during the tenure of Col. Chew, for the purpose of hanging a door so as to bar the access to the old retreat. This became necessary on account of the frequent visitors who came to view the spot. Upon either side of the opening two large trees have grown, and now stand like silent sentinels to guard the scene.

A few yards from the entrance to the cell, just beyond the fence shown in the accompanying photographic reproduction, is the crystal spring, which in Kelpius' time gushed forth from amid the roots of an ancient cedar tree. The water is still as clear and cold as of yore, and invites the thirsty pilgrim of to-day to quench his thirst out of its rock-bound basin. It is still known as "the Hermit's Spring." [241]

The old hut, as described in the account above quoted, was repaired and enlarged, shortly after the sketch was written, by another room and an additional story. It now

---

[241] Or "Kelpius' Spring."

serves as a comfortable "tenant" house for the hired help or "farmer" of the estate. The size of the original cabin may, however, easily be traced from the dimensions of the cellar or basement beneath the house. This cabin, similar to the anchorite cell, was built against the hillside, and faced towards the south.

There is but little to impress the chance visitor with the fact that any part of this structure ever served as the solitary habitation of the recluse philosopher or Theosophical student who here passed his days in voluntary seclusion and exile for the purpose of perfecting himself in spiritual holiness and aiding his fellow-countrymen, who had journeyed so far from the Fatherland, to better their condition and enjoy the promised religious liberty.

Of the Tabernacle no trace whatever could be found. There is a vague tradition that the present mansion, now temporarily deserted and tenantless, stands upon the former site. This has some show of probability, as from the porch, when the trees are leafless, may be seen the former camping-ground of the Hessian troops, beyond the Wissahickon, during the British occupation in 1777–78; a fact which appears to agree with the Hessian letter, written at camp about the time of the battle of Germantown, wherein the writer states that the former "*Kloster*" of Kelpius was visible from their camp.[242]

But by far the most interesting spot within the bounds of the Hermitage estate is the level wooded glen a few yards west of the Kelpius cave, which tradition points out as the spot where the public gatherings and open-air services were held during the favorable seasons. This spot, now after the lapse of two centuries, is as secluded, romantic and beautiful as it was when the Theosophical Mystics

[242] Ephrata MSS.

wandered among its shadows, enjoying the breezes and quenching their thirst from the springs that bubble forth here and there and unite in rills to feed the Wissahickon. One such rill is known even to the present day as "Hermit Run."

Except that some of the primitive forest trees are now replaced by those of second growth, little or no change has taken place in this romantic spot. The hand of modern art has not yet defaced any of its prominent features. The same wealth of wild flowers covers the ground during the spring and summer, while an occasional bird sings his song high up amid the verdant branches. Thus it presents almost the same vast, silent and unmolested solitude as when Kelpius, Falkner, Seelig and Matthai, here in one of God's first temples, wandered among the trees and sought spiritual inspiration amidst the beauties of primeval nature.

The photographic reproduction will give some faint idea of the beauty of the glen. Could the stones and older trees but speak, they might tell of many a mystic incantation and magical exorcism here performed during the hours when graveyards were supposed to yawn. Perchance they could give reports of questions in occult philosophy and alchemy once argued and mysteries of unwritten Cabbala communicated by word of mouth from magister to neophyte under obligations of secrecy.

The steep hillsides that extend from the glen and plateau down to the Wissahickon are still covered with trees of a primitive growth. But few thus far have fallen victims to the axe of the wood-cutter, except for a stretch directly in front of the Prowattain house, where the owner had a vista cut, so that from his porch he could see the park drive.

As to the burial-place of Kelpius and Matthai nothing definite was to be ascertained. Several records state that the former was buried within the garden of the Community. Two direct records state that Matthai was buried at the feet of his former Magister.

From the Moravian records the writer is inclined to believe that the above traditions are true, and that both philosophers were buried in the large orchard, planted under the direction of Kelpius and Falkner on the plateau north or west of the present Hermit Lane.

The strip of land bordering on the Wissahickon and originally a part of the Hermitage property, was taken some years ago for public purposes, and is now included within Fairmount Park. It includes the gorge at the base of the hill, and extends up as far as the red bridge.

This glen or gorge on the north bank of the stream is now a favorite resort for family picnics and children's parties, coming during the hot season from the built-up parts of the great city to enjoy the cool and rustic retreats afforded by the shady shore.

Few among the tens of thousands are aware of the legends hidden in the signs erected by the Park Commission: Hermit Glen, Hermit Bridge, Hermit Lane.

PART II.

THE HERMITS ON THE WISSAHICKON,

1708 - - - 1748.

Johannes Kelpius Transylvanus

MAGISTER JOHANNES KELPIUS.

KELP VON STERNBERG.

JOHANNES KELPIUS will always remain one of the most picturesque characters of our early history; the more so on account of a certain air of mystery and romance which has thus far enshrouded his personality.

But few of his labors in America have been recounted in these pages. Unfortunately, in his modesty, he left but little written record of the great work performed by him during the fourteen long years that he lived on the banks of the romantic Wissahickon. How earnestly he sought to improve the morals and spiritual condition of the rude and heterogeneous population that was then scattered through Eastern Pennsylvania, is shown by the many traditions and legends that have survived for two centuries.

By reason of his scholarly attainments, devout life, independent bearing, and, it may be said, broad humanity, together with his repeated refusals of worldly honors and civil power, that were at various times thrust upon him,

Autograph of Kelpius, from Mumford letter, p. 129–136.

the Magister on the Wissahickon stands out in bold relief as a prominent example of piety and disinterestedness.

There can be but little doubt that this devout scholar, who thus voluntarily banished himself from the Fatherland, home and friends had many difficulties to contend with, both within and without the Community, and that his position at the head of such a Fraternity was anything but a sinecure. There were conflicting interests to equalize and, upon more than one occasion, stubborn minds to combat. When internal dissensions threatened the Fraternity it was always left to Kelpius to use the olive branch.

Thus far but little was known of the Magister's antecedents, except that he was a native of Transylvania (*Siebenbürgen*). Now, after the lapse of two hundred years, it has been the good fortune of the writer, during a late visit to Europe, to gain at least a slight insight into his history.

After considerable inquiry it was learned that a book on Transylvanian *savans* had been published sometime during the last century. Diligent inquiry, however, failed to obtain either a copy of the coveted volume or any information of value.

It was during the weary search for this work that the writer strolled into an *antiquariat* in the ancient city of Halle.[243] Turning over many volumes, almost ready to give up the search, he found an old book, not catalogued and apparently much the worse for wear. It proved to be the one so long sought for.[244]

From this book it is learned that our Magister was the son of Pfarrer George Kelp, of Halwegen, who at the time of his death, February 25, 1685, was the incumbent at

---

[243] F. W. Schmidt, Halle, a S.

[244] Sievert's Nachrichten, von Siebenbürgischen Gelehrten und ihren Schriften. Pressburg, 1785.

Denndorf, a town in the district of Schässburg (*Segesvar*) in Transylvania.

Pfarrer Kelp had three sons: Martin (1659–1694), George and Johannes, the subject of our sketch, who was born in 1673. The exact birthplace of Johannes is not known to a certainty, but it was probably Halwegen, a town in the same district as Denndorf. At the time of Martin's birth the father was resident pfarrer at the former place.

Shortly after Pfarrer Kelp's death, Johannes, who was of a studious nature, received an offer of assistance from three of his father's friends.[245] The young orphan then determined to continue his studies, but away from his native heath, and selected the high school at Tübingen. But on account of the warlike movements in that vicinity and the troublesome times it was concluded to send the young student to the renowned High-School or University at Altdorf, a town near Nüremberg, in Bavaria, then at the height of its fame.

Here the young student received a thorough scientific and religious education. He graduated in 1689, at the youthful age of sixteen, and was honored with the title of Magister, or, as it is stated in the old records of the former University, "*der freien Künste und Weltweisheit Doctor*," doctor of philosophy and the liberal arts.

His thesis upon this occasion was a treatise on natural theology:

"*Theologiæ Naturalis, seu Metaphysicæ Metamorphosin, sub moderamine Viri-M. Dan. Guilh. Molleri, pro summis honoribus, & privilegiis philosophicis legitime obtinendis, die 15 Jun., 1689. Altdorfii.*"

This thesis was published in several editions, both quarto

[245] Count Valentine Franck, Burgomaster Michael Deli, and Notarius Johann Zabanius.

and octavo. It was while a student at Altdorf that the young philosopher attracted the attention of the principal tutor of the institution, the Reverend Johannes Fabricius [Altdorfinus], and in the year following his graduation (1690) a book was printed bearing upon the title-page the names of both master and scholar, which at that day was an almost unheard-of honor to a student.

The title of this work, which is divided into eighteen chapters, is

"*Scylla Theologica, aliquot exemplis Patrum & Doctorum Ecclesiæ qui cum alios refutare laborarent, fervore disputationis abrepti, in contrarios errores misere inciderunt, ostensa, atque in materiam disputationis proposita, a Joh. Fabricio, S. Theol. P. P. & M. Joh. Kelpio. Altdorfii, 1690, octavo.*

This work is divided into sixteen chapters and a summary. The former treat on Tertullian, Pope Stephen I, Gregory Thaumaturgus, Arius, Marcellus, Jovian, Jerome, Augustine, Pelagius, Faustus, Bishop of Riez, Eutyches, Berengarius, Amsdorf, Stancar of Illyricum, Flacius and Huber. The concluding chapter or summary deals with the royal road between Scylla and Charybdis.

This work was followed in the same year (1690) by a third book. It was an essay on the question whether heathen ethics [meaning the Aristotelian] were fit for the instruction of Christian youth. Printed at both Nüremberg and Altdorf, entitled:

"*Inquisitio, an Ethicus Ethnicus, aptus sit Christianæ Juventutis Hodegus? sive: An juvenis christianus sit idoneus auditor Ethices Aristotelicae? Resp. Balthas. Blosio, Norimb. 1690.*"

This valuable treatise, to which is added the poetic congratulations sent to him upon the attainment of the degree of Magister, went through several editions, octavo and quarto. Some of them are dedicated to his patrons who sent him to the University, viz., Count Valentine Franck, a noble of the Saxon nation; Michael Deli, Burgomaster of Schässburg; and Magister Johann Zabanius, provincial notarius at Hermannstadt. Other editions have a somewhat different preface, and are dedicated to his Nüremberg patrons—Paul Baumgartner, Karl Welser von Neunhoff, J. Paul Ebner von Eschenbach, and Joh. Christoph Tucher.

Among the learned men then in Nüremberg whose attention was attracted to the young philosopher's writings was one Magister Johann Jacob Zimmerman, late Diaconus at Bietigheim, in Würtemberg, a pupil and follower of the noted M. Ludwig Brunnquell, and who in addition to his sacred calling was one of the best mathematicians and astronomers in Europe. So great was the esteem in which Magister Zimmerman held the young Transylvanian, that when he subsequently organized a Chapter of Perfection or Collegium Pietatis for the purpose of emigrating to the New World, there to meet the great Deliverer, we find Johannes Kelpius, as we will now call him, the second in command, or Deputy Master; and upon Zimmerman's untimely death at Rotterdam on the eve of embarkation (1693) he became Magister of the Chapter.

BIBLIOTH. PUBL. REG. STUTTG.

It was under the guidance of Kelpius that the journey to the New World was safely accomplished, where they expected to witness the Millennium, which, according to Zimmerman's astronomical calculations, was to take place in the fall of the year of grace 1694.[246]

Martin Kelp, our Magister's elder

[246] Hartmann, Magister-buch, 1477–1700, MS. folio, 499, Königliche Bibliothek, Stuttgart.

brother, also became known for his learning.[247] He finished his education under the patronage of Elias Ladiver and Magister Schnitzler, and studied at Hamburg and Leipzig, where he received the degree of Magister. He too died at an early age, the year after his brother left the Fatherland for Pennsylvania.

The remaining brother, George Kelp,[248] also received a liberal education, and subsequently became Burgomaster of Schässburg, the chief city of his native district. He married into the noble Sternberg family, and afterwards, together with his sons, was knighted, since which time the family has been known as Kelp von Sternberg. It is from this fact that Johannes Kelpius, the Magister on the Wissahickon, in the later Moravian records is alluded to as "Baron Kelpio."

For some reasons unknown, Kelpius, after he came to Philadelphia, failed to keep in touch with his family in Germany. The Transylvanian chronicler, in closing his

---

[247] Rector Martin Kelp was the author of the celebrated work,—

"*Natales Saxonum Transylvaniæ, Aposciasmate Historico collustrati. Resp. Joach. Christiano. Westphal, Neo-Rupin-die 22 Mart., 1684. Lipsiæ. 4to.*

[248] Uffenbach in his Memoirs gives the following interesting information about George Kelp, the brother of our Magister, who then seems to have been living at Lüneburg, in Hanover:

"January 28, 1710, I learned from a resident pastor that a certain person here, named Kelp, had purchased the library of Herr Horn, and then sold the books at auction. The sale of the Manuscripts, however, had been forbidden by the Magistrates, as there were many of local interest among them. My informant further assured me that Kelp, who had married a daughter of the "Stern" family, was wont to gather together many good things, but afterwards sold them dear enough.

"January 30, 1710.—Called again on the above Herr Kelp and purchased from him, at a high price, various books and manuscripts. He is a young, pleasant but capricious man, and notwithstanding the poor appearance of his house, acts big and does not urge one to purchase from him.—Uffenbach Reisen, vol. i, 483, 506.

Johannes Kelpius

FROM THE ORIGINAL CANVASS BY DR. CHRISTOPHER WITT,
NOW IN THE HISTORICAL SOCIETY OF PENNSYLVANIA.

biographical sketch, adds: "Afterwards he journeyed to Pennsylvania, and his Fatherland heard nothing more of him."

This statement may be true so far as his immediate family is concerned, for a regular correspondence was maintained between Kelpius and the leading representatives of similar convictions to his own in England and Germany.

This is shown by copies of a number of letters entered in the back of his Journal—one of the two manuscript books in his handwriting that have come down to us.

This Journal, as it is usually called, contains 101 closely written pages, in addition there is a note upon two of the fly leaves. The first is apparently a quotation from Seneca, and is headed "*Seneca de refor.*"

[Translation.]—"I cannot go beyond my country: it is the one of all; no one can be banished outside of this. My country is not forbidden to me, but only a locality. Into whatever land I come, I come into my own: none is exile, but only another country. My country is wherever it is well; for if one is wise he is a traveller; if foolish an exile. The great principle of virtue is, as he said, a mind gradually trained first to barter visible and transitory things, that it may afterwards be able to give them up. He is delicate to whom his country is sweet; but he is strong to whom every single thing is his country; indeed he is perfect to whom every single thing is his country; indeed he is perfect to whom the world is exile."

The next leaf may be called a title, and sets forth that the following are "Literal copies of letters to friends in and out of Pennsylvania, sent from the Wilderness by Johanno Kelpio, Transylvania. 1694–1703–4–5–6–7."

The first seventeen pages of the book proper contain a Latin *diarium* of his journey to America. It represents however, but a small portion of the voluminous correspondence which he is known to have maintained with the Theosophical Fraternity in Europe.

The contents of this Journal are as follows: Diarium, 17 pages;[249] German letter to Heinrich Johann Deichmann in London, dated September 24, 1697, four pages; another to the same, dated May 12, 1699, 13 pages; with a seven-page postscript by Seelig. Then follows the well-known English missive to Stephen Mumford, December 11, 1699, seven pages; a Latin letter to Rev. Tobias Eric Biörck, 13 pages; a twenty-two-page German letter to Maria Elizabeth Gerber in Virginia, dated October 10, 1704; one in German of five pages, dated July 1, 1705, to his old tutor, Prof. Fabricius, who was then at Helmstadt; another to Deichmann, of two and a half pages, dated July 23, 1705; and, lastly, the English missive of eleven pages to Hester Palmer, in which he describes the "Threefold Wilderness State."[250]

The Latin missive addressed to Rev. Tobias Eric Biörck unfortunately bears no date, but as it is inserted between the Mumford letter (December 11, 1699) and the Gerber missive (October 10, 1704) it was undoubtedly written during the period when Rudman and Justus Falkner were active in New York, and appealed to Kelpius and his party for pecuniary assistance.

The allusion to money evidently relates to the repayment of a loan made to either the struggling Dutch congregation in New York or the Swedish churches on the Delaware.

The first page of this letter is reproduced in *fac-simile*, together with a translation. A spirit of the true religion

[249] The first page of this diary is reproduced in *fac-simile* on page 14 of this work.

[250] Letter in full, pp. 180–191, *ibid.*

pervades the whole letter, and the allusion to the pious Rudman illustrates the intimacy between the mystical Pietists and the Orthodox clergymen in the Province.

[TRANSLATION.]

"TO REV. MAGISTER ERIC BIÖRCK,

"PASTOR AT CHRISTIANNA.

"IMMANUEL.

"May Jehovah remember thee, that thou mayest see the good things of his elect; may he remember thee for the sake of his favor toward his people, that thou mayest rejoice in the joy of his nation. May he visit thee in his salvation, that thou mayest glory in his inheritance. Amen!

"Psalm cvi. 4 and 5.

"*Very reverend Sir and Friend, Master and friend in Jesus our Saviour, ever to be regarded by me with fraternal love:*

"In your beloved letter, written on January 10, and received on January 17, through Mr. Jonas B———, I got a twofold proof of your fraternal love, the epistle and the money. Would to God I were truly such as you have outlined, or such as you have judged me with my most beloved Rudman. By day and by night I attend, indeed, that I may cleanse myself from every blemish both of body and of soul, and I perform my rites in the fear of the Lord, and that I may obtain, by grace alone, that which is my pattern by nature, through sincere imitation of Him; to wit, the adoption as a son, the redemption of our body (Rom. viii, 23. Compare 1 John iii, 1–2; Phil. iii, 11–15; Gal. iv, 5; Apoc. xix, 8; 2 Tim. iv, 8). How many parasangs[251] as yet

[251] Parasang is a Persian measure of length, which, according to Herodotus is thirty stadia, or nearly four English miles. But, in different times and places, it has been 30, 40 or 60 stadia.

Ad Rev. Dn. Ericum Biörk
Pastorem ad Christinam

Immanuel!

Jehovah recordetur Tui ut Electorum suorum bona videas recordetur Tui pro suo erga populum suum favore, ut laeteris in laetitia gentis suae visitet Te in salute sua, ut gloriere in haereditate ejus Amen!
(Psal. 106 45.)

Vir Rev.e adm. & Cl. Dne & Amice in Jesu Salvatore nostro fraterno amore semper mihi prosequende

Amoris Tui fraterni duplex accepi τεκμήριον literas amantissimas & monetam per Dn Jonam B 10ma Cal Febr exaratas, pro quibus gratias ago. Utinam vero is essem quem delineasti, qualemve cum amantissimo meo Rudmanno me esse judicasti! Perdius equidem & pernox id ago ut menute ipsa ab omni & corporis & animae labe purgem sanctimoniam cum Deo metu fungar, atque id quod complex mihi natura est, ego per sinceram ejus non solâ gratiâ adipiscar scil τὴν υἱοθεσίαν τὴν ἀπολύτρωσιν τοῦ σώματος Rom 8,23 conf. 1 Joh. 3,1.2 Phil. 3,11–15 inclus. (Gal 5,5. Apoc 19,8. 2 Tim 4,8.) Verum multis autem parasangis adhuc absum a praefixo mihi scopo, cum illis omnibus qui Χριστῷ συνεσταύρωνται καὶ συνετάφησαν Gal 2,20 Col 2,12 & quos Deus nunc fecit ob divitias τοῦ Χριστοῦ συνεζωοποίησε, καὶ συνήγειρε, καὶ συνεκάθισεν ἐν τοῖς ἐπουρανίοις ἐν Χριστῷ Ἰησοῦ Eph 4,19. melius memetipso nemini excepto solo cordium renumque scrutatore innotescat quodve dilectus noster Rudm. de me testatus fuit, ipsi potius, charitatique divinae quâ cor ejus affectum fuit tribuenda sunt: haec n. teste Paulo 1 Cor. 13. omnia tolerat, omnia credit omnia sperat, omnia sustinet.

non

I mây be distant from the scope (aim) prefixed for myself, becometh known to the fellow-soldiers (Associates) of those crucified and buried with (in) Christ (Gal. ii, 20), and whom God, rich in mercy through Christ, kept secret (in silence) and awakened and placed in the heavenly [places] in Christ Jesus (Eph. i, 20). Better than myself no one knows [my shortcomings] save alone the searcher of hearts and minds; for that which our beloved Rudman bore witness concerning me, is to be attributed rather to himself (Rudman) and to divine charity, wherewithal his heart was affected: these things also, Paul being a witness (I Cor., xiii). He endureth all, believeth all, hopeth all, sustaineth all."

[End of the first page.]

Another interesting missive in this old diary, and one of the most important, is the German letter written by Kelpius to his former tutor, Magister Fabricius, then at the head of the Helmstadt University. It runs thus,—

[TRANSLATION.]

"July 23d, 1705.

"*To Dr. Fabricius, Prof. Theol. at Helmstadt:*

YOUR MAGNIFICENCE:—The joy your letter afforded me I am unable, at present, to describe. I did behold in it, as in a mirror, the sincerity & uprightness of my good old mastor, Dr. Fabricius. What dear Mr. Ingelstätter, *ex-rettore dei Falkein*, reported, is true, so far as appertaineth to the principal point, namely, that I have not become a Quaker. Such an idea hath never come into my mind, albeit I love them from my inmost soul, even as I do all other sects that approach & call themselves Christ's, the Paptists even not excluded, &, with Peter, I have found out, in deed & truth, that God regarded not the person, but in all sorts of work & religion. He that feareth Him, & doeth what is right, is agreeable to Him. I could report of magnalities (if space permitted) which this great God hath wrought even amongst the Indians, whereof there is some printed notice in the Memoirs of the Phil. Soc. in London, & how they are brought to grief now & then by blind-mouthed Christians. Yet one instance I will report, as abashed Sir W. Penn, when he was here last, Anno 1701 (if I remember rightly) when he wanted to preach to them of faith in the God of Heaven & Earth, at their *Kintika* (thus they call their festivity). After having listened to him with great patience, they answered: 'You bid us believe in the Creator & Preserver of Heaven & Earth, though you do not believe in Him yourself, nor trust in Him. For you have now made your own the land we held in common amongst ourselves & our friends. You now take heed, night and day, how you may keep it, so that no one may take it from you. Indeed, you are anxious even beyond your span of life, and divide it among your children. This manor for this child, that manor for that child. But we have faith in God the Creator & Preserver of Heaven & Earth. He preserveth the sun, He hath preserved our fathers so many moons (for they count not by years). He preserveth us, and we believe & are sure that He will also preserve our children after us, & provide for them, & because we believe this, we bequeath them not a foot of land.' Whenever we shall be made worthy to see the many and varied dwellings in our Father's house (for who would be so simple, to say these dwellings were all of one sort), it is my belief we shall then see that the same Architect cared little about our common formula & systematic architecture. And, I trow, many disciples of Moses & Christ, when in want or dying, might be glad if they shall be received in any of the huts, described above, by him, whom they perhaps accused of heresy in this life. I hope that God, who maketh happy both man and beast, & hath mercy on all his children, will, at last, make all men, as died in Adam, alive in the other. But life & death are further distinguished from change, so that those that have been made to live in Christ, must be delivered from the second death. I know that some cranks, *spiriti Divines*,, trouble & crucify themselves concerning this *Lexion theologiæ* (as they call it), but especially the Reprobratites, because these (Restitution of all things) [252] cancel & crucify their dogmas so very frequently. Meseems, however, their little faith hath its origin in the misunderstanding of the word *Eternity*, which neither in Greek nor in Hebrew denoteth a time but an end, but rather the contrary as they have both singular & plural numbers, & Paul even speaketh of the birth of Eternities. But just as the luminaries of the firmament are the dimensions of our time, so it seemeth that the Eternities have, also, their dimensions, which, however, those (sensual Man's having not the spirit) cannot well see, wherefore allowance must be made, if they, perchance, judge hereof as the blind do of colors. But if the Lord from out His infinite plentitude should give them the spiritual mind, they will, no doubt, judge otherwise. How wroth I formerly would wax toward those who would not accept the sayings of Schertzer or Calov [253] as Oracles. And I trust in

[252] The doctrine of "Restitution of all Things" is still adhered to by the German Seventh-day Baptist Church in Pennsylvania, and who are the direct descendants of the secular congregation of the Ephrata Community. They believe in "The full restoration of all things to the primeval condition, as it was before the fall, by Christ, that they may be one as we are."

This is based on the following passages in the Holy Scriptures: John xvii, 2; 1 Cor. xv, 28; Eph. i, 10.

the infinite mercy of God (& your Magnificence also had great patience with me & to me, indeed, publicly, whereof I have since often been ashamed, but admired your Magnificence's humility & prudence), why should I then look with evil eye upon my blind neighbor, because God hath, perchance, showed me beforehand the abundance of His Mercy, by opening mine eyes before theirs? Not to speak of, that I see but little fragments of the fragmentary work & the men of the creation as trees! But, especially, because I hope to become one in God through Christ both with those who do not yet see as I do, and with those that see much better and farther than I.

"Although I proffer this common love in the brotherly love, yet the brotherly love, the Philadelphiac, remains with me on a firm foundation; whence I was wronged, if I have been called a Quaker on account of the former (common love), or even furthermore, a Papist, as has been done by the Quakers in this country, as I was unwilling to enter the married state, however advantageous the connection, wherefore I was either a Jesuit or an Indian Deitist, although, by the grace of God, it is easy for me to be judged from a human standpoint. Nevertheless I have mercy on such untimely judges and condemners, who are oblivious of the express prohibition of Christ & Paul, though professing to be his disciples; therefore I can harmonize as little with the canon of the Anglical Church (Confession), as with the anathema of the Council of Trent,

[253] Abraham Calovius (Kalau), born April 16, 1612, was one of the most celebrated divines of the 17th century, and a native of Morungen, in East Prussia; died February 25, 1686, while General Superintendent and Professor of Divinity at Wittenberg. He was one of the leading controversional writers of the period, and as the representative of the scholastic and zelotic Lutherdom opposed the union of the Protestant Church, in consequence of which his followers were called *Calovians.*

D. JOANNES FABRICIVS
Altdorfinus

PORTRAIT OF MAGISTER FABRICIUS,
TUTOR AND FRIEND OF KELPIUS.

FROM AN OLD COPPERPLATE AT HELMSTADT.

though having no part in the errors mentioned. To the honor of the Anglical Church, I must confess, that they practice the Doctrine of universal grace much better than the Lutherans.

"Their 39 Theses, or Articles (I had almost said 40 less one) are so mild and general, that they can be accepted by any one, who is not too narrowminded and of too little faith. If any one amongst them have but a private view, as, for instance, concerning the universal restitution, the Millennium, the Metemptosis,[256] etc., he is, on that account, not excommunicated forthwith, especially, if he make them but serviceable to the practice of piety, not for the instituting of Sects, although they deem the Quaker Sect the last, & that the Lord would now soon come to His Temple, forasmuch as the opinion concerning the Millennium is quite correct both amongst them and the Presbyterians, or Calvinists, both in Old and New England, as well as here, and even amongst the Quakers themselves a few years ago. It is consequently wrong to place all these into one category. The majority of them are just as worldly in their opinions, as any of the great divisions may be, & if all their members should be subjected to a particular examination on some points of Religion—the result would be, as amongst others—so many heads, so many opinions, as I have found out in mine own experience." [Here the letter ends abruptly.]

Most of the letters in this volume are somewhat rhapsodical, and filled with obscure illusions to mystical subjects and scriptural quotations.

A vein of true piety, however, pervades every missive, the whole being an evidence of the survival of superstition at that late day, strangely mingled with the observed facts of science, which, as a late writer states,[254] is one of the curiosities of spiritual development in all times.

This unique book is now in the possession of Mr. Charles J. Wistar, of Germantown. Well-founded traditions state that some years after Kelpius' death the book was given to Johannes Wüster, an ancestor of the present owner, either by Seelig or by Matthai; most probably the latter, as Wüster cared for the old recluse in his declining years.

The other book contains a number of hymns, written both in German and English, and in most cases the musical score of the melody is neatly written at the commencement of the hymn, showing that Kelpius was a practical musician as well as a poet and philosopher. This hymn-book is about 5 x 7½ inches in size, and is a specimen of Seelig's proficiency in the bookbinder's art. It was for many years in possession of the Warmer family of Germantown, and eventually passed successively into the hands of William W. Leibert, who gave it to A. H. Cassel, of Harleyville, Montgomery County, from whom it finally came into the collection of the Historical Society of Pennsylvania, where it has now found a permanent resting place.

This unique volume of seventy pages contains twelve hymns and melodies. It is evidently a duplicate of a similar manuscript collection, or else it is a compilation from loose sheets upon which were originally written such hymns as were in common use in the services at the Tabernacle. The hymns are written in German on the left hand pages, while on the opposite pages is an attempt at a metrical translation in English. The musical score as well as the hymns are all in the peculiar handwriting of Kelpius, and, like his diary, the book affords us an insight into his religious fervor.

---

[254] Francis Howard Williams.

Most of the hymns are written somewhat after the style of the celebrated Christian Knorr, Baron von Rosenroth,[255] whose name is quoted in connection with the melody of several of the compositions.

Kelpius became acquainted with Knorr during his sojourn at the university, and it is supposed that he first introduced the youthful student into the secrets of Cabbalistic philosophy.

The title, together with a specimen page of the Kelpius hymn book, in both German and English, is reproduced in *fac-simile.* An additional value is imparted to this quaint little book from the fact that it is evidently the first book of hymnology or German poetry and music that was composed and written in the western world. It is, however, just to state that Kelpius was not the only poet and composer among the original party of Theosophical emigrants; Köster, as well as the Falkner brothers, also composed hymns that have survived until the present time, as will be shown in a future chapter.

The English translations are mere paraphases, and fail to convey the full fervor and meaning of the German original.

---

[255] Christian Knorr, Baron v. Rosenroth, was born at Altrauden, in Silesia, July 15, 1636. After studying at the universities of Leipzig and Wittenberg, he made an extended tour through France, England and Holland. At Amsterdam he became acquainted with an Armenian prince; with the chief Rabbi, Meir Stern, from Frankfort; a M. Dr. John Lightfoot, Dr. Henry More, and others, and as a result devoted himself to the study of Oriental languages, of chemistry and of occult and Cabbalistic philosophy. He edited various Rabbinical writings, published several Cabbalistical works, notably his *Kabbala Denudata* (2 vols. Sulzbach, 1677). He, however, is chiefly known by his hymns, published in Nuremberg, 1684, under the title "*Neuer Helicon Mit Seiner Neun Musen; das its, Geistliche Sitten Lieder, &c.*" A number of these hymns were incorporated in the Halle Hymnal, 1704 (*Geistreicher Lieder*), since when they have been translated into different languages, and are now used by nearly all Protestant denominations throughout the world.

I. N. I
The Lamenting Voice
of the
Hidden Love,
at the time
When she lay in Misery & forsaken;
and oprest by the multitude
of Her Enemies
Composed by one
In Kumber.

Mich. VII 8. 9. 10

Rejoyce not against me O mine Enemy: when I fall, I shall arise; when I sit in darkness, the Lord shall be a light unto me. I will bear the indignation of the LORD, because I have sinned against him until he plead my cause, & execute judgment for me: he will bring me forth to the light, & I shall behold his righteousness. Then [illegible] She that is mine enemy shall see it, and shame shall cover her which said unto me, Where is the LORD thy God? mine eyes shall behold her: now shall she be trodden down as the mire of the streets.

Hester signifies Secret, or Hidden, & Haman, by multitude of troubles.

Pennsylvania in America 1705

N.B. That Cumber is, here above, spel'd with a K, & not with a C, has its peculiar Reason.

ENGLISH TITLE OF THE KELPIUS HYMN BOOK.

This applies to the titles as well as to the poetry. The titles are therefore given here in both languages:

The German title reads,—

"*I. N. I. || Die Kläglige Stimme || der || Verborgenen Liebe || zur zeit da Sie || Elend und Verlassen || darnieder lag || und von || Der Menge ihrer Feinde gedranget und geanchstiget || Wurde von einemn in Kummer Schwebenden. || Entworfen.*"

The titles of the hymns are as follows:

(1) "*Von der Wüsteneÿ der Jungfräulichen || Heimlichen Creutzes Liebe.*"

"*Parodie || Die Seele ging zu Nechst.*"

Musical score.

[Of the Wilderness || of the Secret or Private || Virgin Cross Love.]

It is divided into three parts, of 9, 23 and 21 stanzas respectively.

(2) Musical score.

"*Process || der in Tode grünenden || Liebe || Bey gelegenheit eines freundes, so mich hassen wolte.*"

An explanatory note states that "The first & third part may be sung on the following, & Ye Second and last part on Mel. page 1.

[The Process of Love || growing in Death || By occasion of a Friend that would hate me.]

This hymn is colloquial, and is in three parts and twenty-four stanzas, viz., part 1, "Johannes" 10 stanzas; part 2, "The Friend" 4 stanzas; part 3, "Johannes" 9. Both together, 1 stanza, viz.—

"Since then our friendship has in trying times stood even
The Lord increas it more & strengthen it from Heaven
So that it fear no Might nor Pow'r of Death to come,
But may Triumph above by God in Christ's Kingdom."

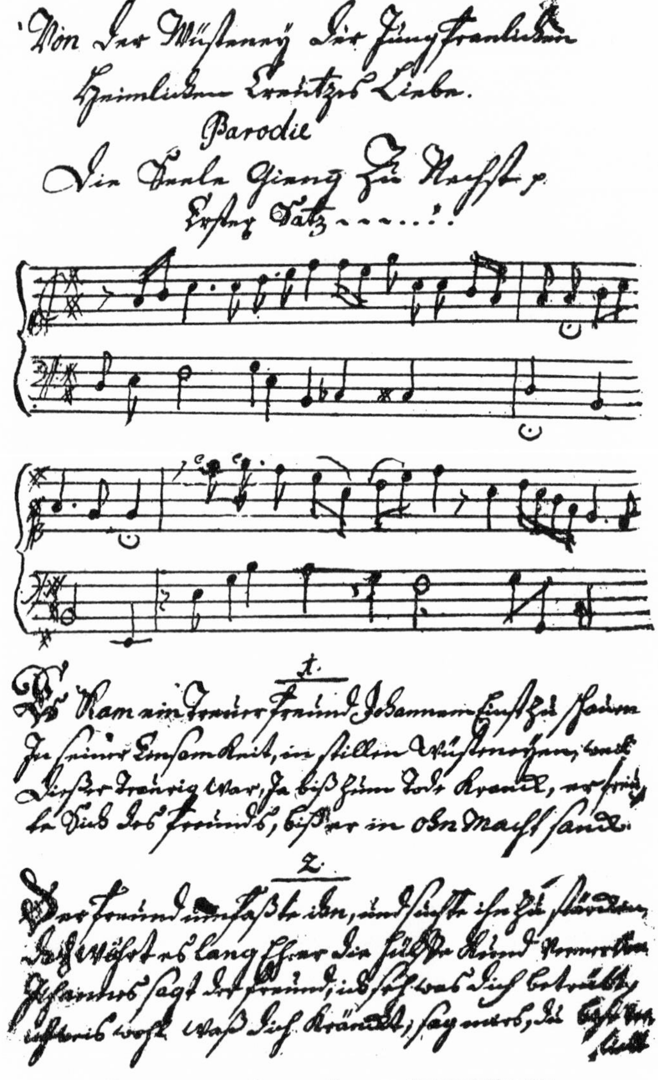

FAC-SIMILE OF A GERMAN PAGE OF KELPIUS' HYMNAL.

(3) "*Bitter Süsse Nachts Ode* || *der sterbenden* || *Todes sich vergnügenden* || *Liebe.* || *Bey der betrachtung dass ihr Creutz sey der Liebe Pfand* || *von der hand Sophia ihr zu gesandt.*"

"*Parodie Rosen:* || *34 Du hast o Seelenfreund:* || *p. 9.*"

[Bitter Sweet Night Ode || of the dying || But contented || Love || By the consideration that the cross is the Pledge of Love, sent to the Soul from Sophia.]

The hymn proper consists of 12 stanzas, at the close the composition assumes a dramatic form, the stanzas being rendered alternately by a "Speaking Voice" and "The Soul," the purpose being to introduce "Contradictions" and "Objections" and "Conclusions" after the manner of the theologians of the seventeenth century.

(4) Musical score.

"*Das Paradox*e *und Seltsam* || *Verguügen* || *der gottlich Verliebten.* || *In eine Antwort auf einen Brief so voller* || *Liebe, trost und Demuth.*"

Mel. "*O Gott du frommer Gott wie folget:*"

[The Paradox and Seldom || Contentment || of the God-loving Soul.]

This hymn contains twenty-one stanzas.

(5) "*Gespräch der Seelen mit* || *sich selbst* || *Uber ihren lang Wehrenden* || *Reinigung* || *Gestillet in Traurigen Verlangen* || *in der Wüsten* || *Anno 1698* || *30 Jan.*"

"*Parodie Rosenroth 18, Hier lieg ich gefangen.*"

Musical score.

[Colloquim of the Soul || with its self || Over her Long || during || Purification || Set in a pensive Longing || in the Wilderness || Anno 1698 Ye 30 Jan.]

This also contains a series of objections, queries and answers.

(6) "*Von der Ruhe || als ich mich einstens in der Wüsten bey || der Armuth so Müde gearbeitet 1697, Octob.*"

"*Im Thon: 'So wünch ich nun eine gute nacht: wie folget.'*"

Musical score.

[Upon Rest || As I once in the Wilderness, in Poverty || had made me weary with Labour || in October, 1697.]

(7) "*Von Den neuen Jungfraülichen || Kraft Leib || worinnen der Herr selbst wohnet || und seiner Geheimnisse offenbahret || wie solcher muste bestellet sein || Gestellet in Sehnlichen Verlangen || Anno 1699, Febr.*"

Melodie p. 17 (same as hymn No. 4.)

[Of the Power of the New || Virgin Body, || where in the Lord himself dwellest || and Revealeth his Mysteries: || How it is to be obtained, || Done in pensive longing, in Febr., 1699.]

The last seven stanzas of this hymn consists of a rythmical prayer.

(8) "*Die macht der Liebe || welche || der Welt der Sünde und dem Todt || Obsinget || in einen || Trauer Gedicht || entworfen || 1705 || N. B.*

"*N. B. Nach dem unterschiedlichen Sätzen kan auch || die Melodie verändert werden; wie folget.*

"*Erster Satz; Melod. 'Die Seele ging zu nächsten.'*

Musical score.

"*Zweiter satz; Mel. 'Du hast O Seele freund,' p. 9.*

"*Dritter satz; 'Die Seele ging, &c.'*

"*Vierter satz; Mel. 'Herr schone Mein.*"

---

[256] *Metemptosis.*—In chronology the solar equation necessary to prevent the new moon from happening a day too late, or the suppression of the bissextile once in 134 years; as opposed to *proemptosis.*

"*5, 6, 7, satz; Mel. 'Die Seele ging zu nachsten.'*

"*Achter satz (This part was to be spoken.)*

"*9 & 10; Mel. 'Die Seele ging &c.'*

"*Elfter satz; Mel. 'O! Gott du fromer Gott.'* [257]

"*Zwölfter satz (To the enlightened souls, yet in Ye first Love).*

"*Melodie || am Ende.*"

[The Power of Love || which conquers the World, Sin & Death || in a Pensive Poem || Composed || 1705.]

(9) "*Ein Verliebtes Girren der || Trostlosen Seele || In der Morgen Dämmerung || Oder von des Willen || auf una absteig || und still stehen.*"

Musical score.

[A Loving Moan || of the Disconsolate Soul || in the Morning Dawn || Or from the Will's Rising, falling & still-stand. || As I lay in Christian Warmer's House, very weak, in a small Bed, not unlike a Coffin, in May, 1706.]

Contents:

"The Soul does desire || To have Nuptial fruit || But as she rose hier || To soon in pursute || The Bridegroom slipt from her, & left her alone || She wish's to be perfect Re-signed, in Moan || So finds she then lastly that most blessed one || 25 stanzas."

(10) "*Trost und aufmnnterungs lied || Vor zwei einsamen Wittwen in sonderheit gestellet || Allheir aber zu gemeiner besten in etwas veränderet || bey gelegenheit einer grossen Verkältung, so || Mich überfallen || 1706 in Julius.*"

Musical score.

"*Mel: 'Was Gott thuet das ist wohlgethan.*"

---

[257] *Geistreicher Lieder*, hymn 303, p. 377, by J. Herman.

57.

A Loving Moan
of the Disconsolate Soul;
in the Morning Dawn
Or, from the Will's Rising, falling, & still stand.
As I lay in Christian Warmers House, very weak, in a small Bed, not unlike a Coffin. in May 1706.

Contents.

The. Soul does desire,
To have Nuptial fruit
But as she rose hier
To soon in pursute,
The Bridgroom slipt from her, & left her alone.
She wish's to be perfect Resigned, in moan,
So finds she then lastly that most blessed one . .

Here lye I submissive
And weak, in a shrine,
O'er come and made passive
With the sweetest pain.

I think

FAC-SIMILE OF A ENGLISH PAGE OF KELPIUS' HYMNAL.

(11) "*Der 121 Psalm David's* || *Tröstlich von einen an dem auser den 5 & 6* || *Gesetz entworfen.*"

[The 121 Psalm of David || comfortably paraphras'd.]

"*Mel.* '*Barmherziger treuer Gott.*' (Chriazo Rosenroth.)

Musical score.

Eight stanzas.

(12) "*Ich Liebe Jesum nur Allein.*"

[The best choice.]

Musical score, Mel.

A late magazine writer, in commenting upon this collection of raphsodical poems, states: "The judicious biographical student who brings to the consideration of the character of Kelpius an appreciative and unbiased mind, will find in these hymns evidence of undoubted sincerity, mingled with a spiritual exaltation bordering on fanaticism. There is little doubt that this lonely man, given to incessant contemplation and continually thrown in upon himself, came at last to regard his mental visions as a veritable new apocalypse; and the position of authority which he early attained,—the spiritual headship which his purity of life and great learning procured for him,—must have tended to fortify his belief in the semi-celestial character of his mission."

Johannes Kelpius was small of stature, slight in frame, and suffered from an affection or paralysis of the left eyelid. It is a curious coincidence that several of the noted religious leaders of the last century had some marked peculiarity about their eyes,—Kelpius, Beissel, Whitefield, Mühlenberg and others. In addition to the above infirmity, Kelpius was of a frail constitntion, which soon broke down under frugal fare and abstemious habits and the extremes of our variable climate.

A succession of heavy colds was the result, aggravated by the custom which Kelpius had of retiring to a cave in the hillside for study and contemplation.

This cave, sixteen feet long by nine feet wide and eight feet high,[258] as before stated, was not a natural formation, but was built for his uses.[259] It was about two hundred yards from the Tabernacle, near a cold spring of water, which to the present day is known as the Kelpius' Spring on the Wissahickon.

According to the Ephrata MSS., this cell or cave was known as the "Laurea," and was originally fitted up with much taste and ingenuity, containing, besides many books, curious utensils for chemical and philosophical purposes.

Finally the repeated colds turned into consumption, and in the winter of 1705–6 he became so feeble that his life was despaired of. It was then that he was removed to the humble home of the Warmer family in Germantown, where he was tenderly nursed by Christiana Warmer. How resigned the devout sufferer was during his illness is shown by the last three lines of the twenty-fifth stanza of his hymn,—

> "Therefore kiss, or correct, Come to me or Go,
> Give Presents, or take them : bring Joy, or bring Wo,
> If I can but have thee, thy will may be so." [260]

It was less than two months after his temporary recovery and return to the Tabernacle (May, 1706), that we again find him suffering from a relapse, having, as he himself writes, a "great cold."

---

[258] From actual measurement.

[259] See frontispiece.

[260] "*Drum Küsse und züchtige, komme und geh,*
Beschenke, entziehe, bring freude, bring weh,
Wann ich dich habe, dein wille gescheh."

[Christian Warmer, the tailor of Germantown, whose wife Christiana was the good Samaritan of the Theosophical enthusiasts, was also strongly imbued with the mystical teachings of Kelpius and his followers, and remained steadfast in his profession until his death, which occurred in the spring of 1728. His peculiar ideas of the future state are well set forth in his last will and testament:

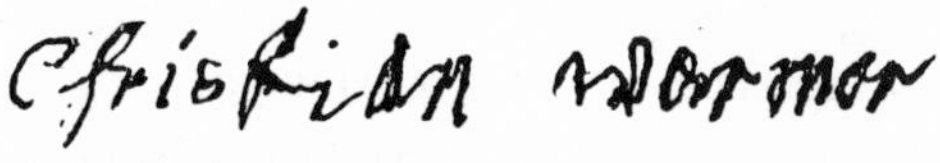

"In the Name of God amen. The 26 day of April in the year of our Lord 1728, I, Christian Warmer of Germantown in the County of Philada & province of Pennsylvania taylor, being of perfect mind and memory (for which I return hearty thanks to God my Heavenly Father) calling to mind the frailty of this Transitory life & that it is appointed for all men once to die Do Make & ordain this my last will & Testant that is to say First of all and Principally I Recomend my soul into the hands of Almighty God, my Heavenly Father who gave it to me & being in a fallen & Degenerate State, has again Espoused it a second time to himself, by & through the Death & sufferings of his Dearly beloved Son Jesus Christ, who has purchased it with his bitter & bloody passion, to be his spouse & bride, with whom I hope to live & Reign Eternally, and my body to the Earth to be buried in a Christian like & desent manner, at the Direction of my Execrs hereafter named, Nothing doubting but at the resurection of the Just through the merits of Jesus Christ, I shall receive the same again, by the mighty power of God, to live & be with my spirit & soul united into one Heavenly Creature with my beloved Saviour & Redeemer & to Reign with him forever & ever.—Amen."]

Thus Kelpius lingered and suffered, the disease gradually but surely gaining the ascendancy, notwithstanding Doctor Witt's "bolus" and the herb decoctions (*haus-mittel*) of the brethren, together with the tender attentions of neighbors and friends, who knelt beside him praying for his soul and watching his failing breath. He finally succumbed in the year 1708, at the early age of thirty-five.

His whole life had been a preparation to meet the heavenly bridegroom, "laying aside all other engagements whatever, trimming his lamp and adorning himself with that white silky holiness and golden righteousness that he might be found worthy."

Among the musty archives in the library of the Francke Institutions or Orphange at Halle, on the Saale, in Saxony, there is an old manuscript that gives a curious account of the death of Magister Kelpius. This paper is in the handwriting of Pastor Heinrich Melchior Mühlenberg, and sets forth that in the year of his arrival in Pennsylvania (1742) Daniel Geissler, a trustworthy man of over sixty years of age, and the former *famulus* and confidential assistant of Kelpius, gave to him the following interesting particulars of the death of the Magister:

"Kelpius among other things was of the firm belief that he would not die a natural death, and that his body would not decay, but that he would be transformed, transfigured, overshadowed and, like Elijah, be translated bodily into the spiritual world.

"As his last hours drew near and the forerunners of dissolution, the Magister spent three long days and nights in praying to God, struggling and supplicating that, in his case, the Lord Sabaoth would receive him bodily as he did Enoch and Elias of old, and that there might be no actual dissolution, but that body and soul might remain intact and be transfigured and received in the flesh.

"At last, on the third day, after a long silence he ceased his pleadings, and, addressing himself to his faithful *famulus*, said: 'My beloved Daniel, I am not to attain that which I aspired unto. I have received my answer. It is that dust I am, and to dust I am to return. It is ordained that I shall die like unto all children of Adam.'

"Kelpius thereupon handed Geissler a box or casket, which was well secured and sealed, and told him to carry it to the Schuylkill, where the water was deep, and cast it into the river. Geissler took the casket as far as the river bank, and being of somewhat an inquisitive nature, concluded to hide the casket until after his master's death, and then possess himself of the secret of its contents.

"Upon his return Kelpius raised himself up and, with outstretched hand, pointing to his *famulus*, looked him sharply in the eyes, and said: 'Daniel, thou hast not done as I bid thee, nor hast thou cast the casket into the river, but hast hidden it near the shore.' Geissler, now more than ever convinced of the occult powers of the dying Magister, without even stammering and excuse, hurried to the river bank, and threw the casket into the water as he was bidden."

The MS. goes on to state that as the mysterious casket touched the water the "Arcanum" exploded, and for a time flashes of lightning and peals like unto thunder came from out of the water.

When Geissler again returned to the bedside of Kelpius at the Tabernacle, the latter told him that now was accomplished the task he had given him. A few days after this episode the pious Magister entered into rest. All tradition seems to agree that his remains were consigned to a grave within the orchard or garden belonging to the Tabernacle over which he had so long and faithfully presided.

Such of the brethren as were left of the original Community performed the last rites according to the impressive ritual of the Mystic Fraternity.

It was shortly before sunset that the cortège with the

bier solemnly filed out of the Saal of the Tabernacle, the Mystics chanting a solemn "De Profundis," ranging themselves in a circle around the open grave. The coffin was then placed over the opening until the orb of day was far down in the west. As the last rays were seen, at a given signal from Seelig, who was now Magister, the body was lowered into the grave. At the same instant a snow-white dove was released from a hamper, and winged its flight heavenward; while the Brethern looking upward and with uplifted hands, repeated thrice the invocation: "*Gott gebe ihn eine seilige auferstehung.*" [God grant him a blessed resurrection.] [261]

The following eulogium, taken from the Ephrata MSS., is attributed to Prior Jaebetz (Rev. Peter Miller, the successor of Beissel). It was evidently written by a scholar, and one who had access to writings of Kelpius which are now unavailable. It shows the estimation in which the pious recluse on the Wissahickon was held during the last century.

"Kelpius educated in one of the most distinguished Universities of Europe, and having had advantage of the best resources for the acquirement of knowledge, was calculated to edify and enlighten those who resorted to him for information. He had particularily made great progress in the study of ancient lore, and was quite proficient in theology. He was intimately acquainted with the principal works of the Rabbins, the Heathen and Stoic philosophers, the Fathers of the Christian Church, and the Reformers. He was conversant with the writings of Tertullian, St.

[261] If this story of the dove is historical, it is a survival of high interest. Dion Cassius, in an impressive account of the funeral by the Emperor Pertinax, of which he was an eye-witness, tells us that an eagle was tied to the funeral pyre. When the flames burnt the rope, the eagle mounted to the clouds, as the soul of Pertinax to the Gods.

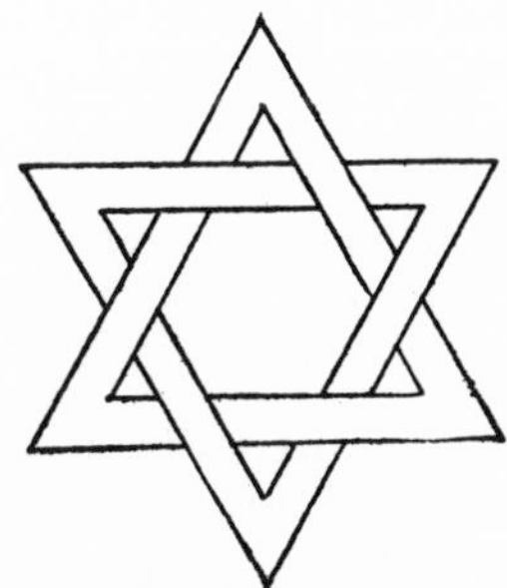

Jerome, St. Augustine, St. Cyprian, Chrysostom, Ambrose, Tauler, Eck, Myconius, Carlstadt, Hedio, Faber, Osiander, Luther, Zwingle and others, whose opinions he would frequently analyse and expound with much animation. He was also a strict disciplinarian, and kept attention constantly directed inwards upon self. To know self, he contended, is the first and most essential of all knowledge. Thales the Milesian, he maintained, was the author of the precept, 'Know thyself,' which was adopted by Chilo the Lacedomonican, and is one of the three inscriptions which, according to Pliny, was consecrated at Delphos by golden letters, and acquired the authority of a divine oracle; it was supposed to have been given by Apollo, of which opinion Cicero has left a record. (Cujus praecipiti *tauta* viz Delphico Deo tributor Cicero.) He directed a sedulous watchfulness over the temper, inclinations and passions, and applauded very much the Counsel of Marcus Aurelius: 'Look within; for within is the fountain of good.'"

Thus lived and died Johann Kelpius, the first Magister of the Theosophical Community on the Wissahickon, whose history is so filled with romance and mystery. Learned and devout, he sacrificed his life in the interests of humanity, and in preparing himself and his followers for the millennium which he believed was near at hand.

SEAL OF THE GERMAN SOCIETY OF PHILADELPHIA.

No other of the early settlers has ever attracted the attention of students of Pennsylvanian history, or excited so much speculation, as this meek and gentle Transylvanian philosopher. Although his last resting-place is unmarked, and known only from vague tradition, his memory has nevertheless been kept green in song and prose. The most notable instance of the former is Whittier's "Pennsylvania Pilgrim," and such parts of it as allude to the subject of our sketch will prove a fitting close to this chapter:

Or painful Kelpius from his hermit den
By Wissahickon, maddest of good men,
Dreamed o'er the Chiliast dreams of Petersen.

Deep in the woods, where the small river slid
Snake-like in shade, the Helmstadt Mystic hid,
Weird as a wizard over arts forbid,

Reading the books of Daniel and of John,
And Behmen's Morning-Redness, through the Stone
Of Wisdom, vouchsafed to his eyes alone,

Whereby he read what man ne'er read before,
And saw the visions man shall see no more,
Till the great angel, striding sea and shore,

Shall bid all flesh await, on land or ships,
The warning trump of the Apocalypse,
Shattering the heavens before the dread eclipse.

HENRICH BERNHARD KÖSTER.

ARMS OF CHUR-BRANDENBURG, 1694.

OF all the characters connected with the Theosophical experiment in the New World none stands out in bolder relief than Henrich Bernhard Köster, one of the original promoters of the enterprise. To the comparative few who thus far knew his name, he is in fact the most heroic figure in the history of the German Pietists of Pennsylvania. Pious, devout, learned, courageous and combative, he not only boldly proclaimed to the settlers of the young province the Gospel according to the orthodox Lutheran faith, but was ever ready to take up the gauntlet when thrown before him. Nor did he hesitate for an instant to follow his opponents into their strongholds, and in their very midst to fearlessly proclaim his convictions, fortifying them with quotations from the Scriptures.

Nation or race made no difference to this devout enthusiast. Casting aside for the time his mystical doctrines and

Rosicrucian speculations, he preached the plain Gospel with untiring energy and zeal among both English, Welsh and Germans.

The seed sown by him at Germantown at the humble home of Isaac Van Bebber, upon that natal day of the holy St. John in 1694, struck root, grew and spread until its influence permeated the whole Province. Upon that day began the movement which was to lead the settlers from the apathy into which they had sunken back to vital religion and established church forms.

It is true that Swedish Lutheran services were held in Pennsylvania for almost half a century prior to Penn's coming, and for some years afterwards. But these were held only for the Swedes. No effort whatever was made either by Fabricius or Lock to extend the faith among the Quakers and Germans who were flocking to these shores.[262]

---

[262] The following documents have come to light since writing the notices of this clergyman in two previous chapters of this book (notes 32 and 99). The first is a letter from Governor Francis Lovelace of New York, and explains itself,—

"FORT JAMES in NEW YORK this 13th day of Ap' 1670.

"CAPT CARR.

"Upon the request of Magister Jacobus Fabritius Pastor of the Lutheran Confession comonly called the Augustan who by the Duke's Lycence hath a Congregation here, I have granted my Pass to him, & his Wife to go to Newcastle or any Place in Delâware River, I pray shew him all Civil Respect when he comes amongst you, & take care he receive no Affront there, & I presume he will comport himself wth gt Civility & Moderacon so as to give no just occasion of offence to others. I am

"Your very loving Friend,

"FRANCIS LOVELACE."

The other document, an extract from the proceedings of the Council, gives us an insight into the subsequent private life and behavior of this clergyman :—

"Att a Councel September 15th 1675.

"Magister Jacobus Fabricius being Ordered by Special Warrt to make his personal Appearance before the Governor here ; to Answer to a Com-

It was left to Köster to take the initiative, and boldly raise his voice immediately upon his arrival among both Germans and English, and to institute services intended to induce the settlers to renew their fealty to orthodox religion; no matter whether to the English Church as by law established or to the faith of the Fatherland.

It is from the advent of the German Pietists in 1694 that we must date the religious revival in the Province. The results of Köster's efforts were widespread: they were not confined to Anglicans and Lutherans, but also stimulated the Baptists, Presbyterians and so-called Sabbatarians to organize in Pennsylvania. Finally, when, after a sojourn of seven years in the Province, the German philosopher became convinced that, on account of the changed religious situation, his usefulness as an evangelist was at an end, he returned to his native country, and resumed his Theosophical studies. He lived to a ripe old age, almost rounding out a century, and died in an institution connected with the Lutheran Church.

Unfortunately our estimates of the character and services of this pioneer have hitherto been based upon the accounts of his religious or personal antagonists, or of such as were ignorant of the true motives that inspired him, and the facts that guided him in his course in America. It is hoped that the matter now presented will place this devout enthusiast in a new light, and give him his proper position among the religious leaders of Provincial Pennsylvania.

Henrich Bernhard Köster (Küster or Köster, as he was

---

plaint made against him by the High Sheriff and Court at Newcastle in Delaware, for causing a Disturbance and Uproar against the Magistrates.

"It is Ordered that the said Magister Fabricius, in Regard of his being Guilty of what is lay'd to his Charge and his former irregular Life and Conversation, be Suspended from Exercising his Function as a Minister, or Preaching any more within the Governmt either in Publick or Private."

generally known in America), was born in November, 1662, in the little town of Blumenberg, in the Principality of Lippe, in Westphalia. His parents were Ludolph Küster, Burgomaster and leading merchant of his native district, and Frau Anna Catherina Blumen von Schwalenberg, a sister of Simon Heinrich Blumen, privy-councellor of Detmold. The Burgomaster was not a man of classical education, but he was endowed with good sense.

The subject of this sketch was the eldest of three brothers who composed the Küster family, and all upon attaining their majority became men of note. Ludolph, the noted literary critic and linguist, was born in 1667, eventually entered the Roman Church, and became the superintendent of the Royal Library in Paris, where he procured the collation of the famous Ephrem Palimpsest.[263]

The youngest brother, Johann, also became a leading citizen in his native district. It was his son, Ludolph, who studied law, and afterwards became noted as the bailiff (*Amtmann*) to the Countess of Schaak at Ingenhausen.

Young Henrich received the rudiments of instruction in the common schools of Blumenberg, where he was taught by Pastor Vogelsang. When the latter was called to Detmold as assistant rector, his student accompanied him, and remained four years under his instruction, perfecting himself in Latin, Hebrew and Greek, beside his other studies.

At the age of fifteen he went to Bremen with the express intention of studying law and philosophy at the Gymnasium of that city. He, however, devoted himself mainly

[263] It was the intention of the parents that young Ludolph should become a merchant and succeed his father. He, however, showed so great a proclivity for books and learning that his elder brother commenced to lead him into classical studies, continuing his supervision over him, even when the latter attended school in Berlin.

to the study of the philosophy of Descartes,[264] and attended the lectures of Schwelings.

After a sojourn there of five years he went to Frankfort on the Oder, where he studied law for three years, leaving the University in 1684, and ending his academic days at the age of twenty-two. Köster had a natural inclination to teach or impart knowledge, and at once started upon a career as tutor. He made his *début* as pedagogue at Küsterin, in the family of Aulic-councillor Polemius, where he remained about a year.

In his curriculum he abandoned the old methods of instruction then in vogue, whereby the minds of the scholars were strained, but attempted rather to interest his pupils by rational discourses, delivered in an agreeable and impressive manner.

This system of instruction became known to Pfarrer Stos, a Berlin divine, who in turn brought it to the notice of the Brandenburger privy-councillor, Baron Orten von Schwerin. The councillor was so much pleased with the new method that he asked Köster to instruct in this manner his three sons, Carl, Friedrich and Orten. A satisfactory agreement having been arrived at, Köster came to Berlin and was installed as resident tutor. This was in the year 1685; he remained in charge for seven years, dividing his time between the estates of his patron in Berlin and Landsberg.

The father of the Baron of Schwerin was a consistent Lutheran, and was greatly grieved at the course of his son in affiliating with the Reformed Church. Every induce-

[264] René Descartes (Kartesius), a celebrated French philosopher, born 1596. Died at Stockholm, February 11, 1650. He advanced far beyond his predecessors, and if he had done nothing besides introducing a spirit of inquiry into the mysterious operations of nature, he would have labored much for the benefit of mankind.

ment was offered to the son to adhere to the faith of his fathers, but even the promise of an increased patrimony failed to alter the course of the Baron. During this controversy between father and son, the former had greatly increased his library, mainly with orthodox standard and controversial theological literature.

To this collection the young tutor had free access, and there came upon the famous English Polyglot,[265] a work that interested him above all others. He now improved his opportunity to perfect himself in Greek and Hebrew, and although jurisprudence had thus far been his specialty, he at once commenced to study such of the Eastern languages as were used in the polyglot translation.

He even went so far as to interest his patron by calling his attention to the preface of Brian Walton,[266] showing him

---

[265] This work, one of the "four great Polyglots," is usually known as the London or Walton's Polyglot, from the fact that it was published in that capital under the editorship of Brian Walton. This great work was completed in the midst of persecution and civil war. It consists of six volumes, folio, with two supplementary volumes (London, 1654–57), exhibiting the text in nine different languages: Hebrew, Syriac, Chaldee, Samaritan, Arabic, Æthiopic, Persian, Greek and Latin. The whole is based upon the Paris Polyglot (Le Jay, 1645), with many additions and improvements. A copy of this work was brought to America by Köster, and formed a part of the library of the Community, where it remained when he returned to Europe. Subsequently it came into the possession of the Sprogel brothers, and is now in the library of Christ Church in Philadelphia.

[266] Brian Walton was born in Cleveland, Yorkshire, in 1600, and was educated at Cambridge, where he took the degree of Master of Arts in 1623. During the Civil War he sided with the King, and was consequently obliged to take shelter at Oxford, where he formed the scheme for his polyglot Bible. Doctor Walton had several assistants in his laborious undertaking, of whom the principal was Dr. Edmund Castell. On the restoration of Charles II, to whom he presented his Bible, with a new dedication (the original one to Oliver Cromwell having been cancelled), he was made one of the royal chaplains; and in 1660 he was raised to the Bishopric of Chester. He died in London, 1661.

how the Briton proved conclusively that the accepted Hebrew text of the Old Testament had been tampered with, and that the Septuagint translation had been made before the interpolations were added, and it therefore contained the veritable Divine Word of the Old Dispensation.[267]

These representations induced Baron von Schwerin to examine the polyglot and read the introduction by Walton. He, too, became of the opinion of his tutor that the deductions of the Briton seemed feasible. He thereupon concluded to refresh his knowledge of Greek, and make a translation of the Septuagint into the German tongue. So patron and tutor studied Greek together, and translated the Old Testament from the Septuagint into German. They began with the Psalms, proceeded with the Pentateuch of Moses and so on, until the whole had been translated and corrected.

After the work was completed, it was finely engrossed upon quarto sheets, illuminated and bound up into several volumes. This monumental work is still preserved in the archives of the Schwerin family.

It is an easy matter to see how close the intercourse and friendship became between the two men, separated as they were by their social positions, and what favors the tutor could have asked, if he had been so disposed, from a patron who had so great an influence with the reigning House of Brandenburg. Indeed more than once was the tutor offered a suitable provision. His reply was, when offered a lucrative appointment under the former prince, "I am a Lutheran, and therefore must not serve a Reformed master, or go to a court where there are so many opportunities for sin."

---

[267] Besides the Latin of the Vulgate there is an interlineary Latin translation of the Hebrew. Though nine languages are used, yet no one book appears in so many. *Vide*, note 265.

It was while at Berlin that Köster became interested in the Pietistic movement, which had taken root and was spreading over northern Germany. Joining a local *Collegium Pietatis*, he became acquainted with Horbius, and through him with John Jacob Zimmermann. When, finally, the movement fell under the bans of both church and state, and it was decided to form a Chapter of Perfection to emigrate to the new World, we find Köster actively seconding Zimmermann in his efforts to secure transportation for the party, and concessions from Penn's representatives in Holland.

After the issuing of the various edicts, the suppression of the *Collegium* at Erfurth, and the expulsion of Francke, it was decided to establish two central rallying-points prior to the final embarkation at Rotterdam. Magdeburg, on the Elbe, in Saxony, and Halberstadt, were the two places selected on account of their accessibility and freedom from judicial interference.

Arms of Rotterdam.

Köster journeyed from Berlin to the former place, and there joined Seelig, Kelp, Biedermann, Falkner, and about twenty others. This contingent elected Köster as their leader, and when the time arrived, started, as was then the custom, on foot, staff in hand, and knapsack on back, upon their pilgrimage to America by way of Holland. Here the two parties were united, and the final preparations were made to embark for the province of Penn, under the auspices of Benjamin Furly.

Arms of Magdeburg.

The success in obtaining transportation for so large a party was mainly due to the efforts of Köster. It appears that Benjamin Furly and Ludolph Köster, then living at Amsterdam,[268] were intimately acquainted; and it was mainly through the intercession of the Köster brothers that the experiment was made possible. How on the eve of embarkation, the chief promoter, Magister Zimmermann, died, and Kelpius was chosen in his place, together with the eventful voyage on the "Sara Maria" has all been fully told in previous chapters.

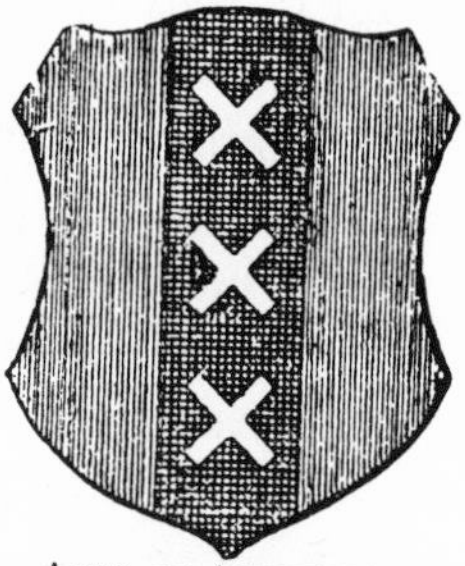

ARMS OF AMSTERDAM.

The Rev. Ernest Ludwig Rathelf, pastor of Langenhausen, near Hanover, was a close friend of Köster after his return to Europe. In referring to the period we are now concerned with, Rathelf, under whose charge Köster was then living at the Hanover Orphanage, states: "Our Herr Köster is a Lutheran, and has always adhered strictly to the dogmas and teachings of his church; carefully investigated them, and held fast unto them. In his youth he was taught the two sacred languages, and he was thus able to read God's holy Word in their original tongues and purity. In his study of jurisprudence, he never neglected an opportunity to obtain a clear insight into theology."

While in the employment of the Baron of Schwerin, the finding of the polyglot not only urged him to perfect himself in the two languages, but also to learn to speak and read other tongues, and to inquire further into spiritual philosophy.

Köster was endowed with a remarkable memory, without which no linguist can succeed. His mind retained

---

[268] Memoirs of Zacharias von Uffenbach.

everything which was entrusted to it, and the matter could be recalled with ease and rapidity. He could repeat *verbatim*, in Hebrew and Greek, all the Psalms, the whole of Isaiah, and other books of the Old Testament. He was equally felicitous in his knowledge of the New Testament. It was far easier for him to recall any quotation from the Bible than to find it in a concordance. This peculiar property of his mind enabled him to repeat to others his spiritual deductions, and to defend himself in controversy.

The society with which he went to America therefore elected him as their general instructor; and he acceded to their wishes. He frequently spoke to his fellow-passengers about spiritual matters, and when Sunday came he preached to them a regular sermon, wherein he especially exhorted them to remain steadfast to the Lutheran Church. Several of his company were somewhat clouded, and seemed deficient in holiness, and in certain articles of the faith. Moreover, he foresaw trouble when these persons would come to a country where they might be led astray by the Quaker doctrine. He therefore devoted all his energies to lead the erring ones aright, and fortify them against all such temptation. What he had done on shipboard he continued in Germantown, where there was a lack of spiritual teachers. As previously stated, Köster did not confine his ministrations to the German-speaking population, but also went among the English, preaching both in Germantown and Philadelphia, as soon as he learned that his English hearers were sincere in their search after spiritual enlightment.

Rathelf mentions that George Keith took passage for Europe about the same time that Köster sailed for America, and that the former left many followers behind him, who now wandered about like unto sheep without a herdsman. When Köster arrived he knew nothing about, or the peculiar schism that had been fomented among the Quakers.

But when he learned of the situation, he at once began to instruct his people and friends upon Sunday and other days, and to impress upon his hearers such doctrines as the Quakers failed in.

The Keithians soon found this out, and when they heard that he preached to the multitudes of the Saviour's death, His merits, His ascension, the use of the Scriptures and of the ordinances they flocked in crowds to listen to his sermons.

It was these Keithians whom Köster, not knowing them at first, took for enemies. But he soon learned to know both them and their sentiments, and led them straightway from the ways of the Quakers. The large number of Bibles and prayer-books [269] which he received from England were a material aid to him, as they were scarce among the Keithians.

The Friends naturally made every effort to heal the old schism, and induce the seceders to return. But the regular Church services organized by Köster, and the Orthodox Lutheran doctrine preached by him, considerably changed the situation. It inspired new hope and courage in the Keithians, and they even went so far as to again enter the meetings, and boldly refute some of the Quaker tenets.

The teachings of Henrich Bernhard Köster, however, had even a more extended effect upon the religious situation of the Province, for they increased among the English and Welsh, a longing for regular services according to the ritual of the English Church. This was the case not only in the hearts and minds of the followers of Keith, but

---

[269] This incident has already been noticed at length on page 68 of this work. There can be no question whatever that Köster used the Book of Common Prayer in his English services, as did the Swedish pastors, Rudmann, Sandel and others under similar circumstances.

also in others who had been brought up in the Church prior to becoming followers of Fox and Penn. This longing for church services as by law established took shape under the guidance of Köster, and within eighteen months after his arrival in the Province (November 15, 1695), a piece of ground was secured in the city of Philadelphia for church purposes, subject to an agreement between Griffith Jones and Joshua Carpenter.

This lot, upon which Christ Church now stands, contained one hundred feet fronting on Second Street, and one hundred and thirty-two feet in depth.[270]

The pecuniary consideration was a yearly rental of "tenne pounds of curant silver money of ye Province." This ground rent could be extinguished for £150 at any time within fifteen years. There was nothing whatever stated in the indenture to show or prove that the ground was secured for church or burial purposes.[271]

---

[270] A strip of land of forty feet on Second Street north of this lot was eventually purchased, making the total frontage of the Church property 140 feet.

[271] It will be noticed that the conveyance, although dated on November 5, 1695–6, was not consummated until four months later, March 5, 1695–6. There is not a single word in the indenture to indicate that the ground was to be held for any specific purpose. Upon the face it is a conveyance in fee-simple from Griffith Jones to Joshua Carpenter, subject to the above-mentioned ground-rent, which, had it not been extinguished within the limit of fifteen years, would have become an irredeemable incumbrance. It was extinguished by a deed made April 4, 1702, and acknowledged in open court in a Court of Common Pleas, June 4, 1702. (Deed not on record.)

On the 20th of July following, Joshua Carpenter signed a declaration which set forth the uses for which this ground was originally intended. After reciting the original deed and its extinguishment, it sets forth:

"*To all Christian People to whom these presents shall come:*

"And Whereas, fifty pounds part of the consideration money was the proper monys belonging to the comunity of the church and the other

The witnesses to this historic document were Samuel Holt, James Trewalla, Jeremiah Price and J[ohn] Moore. It was acknowledged in open court on the 5th day of March, 1695–6, and has never been placed upon record.

This attempt to establish the Church of England in the very stronghold of Quakerdom naturally added fuel to the flame of religious excitement in the Province, and increased the bitter feeling which the Quaker leaders bore against the German religious enthusiast. So great became the hatred of the Friends and others against the Lutherans, on account of Köster's successful efforts in establishing the congregation, that when William Davis, in one of his numerous disputes with the Orthodox Friends, suggested the appointment of a Swedish pastor as referee, the request

---

hundred pounds residue thereof was advanced and taken upon interest by the said Joshua Carpenter for the use of the said church and the said Joshua Carpenter's name from time to time used only in trust the said piece of ground being always designed to be appropriated for a Church and Cemetary and the buildings and other improvements being compleated with the stock and joint charge of the members thereof:

"NOW know Ye that the said Joshua Carpenter doth hereby acknowledge and declare that his name was used in the aforesaid deeds by the speciall nomination and appointment of the community of the said Church and for their use and benefitt and the Sd part of the lott of land is intended for a Cemetery or Church-yard and the Church and other premises are to be perpetually appropriated and used for the publick worship of God and for the better instruction of the people inhabiting and to inhabit in Philadelphia aforesaid in the true Christian religion as it is now professed in the Church of England and established by the laws of the said Realm and to no other use or uses whatsoever the Wardens for the time being paying interest to the Sd Joshua Carpenter his executors administrators or Assigns from time to time for the sum of one hundred pounds till the principall mony shall be paid in out of the publick stock.

"In witness whereof the said Joshua Carpenter hath hereunto sett his hand and seal this twentieth day of July 1702."

The witnesses to the Indenture were Jonathan Dickinson, Charles Plumly, John White, and John Moore.

The document is not upon record.

was refused, with the remark that the Lutherans were as "bad as Indians or Heathens.[272] Köster, however, was not to be diverted from his course; and in the absence of any English clergyman held services according to the Book of Common Prayer, whenever a suitable room was to be obtained.

In referring to this movement he states:—"Here, then, there is an opening for a great harvest, which the Lord opens for us wider and wider, giving us strength to make his Philadelphiac Word a foundation on which Jerusalem can descend from above."

This feeling against the Lutherans, upon the part of the Quakers, was not a new thing, but dates back to some time prior to the arrival of the German Pietists. It arose in this manner. One Charles Christopher Springer, a Swedish schoolmaster at Wicacoa, who, as the old record states, was "a plain, honest, pious man, but devoid of talents,"[273] made a determined effort, after the incapacity and death of Fabritius, to maintain some show of church services among his countrymen, until a regular pastor should arrive from Sweden in response to their repeated petitions.

These services were strictly according to the Lutheran doctrine, the sermon always being read from Luther's "Postilla." It appears that they attracted the notice of the Welsh beyond the Schuylkill river, and the Quakers, fearing that this might alienate the former from their fold, attempted to prevent both the Welsh and the Swedes from crossing the Schuylkill on Sundays, so that they could not attend the services.

---

[272] "Jesus the Crucifyed man," p. 18.

[273] As a matter of fact Springer appears to have been a man of thorough education, as he was an attaché of the Swedish minister in England, whence he was abducted and carried off to Virginia, where he was sold into bondage. After serving as a slave for five years he made his escape, and found a home with those of his own nationality on the Delaware.

This action upon the part of the local authorities was met by a protest and petition from the Swedes to Gov. Benjamin Fletcher of New York, as soon as the news came of his appointment to the governorship of Pennsylvania under the Crown.

This petition was read before the Provincial Council on May 11, 1693, his Excellency Gov. Fletcher presiding. In this paper "they sett forth that their meeting house is on the other side the river: that they live three miles distant from the ferry, and that they are restrained from passing the river the nearest way to their worship on Sundays & Holydays by Philip England, keeper of the ferry att Schuilkill."[274]

Governor Fletcher, as the minutes of the Council state, "did offer his Inclinations to remove any obstruction that might be given to the worship of God, and his regard to the Interest of the proprietarie in the ferry, desiring the Councill's advice."

The members of the Council present at the meeting—Andrew Robeson, Robert Turner, Pat. Robinson, Lawrence Cock, Wm. Clarke—gave as their opinion, "That the petitioners may have Libertie granted them to transport themselves over the river to & from their worship, provided they doe not abuse this Libertie to other ends, to the prejudice of the ferry."

Köster's course of action, together with the opposition of the Quaker leaders, made many enemies for him among his countrymen as well as among the English, and culmi-

---

[274] Philip England established the first regular ferry across the Schuylkill. He held his license under the hand and seal of William Penn, dated the 16th of 8ber, 1683. This grant was confirmed by order of Gov. Fletcher, dated the 29th of April, 1694, and further by a lease from the Lieut. Governor, in behalf of the Proprietor, for a certain term of years at an annual rental of seven pounds.

nated in a disagreement with his fellow-mystics on the Wissahickon, and his retirement with a few others from the Community in the forest.

How he attempted to start a somewhat similar Community in Plymouth, under the name of "the Brethern in America" or "the True Church in Philadelphia," has been fully detailed in a former chapter.[275]

Pastorius, in his so-called "Rebuke," refering to Köster and his followers (1697), writes:—"They stile themselves the Brethern in America, the True Church of Philadelphia or Brotherly Love, etc.

"This sounds mightly afar off, and some silly Women in Germany, who may happen to see their pamphlet, which probably for that end and purpose was printed in the *high Dutch tongue*,[276] besides the English will be ready to think this Church or Brotherhood something real and considerable. But to undeceive those, who prefer Truth before fictions and falsehood, I herewith must inform them that all these specious Names and Epithets in the pages above quoted, and more others, are mere Kosterian Chimera, an idle fancy. He, the said H. B. Koster, arriving here in Pensilvania, his heart and head filled with Whimsical and boisterous Imaginations, but his hands and Purse emptied of the money, which our Friends beyond Sea imparted unto him, and some in his Company, was so cunning as to intice four or five to a Commonalty of Goods, and so settled a Plantation near German-town, upon a tract of Land given unto them, calling the same IRENIA; that is to say, the house of Peace, which not long after became ERINNIA, the House of raging Contention, and now returned to the donor, the Bretheren of America being gone

[275] Page 84–92, *ibid.*

[276] This was the first book printed in the German language in America.

and dispersed, and the Church of Philadelphia (falsly so called) proving momentary, and of no moment; Mark iii, 25."

Among the men whose enemity Köster evoked was the above-named Daniel Francis Pastorius of Germantown. The controversy thus engendered between the two leaders became very bitter, and was aggravated still more by the occurrences of the following year.

The breach between the Orthodox Friends and the Keithians gradually widened toward the time of Yearly Meeting; but the tact of the Friends prevented the seceders from making themselves heard or disturbing their annual gathering. In the next year (1696), however, when the meeting was to be held at Burlington, New Jersey, some of the more aggressive among the Keithians devised a scheme to make themselves heard. There were six in the party, among whom were Thomas Rutter, Thomas Bowyer, and William Davis.[277] As the time approached they called on Köster, and invited him to accompany them, but without unfolding their plan of action. They merely told him that, as Burlington was in West Jersey and was a Protestant town and not under Quaker supremacy, they could there refute the Quakers assembled without fear of arrest as disturbers of public worship.

According to Köster's account, the Keithian party, on the 23d day of September, 1696, took their English Bibles, and another book with which they expected to refute the Quakers, and journeyed to Burlington.

Arriving at the place where the Yearly Meeting was being held, they found the gathering anything but a peaceful one. Even as they were attempting to enter, they were met by a number of Friends who were in the act of expell-

[277] For sketch of William Davis see page 164.

ing from the building an old Keithian, a Scotchman by the name of George Hutchison.[278] The latter then told the party that the meeting had refused to hear him, and as he had presisted, had finally expelled him.

Davis and Rutter now unfolded their plan to Köster, requesting him to act as spokesman. This he refused, stating that the Quakers would accord to him the same treatment as to the luckless Scotchman, and that if they did, he would not submit so tamely.

The Keithians, however, called his attention to a sentence in a book by Edward Burrough, wherein he states that according to the rules of discipline, any one, when moved by the Spirit, can go into a meeting and refute the speaker.

Four contemporaneous accounts of what followed have come down to us. The first is in Köster's own printed narrative of what took place. The others are: the MSS. of Phineas Pemberton, who was present; the epistle sent by the meeting to the governing body of London; and an entry in the minutes of the ministering Friends. They all agree in the salient points.

Köster's narrative is perhaps the most reliable, on account of his extraordinary memory. But as a matter of history, Pemberton's account is also printed, thus presenting both sides of this controversy, the effects of which proved so widespread and portentous.

Köster, in his account, states that as he still hesitated to enter the meeting, the Keithians asked him how they could best controvert the doctrine of a spiritual Christ. He answered that they must take a clear and convincing verse from the Scriptures. While he was speaking he recalled

---

[278] George Hutchison (also spelled Hutcheson and Hutchinson) died in 1698, and on the ninth of the third month was buried in the Friends' ground at Fourth and Arch Streets.—*Friends' Records.*

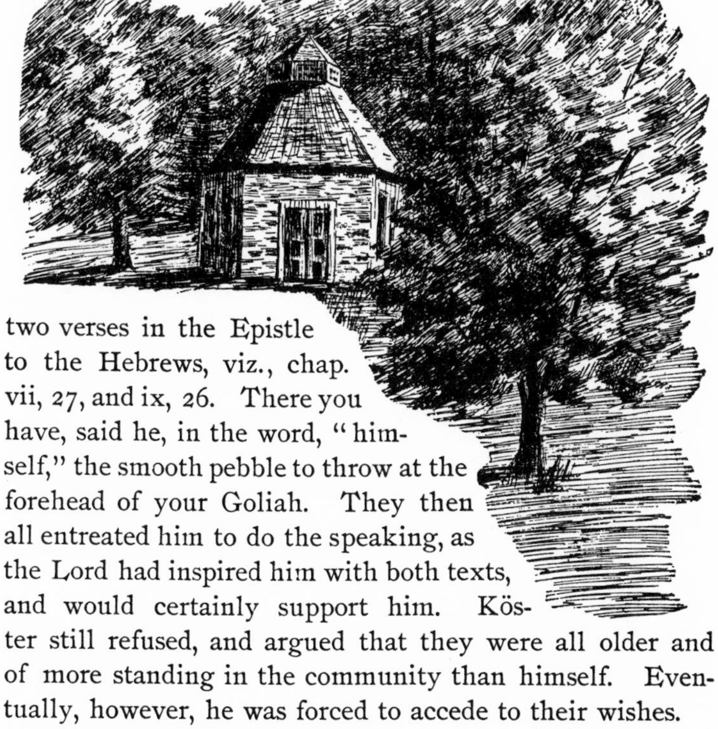

two verses in the Epistle to the Hebrews, viz., chap. vii, 27, and ix, 26. There you have, said he, in the word, "himself," the smooth pebble to throw at the forehead of your Goliah. They then all entreated him to do the speaking, as the Lord had inspired him with both texts, and would certainly support him. Köster still refused, and argued that they were all older and of more standing in the community than himself. Eventually, however, he was forced to accede to their wishes.

So they went into the building and mingled with the people. The meeting, continues Köster, was almost 4000 strong,[279] and about thirty Quaker preachers were upon the raised benches.

---

[279] This must be an error. The old meeting-house at Burlington, built in 1683, was a haxagonal structure, or, as the original draft in the Friends' records state, "a six square building of Forty feet square from out to out," for which Francis Collings, the builder, received £190. A brick addition of 30 feet was subsequently (1696) added to this structure, but under no circumstances could a building of this size have held anything like that number of people. A sketch of this old meeting-house, the scene of the Köster episode, is here reproduced; it is copied from an original painting which is still extant.

The six Keithians stood around him, so that the people could not crowd on him when he began to speak. Their plan was first to read a quotation from the Quaker book, and then ask three times for an audience. Then the German was to make the address.

It was the custom at the Yearly Meetings for the Friends to preach in succession. A number had already spoken; and as one ceased, before another could commence, one of the six Keithians (William Davis) addressed the meeting thus: "We beg of you, Friends, that you will permit us to edify you from the Scriptures." The Quaker, however, whose turn it was to speak continued to talk. As he finished, the Keithian again raised his voice: "We beg of you, Friends, once again that we may edify you with some quotations from the Scriptures." Again the request was ignored, and the next Friend in turn commenced his address. He was not interrupted, but when he had done they immediately arose once more, and said: "We beg of you, Friends, for the third and last time that you may hearken unto us. If you heed us not, we will make ourselves heard." The Friends, however, paid no attention to the request, and the speaker next in order commenced to preach. Then one of the six Keithians stood upon a bench, and read in a clear voice the words from the Quaker discipline: that, according to their own laws, they were bound to listen unto them.

Hereupon Köster stepped out, and began to speak. The Friend who was preaching had a weak voice; Köster, on the contrary, had a strong and penetrating one, which he now exercised to its fullest extent.

The volume of sound from the robust German completely drowned the weak voice of the Public Friend, who was forced to desist. Immediately all the preachers in the gallery stood up, and thereby thought to silence the fearless Teuton, but he was not to be frightened. His address opened with this introduction: "We have begged you thrice for a hearing, and did not wish to interrupt any speakers. But as you would not have it otherwise, so now we shall make ourselves heard.

"I raise my voice against you in the full conviction of the Word of God, to refute from the Holy Scriptures your blasphemous doctrine, which is worse than that of the heathen of America, namely the doctrine of your spiritual Jesus, and that whatever was human in Jesus was dispersed among the clouds during his ascension into Heaven." He thereupon called their attention to the two quotations from the Epistle to the Hebrews: "For this he did once for all when he offered up himself" (vii, 27); and, "now once at the end of the ages hath he been manifested to put away sin by the sacrifice of himself," (ix, 26). Köster pointed out to them that He who made the offering and the sacrifice was the entire Jesus; that the Diety could not have become a sacrifice without humanity; and that since this Jesus has once offered Himself, therefore His humanity must be imperishable.

This testimony lasted about half an hour. Finally he closed with these words: "Now to-day has the light of the Scriptures appeared in the second American darkness, and its strength you shall learn, not only here in Burlington, but in all the Colonies. I stand prepared to give you an account either in writing or orally of my words, and you shall learn that you must flee before these two quotations of Scripture."

With these words as a parting admonition, Köster with his party left the meeting. The Friends immediately spread the report that a number of lunatics had come to the meeting, and had jabbered much that no one could understand. This proceeding induced the Keithians to ask Köster to furnish an account of the affair, which he did and it was printed with his consent.

The full title of this curious work is: "History of the "Protestation, done in the publick yearly meating of the "Quakers at Burlingtown in the year 1696, by the witness "of two remarkable passages, Hebr. vii. 27, and viiii. 26, "aginst the false doctrine of the Quakers, whereby they "revile the blessed human nature of Iesus Christ and its suf- "fering, resurrection, ascension, rule over the church and his "coming again and the doctrine of the holy sacraments, "depending thereupon. Printed and sold by William Brad- "ford at the Bible in New York 1696."

The Friends' side of the controversy is thus told by Phineas Pemberton, who was present as clerk of the Meeting:[280]

"No sooner had George Hutchinson done and left us, but up steps divers Germans and Others, who Indeed were very Fierce & Violent Opposers, the Chiefest of them was one of those called Pietists, his name Henry Barnard Coster, whom Friends in London as we hear assisted in their Comeing here which (if True) they are very Ungrateful, and Forgetful of their Kindnesses Received, For divers of them have given Friends here much Exercise & Trouble but especially at this Meeting, where they brought divers Friends Books with them, some of E. B. Some of W. P's & the Clamour that they made against us was, that 'We deny the Lord Jesus Christ & they were there to Prove it out of these Books but Friends thought it not fit to gratify their Jangling Restless Spirits but Continued their Testi-

[280] *Verbatim* transcript from epistle sent by the Yearly Meeting at Burlington to the Yearly Meeting at London, 7mo. 23, 1696, O. S.

THE "PENNY-POT" HOUSE AND LANDING (VIDE PP. 274-77)

FROM AN OLD SKETCH IN THE PHILADELPHIA LIBRARY.

monys over their heads Raising their Voices & Speaking Two or Three or more sometimes together, but the Lords Power Weighed & Chained them down & they left us. After which we had in the Close of our Meeting a Sweet & Quiet time in which Friends were much Solaced & United in the Love and Life of Truth."

The above, continues Rathelf, is not the only thing that Köster and the Keithians undertook against the Orthodox Quakers. The heart of the former and the courage of the latter were strengthened by these various occurrences.

The Quakers now began a new line of attack, and accused the Keithians of being people who failed to practice what they preached. The charge was that while they continued to advocate the Holy Baptism and the Eucharist, they failed to administer either rite.

"However," continues Rathelf, "the Quakers failed to consider that George Keith was a Briton,[281] and had natur-

---

[281] George Keith was born about 1639 in Scotland, probably in Aberdeenshire. He was educated at Marischal College, Aberdeen, where he graduated M. A., 1653–7. He was designed for the Presbyterian ministry, but it is uncertain whether he was ever ordained. About 1662 he adopted the tenets of the Quakers and promulgated their doctrines, and exercised an important influence by providing Barclay with illustrative material for his great "Apology." Keith suffered several terms of imprisonment for his conscience sake, after which he, together with Penn, Barclay and Furly, made the memorable tour through Holland and Germany; Furly acting as interpreter for the party. Returning to England he was again imprisoned.

In 1682 he emigrated to East Jersey, where he was appointed surveyor-general. Shortly after Penn's arrival he came to Pennsylvania, and engaged extensively in writing and propagating the sentiments of the Quakers. In 1689 he taught school in Philadelphia. His career here was a turbulent one, and ended in the so-called Keithian schism and the establishment of the "Christian" Quakers, who afterwards became Sabbath-keepers, or Sabbatarians. Keith returned to Europe early in 1694, and set up a separate Meeting in London; he subsequently took orders in the Episcopal Church, and returned to America as a missionary in 1702;

ally been imbued with English ideas regarding the necessity of priestly ordination; that without such, none could administer either ordinance,"

Our Köster, however, was a Lutheran, and had entirely different conception respecting priestly ordination. He believed that in cases of emergency, where no ordained priest was to be found, any Christian was justified and had the right, when it was required of him, to baptize and administer the Holy Eucharist.

To remove the above aspersion and refute the charges of the Quakers, Köster resolved to publicly baptize such of the Keithians as were born within the Quaker fold, and had therefore not been baptized. The Keithians, in considering this matter, concluded to conform to the Scripture text as nearly as possible, and asked that the ordinance be administered in the Apostolic manner, by immersion, to such of their number as presented themselves.

The place selected for this public profession of faith was the river Delaware, just above the city.[282] However, as the time approached, there were only a few men who remained steadfast and were willing to offer themselves as living examples of their convictions in the face of the ridicule of their Quaker relatives and neighbors.

---

returning to England in 1704 he was offered the rectory and charge of Edburton in Sussex, which he thankfully accepted, although the situation was one of comparative seclusion. He left no opportunity pass to enter the lists against the Quakers. He served his cure until about 1711, when his bodily strength began to fail and he became bedridden. He died on the 27th of March, 1716, and was buried within the chancel of the church at Edburton. Strange to say his remains, like those of his two co-workers in Pennsylvania, Evans and Club, rest in an unmarked grave. Even the precise spot cannot at the present time be traced. There is a stone of Sussex marble within the chancel at Edburton which it is supposed was placed there to protect his grave.

[282] The city of Philadelphia then extended only from South or Cedar Street to Vine Street on the north. The district above Vine Street was known as Liberty Lands.

The spot selected was the sandy beach, just above the "Penny Pothouse" landing. This was a little north of the present Vine Street, which was then the extreme northern boundary of the city. Just above the inn there was a ship-yard upon the shore, and several sheds offered shelter for the uses of both priest and postulant.

When the day and hour arrived, according to Rathelf, "the Quakers were present in large numbers, long before the appointed hour, to see if any of the seceders would remain steadfast; what they would do and have to say; and which of the leading Keithians would fail to appear at the last moment."

There were also many friends and adherents of the candidates present, together with numbers of avowed churchmen—Swedes, Germans, and a few of Köster's former companions.

The day proved mild and serene. The populace upon the beach in their various costumes; the broad expanse of water in the foreground, with the building brig upon the stocks; the primeval oaks and pines for a background,—all tended to form a pleasing picture. The chief interest, however, centered in the figure of the enthusiastic German evangelist, as he stood upon some elevation, surrounded by his postulants. Tall and erect, robed in a long black gown, and with a fearless and flashing eye, he opened the services in the name of the Trinity, and made a stirring supplication in English showing the necessity for baptism, and giving his reasons why he at that time felt justified in administering the Holy Ordinance after the manner of the Apostles and early Christians. After his address was finished, he demanded a public profession of faith from each of the nine candidates.

He then, to make the ceremony still more impressive,

after the manner of the Lutheran Church, and according to the Prayer Book of Edward VI, pronounced the exorcism of "the Devil and the seductive spirit of Quakerism" [*der Teufel und Quäcker Irrgeist*]. This was delivered with all the power of the German evangelist:

"I command thee, unclean spirit, in the name of the Father, of the Son, and of the Holy Ghost, that thou come out, and depart from these thy servants, whom our Lord Jesus Christ hath vouchsafed to call to His Holy Baptism, to be made members of His body, and of His holy congregation. Therefore, thou cursed spirit, remember thy sentence; remember thy judgement; remember the day to be at hand wherein thou shalt burn in fire everlasting, prepared for thee and thy angels, and presume not hereafter to exercise any tyranny towards these persons whom Christ hath bought with His precious blood, and by His Holy Baptism calleth to be of His flock."

When this impressive exorcism was concluded, the party to be baptized, with Köster at their head, formed a procession, and walked down to the river's edge and into the stream, until they were about waist-deep in the water. After a short invocation they were immersed one after the other in the name of the Holy Trinity, and were finally dismissed with the command in Matthew xxviii, 19: "Go ye therefore and make disciples of all the nations, baptizing them into the name of the Father and of the Son and of the Holy Ghost." [283]

Thus ended the first public administration of the Scriptural ordinance of Baptism within the Province of Pennsylvania. Köster himself declares that he never afterwards administered it in America.

The Keithians were now more anxious than ever to have Köster as their regular pastor. But this he refused, on

[283] Text according to the Greek original.

account of their tendencies toward the Sabbatarian and Anabaptist doctrines. They then selected their teachers from among the number baptized by the German evangelist, who, however, administered the Holy Communion to such as demanded it.[284]

The only names that have come down to us as having been among this party of converts are: William Davis, Thomas Rutter, Thomas Peart and Thomas Bowyer. The other five are unknown. This small party formed the nucleus for two Sabbatarian congregations, viz., the church at Oxford[285] which chose William Davis for pastor; and the First Church of Philadelphia, which chose Thomas Rutter. The latter congregation kept charge of the Keithian meeting-house[286] which had been erected some years previous on Second Street, a little north of where Christ Church was afterwards built. Edwards, in his "Materials," referring to this church states: "Another society of Keithian Quakers who kept together (after Keith's departure) was that of Philadelphia, where they builded a meeting-house in 1692. * * * Nine persons united in communion on June 12, 1698, having Thomas Rutter to their minister. They increased and continued

[284] Rathelf page 501.

[285] See page 164, *ibid.*

[286] The only direct official record relating to this building that has come down to us is the correspondence of the Rev. Thomas Clayton in connection with his attempt to bring back the Keithians into the fold of the Church, and at the same time to recover the land and buildings held by them for the uses of Christ Church. A copy of this correspondence may be found among Morgan Edwards' "Materials."

together for nine years. But some removing to the country (Thomas Rutter[287] among the number) and the unbaptized Keithians falling off, the society in a manner broke up in 1707; for then the few that remained invited the regular Baptists to join them, and were incorporated with them."

The course of Köster, together with the publication of his pamphlet on the Burlington controversy, excited the ire of Pastorius, who sided with the Orthodox Friends, and lost no time in denouncing the German enthusiast as well as his converts.

These public denunciations brought forth another pamphlet by Köster, in which Pastorius was severely handled. This pamphlet was issued early in the year 1697, and was published in English and German under the following title:

"Advice for all Professors and Writers. By Henry Bernhard Köster."

"*Ein Bericht an alle Bekenner und Schrifftsteller. Von. Henrich Bernhard Köster, 1697.*"

This controversial work, printed by William Bradford in New York, was not only the first high-German book written and printed in America, but also the first work that was issued in America in two languages.

According to Pastorius' "Four Boasting Disputers rebuked," p. 2–3, this pamphlet in the *high-Dutch tongue* was printed for circulation in Germany. As a matter of

---

[287] Thomas Rutter remained in Philadelphia and vicinity until 1716, when he removed to the vicinity of Pottstown, where he built a forge and commenced the manufacture of iron, the first that was made in Pennsylvania. His lands were outside of the present limits of Pottstown, and his works are supposed by some to be identical with the old Pool Forge, on the Manatawney, about three miles above Pottstown, though it might have stood at the confluence of the Schuylkill and Manatawney, where traces of an old forge formerly existed. Thomas Rutter, after his eventful career, died in 1729.

fact, such copies of the German edition as were not used among the Germans in Philadelphia and Germantown were circulated in Germany and Holland, while the English edition was distributed broadcast throughout the Province and the adjoining colonies.

In this pamphlet Köster boldly challenges every opposing writer and professor, with the proviso "that none who will not be accounted by them as a vagabond Egyptian, and his answer as a railing pamphlet, must write again, unless he hath first appeared upon the publick Theatre and Stage of the Church and of the world unto a dispute at Philadelphia, etc."[288]

---

[288] The following fragmentary quotations are all we have of this interesting pamphlet. They were used by Pastorius in his so-called refutation:

Page 1.—"Brethren in America," "Poor dark devil (meaning Pastorius) without a body."

Page 2.—"That the root of Anti-christianity, that is to say, the Deneyal of Jesus in the flesh, is to be found among the Quakers."

Page 3.—"The Councils, and Clergies, and Universities of Babylon." "They tell how they entered the 22d day of September, 1696, into the yearly Meeting at Burlington, and there lifted up their Voices like Trumpets, and broke our Friends' Voices in the Air."

Page 4.—"The Babylonian Churches."

"That the Quakers deny Jesus to be properly the Son of God."

"That the Quakers say Christ had offered that which is not himself, but only a Garment," etc.

"That the Quakers deny God in his most high Spirits and Godheads power to be the Father of Christ's body and Mary the Mother."

Page 5.—"That many of the Quakers in preaching and writing revile the Baptism and Supper of Christ, &c. Desiring us to show them by what second degree and message of Christ and his Apostles the union of the Spirit with the outward creatures, or water, bread, wine and the like, has been abrogated."

Page 7.—"The Babylonian Beasts."

"Quakerian Spirits."

"The true church of Philadelphia or Brotherly love," etc.

Page 8.—"The four chief Quarters of Babylon."

"That the body of Christ is absent from the Saints on earth."

[There is no doubt that many extravagant utterances of the early

This was evidently intended by Köster to draw out such of his opponents as had already been engaged in the controversy, and induce them to put their answers in writing. In this scheme he was partially successful, as a number of members of the Yearly Meeting, smarting under the continued attacks of the Keithians, and aggravated by the charges hurled at them by Köster in his last pamphlet, induced Pastorius to prepare a counter-pamphlet. A *fac-simile* of title is here reproduced, it reads:

"Henry Bernhard Köster, William Davis, || Thomas Rutter & Thomas Bowyer, || Four || Boasting Disputers || of this World briefly || REBUKED || And Answered according to their Folly, || which they themselves have manifested in a || late Pamphlet, entitled, Advice for all *Pro- || fessors and Writers.* || Colophon:—Francis Daniel Pastorius. || Printed and Sold by William Bradford at the || Bible in New York, 1697."[289]

That this work was issued with the full knowledge and consent of the Orthodox Friends, is shown by the following *verbatim* extract from the minutes of the Ministering Friends. The original is among the archives of the Philadelphia Yearly Meeting:

"Att a Meeting of Ministering ffriends held att Burlington at ye House of Saml Jennings ye 5 of ye 4 Mo. 1697.

"Where after some time spent in a Silent retire^mt^ before ye Lord & divers good Testimonies from friends did in a Weighty & Orderly manner proceed to business, where y^e^

Friends betrayed a tendency, always present among them, to deny historical Christianity. Thus we read that Dennis Hollister, a Bristol Baptist, said at a church meeting, after he had become a Quaker, that the Bible was the plague of England.—*Records of the Broadmead Church, p. 44, London, 1847. From the original MS. of Soc., xvii.*]

[289] A photographic *fac-simile* of this unique book, made by the present writer, is in the library of the Historical Society of Pennsylvania.

Henry Bernhard Koster, William Davis, Thomas Rutter & Thomas Bowyer,

FOUR

Boasting Disputers

Of this World briefly

REBUKED,

And Answered according to their Folly, which they themselves have manifested in a late Pamphlet, entituled, *Advice for all Professors and Writers.*

BY

Francis Daniel Pastorius.

Printed and Sold by *William Bradford* at the Bible in *New-York*, 1697.

TITLE OF PASTORIUS' "REBUKE."

first thing that occurr'd was a small Manuscript from Fran: Danll Pastoras presented to this meeting in Answer to a vile Pamphlet under the Names of H. B. C., W. D., T. R., T. B. wch said answer was by him Submitted to Judgemt of ye sd Meeting to be made Public or otherwise as they should judge meet; who upon a Serious perusal of it did Judge it Servicable to be printed, & accordingly Thos. Ducket & Nicho: Walln are to acquaint him wth it, only ye Meeting desires he would Explain those two ffrds that Concerning some comming into ye Meeting & Smoaking Tobbacco there to ye disturbing of ffriends,[290] the sd two ffriends are also to let him know yt friends will defray ye Charge of ye Press on ye acctt aforesaid." [*Verbatim* extract from minutes of Ministering Friends].

The following quotation from this "Rebuke" will convey an idea of the tenor of the work:

"They tell how they entered the 22d day of September, 1696, into our yearly Meeting at Burlington, and there lifted up their Voices like trumpets, and broke our friends' voices in the air, &c.

"That at such a time and place (we being Assembled not to quarrel with any Brawlers, but to worship the living God in Spirit and in Truth, waiting for the enjoyment of his Comfortable presence) H. B. Köster, with some not much unlike unto himself, came into our Meeting-House, and there as Trumpets of an uncertain sound, were blown by the Prince of the Power of the Air, who ruleth and operateth in the Children of Unbelief, we do not deny.

"Neither is the Impudency of these our Adversaries a

---

[290] This matter seems to have been eliminated, as it does not appear in the book.

New thing unto us; For several others before them, acted likewise by him, who made bold to appear in the midst of the Sons of God when they came to present themselves before the Lord, Job 1–6, entered into Friends Meeting Houses, and by their ill-behaviour and disorderly interruptings, attempted to disturb the People religiously therein gathered.

"With these troublesome men of Belial, H. B. K., W. D., T. R., T. B., and the rest of their Fraternity, in whose behalf they have signed their Pamphlet, may some cut their own shame as (among us) they will. We, measurably quickened with Christ, are set down in a safe and heavenly hiding place, viz:—his powerfull Name, having that satisfactory assurance, that there the Enemy and his wicked instruments cannot approach nor hurt us, Praises to the Lord our God forever."

An immediate outcome of this controversy was that a number of German Quakers petitioned Pastorious in his official capacity, as the head of the settlement of German Township, to suppress or disperse the whole community of Mystics and Pietists within the bounds of his bailwick. Pastorius, however, skillfully evaded this dilemma by stating that he would refer the whole matter for adjucation to the Proprietor on his arrival, which was then shortly expected. He also admonished the petitioners in the meantime to exercise patience, forbearance, and with meekness to maintain unity.[291]

He gave vent to his own feelings in a piece of poetry founded on 1 Cor. xi, 16: "But if any man seemeth to be contentious, we have no such custom, neither the churches of God."

---

[291] Ephrata MSS.

Die Fehler meiner Brüder
Sind Mir zwar ganz zuwieder
Doch wegen eines worts
Ihr zeugniss zu vernichten
Und freventlich zu richten
Find Ich nicht meines Orts.

[The errors of my Brethern
Are to me indeed wholly repugnant.
However, for a single word
Their testimony to destroy,
And wickedly to judge,
I do not find within my duty.]

It was during this period of intense religious excitement that Köster wrote his "*De Resurrectione Imperii*," noticed at length in a previous chapter (pp. 88–92). One of the favorite methods of the German enthusiast was to close his exhortations with a quotation from the celebrated revival hymn of Nicholai: "*Wachet auf: rufft uns die Stimme der Wachter, sehr hoch auf der Zinne*," already mentioned on page 92 of this work.[292]

Another important result of this peculiar religious condition of the Province was to form a closer union among the thirty odd English churchmen in the city and vicinity.[293]

The leading spirit among this embryo congregation was Colonel Robert Quarry who, with the encouragement received from Governor Francis Nicholson of Maryland, in the latter part of the year 1696, commenced the erection of a substantial brick building[294] for church purposes upon

[292] There is a beautiful translation of this hymn by Miss Winkworth, in universal use: "Awake! Awake! for the night is flying."

[293] The names attached to this memorable petition were,—

Francis Jones, Jasper Yeates, Willm Grant, Saml Peres,
Jarvis Bywater, Thos Briscoll, Darby Greene, Thomas Harris,
Fard'do Dowarthy, Enoch Hubord, George Fisher, John Harrison,
Thos Walter, Thomas Craven, Thos Curtis, John Willson,
Anth'y Blany, Edwd Smout, Robt Quarry, Charles Sober,
Joshua Carpenter, Sam. Holt, Robt Snead, Wm Dyre,
Edw. Bury, Jeremiah Price, Addam Birch, Thos Stapleford,
Jeremiah Hunt, John Sibley, John White, Geo. Thompson,
Robert Gilham, John Gibbs, John Moore, John Herris.

[294] Col. Quarry to Gov. Nicholson. Historical collections of the Colonial Church (Pennsylvania), p. 6–7.

the lot on Second Street, which had been secured by Joshua Carpenter late in the previous year.

Reports of these disturbances and the unsettled condition of religious affairs in the great Quaker Province soon spread over the adjoining colonies in an aggravated form, and became known in England, where they attracted the attention of the Metropolitan of Canterbury, and of the Bishop of London.

The subject was at once referred to the Rev. Thomas Bray,[295] who had but lately been appointed commissary, and had been especially charged by the Archbishop of Canterbury to prepare a report upon the state of the Church in the various colonies. It was at his instance, and upon the representations of Bishop Compton of London, that eventually Rev. Thomas Clayton was appointed a stipend of £50 a year, and ordered to prepare for a journey to Philadelphia, where he arrived some time during the first half of the year 1698.

---

[295] The Rev. Thomas Bray, D. D., was a native of Marston, Shropshire, educated at Hart-Hall, Oxford. He was patronized by Lord Digby and by Bishop Compton, by whom he was sent out as commissary to settle the church affairs of Maryland and Virginia. He behaved in this employment with all that zeal and disinterestedness which characterizes the true Christian, he instituted libraries in several parts of America for the information of the missionaries employed in preaching the Gospel, and every method was pursued to render the conversion of negroes and pagans to the Gospel easy and certain.

Upon his return to London he published several papers relating to the state of the Church in America. The most important of which were the "Memorial of the state of the Church in America." "The acts of his visitation in Maryland." "A circular letter to the Clergy in that Province."

The publication of these papers caused much excitement among the Quakers in London, and an attempt was made to answer and refute the statements of Dr. Bray in a quarto of some fifty pages. This was entitled, "Remarks on Dr. Bray's Memorial, &c., London, 1701." A copy of which may be found in the Philadelphia Library.

In the meantime the congregation in Philadelphia was occasionally served by Köster, and in his absence, for at least a part of the time, prayers were read by a Mr. I. Arrowsmith, a schoolmaster who taught the church school which had been started by the congregation.[296] When the new clergyman arrived in Pennsylvania he, at the desire of his superiors, at once sought out Köster for the purpose of obtaining from him an exact knowledge of the situation. To return to the German account.[297] "The minister, who was named Thomas Clayton,[298] was to undertake the task. He settled in Philadelphia. The commencement of the English congregation was very meagre, and consisted of hardly twenty members.[299] But they kept on increasing. Our Herr Köster went about with the pastor and instructed him in the refutation of the teachings of the

Dr. Henry Compton, Lord Bishop of London, 1675–1713.

Beside the money subscribed by individuals or corporations, Dr. Bray contributed the whole of his small fortune to the support of his liberal plans, better gratified in the promotion of public happiness than in the possession of private wealth. To his great exertions many of the societies in London owe their institution; especially that for the Reformation of Poor Proselytes, that for the Reformation of Manners, and last, but not least, that for the *Propogation of the Gospel in Foreign Parts.*

This good man, whose life was devoted to benevolent purposes and who deservedly received the thanks of both King and Parliament, died in 1730, aged seventy-three years.

Quakers. Clayton was a young man, and willingly and cheerfully took the advice of a man who had often dealt with such people; and thus one by one the Keithians were drawn back into the fold of the Church."

Thus it will be seen that the German evangelist, in addition to instituting the Orthodox Lutheran services among the Germans, was instrumental in starting two English Sabbatarian congregations, as well as being prominent, if not the chief factor, in establishing the oldest Episcopal one within the State. Thanks to the efforts of Henrich Bernhard Köster, the German Pietist, the Rev. Thomas Clayton, upon his arrival in Pennsylvania, found a substantial church-building almost ready for consecration and the well-organized nucleus of a congregation.

One of the first visible results of the labors of the new clergyman, coached as he was by the German Theosophist, was the organization of a regularly constituted vestry, and the completion and solemn dedication to its pious uses of the plain brick structure on North Second Street. An old document states: "Though humble in its size and archi-

---

[296] "Perry's Historical Collections," vol. ii, pp. 7 and 15.

[297] Rathelf, p. 501.

[298] Rev. Thomas Clayton, a young clergyman of the Church of England, was the first minister of that faith who was regularly sent out to Pennsylvania.

Shortly after Dr. Bray's appointment as commissary in 1696, the peculiar situation in Pennsylvania became known in England. Urgent appeals for clergy were also received from South Carolina at the same time.

It was, however, not until the year 1698, that two men were selected for these missions, Thomas Clayton and Samuel Marshall, the latter was selected for Charleston. Both, as an old record states, "as pious and happy in their conduct as could have been found." They both started on their journey together. Clayton's career in Philadelphia was a short one, as it was terminated in the year after his arrival (1699) by the yellow fever.

[299] Such as lived within the city limits.

tecture, it was a goodly structure for a city then in its infancy."

[There is no proof whatever for the statement that Christ Church was a wooden structure, and as small as is represented by the same authority. The foundation for this tale, which has been repeated over and over again in print, is but the incoherent mutterings of an old negro, "Black Alice," who was then (1802) over a century old, and no doubt confused in her mind the first Keithian meeting-house, which was built of frame and located in the immediate vicinity, with Christ Church. Gabriel Thomas, in his account of 1698, says that the Church of England built a very fine church in Philadelphia, etc.

Then in the old cash book of the congregation, under date of May 11, 1711, there is an entry or charge for 37,000 bricks for an addition to the church, and at the same time a charge for "pulling down the gable-end and cleaning the bricks." It is hardly probable that so many thousands of bricks would be used in enlarging a wooden church of such small dimensions as quoted by Watson in his "Annals."]

Christ Church was the name applied upon that occasion to both church and congregation. The name of the church and its associations have became historic, not only in the annals of our State but of the whole nation.

Köster continued to preach and exhort in both English and German, but now spent much of his time in retirement and study upon his little farm in Plymouth,[300] where he

---

[300] The location of the Tabernacle of the rival Community known as "Irenia" or the House of Peace, is somewhat obscure, all of the German accounts state that it was at Plymouth, and one or two writers state particularly that it was beyond the jurisdiction of Pastorius. It was probably on part of Thomas Fairman's land in that vicinity.

Pastorius in his "Rebuke" calls it "a plantation near Germantown." *Vide* p. 87, *Supra*. Rathelf, p. 487.

CHRIST CHURCH, PHILADELPHIA.

PRIOR TO THE REVOLUTION.

ORIGINAL IN THE COLLECTION OF THE PENNSYLVANIA HISTORICAL SOCIETY.

INTERIOR VIEW OF CHRIST CHURCH PRIOR TO THE REVOLUTION.

COMPLETED 1745.

FROM A PHOTOGRAPH OF THE ORIGINAL SKETCH.

also taught children and gave spiritual instruction to adults. During the long winter nights he wrote several theological works, one of which has been noticed at length in a previous chapter.[301] He also composed a number of hymns, which were printed upon his return to Europe.[302]

As the time passed the epidemic of yellow fever spread over the land in 1699, numbering among its victims the Rev. Thomas Clayton.[303]

Shortly after the death of Clayton, Evan Evans arrived from England. He had been sent to Pennsylvania by the Bishop of London, with special reference to the Welsh Quakers who, it was understood, had also became restive under the Quaker rule. Evans at once resumed charge of the Church affairs in the Province.

Köster, in viewing the situation, now felt that the term of his usefulness among the English colonists was about completed, unless he absolutely joined the Sabbatarian movement, which embraced such of the Keithians as had not returned to the Church of England. This he refused to do, for it would have necessitated a sacrifice of his Lutheran principles: he therefore conceived a desire to return to his native land. As one of the members of the original Community, who had married, intended also to return, Köster was persuaded to accompany him. His troubles, however, were not yet at an end. In December, 1699, the little party started for Virginia, where they were to take passage on a tobacco ship for England. Köster left all the arrangements for the voyage to his companion who, he

[301] Page 88, *Supra*.

[302] Some of these hymns were incorporated by Gottfried Arnold in the "Poetische Samlung," *Ratione meditationes hermenevticea*.

[303] Rev. Thomas Clayton died at Sassafras, Maryland, where he had gone to escape the scourge, and at the same time consult with some of the Maryland clergy on the state of the Church.

states, was an "eccentric character with but little sense, and subject to sudden impulses."

The vessel in which the passage was secured was an old one, besides being heavily laden. To make matters worse, the captain suffered from rheumatism in his feet and was often helpless. The weather was stormy, it being midwinter. To crown all, Köster had given his money, the proceeds from the sale of his property, to his companion for safe-keeping, and the latter attempted to exchange the currency for specie. But the broker, "a wicked Scotchman," handed him in return the amount in Spanish dollars, which proved to be copper silver-plated counterfeits.

Köster was hereupon urged to remain in the country at least until spring. But as his companion refused to acquiesce, they embarked on the vessel as originally intended. The season and passage proved a stormy one, as was shown by the numerous wrecks that were seen upon the Goodwin Sands, and Köster states that he felt they also would go hence into eternity unless the Almighty would help. Fortunately the storm suddenly abated, and the old ship dropped her anchor safely in the Thames. They arrived in London at the close of January, 1700.

It is hardly necessary for our purpose to trace at length Köster's long and eventful course in Europe. From London he journeyed to his native land by way of Holland. When in Amsterdam, he published an octavo against the Quakers under the title:

"*Aufgeschlossene Prophetia der Hebräer, oder der von anno 1692 an, vom Himmel aus dem Rath der Wächter herabsteigende Bliz und der von a, 1697, 1700, 1703, 1707 an, bis an alle Ende der Himmel und Erden, darauf folgende Donner. Amsterdami, 1700. 8 vo.*"

About the same time he also became interested in Oliger

Pauli, and in the following year published a pamphlet upholding that visionary:

"*Der Hebreer Schechina, d. i. die persönliche Einwohnung der göttlichen Herrlichkeit in dem Messia an Oliger Pauli. Amsterdam, 1701. 8vo.*"

From Holland he journeyed to Germany, and in the next year published at Lemgo the Latin thesis he had written in Philadelphia prior to his departure. The full title and description of this curious composition have been given in a previous chapter (page 88).

When Köster heard that the Baron of Amazone, whom he had formerly known in Berlin, was now upper tutor to the Abbess of Hervorden, Charlotte Sophia, a born princess of Curland, he went there to visit his former friend. The Duchess who had a claim upon the ruling Duke of Curland, Ferdinand, asked Köster to act as her ambassador and press the claim. For this purpose he went to Stockholm, where he arrived at the end of the year 1702. Here they directed him to the King, who was then with his army in Poland. Köster found the King the following year in the camp before Thorn, and was so successful in his efforts that the Duke was compelled to pay a part of the money owed. Such a service deserved a reward, but the Abbess was soon after compelled to leave Hervorden and flee to Verden, where she was not in a situation to show herself grateful to him. Köster nevertheless remained with her several years in Verden, and afterwards went to Hamburg, where he acted as tutor for a short time, until the Danish ambassador to England, Baron von Schaak, who was about to leave for that country, took him as tutor to his sons. He was sent from Hamburg to Copenhagen, and thence to Schwanholm, where the family resided.

Here he remained for seven years, and in 1714 he went to

Berlin, where he took up his abode with a country curate named Rindfleisch. In 1724 he went to Berleburg, which at that time was a rallying point for religious visionaries and enthusiasts of all kinds.

The Count Casimir von Sayn and Witgenstein, who granted them religious liberty within his domain, was so well pleased with Köster that he asked him to remain at court during his pleasure. Köster now set to work to complete his greatest work, one that he had had in hand for a long time, for he had worked upon it even during his sojourn in America. It was called:

"*Schlüssel* || *der ersten und letzten* || *Hebräisch Griechisch Teutschen* || *HARMONIE:* || *welche nicht nur in einer* || *Probe von tausend Wörtern* || *an Bedeutung und Klang eine nahe Verwandtschafft zeiget; durch welches Mittel man die Hebräischen Wörter eher behalten, und sich vieler* || *ursprünglichen Wahrheiten errinnern mag, &c. Henrich Bernhard Köster,* || *Jünger der vollstandigen Rede des Logu Alpha und Omega.* || *Berleburg, zu finden bey Johann Jacob Haug. Anno 1724, 8vo., 568 pages.*"

An edition of a thousand copies was ordered to be printed at the expense of the Count Casimir, to whom the volume was dedicated, with display type in all the verbose and laudatory style of the period. The only known copy of this interesting work, the title of which is reproduced in *fac-simile*, and is in the library of the writer, bears the curious endorsement upon the title that the author was a scientist of a peculiar kind; and as no University would call him to a professorship, he signs himself: *Professorum Extrac* * * * *Linguâ Orientale Occidentalium per Universa* * * *.

The main title of the work, "Key of the first and last Hebrew-Greek, German Harmony," sets forth its import,

Schlüssel
der ersten und letzten
Hebräisch-Griechisch-Teutschen
Harmonie:
welche nicht nur in einer
Probe von tausend Wörtern
an Bedeutung und Klang eine nahe Verwandtschafft zeiget;
durch welches Mittel man die Hebräischen Wörter eher behalten/ und sich vieler
ursprünglichen Wahrheiten erinnern mag:
sondern auch
aus dem Orient durch den Mund und durch die Feder des Geistes GOttes und aller
H. Schreiber/ Apostel und Propheten/ und also des wahren Mosis/ Davids und Jesaiä/ zuerst
durch die rechte 6000 Jahre von der Schöpffung an bis zur Offenbahrung JEsu Christi an Johannes/ mit der ersten
lauteren Bibel allein regieret/ und weit über die Verfälschungen der Chaldäischen Masorethen des Barcochbischen Stern-Geistes/
und aller daraus entstandenen Irrthümer/ die Zeugnissen und Schrifften der Märtyrer und Kirchen-Lehrer der ersten 400 Jahre/
namentlich der 144000 lebendigen Aufgangs-Pfeiler der An. Christi 290. früh neugebohrnen christlichen Mittags-Welt/ erfüllet
hat; auch daher noch in Griechen- und Morenland/ Egypten/ Arabien/ Armenien/ Türckey/ Persien/ Ost-Indien/ Tartarey/
Moscovien/ Moldau und Servien/ und bey dem von Ihro Kayserl. Majest. selbst aufgenommenen Raitzischen Patriarchen und bey
der von Ihro Kayserl. Majest. durchleuchtigsten Feld-Herrn jetzt tapffer und treu erfundenen Raitzischen Nation/ stehen bleibt;
letztens auch im Abglantz und Abend-Schein die edleren Gemüther Teutschlandes/ Preussens/ Sachsens/
Hollands/ Engelands/ und Franckreichs/ erleuchtet hat:
Aus den Schatzen des Alterthums des Alpha und Omega/
dessen allmächtiges Reich erst zu erscheinen kommt in dem
Regenbogen der Harmonie seiner Völcker und Sprachen/
mit der Krafft des Mundes seiner Unmündigen/ wodurch er bereit stehet alle Widersprecher mündlich
und kürtzlich zu widerlegen/ schrifftlich zusammen-getragen von
Henrich Bernhard Köster/
Jünger der vollständigen Rede des Logu Alpha und Omega.

Berleburg/ zu finden bey Johann Jacob Haug. Anno 1724.

Fac-simile of Title Page (reduced), original in Library of the Writer.

as the writer seeks to prove by one thousand examples the existence of a mutual relation between the three languages. In addition, however, he introduces a number of mystical charts and occult problems bearing upon the Trinity, the Incarnation of Christ and the Apocalypse. Regarding the latter, Köster touches upon an entirely new and unique theory,—one that he would here gladly communicate to the world at large, if such were possible. Upon the title page he calls himself "a disciple of the complete counsel [of the] Logos,—Alpha and Omega."

In the main he leans toward those who receive the Apocalypse as a portrayal of the destiny of the church of Christ. Yet in his divisions of the periods and explanation of the scenes described he differs from all other expounders.

A number of hymns of a mystical character are also introduced in the latter part of the work, showing him, in addition to his other accomplishments, to have been a poet of no mean order. This book was thought worthy of a special mention in the "*Bibliotheque raisonnee.*" The reference will be found upon page 59 of volume xviii.[304]

Rathelf, in speaking of his (Köster's) poetical powers,[305] mentions that he held in special reverence St. Bernhard's hymn,—

"Iesu dulcis memoria,
Dans cordi vera gaudia,
Sed super mel et omnia
Eius dulcis praesentia."

This he paraphased and published as a *decachordon* or hymn of ten chords, in the Latin, Hebrew, Greek, German,

---

[304] "*Tel a été encore Henri Bernard Köster, qui dans un autre livre allemand, imprimé a Berlebourg en 1724, promettoit de démontrer, par des calculs d'arithmétique et de géométrie, les mystères de la trinité, de l'incarnation, etc., jusqua'a ceux de l'Apocalypse.*"

[305] Rathelf, page 510.

Figur

der Dreyeinigen göttlichen Er-scheinung auf dem heiligen Berge/

gemäß dem Dreyangel/ wovon auch etwas bey Kottero im Anfang zu sehen.

Figur Alpha.

Der obere Theil des Alpha A, der Dreyangel/ die Dreyeinige Vereinigung ieder Personen des gött-lichen Wesens mit einander.

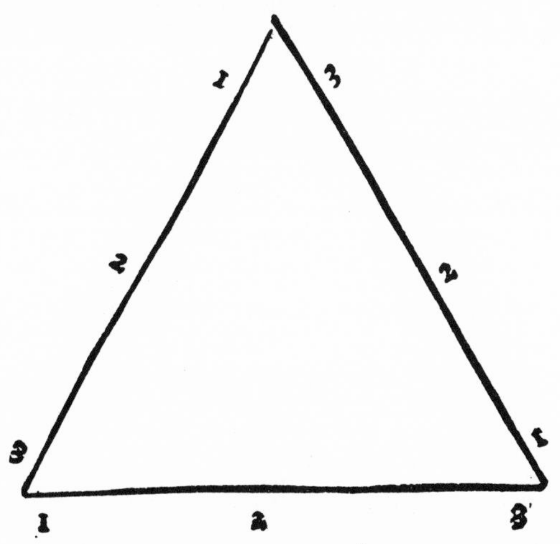

FAC-SIMILE OF MYSTIC CHART IN KÖSTER'S "HARMONIE."

French, English, Dutch, Sclavonic, Arabic and Persian tongues.

The three standard Lutheran hymns: "*Vom Himmel hoch da kom ich her;*" "*Eine feste Burg ist unser Gott;*" and "*Behalt uns Herr bei deinem Wort,*" were also paraphrased by him, and published in the same manner in the following tongues: German, Hebrew, Greek, Latin, French, Swedish, Danish, Sclavonic, English and Dutch.

After Köster, for some unknown reason, became tired of Berleburg, he went successively to East Friesland and Holland, back to East Friesland again, and thence to Bremen; and finally, in 1735, he came to Hanover, where he instructed the son of Pastor Buschen and others in the languages. As the old Theosophist became weaker, the Hanoverian *Magistrat* gave him a living in the Lutheran Orphanage. Becoming gradually feebler in body and mind his wants were carefully provided for.

Arms of the City of Hanover.

Notwithstanding the encroachments of age, he still stoutly maintained that he had solved the problem of life, and that he would not undergo a physical death,—a claim which certainly seemed to gain credit as the lamp of his life continued to flicker until the century mark was almost in view.

"This," continues his friend and biographer, Rathelf (1739), "is the life of our old Herr Köster, a man who is familiar with most of the languages of this world, and who not only understands them, but can speak them. To give an example: his custom is to repeat his daily prayers in the Hebrew, Greek, Bohemian and German languages, which he considers to be the four holy tongues."

THE BREITENHAUPT HOUSE IN NORDHEIM, GERMANY.

AT ONE TIME THE ASYLUM OF KOSTER

However, the best proof of this is his numerous writings, both those printed and those still in manuscript. Besides the works already enumerated, the following title is known: "*De Uitlegging der 22 lettres des heiligan Hebrewischen, en der 24 letters des heiligen Griekschen, en des daarmede overeenkommenden Boheemischen Hoogh-en Nederduitschen Alphabeets.*" Printed at Amsterdam in octavo.

Köster, notwithstanding his physical infirmities, continued to teach languages and to expound his mystical deductions until the end of his eventful life.

For a short time he seems to have been an inmate of the Breitenhaupt institution in the ancient Hanoverian city of Nordheim: a charitable home which had been founded by the celebrated Senior Breitenhaupt, with whom we became acquainted in the earlier chapters of this narrative.[306] He finally returned to Hanover, where he ended his days in the year 1749, at the ripe old age of eighty-seven years.[307] Tradition tells us that the old Mystic was buried as was then the custom, by torchlight, according to the Lutheran ritual, within the precincts of the old God's acre that formerly surrounded the Aegidien Kirche in Hanover.

Arms of the Ancient City of Nordheim.

Resting far away from the scenes of his early struggles and triumphs in the western world, though ridiculed by contemporary writers[308] and forgotten by his kin in the Fatherland, his memory still lives in the history of the Pennsylvania Germans.

Hermit Spring and Hermit Lane, within the bounds of

---

306 Page 54, foot note 69, *ibid.*

307 "*Zuverlässige Nachrichten von Jüngstverstorbenen Gelehrten.*" Schmersahl, Zelle, 1751.

308 Adelung, "*Geschichte der menschlichen Narrheit,*" vol. vii, p. 86, *et seq.*

one of the finest natural parks in the world, still refer to the band of mystic philosophers who settled here, of whom the subject of our sketch, Henrich Bernhard Köster, was once a leader. The congregation of Christ Church in Philadelphia, in the establishment of which he was so prominent a factor, even at the present writing is celebrating its bi-centennial.

Psal. 87, 5. 6.

Die Mutter Sion wird sagen: Ein Mensch und ein Mensch ist in ihr gebohren/ und er selbst/ der Höchste/ hat sie gegründet. Jehovah wird es in der Schrifft der regierenden Völcker und Herren nach seinen Weißheits-Zahlen ausgerechnet erzählen; derer nemlich die in ihr gebohren sind.

1. WAch auf mein Hertz/ und schau dorthin/
Da GOttes Licht von Anbegin
Von Juda Stamm und Reich bekannt
Erschallt ins grose Himmels-Land!

2. Hinauf/ da Licht und Wonne blinckt/
Dahin der rechte Aufgang winckt/
Da Sem in Zämachhs Erde blüh't/
Da Japheth mit Messia ruh't!

3. Zum Lebens-Sieg! zur Freuden-Welt!
Zum göldnen Schwerdt im Pracht-Gezelt!
Erweckter Geist/ neu Pasia-Lamm!
Des neuen Saleins Glantz 'Olam.

4. Des Jaspis neu-besprengte Au
Mit seinem weiten Sapphir-Blau,
Eröffnet dir dein Hertzens-Hirt
Eel Jeschirun/ der Alles wird.

5. Er Logos aller Reiche Reich
Macht Sions Armen wahrlich reich!
In einer Red'/ in einem Wort/
Erhält er all s/ der treue Hort.

6. Denn seine Gründe steh'n/ er ist/
Er war und kommt/ JEsus der Christ;
Im Offenbahrungs-A und O:
Zämachh der Aufgang macht uns froh.

❋ ❋

Frölich bin ich alle Stunden/
Voller Trost und hertzlich froh/
Weil ich habe den gefunden/
Der das Alpha ist und O
Der den Schlüssel Davids hat/
Und mir zeigt des Himmels Pfad.

FAC-SIMILE OF ONE OF KÖSTER'S HYMNS IN THE "HARMONIE."

Daniel Falckner

DANIEL FALKNER.

Der Mitkämpffende / Mitleydende / und Mithoffende an dem Leibe JEsu / eingepflantzte Mitknecht / erwartend meines Ertz-Hirtens und Himmels-Königs in sehnlichem Verlangen

Daniel Falckner / Burger und Pilgrim in Pensylvanien in Norden America.

FROM FALKNER'S MISSIVE TO GERMANY, 1694.

NEXT to Kelpius and Köster, Daniel Falkner (Falckner) was the most prominent character of the Theosophical Brotherhood in America. He was not only one of the leading spirits of the movement in Europe, under whose auspices the Chapter of Perfection for the New World was organized, but he was also after their arrival in Pennsylvania, the executive and financial head of the party, and upon him devolved the arduous task of locating the Community and providing for their shelter and sustenance.

Shortly after his arrival in 1694, he thus gives his impression of the social and religious condition of the Province.[309]

"It is a country that supports its laborers abundantly: there is plenty of food. What pleases me most is that one can be peasant, scholar, priest and nobleman all at the same time without interference, which of all modes of living has

---

[309] Sendschrieben, August 7, 1694.

been found to be the best and most satisfactory since patriarchial times. To be a peasant and nothing else, is a sort of animal life; to be a scholar and nothing else, such as in Europe, is a morbid and self-indulgent existence; to be a priest and nothing else, ties life to blunders and responsibilities; to be a nobleman and nothing else, makes godless and riotous.

"The religion most generally professed in this Province is that of the Quakers, who have their name from quaking or trembling. Having in their collective body been active for a long time in holding up to the kings and nations of Europe the signal of contrition, they now must themselves passively confirm the truth of this signal on account of the pride and foolish arrogant ignorance of their members."

After making mention of the Keithian schism, he continues: "Here, then, there is an opening for a great harvest, which the Lord opens for us wider and wider, giving us strength to make his Philadelphic Word a foundation on which Jerusalem can descend from above.

"Ye European Churchwomen, consider, unless you put off your soiled garments of religion you cannot enter into the Philadelphia which the Lord awakens anew out of a little pebble and a paltry mustard seed, rather outside of your European Babylon than within it, as the future will show."

Our knowledge of Daniel Falkner has thus far been mainly based upon certain defamatory entries and epistles made by Daniel Francis Pastorius, who was his bitter opponent.

That the founder of Germantown may have had some cause for his enemity towards some of the Theosophical enthusiasts who established themselves upon the borders of his bailwick may be assumed, as upon the very day of their arrival they commenced regular Church services in opposition to the gatherings patterned after the Quaker meetings and presided over by Pastorius.

Then followed the bitter controversy between Köster and the Friends, wherein Pastorius acted as champion for the latter. Now, even before the wounds had healed that were inflicted upon him by the bold and impetuous Köster, Falkner returns to America, and without any preliminary notice to Pastorius supercedes him as agent for the Frankfort Company, and asks him to account unto him for his stewardship.

The old strife between Pastorius and the Mystics on the Wissahickon was now renewed with all its acrimony on the part of the former, and as Kelpius refused to be drawn into the controversy, Pastorius aimed the darts of his fiery temper at Daniel Falkner who, however, like his fellow-mystic Köster, was equal to his opponent.

That the Saxon Theosophist was by far the abler politician and diplomat of the two, and that Pastorius was outgeneraled by his opponent, has already been fully set forth in these pages, and will be still further illustrated in the following sketch.

It will also be shown that Daniel Falkner was not quite so dissolute a character as Pastorius would make him appear. The facts here given are based upon various official documents and Church records, most of which have been undisturbed for more than a century, and were unearthed by the writer only after a long and tiresome search upon both continents.

"Daniel Falkner, Citizen and Pilgrim in Pennsylvania in North America. The fellow-struggler Compassionate and expectant of the body of Jesus. A transplanted fellow-servant, awaiting the Arch-shepherd and King of Heaven with ardent longing." Thus the pious pilgrim signs himself during his visit to Europe.

The two Falkner brothers, Daniel and Justus, were Saxons from Langen-Reinsdorf (formerly known as Langen-Rehnsdorf, and Langeramsdorf), near Crimmitschau, Diocese of Zwickau, situated in that part of Saxony formerly known as the Markgravate of Meissen, and they were scions of an old Lutheran family. Their ancestors on both sides had been ordained Lutheran ministers.

Their grandfather Christian Falkner, (died November 5, 1658), as well as his son Daniel Falkner (died April 7, 1674), father of the subjects of our sketch, were both pastors of Langen-Reinsdorf. The latter left four children, viz.: Paul Christian, born February 2, 1662; Daniel, born November 25, 1666; a third child of which we have no record; and Justus, born November 22, 1672.

All the sons were educated with the same object in view, and were eventually ordained to the holy ministry.[310] It is, however, an open question whether the subject of our sketch was ordained prior to his departure to America in 1693 or during his visit to Germany in 1698–1700. But it is more likely that it was during the latter period.

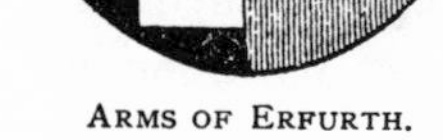

Arms of Erfurth.

Daniel Falkner's connection with the Pietistical movement in Germany dates from its introduction into the ancient city of Erfurth, where he was a licentiate, and presumably attended or taught at the University, and we find him not only seconding Diaconus Augustus H. Francke in the formation of the

[310] According to the Berkenmeyer papers there can be no doubt whatever as to Daniel Falkner's regular ordination.

local *Collegium Pietatis*, but also a believer in, and sympathizer with, Anna Maria Schuckart, *alias* "the Erfurth Prophetess." This woman was the ecstatic servant of Licentiate Johann Gottfried Schmaltz (not "Lieutenant," as erroneously stated on p. 21 *supra*), who was also proscribed as a Pietist. She attracted much attention by her extravagant utterances while in an ecstatic condition. Among other prophecies, she foretold the future greatness of Francke and the success of the American enterprise.

THE OLD UNIVERSITY AT ERFURTH.

She becomes of importance in our narrative from the fact that Kelpius, in his Diary, mentions the excommunication by Köster of both Falkner and the Erfurth Prophetess upon the very day that the "Sara Maria" passed into the Capes of Virginia. This entry in the Kelpius Diary has always been somewhat of a conundrum to students of Pennsylvania-German history, and has led at least one writer to suppose that the woman was among the passengers on the ship. There is nothing, however, to give color to this assumption, or that she ever left Germany.

Spener, in a letter to Francke dated May 8, 1693, writes that Falkner had confessed to him that he awakened the religious ecstasy in Anna Maria Schuckart through an

---

311 Cramer, *Beiträge*, p. 302.

Intensa imaginatio in divine matters.[311] Here we may find the solution of the conundrum in Kelpius' Diary.

There can be but little question that Falkner, during the voyage, repeated this confession or statement, and when it came to the knowledge of the austere Köster, who acted as the chaplain or spiritual director of the party, the latter publicly read the ban of excommunication to Falkner who was present, and *in absentio* over the Erfurth Prophetess in Europe.

[There were a number of woman who became identified with the Mystical and Pietistic movements of that day. Mention has already been made in the course of this work of Jane Leade, Johanna von Merlau, and Rosamunde von Asseburg (p. 61 *supra*).[312] Francke mentions three maid-servants in connection with his work at Erfurth who were subject to trances, ecstasies and visions. He designates them as "beautiful examples of God's mercy."[313] They were Katharine Reinecke, servant to Oberkommissar Pratorius in Halberstadt; Magdalena Elrichs, servant to Pastor Sprögel in Quedlinburg; and Anna Maria Schuckart, servant to Licentiate Schmaltz in Erfurth.

The last-named prophesied in 1691 that the city of Erfurth would suffer great misfortune for the banishment of Francke. She further claimed to have the power to distinguish devout from wicked persons by the mere sense of feeling.

---

[312] Rosamunda Juliane von der Asseburg, born 1672, was the most celebrated of the ecstatic women of that period. Her alleged visions of Christ and the Deity were credited by a number of leading divines, notably Dr. Peterson and his followers.

It is a curious fact that she was a descendant of the Countess von Asseburg, whose picture is shown in the Cathedral at Magdeburg, and who, according to the old legend, returned to life after her burial during an attempt at grave robbery by the sexton.

[313] Cramer, *Beiträge*, p. 162; Sachsse, *Ursprung*, etc., p. 241.

After Francke's expulsion from Erfurth[314] the woman followed him to Halle, and in a letter to Spener[315] he writes: "As I prayed with them, Anna Maria fell into extasies, and in this condition recited many lovely verses in the regular cadence of the strophe, and with a right elegant action of her hands; which moved me more than anything I had thus far heard or seen. But a short time before I had spoken to her privately about such of her failings (*gebrechen*) as were known to me, which she received well from me." Upon a subsequent occasion he writes: "With Anna Maria still more wonderful things have happened than at Erfurth. Upon different occasions here, in the presence of many witnesses, she exuded blood from her forehead and hands, so that it streamed from her. The blood was not only seen upon her, but was distinctly noticed to exude from her skin like perspiration. As various persons were present who

STREET VIEW IN OLD ERFURTH.

expressed some doubt as to the actual circumstances (*beschaffenheit*), they were now convinced by their own evidence. Yesterday she sang a hymn continuously for two hours, during which time a number of peculiar matters took place."

In the year 1692 a book was published laudatory of these three ecstatic women, under the signature of Francke, "*Eigentliche Nachricht von Begeisterten Mägden, 1692.*" A year later, after Francke became connected with the new University at Halle, he repudiated this work together with any endorsement of the ecstatic visionaries.]

When Daniel Falkner returned from Europe it was without doubt his intention to resume his interest and activity in the Theosophical Community which had been established by his instrumentality. In addition to the power of attorney, empowering him to act for the Frankfort Company and Benjamin Furly, as before mentioned, Falkner brought a deed of gift for 4000 acres of land from Catherina Elizabeth Schutz, widow of Jacob van der Walle, who was one of the original purchasers of the German tract.

This indenture, dated the first of March, 1700, sets forth that she hereby gives her share of land, consisting of 4000 acres, unto some pious families and persons (by which no doubt the Community is intended) who are already in Pennsylvania, or intend to go thither this year, as likewise unto such as shall follow them in time to come; among whom Daniel Falkner, who hath settled there already, and Mr. Arnold Stork, who dwells at present at Duisburg, but will

---

[314] *Vide*, Acta des Magistrats zu Erfurth. Acta der Stadt Archiv, Erfurth, Abtheilung X. A I., No. 13. Untersuchung gegen die, den Pietismus anhengenden Personen abt. X. A. I., No. 15. Francke returned to Erfurth, June 17, 1695, to attend the trial of Christina Hirshhausin. Records examined by writer August, 1894.

[315] Cramer, *Beiträge*, 263.

shortly transport himself, shall be constituted and appointed as attorneys, as well for themselves and their families, to take part thereof as also according to their good pleasure and conscience to cause to participate other pious families, especially the widows among the same, viz., the widow Zimmermann,[316] and other two widows with their children being of Duisburg, etc.

It also contains the following provision: "Forasmuch as I also understand that George Müller of Friedrichstadt is resolved to transport himself with his family unto Pennsylvania, my will is that he with his family shall be one participant of this donation." This deed, according to the records, was presented in open court, on the 16th day of the 12th month, 1702–3.

Signed Sealed & delivered in the presence of
Francis Daniel Pastorius.
Daniel Falkner

FROM AN OLD DEED IN THE PENNYPACKER COLLECTION.

We have here the first effort, so far as known, looking toward the establishment of a trust for the aid of indigent widows in Pennsylvania. Just what benefit, if any, the intended beneficiaries derived from the gift cannot be told. That the charitable scheme miscarried, however, was no fault of the subject of this sketch. When, towards the end of August, 1700, Daniel Falkner arrived in Germantown, together with his brother Justus and his companions (among whom were Johann Jawert and Arnold Stork), the former at once, in the name of the Frankfort Company, demanded from Pastorius an account of his stewardship and a delivery of the company's property.

---

316 The widow of Magister John Jacob Zimmermann, *vide* page 47, *supra*.

It was only after a considerable demurrer upon the part of Pastorius, nominally on account of Kelpius' refusal to act, that the transfer was made to Falkner and Jawert. This property consisted of the land, houses, crops in and above ground, horses, cattle, household goods, farming utensils, and other property, besides arrears in rent and other good debts due and payable to the said company, amounting to over two hundred and thirty pounds sterling.[317] Falkner at once took vigorous hold of the tangled affairs of the company and attempted to straighten them out. He also

Francis Daniel Pastorius.

AUTOGRAPH OF PASTORIUS.

took a lively part in the civil government, all of which tended to sever the fraternal ties that once bound him to his former companions.

It has been repeatedly stated that Falkner's power of attorney from Furly was void, as a similar document had been given to Reynier Jansen, which antedated the former's. The truth is that the Jansen authority had been revoked by Furly, but by an oversight the fact was not mentioned in Falkner's document. This, however, was subsequently rectified. In August, 1702, a new letter was sent by Furly to the Falkner brothers, and in the accompanying letter of explanation we read:

---

[317] Pennypacker's *Colonial Cases;* Pastorius MSS; Penna. Papers; Archives S. P. G; London Letter Book, xii, folio 206.

"That my last letter of Attorney sent you, is owned, at last, as sufficient tho not signed by 2 there willing, tho the things were too generally therein mentioned, nor my letter of Attorney to Renier Jansen were not therein revoked. * * * I told you finally that I would have sent you a Letter of Attorney, in the manner of the Governours to Me, but that I had no skill, nor time to do it. But should take care to have it done in England Authentikely and now having received from England a copy of a Letter of Attorney so ample to all intents and purposes as possible.

"In which all care is taken to obviate all objections, & to give you all power, as 1, all former letters of Attorneys are revoked, in so far as they have not been executed & confirmed in so far as anything by Virtue thereof has been legally done, etc." [318]

FAC-SIMILE OF HEADING AND SIGNATURE OF THE ORIGINAL LETTER.

[318] Letter in full, "Pennsylvania Magazine," vol. x, pp. 474-5.

It will be seen from the above document that all the charges made by Pastorius and others, in reference to the invalidity of Falkner's right to act for Benjamin Furly,

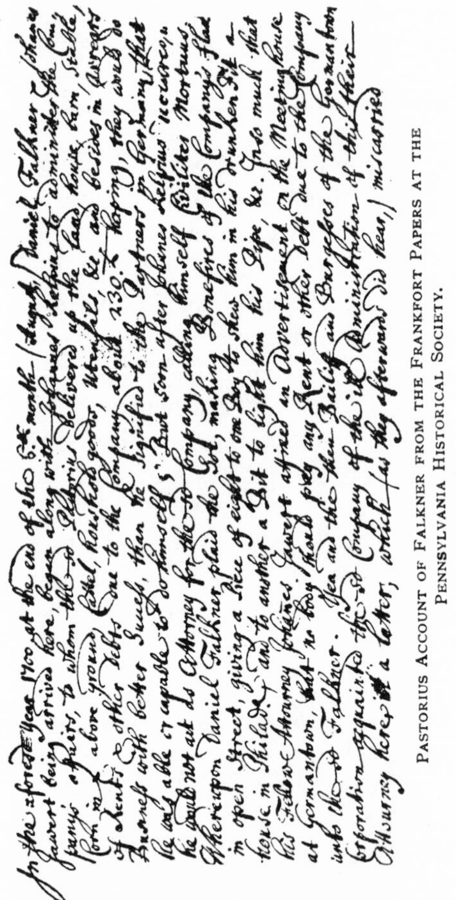
In the aforesd year 1700 at the end of the 6th month (August) Daniel Falkner & Johannes
Jawert being arrived here, began along with Johannes Kelpius to administer the Company's affairs, to whom the sd Pastorius delivered up the Land, house, barn, stable,
Corn in ye above ground, Cattel, household goods, Utensils, &c. and besides in Assign-
ments of Rents & other Debts due to the Company about 230£, hoping they would do
business with better success than he signified to the Partners in Germany, that
he was able or capable to do himself; but soon after Johannes Kelpius renouncing
he would not act as Attorney for the sd Company, calling himself Cælibatus Mortuus;
Whereupon Daniel Falkner plaid the Sot, making Bonefires of the Company's Flax
in open Street, giving a piece of eight to one Day to shew him in his drunken fit a
house in Philada; and to another a Bit to light him his Pipe, &c. Inso much that
his Fellow-Attorney Johannes Jawert affixed an Advertisement on the Meeting house
at Germantown, that no body should pay any Rent or other Debt due to the Company
unto the sd Falkner. Yea and the then Bailiff and Burgesses of the Germantown
Corporation acquainted the sd Company of the ill Administration of this their
Attorney here by a Letter, which (as they afterwards did hear,) miscarried

Pastorius Account of Falkner from the Frankfort Papers at the Pennsylvania Historical Society.

are without any foundation. Pastorius intimates that after Falkner's accession to wealth and power he entered upon a life of dissipation. As many of Falkner's acts, together with his efforts to recover the company's property, are matters of record, it is well to receive these statements with some allowance.

The immediate cause for the final rupture between Falkner and his former companions in no manner reflects upon the former. It happened within a year or two after his return to America, when he renounced his profession of celibacy, married, and evidently settled down to become a farmer and a useful citizen.[319] There seems to be no record of his marriage or who his wife was. The first positive information upon this episode in his career is the memorandum found in Pastorius' writing, among the Frankfort papers, which states that "his own wife desired others to look for him in the woods, where it was thought he might have killed himself, he being above a week from home and nobody knowing where to find him."

So much for Pastorius. In our sketch of the Community, the civil career of Daniel Falkner was traced down to the year 1704, when the last mention of his name appears in connection with the local affairs of Germantown. That he still remained in the Province and pressed the claims of his principals in Europe, for whom he acted as attorney, is shown by the official records of the land office.

In a previous chapter extracts were given from the records to show how energetic Falkner was in settling the tangled affairs of the Frankfort Land Company, which had evidently been overlooked or neglected by Pastorius. The Furly claims were also vigorously pushed, as is shown by the old minute book "G," where we find several entries bearing upon the subject.

---

[319] According to the court records, October 14th, 1704, he was fined 6s. for having bad fences.

Early in the year 1705, Daniel Falkner, together with Jawert, who in the mean time had also married, made another effort to recover the land company's property. To counteract the continual charges by Pastorius that the power of attorney given to Falkner was void, on account of the refusal of Kelpius to act (as the document called for three persons to act jointly and not severally), the two remaining persons, upon legal advice, on March 29, 1705, substituted one George Lowther, a Philadelphia attorney, in the place of Kelpius.

On the 22nd of the 8th month, 1705, Daniel Falkner went before the "Board of Property,"[320] and "by order of Benjamin Furly, Informs that by the said Benjamin's letter he finds the Prop'ry had Promised him 2 lotts in the City Philad'a. for his 2 sons, Jno. and Arent Furly, and gave him an Expectation that he had wrote to the Sec'ry about it, y'rfor by his Petition, Requests the said lotts, but the Sec'ry nor any Other Person haveing Rec'd any Orders about them 'tis referred till such Orders arrive."

That the substitution of Lowther as the third attorney did not meet with entire success is shown by Pastorius' sworn report to the land company in Germany,[321] where he states that in November, 1705, Jawert, who by this time had located permanently on the Bohemia Manor in Maryland, returned to Germantown, and upon the ninth of that month affixed a public proclamation against the Court-house door,[322] by which he notified all persons not to pay any rent or other debt unto the said Daniel Falkner on the company's account.[323]

Notwithstanding the above manifesto, George Lowther,

---

[320] Penna. Archives, second series, vol. xix, p. 465.

[321] Pennsylvania Papers, S. P. G., London, Book 12, folio 206.

[322] Another account states it was the meeting house of the Friends.

four months later, March 26, 1706, notified all tenants to meet him at the house of Joseph Coulson, on Friday, April

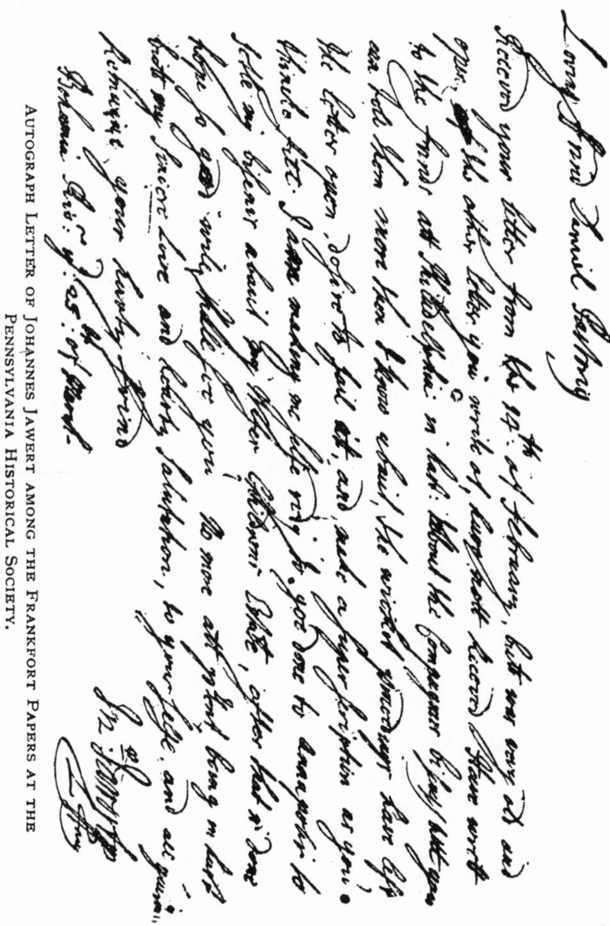

Loving Friend Daniel Pastorius

Received your letter from the 14th: of february, butt was very old and open, the other letter you write of, have nott Received. I have writt to the friends att Philadelphia in hast: about the Companyes business but you can tell them more then I know about, the wicked proceedings have left the letter open, desire to seal it, and make a superscription as you thinke fitt. I am making me selfe ready to goe done to Annapolis to settle my business about my Wifes Childrens Estate, after that is done hope to goe [illegible] will see you. No more att present being in hast butt my Sincere Love and hearty Salutation, to your selfe, and all yours. Remaining your hearty friend

Jn.o Jawert

Bohemia Riv.r ye 25th of March

Autograph Letter of Johannes Jawert among the Frankfort Papers at the Pennsylvania Historical Society.

5th, and make settlement of the debts due the company.

323 An explanation of this action may be found in the fact that Jawert had become a member of the Society of Friends, and then joined forces with Pastorius against Falkner, who adhered strictly to his Lutheran faith.

Under such circumstances, the lot of the German tenants was not a happy one; neither was the position of Falkner a sinecure.

The continuous opposition of Pastorius to Falkner's administration and the challenging of his authority to act, culminated about this time in a letter, inspired by Pastorius, from the Bailiff and Burgesses of the town, asking the company to dismiss Falkner and restore Pastorius to his former position. This missive failed to accomplish its purpose. For the next year or two, as Pastorius himself states, matters were quiet; Falkner doing the best he could under the adverse circumstances.

In the meantime a new condition arose to complicate still more the affairs of the land company. The property belonging to this organization during the past years had steadily increased in value. The unsettled condition of its affairs in the Province, for which Pastorius was mainly responsible, attracted the attention of various persons who wished to possess themselves of this now valuable franchise. A conspiracy was the result, the chief actors in which were Johann Heinrich Sprogel, David Lloyd,[324] and Thomas Clark, the last acting as attorney for Sprogel.

In the investigation of this celebrated case the finding of the Provincial Council, March 1, 1708–9, was that "it appeared that David Lloyd was principal agent and contriver of the whole, and it was affirmed that he had for his pay a thousand acres of Benjamin Furly's land, which he, the said Benjamin, was so weak as to intrust Sprogel with the disposal of." [325]

Sprogel,[326] who was the son of the well-known theolo-

---

[324] For biographical sketch of David Lloyd, see "Penna. Magazine," vol. v, pp. 187–8.

[325] Minutes of Prov. Council, Col. Rec. ii, p. 432.

gian of the same name, appears in anything but an enviable light. From certain correspondence between Benjamin Furly and others which has lately come to light, it appears that Sprogel was a schemer of the first order, and anything

AUTOGRAPH OF JOHN HENRY SPROGEL.

but a man of honor, character or principle. In fact, Furly accuses him not only of forgery, but of larceny as well.[327] Sprogel came to America either with the Falkner brothers or shortly afterwards, as his name appears upon the public records as early as 18th 11 mo., 1702.[328]

The climax of the conspiracy for which Daniel Falkner has thus far been blamed occurred on the 13th of January, 1708–9.[329] According to Pastorius,[330] "the said Falkner appeared in an adjourned court held for the County of

[326] John Henry Sprogel, was born February 12, 1679. His father, an eminent author and clergyman of the same name, was teacher of the seminary at Quedlinburg. His mother, Susanna Margaretta, was a daughter of the celebrated composer of music Michael Wagner, and the Church historian Godfried Arnold, who wrote the "*Kirchen* and *Ketzer Historiæ*," married his sister. Sprogel was naturalized in 1705, and for a time figured as a shipping merchant and became quite a land owner, as in addition to the Frankfort Company lands he acquired several large tracts on the other side of the river. He died at his home at the mouth of Sprogel's Run at Manatawney, which was a part of the land to the present suit, wherein he had subsidized all the lawyers who were then in the Province, viz.: David Lloyd, George Lowther, Thomas Clark and Thomas MacNamara.

The borough of Pottstown is now upon a part of this land.

[327] Furly's letters in the collection of the Penna. Historical Society.

[328] Minute Book G.

[329] A full account of this case will be found in the report of Colonial Cases, by Hon. Samuel W. Pennypacker.

[330] Archives of S. P. G., London, Letter-book xii, p. 206.

Philadelphia, where it is said he swore that the Frankfort Company was many hundred pounds in his debt, and that he therfore must sell their land to *Ditto* Sprogel; to whom the said court immediately granted an ejectment. When as neither Johannes Jawert nor the aforsaid Pastorius had the least knowledge of it, and the tenants in possession never were summond to any court.

"The 24th of January, 1708–9, the sheriff, by virtue of a writt signed Joseph Growden, Esq., delivered unto the said Sprogel possession of the said company's house & land in Germantown and Atturned unto him the said Sprogell some of the Ten'ts in the German Township. The greatest part then refusing to acknowledge him for their Land Lord, who never the Less were afterwards successively persuaded so to do.

"Thereupon the said Jawert and Pastorius, Petitioned the Hona'ble Govern'r Charles Gookin Esq. and Councill, Anno 1709 for to assign a Lawyer, in Order to have the wrong redressed, for as much as the said Sprogel had feed most of them, if not all & However Thomas Clark affirming before the Hona'ble Board, That when he did Rise in the above said Court, he was promised 40 shillings But never had the same paid to him, he was to do the Company's business. Now in what manner he acted the said Johannes Jawert who gave him a Tenn pounds Fee, Can tell best and Judge Growdon Then owned at the said Board that the court had been surprised by the Lawyers."[331]

Now the true facts of the case are that Sprogel, by virtue of forged letters, he together with David Lloyd imposed upon Falkner, actually had him imprisoned in the common goal, and released him only upon conveying the Frankfort

[331] Minutes Prov. Council, March 1, 1708–9, Col. Rec. ii, 430.

claims to them, as is shown by his own declaration to the representative of the Governor.[332]

Some years later the survivors of the old Frankfort Company, owing to the unsatisfactory condition of their affairs in Pennsylvania and the lack of any returns from their investments there, offered to give all of their lands in Pennsylvania to the Venerable Society for the Propagation of the Gospel in Foreign Parts,[333] which had been formed in London. This offer, it appears, was accepted and an attempt was made by the society to recover the same.

In connection with the investigation that followed, a report was made by Captain Vining, who was deputed to look up the matter and report the true facts of the case to Governor Gookin. In this report he states:[334]

"I have waited on Francis Daniel Pastorius, Severall times but he's Apprehensive of his own ill Administration, and others have forbid him whose Circumstances are as bad as his, I have herewith sent an Exemplification of 22377 acres in Mannatanny with the survey of it from the surveyor General's office, also an exemplification (here follows a list of the Company's property) But by Dan'l Falkner was this day informed that Pastorius sold all that (land) but gave no titles, the said Faulkner further saith that he sold[335] the 22377 acres of land to Sprogell by force being

---

[332] Records S. P. G.

[333] The credit for the discovery of these valuable documents, stored in the archives of the London Society, is due to the Rev. Roswell Randall Hoes, Chaplain U. S. N. Rev. Mr. Hoes, who is considered one of the most thorough investigators and geneologists of the early Dutch settlers, is best known by his publication of the Baptismal and Marriage Registers of the Old Dutch Church of Kingston, Ulster County, N. Y., formerly named Wiltwyck and familiarly called *Esopus*. New York, 1891.

[334] Archives S. P. G. Letter-book xiii, Penna. Letters, folio 281.

[335] This should read surrendered, as Falkner received no consideration whatever for the transfer of the property.

sued and in Goal, and many years after Jawert and Kelpius had renoun'd acting and that he knew himself weak and of no power to sell but was poor and forced to do it by David Lloyd and Tho' Clark, Sprogell's Attorney he Adds that 100 acres of Liberty lands was laid out Between the Two Ferrys Rocks and benjamins, w'ch he sold to Dr. Sober also 120 acres do Land near Derby which he sold to John Ball which he now lives on but observe that in all the sales of Land he sold it was by his own power of and no joint power of Jawert, Kelpius, and the Falkner the records do not afford a copy of the power of Attorney by which these men acted, or at least I cannot come at them however Mr. Pastorius assures me that he often saw the power granted to Jawert, Kelpius and Falkner and that they were to act jointly together, but severally not at all. The same did this Daniel Falkner confess to me this day but is poor and believe could be got for a small gain to discover the whole plott and in the presence of Edward Farmer Esq. promised he would."

From the above it will be seen that Falkner profited little or nothing by his attorneyship, and that in the end he was a victim of Sprogel's machinations; further, that whatever loss resulted to the parent company was due to Sprogel, who remained in possession of the property.

Sprogel, in the year 1713, sold 1000 acres of this land to Rev. Evan Evans, then rector of Christ Church in Philadelphia, and who was the most active clergyman within the Province. Six hundred acres, deeded July 10, 11 of above year, were to be known as *Rhyd y Carw* (the Deer's Trail). The remaining 400 acres adjoining the above, conveyed July 29, 30, 1713, were named by Evans "*Trefeglwys*," or Churchtown. The consideration being £180 lawful silver money of America, in addition to the usual quit rent. The latter tract is in Caernarvon Township, Lancaster County. Here an Episcopal preaching station was established by Evans, which is still known as Christ Church, Churchtown.[336]

The Frankfort Company, in view of the new evidence that has come to light, certainly seems to have been unfortunate in the selection of its official representatives in America. Daniel Falkner seems to be the only one of the three who retired poor at the expiration of his stewardship.

The title of the Frankfort Land Company to the Manatawney tract of 22000 acres, confirmed October 25, 1701, is supposed to have been settled by Germans as early as 1700, emigrants who came over with Daniel Falkner upon his return. The development of this tract, which still partly bears his name "Falkner's Swamp,"[337] occupied much of the time and energy of the German Mystic, and as a result he gradually lost his interest in Germantown civil affairs, as well as in the Community he had been instrumental in establishing upon the Wissahickon.

The earliest direct evidence of this congregation known to the writer, is a Swedish account of a visit made to Manatawney by Pastor Sandel in company with Daniel Falkner in the autumn of 1704, wherein it is stated that

---

[336] *Vide*, Historical Collections of American Church, vol ii, p. 73.

[337] According to Henry S. Dotterer, the boundaries of Falkner Swamp may be given in a general way as follows: on the north are the South Mountains, on the south are the Stone Hills, on the west the Fox Hills, and on the east the ridge rising from the left bank of Society Run. Swamp Creek, having as its tributaries Society Run, Spack Run, Minister Creek (the old Pfarrer's Bach), Schlegel's Run and Goshenhoppen Run, flows in a winding course through the Valley. The first official name given to any portion of the Swamp Creek Valley of Falkner's Swamp was Hanover Township. Afterwards Frederick Township was set up, and later Douglass Township, and still later Hanover was cut up into New Hanover and Upper Hanover.

the former assisted Falkner at the Church services on Sunday, October 15th.[337] One of the first things he did in

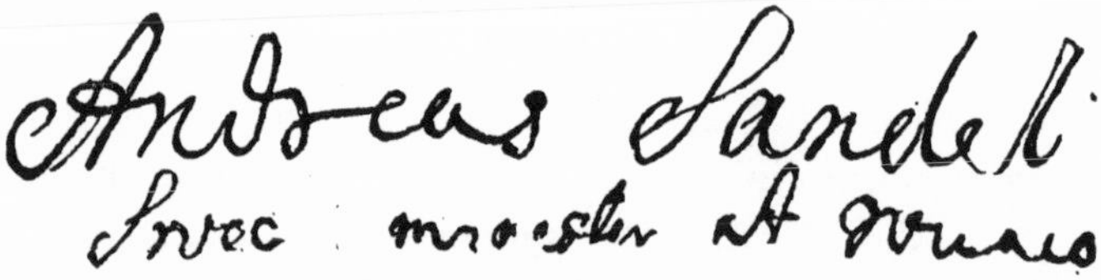

AUTOGRAPH OF REV. ANDREAS SANDEL.

the new settlement was to organize a congregation, build a church, and hold services according to the Lutheran ritual.

This humble structure, a mere rude log-cabin, without any attempt at ornamentation or architectural beauty, with its sparse congregation and enthusiastic preacher, has the distinction of being the first regular *German* Lutheran Church and organized congregation in the Western World. It served the congregation until 1721, when a more pretentious building was erected, also of logs. In 1719 the church was endowed with 50 acres of land for church and school purposes by Sprogel, who succeeded Falkner to the land.

[The circumstances connected with this interesting gift are as follows:[338] In the latter year John Henry Sprogel requested Henry Pannebecker to lay out and survey fifty acres for the purpose, which survey was completed April 17, 1719, and George Boone, to prepare a deed, but through some neglect this important paper was never executed. The Lutherans entered into possession, raised a contribution among themselves, built a church and a schoolhouse, and had them completely finished in 1721. About the same year, becoming more numerous and the congre-

[337] Corroborative evidence appears in Sandel's Diary.

[338] Henry S. Dotterer in the "Perkiomen Region, Past and Present," vol. i, pp. 4-5.

gation being to large for the building, they raised another contribution and erected a larger church and school-house "far preferable to the former." In 1746 they awoke to a knowledge of the fact that Sprogel was dead, and that "owing to the Sloath and Neglect of the Elders and Church wardens" they had no title except it was shown by Sprogel's conveyance of other lands described as adjoining those of the church. Henry Pannebecker, Valentine Geiger, George Jerger, Johanna Christiana Sprogel, widow of John Henry Sprogel, Jr., John Frederick Richards and Anna Elizabeth Hoppin, sister of Spogel and a widow, February 10, 1746, united in a certificate of these facts, and appearing before John Potts, one of his Majesty's justices, declared they were "Real Truth." Upon this paper the title depends.]

It may be well to state here incidentally that Justus Falkner was not ordained at Wicacoa as pastor of this church, nor did he ever serve or preach here after his ordination. How long Daniel Falkner continued his interest in either this tract or the church is not known to a certainty, but it could not have been long after he was dispossessed of the property by Sprogel, as is recited at length elsewhere in this sketch.

[The next German preacher of whom we have any record as ministering to the Falkner Swamp congregation is Gerhard Henkel[339] who served the congregation for several years after his arrival in 1717.[340] From March, 1720, to October, 1723, the church was served by Rev. Samuel Hesselius, the Swedish pastor at Wicacoa, after which time the congregation was served by various preachers at irregu-

[339] It is a question whether Gerhard Henkel was ever ordained. *Vide*, Rev. J. W. Mann, "Annotations Hallische Nachrichten," vol. i.

[340] "Halleische Nachrichten," p. 831.

lar intervals until they united with the congregations at Trappe and Philadelphia in an urgent call to Europe,[341] which was responded to by the Rev. Henry Melchior Mühlenberg in 1742.]

Daniel Falkner, now thoroughly disheartened and bereft of all his property by the conspiracy of Sprogel and Lloyd and the continuous opposition of Pastorius and his followers, and seeing that the Brotherhood, after the death of Kelpius, was in a state of disintegration, determined, at the first opportunity, to bid farewell to the scenes of his struggles and disappointments. He did not have long to wait, as his brother Justus asked his assistance in ministering to the Germans who were scattered over a large territory in East Jersey, and had started several congregations on the Raritan and its tributaries. The records of this are to be found upon the old register of the New York congregation, where they were entered by Dominie Justus Falkner (1703-1723), as a part of his *notitia parochialis*.

According to an extended investigation lately published[342] relative to the German Lutherans in New Jersey, it appears that the earliest known local record of any act of service by a German Lutheran pastor in that colony was a baptism held August 1, 1714, at the house of "Ari van Guinea" a Christian negro on the Raritan, upon which occasion was baptized a child, born March 25, of John Peter Applemann and his wife Anna Magdalena.

Unfortunately the chronicler neglects to give the entry *verbatim*, or even to name the pastor who performed the sacred function, or where the original record is to be found. Which of the two Falkner brothers officiated upon this

---

[341] "The Old Trappe Church," Kretschmann, 1893, p. 5.

[342] "The Early Germans in New Jersey," by Theo. Freylinghausen Chambers.

occasion is an open question. It was most probably Daniel, as Dominie Justus would have entered the fact upon his own register in New York.

Then again Ari and his wife Jora, both negroes, were originally from New York, and in the entry of the baptism of their child in 1705, Dominie Falkner calls them both Christian members of his congregation.[343] After their removal to the Raritan Valley, they remained true and steadfast to their Christian profession according to the Lutheran doctrine, which is further instanced by the facts of their humble home being selected for the administration of the sacred ordinance, and that the name of their son, "Ari van Guinea, Jr.," subsequently appears upon Falkner's subscription list as a contributor towards the re-building of the Lutheran Church in New York.

To return to the subject of our sketch, it was shortly after the interview mentioned by Captain Vining that we find Daniel Falkner installed as the regular pastor of two or more congregations in the valley of the Raritan, and his family permanently settled in New Jersey, where two of his daughters eventually married parishioners; Mollie married Wilhelm Dern, a brewer, and the other married Johannes Kasner, who was a farmer. Both were active men in their respective congregations.

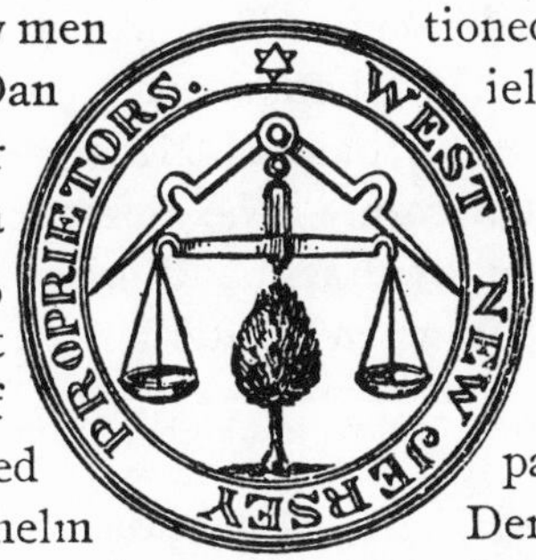

SEAL OF WEST JERSEY.

From now onward the history of Daniel Falkner becomes a part of the Lutheran Church record of New Jersey and New York. The congregations served by him were known

343 *Vide*, extracts Baptismal Register,—sketch of Justus Falkner.

as *Rareton* (Raritan), *Im Gebirge* (in the Highlands), *Mühlstein*, *Uylekil*, *Remrepugh*, (Wallkill) or *Ramapo*,[344] (Remmerspach), *Hanover*, and *Racheway*.

[*Racheway*, now Rockaway, originally *Rahawaich*, the Indian name of a tributary of the Raritan in Hunterdon County. It was upon the east bank of this river, two miles west of the present New Germantown, that the small log church of the Racheway congregation was built.]

Of these stations at the time of Falkner's activity, according to the old records, Mühlstein must have been the most important Lutheran settlement at that day. The Rev. E. T. Corwin, D. D., of New Brunswick, who lived in the Mühlstein section for a quarter of a century, and spent much time in investigating the history of that region, states that the place now called Harlingen was, from 1728–1788, called Millstone (Mühlstein), because it was *op de Millstone* (over the Millstone). The Millstone River[345] is said to have been so named because of a hollow stone on the bank, in the present village of Millstone,[346] where the Indians pounded their corn. The reference to the Raritan, according to the same eminent authority, means the country about New Germantown in Hunterdon and Warren Counties.

---

[344] Ramapo, in Bergen County, is a high hill on the river of the same name.

[345] The Millstone River rises near Paint Island Spring, in Upper Freehold Township, Monmouth County, and flows thence by a northern course of about five miles to the line between Monmouth and Middlesex Counties, thence N. W. about 14 miles through Middlesex County to the mouth of Stony Brook; thence N. E. by way of Kingston into Somerset County, and after a course of 16 miles empties into the Raritan. It is a strong rapid stream, receiving the waters of an extensive country, and runs in many places through narrow valleys and consequently is subject to sudden and great overflows.

[346] The village of Millstone is in Hillsboro Township, Somerset County, on the left bank of the Millstone River. It is about five miles south of Somerville.

According to late investigation,[347] the congregation "*Im Gebirge*," *i. e.*, in the highlands or mountains, also called in the German reports the *Berg Gemeine* or Hill Congregation, built a church[348] at an early day which stood about one mile east of Pluckamin.[349] The Rockaway Church, according to the same authority, was in Potterstown,[350] and is spoken of in a deed given for land "next to the church lot" by *Aree van Genee*,[351] in 1741, to Matthias Scharfenstein.

As to the Hanover Church there seems to be some doubt and uncertainty about its identity. Recent investigations, however, all seem to point to the locality of *Fuchsenberg* or Fox Hill as the one here alluded to.[352] According to the Halle Reports, the original log church was located on the northern slope of this tract of elevated country, and was used by those of both the Lutheran and Reformed faith.[353]

In addition to the above enumerated stations, Daniel Falkner for a time served all the congregations, German and Dutch Lutheran, between Albany and Staten Island. This was after the death of the Rev. Joshua Kocherthal in 1719, and of his brother Justus in 1723. In the old Kocherthal Church Register appears the following entry in his handwriting:

---

[347] Theo. Freylinghausen Chambers in "The Early Germans in New Jersey," Rev. J. W. Mann "Annotations Hallische Nachrichten," vol. ii, p. 227.

[348] This church was replaced in 1756 by a stone one built in Pluckamin, upon the site now occupied by the Presbyterian Church. *Ibid.*

[349] Pluckamin is a town in Bedminster Township, Somerest County. It is pleasantly situated at the foot of Basking Ridge. It is about six miles northwest of Somerville.

[350] Potterstown or Pottersville is in Hunterdon County on the road leading from Somerville to Philipsburg.

[351] Ari van Guinea, *vide*, p. 323, also sketch of Justus Falkner.

[352] An exhaustive argument upon this subject will be found in the previously quoted work of Mr. Chambers.

[353] "Annotations Hallische Nachrichten," vol. ii, p. 226.

"*Anno 1724 ultima Die Mensis Septembr beate defunctorum et Kocherthalii et Fratris partes exolvere vocatus Baptizavi Seqventes* Daniel Falckner. *Past. ad Mühlstein et in Montib. prope flumem Rareton.*"

[In the year 1724, on the last day of September, called in the place of the saintly deceased Kocherthal, and my saintly brother, I, Daniel Falkner, pastor at Mühlstein and on the river Raritan, baptized the following.][354]

In this extended field of labor did the German Theosophist serve well and faithfully until the arrival from Europe of the Rev. W. C. Berkenmeyer, nor did his zeal and interest abate in the New York congregations after the arrival of the official successor to his deceased brother. For when the question was agitated for building a new and enlarged church in New York city, and the enterprise lagged for want of funds, the now aged Pietist and pastor personally interested himself and others by collecting money from his own charges in New Jersey. It was largely due to his influence and efforts that the task undertaken by the struggling Lutherans in New York city was successfully accomplished. A record of two subscription lists from the Jersey congregations has fortunately been preserved, and both are headed by Daniel Falkner personally. Rev. Berkenmeyer, the pastor in charge, acknowledges the receipt of both lists in the church records under date of June 23, 1727.

"On the 23d of June have I received, at Kalverak, from Falkner, on the second Sunday after Trinity, 1727,[335] * * * at Raritans. At Mühlstein they have for the building of the Lutheran Church caused to be subscribed."

A fac-simile of the original entry, with the names attached, is here given. This interesting record was photo-

[354] List of names missing.

[335] Illegible.

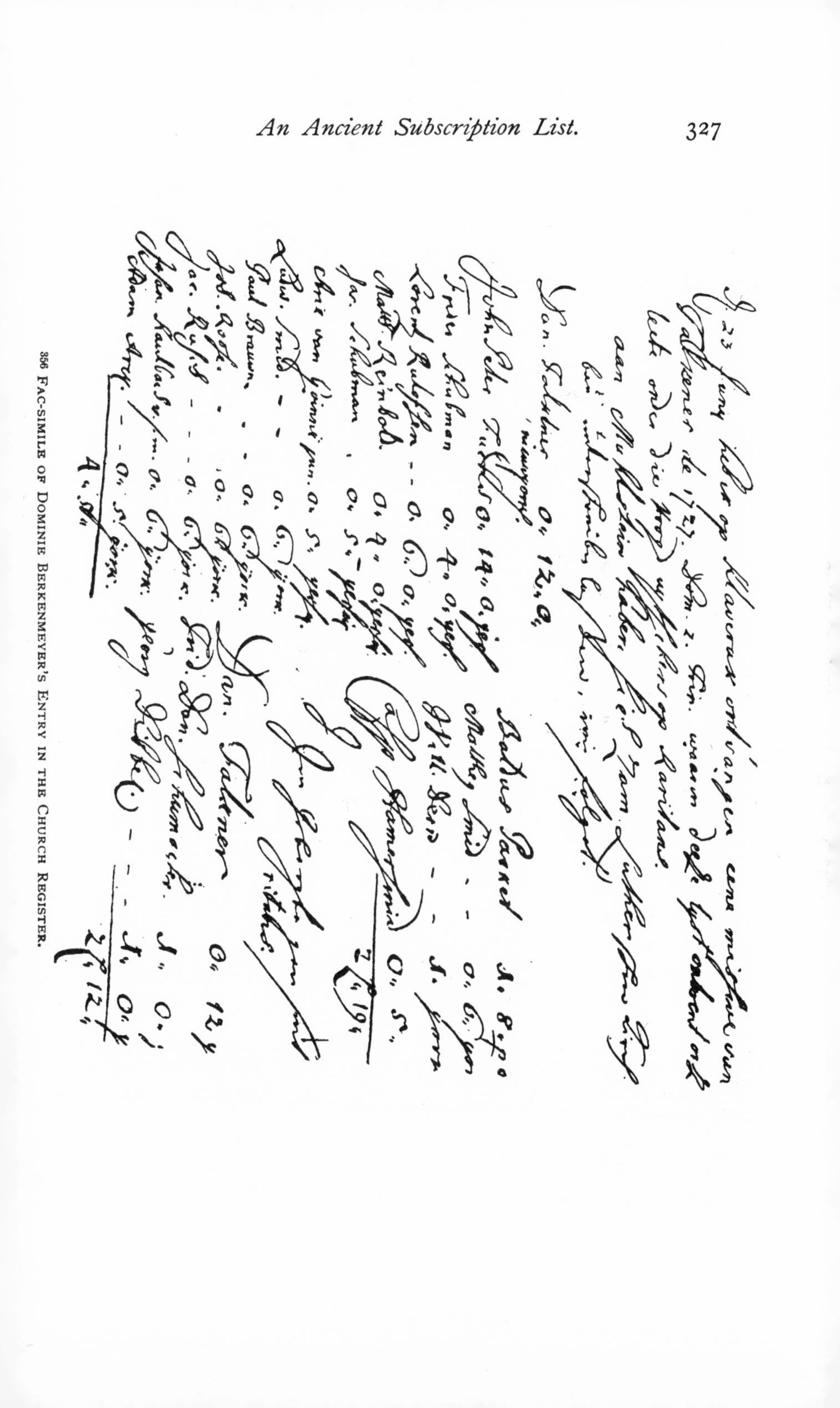

356 FAC-SIMILE OF DOMINIE BERKENMEYER'S ENTRY IN THE CHURCH REGISTER.

graphed by the present writer from the original which is still in possession of the New York congregation.

Attention is here called to the fact that Rev. Berkenmeyer, who was a great stickler for ecclesiastical ethics as is shown in his controversy with Van Diren,[357] never once questioned the validity of Daniel Falkner's ordination or right to perform the sacred functions. This fact is repeatedly proven by his numerous entries in the church records as well as by his correspondence.

When finally the Dutch Lutheran Church at the southwest corner of the *Breit-weg* and *Priester Gasse*[358] was completed and dedicated to its pious uses, on the fourth Sunday after Trinity (June 29, 1729), and named after the Holy Trinity, Daniel Falkner, the former Pietist of Erfurth, Theosophist on the Wissahickon, and now serving as a regular ordained pastor in East Jersey, was one of the most venerable and honored clergymen who officiated at the altar upon that festive occasion. Further, the warmest thanks were extended to Dominie Falkner at the time by Pastor Berkenmeyer and his congregation for the assistance the former had rendered to them.

Strange, indeed, it seems that this should be the same man who was so persistently vilified and maligned by Pastorius, and wronged by Sprogel and his co-partners. Outside of the accusations in the Pastorius MSS. not a word or line can be found to corroborate the charges against this pioneer missionary, who labored in the vineyard of the Lord until the end of his days.

---

[356] In the preceding subscription list the name of Arie van Guinea, Jr., will be noticed. This was a son of Ari van Guinea and Jora his wife, mentioned elsewhere in this book, *vide*, p. 323, *supra* and sketch of Justus Falkner.

[557] Zenger, 1728.

[358] Broadway and Rector Streets.

As Daniel Falkner grew older and became unable to serve his widely scattered congregations with that regularity which had been his custom, he requested two of the congregations to secure another pastor. Before long a candidate presented himself. He was from Pennsylvania, and his name was Casper Stöver. He was willing to assume the charges, provided Falkner would ordain him to the ministry. This the latter refused to do, after hearing Stöver's trial sermon. Consequently the old Theosophist remained in charge for about two years longer, acting not only as clergyman but also as physician.

A letter written at this period represents Falkner as ageing rapidly; but he was still bodily active, his eyes were clear and sharp, and did him good service in gathering herbs and simples for curative purposes. He was, however, somewhat eccentric, and upon that account had more or less trouble with some of his parishioners. The discontented ones finally appealed to Dominie Berkenmeyer, the senior in New York. This resulted in a personal visit to Rockaway on Thursday, September 9, 1731, by Berkenmeyer, with two of his elders, viz.: Hannes Lagrangie and Heinrich Schleydorn.

An interesting account of this journey is found in Berkenmeyer's Diary.[359] It is headed: "*IMMANUEL—Relation von der Raretauner Brief* || *nach Hamburg* || *aus meinen diario und paquet 19 der Neu Yorkische Briefen* || *in diese Continuation des Loonenburgischen, Albanische* || *Protocolli eingeruckt.*"

It states that the trio, on September 9, 1731, went by water to Elizabeth Point, where they were met by members of one of Falkner's congregations. Three spare horses were furnished, and the party rode until nightfall.

---

359 Archive of the Lutheran Seminary at Gettysburg, Penn.

After a short rest, they again started at two o'clock in the morning and proceeded on their journey, as the cool night and the bright moonlight was preferable to the torrid heat of the sun.

Arriving at the end, Berkenmeyer first went towards Falkner's house, where the visitors were met with the unsatisfactory statement that the pastor had left at daybreak and had gone into the woods to gather herbs, also that he had gone on a fishing excursion with his son-in-law. A servant girl, however, was sent out into the woods to search for Falkner, and, as she did not return for some time, Elder Schleydorn also went in search of him.

The search proving unsuccessful, Falkner's daughter offered to go, but just as she was about to start, her father and his son-in-law were seen approaching leisurely from the woods, whither they had gone in search of medicinal herbs, which were supposed to be gathered while the dew was yet on them. Falkner greeted his visitors cordially, and as his morning's occupation was uppermost in his mind, he called their attention to some differences between similar herbs in America and Europe. Botany and curative herbs had but little interest for the three strangers, so they at once broached the subject of their visit. To their joy the old Theosophist, without hesitation, offered to resign any of his charges as soon as a successor should arrive, if such an act upon his part would lead to permanent harmony.

From the hospitable home of Dominie Falkner the trio journeyed to Rockaway (Whitehouse), where the new church building[360] was being made ready for service. They arrived at eight o'clock in the evening (Friday, September 10, 1731), and found their intended host, John Bal-

[360] At Potterstown.

thazar Pickel, busily engaged in arranging the pulpit and seats for the morrow.

On the next day (Saturday, September 11), preparatory communion services[361] were held, and the church was solemnly dedicated to its pious uses according to the Orthodox Lutheran ritual. Upon the following day, Sunday, the Holy Communion was administered to about thirty persons, at which service both Rev. Berkenmeyer and Daniel Falkner officiated.

On Monday, September 13, 1731, a congregational meeting was held at the house of Peter Kasner, *Im Gebirge* [in the hills or highlands] at which, in reply to an address by Dominie Berkenmeyer, the venerable Falkner told the strangers "How much pleasure it had afforded his people as well as himself to have been able to assist them in the building of their new church in the city."

He further stated "that he acknowledged that city to be their modern Athens, whence their help and succor must come in the future. For this reason he had prayed continually and fervently, during both his sainted brother's lifetime and Kocherthal's, that they would not neglect the isolated German congregations in the Jerseys. In conclusion he thanked the Reverend Senior and his deputies for their trouble and offers of assistance in settling any congregational differences that existed or should arise at any future time. As to his own personality, he declared that, although he was without means, he was perfectly willing to resign any or all of his charges so that the congregations should be served better and more regularly. He, however, cautioned them that his charges were precarious, as the congregations were apt to make promises, but they failed to keep their obligations, and there were no means at hand

---

361 *Vor-beichte.*

to ensure sustenance to any man who should come to them from some distant land."

The outcome of this meeting was that calls to London and Hamburg were issued and transmitted to Europe. Both of these documents were signed by Daniel Falkner as *Pastor loci.* Before dismissing the Council, Dominie Berkenmeyer made an address, in which he extended hearty thanks to Pastor Falkner for his love and charity towards the people under him. He then proceeded to admonish the assembled church officers and members to extend all due reverence and courtesy within their power to Pastor Falkner for his consideration towards them. An agreement was also drawn up on this occasion and signed by all present. A *fac-simile* of it is here reproduced from the original draft in the Berkenmeyer Diary.

It was well toward the end of the year 1734 before the Rev. John August Wolff arrived from Europe in response to the two urgent calls sent out at the above meeting. During this *interim* of three years Pastor Falkner continued as best he could to serve his numerous and scattered congregations. The selection of Pastor Wolff proved a most unfortunate one, and it was not long before direct charges were made and proven against the new pastor, who was thereupon debarred from officiating by the church officials.

During these troubles we again find the old Pietist active in supplying the congregations, and raising his voice in the interests of religion and morality as against the conduct of Wolff. Several letters written by Falkner to Dominie Berkenmeyer and Pastor Knoll upon this subject are still in existence.

The last trace which the present writer could find of the now aged and venerable Daniel Falkner, whose years were extended beyond the scriptural limit of three score and

Fac-simile of Entry in Rev. Berkenmeyer's Diary respecting the Agreement of September 13, 1731.

ten, is about the year 1741. He was then living in retirement with his daughter in the vicinity of the present New Germantown, in Hunterdon County.

Just when he was called from the Church militant to join the Church triumphant is not ascertained. Careful research has failed to disclose records which would give information as to either his death or burial. There can be but little doubt that he died in full communion with the church of his forefathers in the hope of a blessed resurrection, as did most of his former brethern of the Chapter of Perfection who established themselves upon the banks of the Wissahickon.

Fortunate, indeed, was the discovery in the Berkenmeyer Diaries, Trinity Church records and Furly correspondence, of the references to Daniel Falkner, as they afford us a true insight into the life and character of this Pietist, Theosophist and student, who was so active in the early days of Pennsylvania's history, and whom hitherto we had known only as a dissolute character from the scurrilities of Pastorius. There is no evidence whatever to show that Daniel Falkner ever revisited Pennsylvania, or took any interest in the affairs of either the land company or such of his former companions as remained on the Ridge. Nor is there any evidence to show that he profited even to the value of a single shilling by his attorneyship.

Perhaps at some future day additional records may be found in connection with the Frankfort Company which will give still further insight into the life of this pious pilgrim: "a fellow-struggler, compassionate and expectant of the Body of Christ awaiting the Arch-Shepherd and King of Heaven with ardent longing" no longer, but now a partaker of the rewards due to the faithful servant in the realms of bliss.

JOHANN GOTTFRIED SEELIG.

Arms of Chur-Braunschweig, 1694.

SEELIG, who for a short time succeeded Kelpius as Magister of the now greatly diminished Theosophical Brotherhood, was a native of Lemgo, a town of some importance in Lippe-Detmold, where he was born in 1668. He was one of the original promoters of the Chapter of Perfection and the scheme of emigration to America. In all contemporary accounts his name is mentioned as one of the principal characters of the Brotherhood. Seelig was a theologian as well as a scholar, and prior to his connection with the Pietistical movement was a licentiate or candidate for orders, who was licensed to preach and teach theology. Seelig was noted for his examplary piety and austere manner, and next to Kelpius was, so far as our knowledge goes, the most gentle and lovely character among the Mystic Brotherhood.

He resisted all offers to return to the world and its temptations with the same determination as his Magister. Wealth and power had no charm for this devout Mystic. Of all the members of the Fraternity, he was the nearest to Kelpius, who was wont to speak of him as his "dear Seelig" (*lieber Seelig*).

Even the honor accorded him by the remaining Theosophists as Magister after the death of Kelpius was too great for him. He practiced the humility that he professed, and said he would rather live the life of an humble recluse, clad in coarse woolen homespun in his cheerless anchorite cell, than be clothed with any show of worldly authority or power; a condition which he held to be inconsistent with his profession.

So after a short time Seelig renounced his right of succession as Magister in favor of Conrad Matthäi, clad himself in pilgrim garb, and retired to one of the small log cabins that were on the tract, where he spent his time in mystical speculations and devout meditations, in which the spiritual bridegroom bore an important part.

The pious ascetic, however, did not live in idleness, but tilled a garden for his support, taught school, instructed adults in religion, and, as he was an expert scrivener, did much of the early conveyancing about Germantown. As a matter of fact it is said that many of the older Germantown deeds are in his handwriting.

Like nearly all German *studiosi* of that period he had been instructed in a handicraft in his youth. In his case it was one that proved itself of great value not only to the old recluse but also to the community at large. This was the bookbinder's art, and he had brought a full complement of tools with him to this country. All the Jansen imprints were bound by him, as were also the earliest editions of the Sauer press. Prominent among the latter was the edition of the *Zionitischer Weyrauchs Hügel, oder Myrrhen Berg*, a hymn book of over 800 pages, printed by Sauer for the Ephrata Community.

There is an Ephrata tradition, which is undoubtedly correct, that Seelig afterwards instructed several of the Zionitic Brotherhood[362] in his art, and thus introduced book-binding among them; so that Ephrata for a time became the most extensive bindery in America. Further, it is more than probable that Seelig had some knowledge of the printer's art, and was one of those who induced Reynier Jansen to assume the responsibility of the Friend's press,[363] and afterwards assisted him in its management.

Not the least of Seelig's labors was the giving of instructtion, religious and elementary, to the young of both sexes. That his efforts in this line bore good fruit is attested by the tribute accorded him by the Patriarch Mühlenberg,[364] who in his reports to Halle writes:[365] "Several years ago an inquiry was made of me from Germany in reference to certain *candidatii theologiæ* who came to this country some considerable time before my arrival. In the first years of my sojourn here I met one of them, Herr Seelig, who lived in the above-mentioned vicinity (Roxborough) eight miles from the city,[366] after the manner of an anchorite, and instructed the children of the vicinity.

"To this old and venerable *candidatus* our fellow-sister[367] went to school in her tender youth, and received through his instructions gentle impressions of true piety."

---

362 A branch of the Ephrata Community.

363 *Vide* p. 105, *supra.*

364 The Rev. Heinrich Melchior Mühlenberg, the first Lutheran minister sent out from Halle. He is usually called the Patriarch to distinguish him from his three sons who were all ordained in the ministry.

365 XIV Continuation, folio 1256.

366 This distance was computed from the old Court House at Second and Market Streets, up Second Street and Germantown Road to Germantown was five miles; thence to Roxborough, as the roads then went, three miles; total eight miles.

367 A member of his congregation. *Vide "Merkwürdige Exempel,"* No. 1, 1769.

On account of Seelig's austere mode of life and the coarse pilgrim habit worn upon all occasions, he became known among the inhabitants as "*der Heilige Johannes.*" As the devout recluse became older, and the inroads of age were making themselves felt, it appears that he left the cabin near the Wissahickon and took up his abode in a somewhat similar structure on the farm of William Levering, which was either especially built for him or else placed at his disposal. Trustworthy traditions in the Levering family,[368] which have been handed down for generations, inform us that this cabin was in the valley back of the present Leverington Cemetery in Roxborough, and was near the home of William Levering.[369]

What the precise relations were that existed between the mystic recluse and William Levering is not known at the present day, except that they were those of intimate friendship. The same traditions tell us that "Seelig, while living on the Levering farm, predicted men's lives, when requested, after the manner of the astrologers of the middle ages."

When the old recluse verged on threescore and ten, he became so feeble that he was frequently confined to his cabin. During this period he was frequently visited by the early Moravian evangelists, Böhnisch, Spangenberg, Nitschmann and Neisser. He was well known to the Count Zinzendorf, who paid him several visits. Seelig was

---

368 "Genealogical Account of the Levering Family," page 19.

369 William Levering was the son of Wigart, the emigrant. He came to Pennsylvania with his father in 1685, when he was eight years old; the family removed from Germantown to Roxborough in 1692; their plantation or farm adjoined that of the Kelpius Community. The Levering family subsequently intermarried with the Righters, who bought the former tract after the disbandment of the Community. Wigert Levering, the emigrant, died February 2, 1744-45, at the age of ninty-seven years; his son, William, died in the fall of 1746, in his seventieth year.

one of the two "Hermits" whom the Count could not persuade to join forces with him in his evangelistic movement.

There is a tradition connected with Seelig, somewhat similar to that of Kelpius. During his last sickness, when he felt that his end was approaching, he expressed the desire to William Levering that his staff (*stab*), a peculiar cane which he had always carried, should be cast into the Schuylkill immediately upon his death. This request was complied with, and as the rod touched the water it exploded with a loud report. His death is thus noted in the Levering family Bible: "John Sealy, hermit, died April 26, 1745, aged 77 years."

In the Ephrata Manuscripts it is stated that he was buried on the farm. But whether on the Levering farm [370] or beside Kelpius and others, who rested under the shadow of the Tabernacle in the orchard on the then Righter plantation, cannot be determined.

From the old record we further learn that it was at the close of a bright spring-like day that the small *cortége* wended its way from the humble cabin in the Levering valley bearing the remains of the devout recluse to the grave. The mourners were sincere, for Seelig, like Kelpius, had been singularly beloved and respected.

Prominent among the number were such as once belonged to the Community on the Wissahickon. The only names, however, that have come down to us of the latter are Conrad Matthäi, who conducted the services, and his two assistants—Daniel Geissler,[371] former *Famulus* to Kelpius, and Christopher Witt, now "Practitioner of Physic" in Germantown. As the last rays of the sun gilded the horizon,

---

[370] There was a private burying ground upon the Levering farm at that time.

[371] Daniel Geissler died a few months after Seelig.

the relics of the old Theosophist were lowered into the gravė, the mystic incantation thrice repeated, while the released dove coursed in wide circles through the air until lost to view in the distance.

The last will and testament of Johann Gottfried Seelig bears date September 17, 1735, and in it he is described as "John Sehlee of Roxborough, in the County of Philadelphia, Gentlemen." He bequeathed the whole of his estate to his "ffriend William Levering Sen[r] of Roxborough," and appointed him executor. The will is witnessed by Matthew Holgate, John Baldt and John Gruber.

The inventory of his estate contains the following items: 25 shirts, 4 coats, 2 jackets, 2 hats, 2 pairs of shoes and slippers, 7 pairs of linen drawers, 3 planes, 2 saws, 1 gluepot, 54 glass bottles, 5 book-binder's presses, 1 Saddle and bridle, 1 scale, gold and silver weights, 5 Bibles, 14 books, 10 works of Jacob Böhme, 120 Latin, Dutch and Greek books.

Justus Falckner

DOMINIE JUSTUS FALKNER.

ARMS OF CHUR-SACHSEN A. D. 1694.

JUSTUS FALKNER, born Nov. 22, 1672, was the fourth son of Pastor Daniel Falkner,[372] the Lutheran pastor at Langenreinsdorf, Crimmitschau, Zwickau, Saxony.

He was the younger brother of Daniel Falkner, who came to America with Kelpius and Köster, accompanied him upon his return to Pennsylvania in the year 1700, and, together with Jawert, Storch, Sprogel and others, reinforced the Community on the Wissahickon. When Justus Falkner left Europe he was yet in his diaconate, and a candidate for orders (*Candidat Theologiæ*). Subsequently he had the proud distinction of being the first person to be ordained to the holy ministry within the bounds of the Province of Penn, if not in the New World. From that time until his death in 1723 he served as pastor of the oldest Lutheran congregation in America.[373]

The earliest record of Justus Falkner, found by the present writer, is recorded in the oldest register of the ven-

[372] *Vide* page 302, *supra*.

[373] The Dutch Lutheran Church of the Holy Trinity in New York City.

JUSTUS FALKNER AS A STUDENT, FROM AN OLD SKETCH AT HALLE.

erable University at Halle, Germany, which bears the following title, viz:

"*Catologus derer Studiosorum, so auf hiesiger FRIED-RICHS, Universität, immatriculiret worden. Nach Ordnung des Alphabet's Eingerichtet.* De Anno MDCXCIII."

The first entry upon the sixth page reads:

"FALCKNER, Justy, Langeramsdorf, Miss."
"P. R. Thomasius, 1693, 20 Jan."

The above entry shows that Justus Falkner was one of the students at Leipzig who followed Thomasius to Halle upon the latter's expulsion from that city.

It has been stated that the reason why Justus Falkner was not ordained in Germany was that the young deacon, upon completing his theological course, felt that the responsibility of the ministerial office in the German Church of that time was too great for him to undertake. This statement is evidently based upon the Latin note in Biörck's "*Dissertatio Gradualis de Plantatione Ecclesiae svecanæ in America,*" in which he states:

"This man deserted his home so as to escape the burden of the Pastorate, yet now he submitted to be brought to himself by Rudmann, Biörck and Sandel, on November 24, 1703."

With the exception of the above note, the present writer has found nothing whatever to substantiate this presumption. In fact, the contrary seems to have been the case, and that he took an active interest in the ministry after his course at the University was completed.

בשם יהוה

DISSERTATIO GRADUALIS,

De

PLANTATIONE
ECCLESIÆ SVECANÆ

IN

AMERICA,

QUAM,

Suffragante Ampl. Senatu Philosoph. in Regio Upsal. Atheneo,

PRÆSIDE,

VIRO Amplissimo atque Celeberrimo

MAG. ANDREA
BRÖNWALL/

Eth. & Polit. Prof. Reg. & Ord.

In Audit. Gust. Maj. d. 14 Jun.
An. MDCCXXXI.

Examinandam modeste sistit

TOBIAS E. BIÖRCK.

AMERICANO-DALEKARLUS.

UPSALIÆ. Literis WERNERIANIS.

That he was in close touch with Rev. Francke, under whom he had studied the Oriental languages at the University,[374] and who was now one of the recognized religious leaders in Europe, is shown by the fact that several of his hymns were incorporated by Francke in his revised hymn book: "*Geistreiches Gesang Buch*," Halle, 1697.

The most noted of Falkner's hymns is the one commencing with the line: "*Auf! ihr Christen, Christi glieder*," on page 430 of the original edition.[375] This hymn is a stirring, vigorous composition of eleven stanzas of six lines each. It was set to the melody "*Meine Hoffnung stehet veste*," and was well calculated to raise the religious fervor of the worshippers.

On a manuscript copy of this hymn, Falkner notes two references to the Scriptures as his theme, or the foundation of its composition, viz.: Eph. vi, 10; 1 John v, 4.[376]

Originally it was designated, "An encouragement to conflict in the Christian warfare," and was retained by Freylinhausen in his *Gesang Buch* of 1704, but it was subsequently relegated to the *Anhang* or appendix.[377]

From the very outset the hymn came into extended use in both Europe and America. It became a favorite revival hymn with the so-called Separatists, or dissenters from the orthodox church, and was incorporated into their hymn books; a prominent instance being the *Davidsche Psalter-*

---

[374] Rev. A. H. Francke was not called to the theological chair of the University until 1699, some time after Justus Falkner had left the institution.

[375] Copy in archive of the Moravian Church at Bethlehem.

[376] Finally my brethern, be strong in the Lord, and in the power of his might (Eph. vi, 10).

For whatsoever is born of God, overcometh the world, and this is the victory that overcometh the world, even our faith (1 John v, 4).

[377] "*Geistreicher Lieder*," Halle, 1731. Hymn No. 634, page 769. Copy in possession of the writer.

395. Mel. Meine Hoffnung stehet 2c.

AUf, ihr Christen, Christi Glieder! die ihr noch hangt an dem Haupt; auf! wacht auf! ermannt euch wieder, eh ihr werdet hingeraubt. Satan beut an den Streit Christo und der Christenheit.

2. Auf! folgt Christo, eurem Helde, trauet seinem starcken Arm, liegt der Satan gleich zu Felde mit dem gantzen Höllen-Schwarm: sind doch der noch vielmehr, die da stets sind um uns her.

3. Nur auf Christi Blut gewaget mit Gebet und Wachsamkeit, dieses machet unverzaget und recht tapfre Krieges-Leut; Christi Blut gibt uns Muth wieder alle Teufels-Brut.

4. Christi Heeres Creutzes-Fahne, so da weiß und roth gesprengt, ist schon auf dem Sieges Plane uns zum Troste ausgehängt; wer hier kriegt, nie erliegt, sondern unterm Creutze siegt.

5. Diesen Sieg hat auch empfunden vieler Heilgen starcker Muth, da sie haben überwundē frölich durch des Lam̄es Blut. Solten wir dann allhier auch nicht streiten mit Begier.

6. Wer die Sclaverey nur liebet, Fleisches Ruh und Sicherheit, und den Sünden sich ergiebet, der hat wenig Lust zum Streit; den die Macht, Satans Macht, hat ihn in den Schlaf gebracht.

7. Aber wen die Weisheit lehret, was die Freyheit für ein Theil, dessen Hertz zu GOtt sich kehret, seinem allerhöchsten Heil, sucht allein ohne Schein Christi freyer Knecht zu seyn.

8. Denn vergnügt auch wohl das Leben, so der Freyheit mangeln muß? Wer sich GOtt nicht gantz ergeben, hat nur Müh, Angst und Verdruß; der, der kriegt recht vergnügt, wer sein Leben selbst besiegt.

9. Drum auf! laßt uns überwinden in dem Blute JEsu Christ, und an unsre Stirne binden sein Wort, so ein Zeugniß ist, das uns deckt und erweckt, und nach Gottes Liebe schmeckt.

10. Unser Leben sey verborgen mit Christo in GOtt alleyn, auf daß wir an jenem Morgen mit ihm offenbar auch seyn, da das Leid dieser Zeit werden wird zu lauter Freud.

11. Da GOtt seinen treuen Knechten geben wird den Gnaden-Lohn, und die Hütten der Gerechten stimmen an den Sieges-Thon; da fürwahr Gottes Schaar ihn wird loben immerdar.

FAC-SIMILE OF HYMN IN THE ZIONITISCHER WEYRAUCHS HÜGEL.

Spiel der Kinder Zions, Berlenburg, 1718. This was the first distinct hymnal published for the use of the Separatists.

In America it was incorporated in the celebrated *Zionitischer Weyrauchs Hügel*, of the Ephrata Community (Sauer, 1738, hymn 395, page 444); also in *Der Kleine Davidische Psalterspiel der kinder Zions* (Sauer, hymn 38, page 41), and a number of other early American hymn books. It is also to be found in the Manuscript Hymnal of the Zionitic Brotherhood, which is known as the *Paradiesische Nadits Tropffen*, 1734 (hymn 11, p. 6).[378] This hymn, after a lapse of two centuries, is still used by nearly all the Protestant denominations in Germany, and is retained in their hymnology in America as well, the latest instance being its retention by the Lutheran Church of the United States in their new German *Kirchen Buch*, wherein it is hymn 331. Especial attention is called to it in Stip's *Unverfälschter Liedersegen* (Berlin, 1851).

ZIONITISCHER
Weyrauchs Hügel
Oder:
Myrrhen Berg,
Worinnen allerley liebliches und wohl riechendes nach Apotheker-Kunst zubereitetes Rauch-Werck zu finden.
Bestehend
In allerley Liebes-Würckungen der in GOTT geheiligten Seelen, welche sich in vielen und mancherley geistlichen und lieblichen Liedern aus gebildet.
Als darinnen
Der letzte Ruff zu dem Abendmahl des grossen GOttes auf unterschiedliche Weise trefflich aus gedrucket ist;
Zum Dienst
Der in dem Abend-Ländischen Welt-Theil als bey dem Untergang der Sonnen erweckten Kirche GOttes, und zu ihrer Ermunterung auf die Mitternächtige Zukunfft des Bräutigams ans Licht gegeben.
Germantown, Gedruckt bey Christoph Sauer.

Julian, in his Dictionary of Hymnology, mentions the following translations into the English language: "Rise, ye children of Salvation" (omitting stanza four) in Mrs. Bevans' "Songs of Eternal Life," 1858, page 10. Three centos[379] have come into use, the translations of stanzas, one, three and nine, in Dr. Pagenstecher's collection, 1864;

[378] Collection of Historical Society of Pennsylvania.

[379] Cento, a composition formed by verses or passages from different authors disposed in a new order.

of stanzas one, five, nine and eleven in the English Presbyterian Psalms and Hymns, 1867; and the Temple Hymn Book, 1867; and stanzas one, five and eleven in *Laudes Domini*, N. Y., 1884.

Another is: "If our all on Him we venture," a translation of stanza three, as stanza two of hymn No. 1064 in the supplement of 1808 to the Moravian Hymn Book of 1801.[380] Another celebrated hymn attributed to Justus Falkner[381] is:

O Herr der Herrlichkeit,
O Glantz der Seligkeit,
Du Licht vom Lichte,
Der Müden süsser Saft,
Des grossen Vater's Kraft,
Sein Angesichte.

This hymn is also to be found in Sauer's *Psalterspiel* (361) and in the *Weyrauchs Hügel* (475, p. 540).

It was toward the close of the young student's academic term at Halle that his elder brother Daniel returned to his native land as an emissary from America, and it was not a very difficult matter for him to induce his younger brother to accompany him on a mission having for its main object the spreading of the Gospel in the "Land of Darkness" (*Abend-land*).

The next official record of the subject of our sketch we find at Rotterdam in Holland, dated April, 1700, where the two brothers accept from Benjamin Furly a power of attorney to act in his stead in America.

As has been before stated, the two brothers, with a number of companions, arrived at Germantown in August, 1700. Shortly afterwards we find him taking a more or less active part in the civic affairs of the German Township,

[380] Hymn No. 509, edition of 1886.

[381] Some credit this hymn to Dr. Petersen.

and serving a term as Burgess. Although we have no direct record of the facts, he without doubt actively seconded his brother in organizing and ministering to the German settlers on the Manatawney tract.

According to the old minute-book "G," before quoted, he appears as joint-attorney with his brother for Benjamin Furly of Rotterdam, and was so acknowledged by William Penn during his second visit to the Province (1699-1701).[382] In a subsequent entry, on the 19th of 11th month, 1701, Daniel and Justus Falkner appear as attorneys for the Frankfort Land Company, and produce a patent for some city property.[383] Upon the 18th of the 12th month, 1701, both brothers again figure before the Land Commissioners in the interests of Benjamin Furly. At different times after the above entry they continue to press the claims of their clients.

On the 30th of the 6th month, 1703, Justus Falkner appears alone before the Commissioners, and as attorney of Furly produces a "return of 1000 acres in Chest'r County, "said to be in Pursuance of our Warr't dat. 16, 12 Mo., "1701, and the Same Land appearing to be an Encroachm't "upon the Welch Tract within their Settlements, and "already granted to David Lloyd and Is. Norris, the same "is Rejected and disapproved of, and thereupon 'Tis "Ordered that the Same be Certifyed by Indorsement On "the said Return under Ye Comm'rs hands, which is accord-"ingly Done."

It is evident from the above official minute that the loss of this parcel of land to Furly was not through any fault of the Falkner brothers, as has been frequently stated by Pastorius. The charge by the latter that they sold the

382 Pennsylvania Archives, Second Series, xix, 243-44.

383 *Ibid*, 249-50.

above land for their own use and benefit is also hereby shown to be without any foundation.

The above entry is the last notice of Justus Falkner upon the official records of Pennsylvania. This attempt to recover the land for its rightful owner was evidently the beginning of the differences with Daniel Lloyd and Isaac Norris, which ended five years later in the Sprogel conspiracy and the dispossession of Daniel Falkner.

That Justus Falkner, during his sojourn in Pennsylvania, was a man without reproach and one of exemplary piety, may be judged from his subsequent career and the fact that his name is not even mentioned by the splenetic Pastorius, who so persistantly vilified the elder brother. Just what part Justus bore in the organization of the Lutheran congregation at Falkner's Swamp (New Hannover, Montgomery County, Penna.), the first German Lutheran congregation organized in America, or how often he was wont to visit the church or minister to his fellow-countrymen, cannot be told to a certainity; nor can his sojourn among the Mystics on the Wissahickon be traced in detail. His intercourse, however, with Kelpius, Seelig, and the Swedish pastors, Rudman, Biörck, Sandel and Auren, is known to have been frequent and intimate.

An important historical error can now be postively corrected, viz.: "That Justus Falkner was ordained for the purpose of serving the German congregation at Falkner's Swamp on the Manatawney tract." It appears from his own memorandum that with the exception of a possible farewell sermon, he never served the Manatawney congregation nor any other one in Pennsylvania after his ordination.

We now come to what is to us historically the most interesting episode in the career of the Saxon Pietist and Pennsylvania Theosophist, and one in which he was the central figure, and that is the first regular Lutheran ordination in the Western Hemisphere. The circumstances connected with the ordination of Justus Falkner at Wicacoa are as follows:

Andreas Rudman, the Swedish pastor at Wicacoa, had received repeated calls for help from the distressed Lutherans in New York, who had been without any clergyman to minister to their wants for some length of time. Consequently, after the arrival of Rev. Andreas Sandel, March 10, 1701–2, Magister Rudman gave their forlorn condition his earnest consideration, and finding their case as bad as had been represented concluded personally to take charge of the extended mission.

In pursuance of this resolve he, on July 5, 1702, installed Sandel as rector of Wicacoa, and on the 19th of the same month he preached his valedictory sermon. At the conclusion of the sermon, he embraced the opportunity of making public Auren's Sabbatarian doctrine and implored his parishioners to be upon their guard and remain true to the Lutheran faith. A confessional service and the Eucharist closed the impressive occasion.[384]

Early on the next day, July 20th, Rudman started for New York, accompanied by Mr. Thomas, a schoolmaster at Christ Church, who was in deacon's orders, and intended to sail for England to receive ordination. A number of Swedes, led by Pastor Sandel, Matz Keen, Peter Rambo and Eric Keen, also accompanied them part of the way.

SEAL OF EAST JERSEY, A.D. 1703.

Rudman, upon his arrival in New York, at once commenced to gather up and organize the Lutherans (German, Dutch and Swedish) who were scattered over the large territory, which, in

[384] MSS. diary of Andreas Sandel.

addition to the embryo city and the valley of the Hudson, included Long Island and East Jersey as far west as the Delaware River.[385]

After Rudman was well established in his new field of labor, he sent to Pennsylvania for his wife and young family, and all went well until the summer of the following year, when the yellow fever broke out in the citadel and town. In the latter part of August Dominie Rudman and his family were prostrated by the terrible scourge, and upon the death of his second son, Anders, he wrote to Philadelphia for aid, stating that both he and his daughter were stricken with the disorder.[386]

In response to this urgent appeal, Revs. Biörck and Sandel at once made arrangements to go to his assistance; but so slow were the imperfect means of communication at that time, it was not until September 13th that a start was made from Philadelphia to relieve the stricken pastor. The party arrived in New York on the afternoon of the 16th, where they found Dominie Rudman recovering, but his daughter still severely ill.[387]

Dominie Rudman never entirely recovered from this attack, and being of a frail constitution he realized, after another year's trial, that on account of the rigor of the climate he could not continue in charge during another winter. In this extremity, not wishing to leave the field uncovered, he bethought himself of the Falkner brothers, and finding that Daniel had married and was occupied with

---

385 Phillipsburg, opposite Easton, was the most westward station.

386 Sandel's Diary.

387 Sandel, in his diary, notes: "Sept. 17, 1702, we went looking about the town that day and saw the English Church and also the Dutch [Reformed?] both of them edifices of beauty.

Sept. 20. "To-day we went calling on all who profess the Lutheran creed; there are very few here."

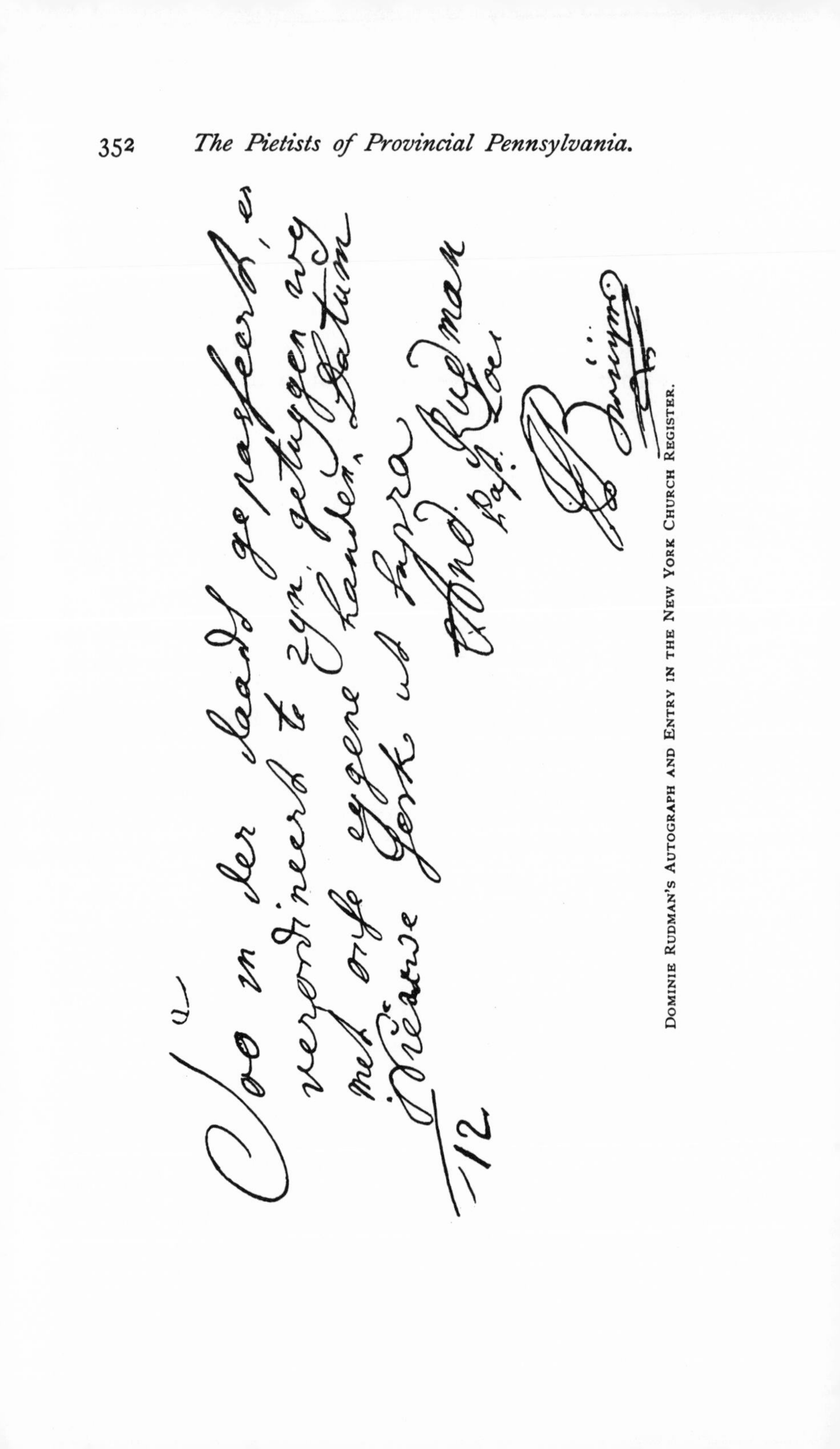

DOMINIE RUDMAN'S AUTOGRAPH AND ENTRY IN THE NEW YORK CHURCH REGISTER.

the civic affairs of the German Township, he invited the younger brother, October 27th, 1703, to come to New York and preach a trial sermon. This was followed three days later by a formal call from the congregation to serve them as pastor.

Justus Falkner acknowledged both letters under date of November 3, 1703, accepting the call, but refused to preach a trial sermon. As the people supported him in this refusal, Dominie Rudman forthwith severed his connection with the New York congregation and returned to Philadelphia, where he acted as suffragan to the Archbishop of Upsala, assisted by Rev. Eric Biörck of Christiana,[388] and Andreas Sandel of Wicacoa.

On Wednesday, November 24, 1703, he ordained the deacon (*Candidat Theologiæ*), Justus Falkner, to the holy priesthood, according to the ritual of the Swedish Orthodox Lutheran Church. The ceremony took place within the consecrated precincts of "Gloria Dei" (Old Swedes) at Wicacoa.

It was a solemn ceremony which was enacted upon that bleak November day within the bare walls of the Swedish church on the banks of the Delaware. The sacred structure, as yet bare and unfinished, lacked both tower and side projections. The interior, with its rough walls and exposed roof, earthen floors and hard benches, well matched the unadorned altar within the recess in the east, separated by a rude railing from the body of the church and its primitive surroundings.

Upon this occasion no pealing organ, with a multitude of stops and pedals, vestured choir, or elaborate music made melody for the service. No long procession of robed

---

[388] Wilmington, Delaware.

clergy, with mitred bishop surrounded by acolytes and led by the Cross-bearer, were present to add dignity to the scene and impress the beholder with awe.

The ceremony of ordination, although simple and devoid of all pomp and glitter, was none the less solemn and impressive. This was greatly due to a number of the Theosophical Brethern from the Ridge, under the leadership of Magister Johannes Kelpius, who had come down from the Wissahickon to give *éclat* to the elevation of one of their number as Presbyter in the Lutheran Church.

The Theosophical Brotherhood, partly clad in the habit of the German University student, others in the rough pilgrim garb of unbleached homespun, occupied the front benches, while the rear of the church was filled with a number of Swedes and a sprinkling of English Churchmen and Dissenters. It is said that even a few Quakers and Indians were attracted to the church, and enhanced the picturesqueness of the scene.

The service was opened with a voluntary on the little organ[389] in the gallery by Jonas the organist,[390] supple-

[389] This is the earliest reference to a church organ in any Protestant church in America. It is not known to a certainty just where or when they obtained it. If it had been sent over from Sweden, that fact would undoubtedly have appeared upon the records. There is a strong probability that this instrument was brought over by Kelpius and his party in 1694, and that it was originally set up in the Tabernacle on the Wissahickon.

The present writer has seen a letter by Kelpius in which reference is made to an organ, but all trace of this paper now seems to be lost. There is also an account that Dr. Witt and others of the Community built an organ at Germantown or Wissahickon at an early day. Among the musical instruments brought over by the Brotherhood was a virginal (a keyed instrument, something like a pianoforte). This afterwards reverted to the widow of Magister Zimmermann, and appears in the inventory of her effects.

The first church organ introduced into Christ Church, Philadelphia, was obtained in 1728 from Ludovic Christian Sprogell, who was one of the survivors of the Brotherhood on the Ridge.

mented with instrumental music by the Mystics on the viol, hautboy,[391] trumpets (*Posaunen*) and kettle-drums (*Pauken*).[392] After this they intoned the Anthem:

Veni Creator Spiritus,
Mentes tuorum visita,
Imple superna gratia,
Quae tu creasti pectora, etc.

While this was being sung, a little procession of six persons entered the church by the west portal. First came two churchwardens, then the candidate for ordination, with Rev. Andreas Sandel as sponser[393] by his side; lastly, Revs. Erick Biörck and Andreas Rudman, the latter as suffragan or vice-bishop.[394]

As the little procession reached the chancel rail, the two wardens (*Eldeste*) stood on either side of the railing, while the suffragan and the two priests entered within the chancel and ranged themselves in front and at either side of the altar, upon which were placed a crucifix and lighted tapers. The suffragan was robed in a girdled surplice, with chasuble[395] and stole, while the two assistants wore the black clerical robe[396] (*Schwarze Taler*). The candidate, wearing the collegiate gown of the German University, knelt before the rail, upon which a chasuble[397] (*chor-hemd*) had been previously placed.

---

390 The earliest mention of Jonas the organist is in Sandel's diary, under date July 20, 1702, as one of the number that accompanied Pastor Rudman part of the way on his journey to New York.

391 Hautboy, a wind instrument, somewhat like a flute or clarionette.

392 *Vide* Kelpius Diary, Falkner, Sendschreiben and "Pennsylvania Magazine," vol. xi, page 434.

393 Sandel also acted as secretary of the Consistorium on this occasion.

394 *Vide* "Hallesche Nachrichten," new ed., pp. 441, 478; also W. C. Berkenmeyer *vs.* Van Dieren, J. Peter Zenger, New York, 1728.

395 This garment was not strictly a chasuble, but a white lace garment similar to the Roman surplice.

396 Similar to the one still worn by the Lutheran clergy.

The anthem being ended, the suffragan, standing in front of the altar facing the congregation, opened the services proper with an invitation to prayer. Then turning to the east, while all kneeled, he repeated the following invocation.

[" Almighty and everlasting God, the Father of our Lord Jesus Christ, who himself has commanded us that we shall pray for laborers in thy harvest, we pray thy unsearchable mercy that thou wouldst send us right-minded teachers, and give thy holy and wholesome Word into their hearts and mouths, so that they without error may both correctly teach and perfectly execute all thy commandments, in order that we being taught, exhorted, comforted and strengthened by thy holy Word, may do that which is pleasing unto thee and useful to us.

"Grant us, O Lord, thy Holy Spirit, that thy Word may always remain among us; that it may increase and bear fruit, and that thy servant may with befitting courage preach thy Word, so that thy holy Christian Church[398] may be edified thereby, and may serve thee in steadfast faith, and forever continue in the knowledge of thee. Through Jesus Christ our Lord. Amen."]

The suffragan then arose and turned to the congregation, after which Rev. Sandel, acting as consistorial secretary, advanced to the chancel rail and read out the name of the candidate and the charge to which he was called.

The suffragan, then addressing the kneeling candidate, said: "Inasmuch as you, Justus Falkner, are called to the Holy office of the Ministry, and in order that you with us, and we with you, may rightly understand the sacredness of this calling, then let us hear the promise and the exhortation

---

[397] Also known as a "Mess-hemd," a short white garment worn over the black robe when officiating at the altar.

[398] Literally, congregation,

of the Word of God." At this point, Rev. Biörck stepped forward and read out the following parts of Scripture:

Matt. xxviii, 18-20; St. John ii, 15-17, xx, 21-23; Matt. x, 32-33; 2 Cor. v, 17-20; Jeremiah xv, 19; Matt. v, 13-16; 1 Tim. iv, 7-8, 12-14, 16; 2 Tim. ii, 15-16, 22-25; 1 Peter v, 2-4.

When this reading was concluded, Vice-Bishop Rudman advanced and said: "May God give you grace that you may faithfully guard these sayings in your heart. May they be a guide for your conversation, and remind you of your responsibility. May *it* increase your watchfulness, uphold your zeal, and now and forever consecrate you to the service of Heaven.

"The Church of Jesus Christ expects of you that, being sensible of the weight of the ministerial office, you yourself shall consider the important duties which this office lays upon your shoulders. The Church of Jesus Christ expects of you that, in believing prayers in the name of Jesus Christ, you implore God for grace and power worthily to exercise it. The Church of Jesus Christ expects of you that you fight a good and faithful fight, lay hold of eternal life and make a good confession. Confess therefore your faith before God and this congregation."

Sandel, as secretary, now advanced and slowly read the Apostolic Creed, each word being carefully repeated by the candidate before the next following one was uttered by the secretary.[399] When this important feature of the ritual was concluded the suffragan said:

"May the Lord God grant unto you grace to stand fast in this faith to the end, and to strengthen those who are your brethern in the faith."

---

[399] The original states that the confession was *spelled* out letter for letter, word for word.

Advancing to the kneeling candidate, the suffragan asked the following questions:

"Do you, Justus Falkner, declare yourself willing to undertake this holy ministerial office in the name of the holy Trinity?"

To which the candidate answered a clear "Yes."

"Will you solemnly promise that this office shall be worthily and rightly administered in all its parts, to the glory of God and the salvation of souls?"

Again the same clear response "Yes."

"Will you always continue in the pure Word of God, flee all false and heretical teaching, preach Jesus Christ according to the Word of God, and administer the Holy Sacraments according to his institution?"

Response, "I will."

"Will you so regulate your life that it may be an example to the faithful, and shall scandalize no one?"

The kneeling man again answered in the affirmative.

The suffragan continuing, said:

"You acknowledge therefore your obligations. You have declared it to be your purpose to fulfill them. Confirm it now with your oath of office."

The obligation was then administered upon the Holy Evangels by the acting secretary.[400]

After which the suffragan continued:

"May the Almighty God strengthen you and help you to keep all this, and according to the power given to me in God's stead by the Church, I hereby confer upon you the ministerial dignity in the name of God the Father and the Son and the Holy Ghost. Amen."

The candidate here again kneeled, while the Brother-

---

[400] Text of obligation is missing.

hood intoned, to the soft strains of instrumental music, the hymn:

> "Veni Sancto Spirit,
> Reple tuorum corda fidelium."

During the singing of this hymn, the suffragan, assisted by the two clergymen, invested the candidate with the chasuble and stole. When this ceremony was completed and the hymn sung, the suffragan repeated the Lord's Prayer, while he imparted the Apostolic succession[401] by the laying on of hands. He then returned to the altar, and said, "Let us pray." Then, turning once more to the east, he read the following invocation:

"O everlasting merciful God; dear heavenly Father, who through thy beloved Son, our Lord Jesus Christ, hast said unto us, the harvest is plenteous but the laborers are few; pray ye therefore the Lord of the harvest that he send forth laborers into his harvest, and who by these words hast made us understand that we cannot procure rightminded and faithful teachers except only of thy merciful hand: we pray thee therefore of our whole heart that thou wouldst mercifully look upon this thy servant who is now ordained to thy service and to the holy office of thy Ministry, and give him thy Holy Spirit, so that he may go forth under watching and be strengthened by thy Word, and be able to stand fast in the fight for thy kingdom, and to execute thy work, teach and reprove men with all humility and learning; in order that thy Holy Gospel may continue among us pure and unadulterated, and bear for us the fruits of salvation and of eternal life. Through thy Son Jesus Christ our Lord. Amen."

Here the sufragan, turning to the kneeling postulant, said: "Bow down your heart to God and receive the benediction."

---

[401] This was according to the Swedish ritual.

After this was given the impressive liturgy was at an end. The Theosophists then intoned the 115th Psalm: "*Non Nobis Dominie*," during which the little procession reformed and as the last verse was sung slowly left the church, and the solemn and impressive ceremonial which marked the first regular ordination of a Protestant clergyman in America was at an end.

The reader may ask: Did the newly ordained pastor keep his sacred ordination vows? This the sequel of our sketch will show. It may, however, be permitted here to say without anticipation that no more active, disinterested or pious clergyman ever labored among the Germans and Dutch during the trying Colonial period than this same Justus Falkner.

On the next day, after the certificate of ordination had been engrossed in due form by Johann Seelig, it was laid upon the altar before which the ordination had taken place, and there was signed by the three officiating clergymen.

And. Rudman

Ericus Tob. Biörck

Andreas Sandel

SIGNATURES OF THE THREE OFFICIATING CLERGYMEN.

It was dated November 25, 1703, and bore the signature of Andreas Rudman as vice-bishop.[402]

---

[402] Rudman and Sandel.

GLORIA DEI (OLD SWEDES) WICACOA.

AFTER ETCHING BY LUDWIG E. FABER.

Thus the new dominie was sent out to minister in the adjoining Provinces; and to the Orthodox Lutheran Church in Pennsylvania is due the honor of having ordained and sent out the first man, a native of Saxony, for missionary purposes in the Western World; who was to labor, not among those of his own kith and kin, but among people who used a tongue foreign to his own.

Pastor Justus Falkner at once made preparations to enter upon his new field of labor. He arrived in New York city on Thursday, the second of December, or just eight days after his ordination. After preaching on the third and fourth Sundays in Advent, he was accepted as their regular pastor by the oldest Lutheran congregation in America.

The first record made by him in the *Kercken-Boeck*, or church register, shortly after his arrival sets forth the facts of his call in Dutch, with a short prayer in classical Latin.

[In the name of Jesus. In the year of Christ, 1703, on the second of December, I, Justus Falckner, born in Saxony, Germany, at Langen-Reinsdorff, in the district of Zwickau, came to Philadelphia, thence to New York, after previous invitation. On the third Sunday after Advent I delivered two sermons in the Lutheran Church here. I did the same on the fourth Sunday after Advent. Thereupon I was received by the Consistorium of the Christian Protestant Lutheran Congregation as their regular pastor and teacher.]

Then followes the invocation:

"*Deus Ter Optimus Maximo qui intrusit me hanc in messem, adsit speciali sua gratia mihi operaio abjecto et admodum infirmo, sine qua pereundum mihi est sub mole tentationum, quae me saepius obrunt. In Te, Domine, speravi, non sinas me confundi! Redde me ad vocationem meam aptum; non cucurri, sed misisti, intrusisti; interim quic-*

In Nomine Jesu!

Anno Christi 1703. Den 2[t] Decemb.
ben Ick Justus Falckner, gebooren in Sassen in Germania
tot Langen-Reinsdorff onder het Ampt Zwickau, van Phila=
delphia hier in Newyorck nae voorgaende Beroepinge, aenge
komen, en hebbe den derden Advents-Sondagh twee Predicatien
in de Lutherische Kercke allhier gehouden; diesgelycken oock
den vierden Advents Sondagh: Daerop ben ick van het
Consistorium der Christelycken Protestantischen Lutherischen
Gemeene, tot haer ordentlycke Pastor en Leraer aengenomen
worden! Deus Ter Optimus Maximus qui intrusit me hanc in messem
adsit speciali sua gratia, mihi operario abjecto et admodum infirmo,
sine qua pereundum mihi est, sub mole tentationum, quæ me sæpius
obruunt! In Te Domine speravi, non sinas me confundi! redde me
ad vocationem meam aptum; non cucurri; sed misisti, intrusisti:
interim quicquid in me inscio, corrupta admiscuerit natura, remit
te, da veniam humiliter deprecanti, per Dominum nostrum imo
meum Jesum Christum Amen!!

Fac-simile of Justus Falkner's First Entry in the Church Register at New York.

quid in me inscio corrupta admiscuerit natura remitte; da veniam humiliter deprecanti, per Dominum nostrum, imo meum Jesum Christum. Amen."

[God, the Father of all mercy, and Lord of great majesty, who hast sent me into this harvest, be with me, thy lowly and ever-feeble laborer, with thy special grace, without which I should perish under the burden of temptation which often overcomes me with its might. In thee, O Lord, have I trusted; let me not be confounded. Strengthen me in my calling. I did not seek it, but thou hast sent me, yea, placed me in the office. Meanwhile wouldst thou grant remission for whatsoever, without my knowledge, a corrupt nature has introduced within me, and forgive and pardon me upon my humble supplication, through our Lord, yea, my Jesus Christ. Amen.]

A *fac-simile* of this interesting entry is also reproduced; it was photographed from the original by the present writer.

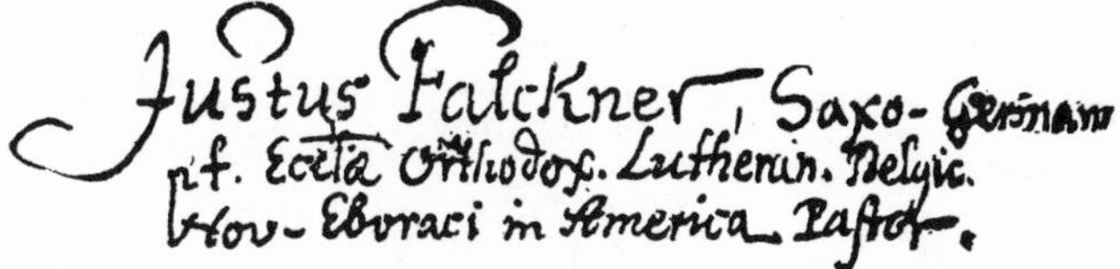

OFFICIAL SIGNATURE OF DOMINIE FALKNER.

The time when Pastor Falkner arrived in New York was far from being a propitious one, as the settlers were in constant fear of attack by both sea and land.[403]

The Hudson Valley from one end to the other was menanced by the enemy. All residents were forced to be constantly prepared to defend their life and property by water as well as land.

---

[403] This was during the war of the Spanish succession, in which England was engaged against France.

Two members of the church council, Church Warden (*Eldeste*) Jan Hendrick and Vestryman (*Vorsteher*) Pieter van Woglom, with whom the new pastor made his home, were military officers. The former was a major of infantry, a highly respected man, who well appreciated the serious aspect of the general situation.

In addition to the above, Church Warden Andreas van Boskerk; *Vorsteher* and Overseer (*kirch-meister*) Laur van Boskerk; the sacristans Hanns La Grangie and Joh. Viet, with Samuel Beekman, reader and sexton, all were liable to military duty when the occasion required their services.

SEAL OF NEW YORK, A.D. 1703.

At the other end of his extended territory, church affairs were, if anything, at a still lower ebb. Pastor Falkner, upon his first visit to Albany, found the congregation there virtually disbanded. A small and dilapidated house was called by courtesy a church, and the membership scattered without officers or organization. It was not until June, 1705, that he succeeded in effecting a permanent organization.

As for any regular stipend in either place, none was in prospect. Church finances were at so low an ebb that bare promises were not even made looking towards the pastor's sustenance. A reliable account that has come down to our time informs us that the situation for a time was even worse in New York than elsewhere.

Dominie Falkner must indeed have been a courageous man as well as a pious one to enter upon this extended field, which he eventually enlarged by serving all the Germans along the Hudson and in East Jersey, from the

Hackensack in Bergan County to the valley of the Raritan, without any prospect of renumeration. Another fact to be taken into consideration, and one that proves more than anything else how earnest, faithful and diligent he was, is that he came here an entire stranger, among people whose tongue was somewhat different from his own, and in the face of the direct opposition of the resident Reformed clergy and laity, who where then numerically in the majority, and received their sustenance from the Amsterdam Classis.

One of the first things done by our pious evangelist was to issue a call for a meeting at the house of his landlord, of the "Protestant Christian Congregation[404] adhering to the unaltered Augsburg Confession,"[405] to take into consideration the dire necessities of the church. At this meeting, after some desultory discussion, it was resolved to send out circular letters asking for assistance. These letters were signed by Falkner and the church officers. Three were sent to the Swedish Lutheran brethern in the South.[406] A fourth circular was addressed personally to Magister Rudman, asking his intercession in their behalf with the Germans and English in Pennsylvania. Still later a similar circular, with special reference to the ruinous condition of the church, was sent to the Dutch Lutherans on the Island of St. Thomas in the West Indies.

Subsequently a sum of money was received in response to this last appeal, but unfortunately with the proviso that it was to be used only towards building a new church.[407]

---

[404] *Christliche Protestantischen Gemeinde, der ungeänderten Augsburgischen Confession zugethan.*

[405] *Vide* page 66, *supra.*

[406] On the Delaware river, viz., at Wicacoa, Christiana and Penn's Neck in New Jersey.

Here a new complication arose: the money was badly needed for congregational purposes, and so was a new church building, but during the prevailing financial stringency there was no way of suplementing the amount received so as to make it available.

In this dilemma another congregational meeting was convened by Dominie Falkner at the house of Reader Beekman, where it was resolved that the old building should be made tenantable with moneys to be collected by the church-wardens, while the St. Thomas funds were to remain intact and be kept as the nucleus of a building fund for a future church.[408]

The Dutch Reformed congregation in New York was in far better shape, and at first it seems strange that no assistance was offered by them to the Lutherans. At this time there was considerable friction in the colony between the Dutch Lutheran and Reformed congregations. The es-

---

[407] The first Lutheran church in New York was built outside of the Citadel about where Bowling Green now is. When New York came once more into the possession of the Dutch, this building was razed for military reasons, in lieu of which a lot was given the congregation at what is now the S. W. Cor. Broadway and Rector Street. The first church upon this site served the congregation until 1729, when a new building was erected, partly by the efforts of Daniel Falkner.

July 6, 1784, the congregation having substituted the German for the Dutch tongue, united with the German Lutheran Church, known as the Swamp congregation, and assumed the name "The Corporation of the United German Lutheran Churches of New York," the services were transferred to the church at Frankfort and William Streets. About 1826 the united congregation moved to Walker Street near Broadway.

By a special act of the legislature, passed March 29, 1866, the name was changed to "The German Evangelical Lutheran Church of St. Matthew." A spacious church was secured at the N. E. Cor. of Broome and Elizabeth Streets, where the congregation now worship.

[408] The second church was not built until some years after Justus Falkner's death, and then only by the personal efforts of his brother Daniel. *Vide* page 326–7, *supra*.

trangement was partly caused by the orthodoxy of the Lutheran pastor and his close adherence to the unaltered Augsburg Confession.[409] Discussions were indulged in, not only by the rival pastors, but by the individual members as well, and heated arguments often resulted.

To place his people in a position the better to uphold their faith and controvert the arguments of the Reformed, Dominie Falkner prepared a little book in the colloquial style of the period, in which he attempted to fortify his readers by quotations from the Scriptures against what he designated "Calvinistic errors."

This book, published by William Bradford, was in the low Dutch language, and was the first Orthodox Lutheran text-book published in America. Falkner was the second Lutheran clergyman to avail himself of the Bradford press; his predecessor having been Heinrich Bernhard Köster, in 1695.[410]

The title of this work reads as follows:

"Fundamental Instruction || upon || certain chiet || prominent articles of the || Veritable, undefiled, Beatifical || Christian Doctrine, || founded upon the basis of the Apostles and Prophets of which || Jesus Christus || is the corner-stone, || expounded in plain, but edifying || Questions and Answers. || By || Justus Falckner, Saxo || Germanus, Minister of the Christian || Protestant so-called Lutheran || Congregation at N. York and Albany. || Printed in New York by W. Bradfordt, || 1708.

A *fac-simile* of this title page is also reproduced. The original is in the collection of the Pennsylvania Historical Society.

In the preface, which is also in Dutch, the compiler

---

409 *Vide* foot-note, page 66.

410 Page 266, *supra*.

GRONDLYCKE ONDERRICHT
VAN
Sekere Voorname Hoofd-ſtucken, der
Waren, Loutern, Saligmakenden,
Chriſtelycken Leere,
Gegrondet op den Grondt van de Apo-
ſtelen en Propheten, daer
Jeſus Chriſtus
de HOECK-STEEN.
IS.
Angeweſen in eenvoudige, dog ſtigtlycke
Vragen en *Antwoorden*,
Door
JUSTUS FALCKNER, *Saxo-
Germanus*, Miniſter der Chriſtelycken
Proteſtantſen Genaemten Lutherſchen
Gemeente te *N. York* en *Alban.en*,
&c.
Pſal. 119. v. 104. (*God*) s *Woort maeckt my
Kloeck*; *daerom hate ick alle valſche Wegen.*

Gedruckt te Nieuw-York by W. Bradfordt,
1708

TITLE OF FIRST LUTHERAN TEXT-BOOK PRINTED IN AMERICA.

commits himself absolutely to the symbolism of the Lutheran Church, the confession of the Fathers; "which confession," he continues, "and faith by the grace of God, and the conviction of his Word and Spirit, lives also in me, and shall remain there until my blissful end."

He further states that it is to be distinctly understood that the contents of this book are to be taken in strict conformity with the teachings, confession and faith of the Lutheran Church, to which his parents and grandparents belonged. He continues: "Both my grandfathers, paternal and maternal, as well as my father, were found worthy by the grace of God to serve in the holy priesthood of his aggressive church."

The body of the book consists, as before stated, of a series of questions and answers. The last two pages are taken up with hymns. The first, of three stanzas of ten lines each, is a Dutch translation of Luther's hymn, "*Wir glauben all an einem Gott.*" This is followed by a hymn to be sung before the sermon, which has four stanzas of four lines each. The last one is a hymn of two stanzas of twelve lines each. These are evidently of his own composition and without doubt are the first original hymns published in the Western Hemisphere.[411]

The whole book is remarkable for its orthodoxy, and it attracted the attention of leading divines in Germany. The celebrated Löscher, in his "Continuations" for 1726, designates this text-book as a "*Compendium Doctrinae Anti-Calvinianum.*

It certainly is greatly to the credit of Dominie Falkner, with his widespread field of labor, that he should have found time to compile the above book. How earnestly he

[411] No traces of these hymns are to be found in the older Lutheran hymnals accessible to the writer.

2. Heer Jesu Christ, Thy Godes Lam!
Wy zyn versaemt in uwen Naem:
Weest dan in 't midden van ons, Heer,
En geeft ons aendacht tot uw Leer.
3. Heyl'ge Geest, ons in waerheyd leydt;
Uws dienaers mondt en tong bereydt:
Laet 't woordt door d'ooren 't hert ingaen,
En help ons doen na uw vermaen.
4. Heer, ons' Godt boven al vermaerd
In drie Persoonen g'openbaert;
Wy bidden U hert'lyck t'samen,
Verhoort doch dees onse beed'! Amen.

HEer Godt dyn trouw met g'naed' verleen
En schick dyn heyl'gen Geest met een
Die ons de waerheydt leere;
En geef verstandt, hert, sin, Heer Godt,
Dat ons uw Woordt niet zy een spot,
Maer gantsch tot U bekeere.
O God, uw g'naed' daer aen bewys,
Dat hem wel schick tot uwen prys,
Al onse doen en laten;
Wat hind'ren mach, dat selve wendt;
Wat voord'ren mach, dat geef behendt,
Te wand'len uwe straten.
2. En stuur ons wel Heer by den tydt:
Wy weten niet hoe seer subyt
Passeeren onse Dagen.
Lucht, g'loof, vrees, vrede liefd'en en trouw
Leer ons uw Geest, die ons nieuw bouw,
Dat wil Hy niet af-slagen.
Hy b'hoed altydt voor valsche leer,
De boose werl'l ook trouw'lyck weer
Dat sy ons niet verblinde:
Hy deel uyt syn Barmhertigheydt,
Toon ons daer voor de Saligheydt,
En help met g'naed' ten ende.

FAC-SIMILE OF THE FIRST ORIGINAL HYMN PRINTED IN AMERICA.

felt for the charges under his care is shown by the fact that he invited his elder brother Daniel to leave Pennsylvania and take charge of the scattered German and Dutch congregations in East Jersey.

Although the chief centers of his activity were Albany and New York, we find this untiring missionary establishing preaching stations at various widely distant points in the Hudson Valley. Geographically speaking, his charge was divided into two parts: one south, the other north of the Highlands of the Hudson. Falkner was wont to serve the former in the summer season, and the latter during the winter months. During the summer, in addition to his city charge, he served the congregations at Hackensack, Raritan, Remmerspach, Piscataway, Elizabethtown and Phillipsburg.

In the north his activity extended from Albany to Loonenburg (Athens), Klickenberg, Four Mile Point, Coxsackie, Kinderhook and Calverack. Wherever Dutch Lutherans settled there Dominie Falkner was found plying his sacred calling. To the above must be added the German congregations founded after the large immigration had set in during the early years of Queen Anne's reign, which were served in their native tongue by the zealous evangelist.

This latter duty became especially onerous during the absence of the German Pastor, Rev. Josua Kocherthal, and his subsequent death in 1719, when the German Lutheran congregations at Quassaik, Rosenthal, Schawanggunk, Langen Rack, Newtown, Tarbush, Queensbury, Rhinebeck and Schoharie were all visited by Falkner at more or less regular intervals.

Among the papers relating to the Palatines, published in vol. iii. of the "Documentary History of New York," is found the following notice: "*Litra* B. In the Books by our Church,[412] Fol. 28, is to be found that our then minister Justus Falkenier has baptized Ao 1710 Ye 19th April in the house of one of the Trustees, *of* which Time he has continued to serve the People there every year without any Profit of the Glebe."

That these stations were not merely small hamlets or isolated farm-houses, is shown by the entries in his register, as he frequently upon the same occasion baptized five, six, eight, nine or ten children. A personal account of his ministrations has fortunately been preserved to us in Biörck's *Dissertatic Gradualis*, before mentioned, published in Sweden, 1731.

Biörck there states: "The care of these churches [the Dutch Lutheran Churches in New York] was therefore [after the illness of Dominie Rudman] committed to Magister Justus Falkner, a German, and the planting of them brought forth, after some time, so plentiful a harvest that seven churches successively ordained in the same way might be enumerated, as Falkner intimates in a letter to Magister Sandel, dated New York, September 28, 1715.

"In the Jerseys, there I visit three small Lutheran con-"gregations[413] living a great distance one from the other, all "these three consist of about one hundred communicants, "the most poor people and poor settlers.

"In the Province of New York I serve four small Luth-"eran congregations, & all these four consist in all of about "one hundred constant communicants, besides strangers "going & coming in the city of N. York, so that in all I "have seven congregations, whom to serve I must yearly "travel about twelve hundred English miles."

---

412 On Quassaik Creek in Ulster County.

413 These congregations were in Bergen County along the Hudson, and evidently do not include those on the Raritan, which were ministered to by his brother Daniel.

Biörck then adds, "Thus these men were punctual enough in meeting, although scattered far and wide. Moreover:

"Mr. Kocherthal resideth as yet for the most time in one place on Hudson's River, but visiteth two places on the other side of the river, where particular Lutheran congregations meet. He has been as yet but once with those Lutheran Palatines that live in the Mohacks' country.

"We have brought forward these things so much out of our way, in order to make it clear that the splendor of the Gospel had already shone in such various places of America."

To reach these widely separated stations was a serious question. No regular conveyances existed; the only means of intercourse was either by canoe on the watercourses or on horseback through the almost trackless forest, unprotected from the elements and exposed to the dangers from wild beasts and a treacherous savage. Still, even these dangers failed to deter this pioneer missionary from his path of duty.

Great as was this widespread field of his ministrations, we have records, that he, in addition, found time to extend his labors and spread the Gospel among the negro slaves in the colony, as well as the Indians who still remained in the vicinity.

The old church records and registers of the venerable Trinity Lutheran Church (now St. Matthew's at the corner of Broome and Elizabeth Streets) give us the best insight into the piety and untiring energy of Justus Falkner.

It is indeed fortunate that these records have been preserved to the present generation. They were saved from destruction during the great conflagration in 1776 by the heroism of the pastor, who rescued them from the burning parsonage at the peril of his life; after which they were securely placed in the cellar of the new church, and were forgotten until found by chance a few years ago; and now, by the courtesy of the Reverend John Henry Seiker, the pastor of the church, they have been placed at the disposal of the present writer.

Dominie Falkner evidently considered the Church Book of the New York congregation as his official register, and copied his ministerial acts upon its pages, irrespective of where they were administered.

This interesting relic had been procured some time previous to the arrival of Dominie Falkner, as is shown by a memorandum or two in Pastor Rudmann's handwriting. No effort seems to have been made by the latter to keep a separate record of his ministerial acts in New York, and they were without doubt entered upon the records of the Wicacoa church, which was his official station.

It was consequently left to Justus Falkner to open the church register of the Trinity Lutheran congregation in New York. This book is the oldest systematic Lutheran record in America, and is in the unmistakable handwriting of the pastor.

On the first page it states that "this is the Church Register (*Kercken-Boeck*) of the Christian Apostolic Protestant Lutheran Congregation, according to the unaltered Confession of Augsburg, in New York, and the other thereto belonging places in America."

Then follows a brief list of contents:

"An inventory of books and papers belonging to the Church, folio 3.

"Baptismal Record (*Doop Register*), folio 79*a*.

"Register of such persons as partook for the first time with our Christian Apostolic Protestant Lutheran Congregation of the Holy Sacrament, folio 87*b*.

"Register of such as have been dismissed by the congregation, folio 109.

KERCKEN-BOECK.

v: de Christelycke Apostolische Protestantische Lutherische
Gemeente toegedaen de onveranderte Confessie van Augsburg
in Newyorck en andern daertoe behoorende Plaetse
in America.

Inhoudt van dit Boeck

Inventarium van de Boecken en papieren, aan de
kerk behoorende. . . . . Fol. 3.

PHOTOGRAPHED FROM THE ORIGINAL.

"Register of such as were married by the pastors of said congregation, folio 145.

"Burial Register, folio 185.

"Register of Church Officers, folio 316.

"Justus Falckner, Saxo-Germano nf. Eccla. Orthodox Lutheran Belvic Nov-Eboraci in America, Pastor."

To the historian the most interesting item on the above page is the reference to an inventory of church papers, then (1704) in possession of the corporation. They consisted of several bundles or packages of documents, and were labelled "Church papers," Packet I, II, etc., respectively. These documents have long since disappeared; the only record of them which has came down to us being Falkner's inventory in the *Kercken-Boeck.*

Among the itemized list, Packet No. 11 would be of exceeding interest if it were still in existence, as it contained, among other documents, the following:

Item No. 5.—The congregational call of Justus Falkner.

" *6.*—Rudmann's letter to Falkner, and Falkner's reply and acceptance.

" *8.*—A personal report from Falkner to Rudmann.

" *9.*—The engrossed certificate of ordination granted to Justus Falkner, and signed by the three Swedish pastors on the Delaware. This document was deposited by Justus Falkner with the congregation upon his acceptance of the charge.

The body of the book is divided, as the table of contents indicates, into six divisions. Reference has already been made to Dominie Falkner's first entry and *votum.*

The first ministerial act recorded was a baptism administered in the barn of Cornelius van Boskerk at Hackensack in East Jersey, on Monday, February 27, 1704. Upon this occasion were baptized three children after a full morning service. On April 17th, following, which was Easter Monday, Falkner baptized a daughter of Pieter A. van Boskerk in the church at New York. These four baptisms were entered upon the register at the same time in the Low Dutch language, with the following *votum :*

"O Lord! Lord, let this child, together with the three

18

Doop Register.

Voor de Christelycke Protestantische Lutherische Gemeente in Newyorck, Nova Caesarea, Albania en andere daertoe, behoorende plaetsen in America Septentrionali

Anno Christi 1704.

Anno 1704 d. 27 Februarii hebb ick gedoopt tot Hackinsack in Novâ Caesarea nae gehoudene voormittags Predicatie in de Schuer van Cornelius van Boschkerck, naevolgende drie Kinderen

1 Dirck jonge Soon van Mattheus Corneliussen en syner Huysvrouw Trintje, geboorn op Hackinsack
Getuygen waren Albert Saborisky en syn Huysvrouw Magdalena

2 Laurens jonge Soon van Laurens van Boschkerck en syner H. Vrouw Henrichje
Getuygen waren Martin Meyer, en Margareta Jansen.

3 Alida jonge Dogter van Rudolph Berg en Catharina syner H. Vrouw
Getuygen waren de Moeder selve en een Michael

4 Anno 1704 d. 17 Aprilis op de tweede Paeschendagh gedoopt in onse Kercke tot Newyorck Antje jonge Dogter van Pieter van Boschkerck en syner Huysvrouw Trintje geboorn op Constapels-Hoeck d. 26. Decemb. 1703. Getuygen waren Heere Major de Bruyn en Gertje de Huysvrouw van Bernt Christiaen-
O Heere, Heere laet dit kint met de boven-

FAC-SIMILE OF EARLIEST BAPTISMAL RECORD.

above written Hackensack Children, be and remain engrossed upon the book of life, through Jesus Christ. Amen."

Almost every one of Falkner's entries closes with a short prayer or *votum* for the future welfare of the person mentioned; showing the deep interest this devout shepherd took in the spiritual welfare of his flock, irrespective of their nationality or social position. Dutch, English, German, negro and Indian all lost their individuality with this pious evangelist, whose only aim and object it was to extend the Church of Christ in the wilds of America, according to the precepts of the Augsburg Confession.

The following short prayers follow the respective baptisms during the first year of his ministration:

"O God, let this child be and remain a child of salvation through Christ. Amen."

"Lord, let this child also remain forever within thy everlasting grace and favor, through Christ. Amen."

"O God, let this child be included and remain in thy eternal favor, through Christ."

"O Lord, we commend this child unto thee, for both temporal and eternal welfare, through Christ. O My God, may this child be and remain a member of thy kingdom of grace and glory, through Christ. Amen."

The baptism of children of English parents was usually recorded in the English language.

"Baptized d. 10 Octobr, 1704 in ye House of Mr. William Chambers, Richard, son of Mr. William Chambers *en* his wife Sarah, born d. 10 ditto.

"Bless, O Lord, this child also with everlasting happiness, through Christ Jesus. Amen.

"Anno 1707, the 1, Juni [literal transcript], being Whitsunday, baptized, in our Lutheran Church at Albany, Elizabeth, young daughter of Lieutenant Richard Brewer & Catherine his wife, born the 11 of March of this year. Godfather was Lieut: Henry Holland, God mother Madam Elisabeth Weems and Mrs. Margareta Kollnis.

"Grant, O Lord, that this Childt never cast away the grace

which thou has Schworn, yea given by the Covenant of Baptism trough Jesus Christ our Lord. Amen."

Among the many interesting items in the baptismal register is the following:

In the year 1705 were baptized a daughter of Are of Guinea, a negro, and his wife Jora, both Christian mem-

ANNO CHRISTI
1704

Syn ten eerstermael tot het Hoogheylige Sacrament des Lichaems en Bloedts Jesu Christi in onse Christelycke Protestantse Gemeente toegelaeten worden naevolgende Personen.

In Newyorck
1 Catharina Vietts Mr. Johan Vietts Huys Vrow
2. Charles Beeckman
3 Elsje La Grancie
In Albanien
4. Maria Johan Evertsen Huys Vrow.
Laet o Heere Jesu Christe dese Personen ware levendige Lidtmaten aen u heylig Lichaem syn en blyven amen!

RECORD OF FIRST COMMUNICANTS.

bers of the congregation.[414] Falkner concludes with this *votum:*

"Lord, merciful God, who lookest not upon the person, but from whom different creatures that fear thee and do right find favor, let this child be clothed in the white robe of innocence and righteousness, and so remain through the grace of Christ, the Saviour of all mankind. Amen."

---

[414] *Vide*, pp. 323, *Supra*.

One of the most impressive incidents during Dominie Falkner's pastorate in New York occurred on Easter Sunday, 1708. It was a clear, bright April day with the harbingers of spring singing in the air, and the warm sun calling all vegetation once more to put on its garb of verdure; indeed a typical Paschal day, when all nature seemed to rejoice.

The church was decorated with budding boughs and spring flowers. The Paschal candles burned brightly on either side of the crucifix upon the altar, all indicative of the glorious resurrection to be celebrated.

It was, however, a gala day in the church independent of its being one of the most joyous festivals. The full order of morning service (*Haupt-gottesdeinst*) was completed, to the reading of the last collect, when a baptism somewhat out of the ordinary course was administered. The candidate was a Carolina Indian, who was a slave held by Peter Woglam.

When the former first expressed a wish to become a Christian, it became a question whether if he were admitted to the Church he could still be held in bondage and treated as a slave. The master naturally objected, in the fear that he might lose his servant. The Indian, however, settled the question by stating that he was willing to remain in servitude in this world, provided he was assured that he would be free and equal in the skies beyond.

Dominie Falkner, when he heard of the circumstances, examined the Indian, found him sincere, and concluded to accept him, and instructed him in the catechism and the tenets of the faith.

Upon the Sunday in question, after the holy Eucharist had been celebrated, the Indian slave, after having been duly prepared, was called up before the altar and publicly catechised in presence of the congregation by the pastor and wardens. He was then asked by Dominie Falkner whether he solemnly promised before the omnipotent Lord and this Christian congregation that he would, after he was received into the Church, continue to serve his worldly master and mistress as faithfully and truly as if he were yet in his benighted state.

Upon the Indian giving his solemn promise that he would, Dominie Falkner proceeded to baptize him, after he had driven out the spirit of evil with the ancient exorcism according to the Lutheran ritual: "*Darum, du vermaledeyter Teufel, erkenne dein urtheil, &c.*"

The name given to the new convert was "Thomas Christian." The ceremony closed with the invocation by the Dominie: "That the Lord would henceforth cause this unbelieving *Thomas* to become a believing *Christian.*" The morning service closed with the benediction.

History is silent as to the fate of this poor Indian slave who thus voluntarily embraced the Christian faith. Presumably he continued to serve his master and mistress, according to his solemn promise, with the same fidelity as before. Whether his bonds were ever relaxed, or whether his subsequent treatment was worse we do not know.

A somewhat similiar ceremony was performed at Albany four years after the above. The convert in this instance was a negro slave. The entry in the old register reads:

"Anno 1712, January 27, baptized at Loonenburg in Albany, Pieter Christian, a Negro and slave of Jan van Loons of Loonenburg, about thirty years of age. He has promised among other things that he will hereafter, as well as he has done before, faithfully serve his master and mistress as servant.

"Grant, O God, that this black and hard Negro-heart be and remain a Christian heart, and may he be numbered among those who are clothed with white raiment before the throne of the Lamb, through the merits of the Lamb of God who bore the sins of the world. Amen."

Under date of 28, February 1710, Dominie Falkner records the baptism of Louisa Abigail, daughter of Pastor Josua Kocherthal and his wife Sibylla Charlotta.

Among the many curious entries in the Baptismal record, the following is interesting as it illustrates the orthodoxy of the Dominie. It appears that during his absence two members of his church called upon the English Episcopal minister, Rev. John Sharpe, to baptize their children. This fact evidently pained him deeply, as will be seen from the appended *votum:*

"Nov. 30, 1712. During my absence Mr. John Sharpe[415] baptized the young daughter of Christian Streit, named Maria Magdalena, born in New York, &c.

"December 28, 1712. Also baptized by Mr. Sharpe, the young daughter of Johann Phillip Tays, named Christine Elizabeth, born in New York, &c.

"Lord, Lord God! Merciful, gracious and forbearing, of great mercy and consideration, which thou showest unto

---

[415] The Rev. John Sharpe, a clergyman of character and ability, was one of the early clergy upon the rolls of the Society for the Propogation of the Gospel in Foreign Parts. His chief station under the Society was in East Jersey. Prior to this he appears to have been stationed in Maryland, probably under orders of the Bishop of London. (Nichols to Stubs.—Perry's Historical Collections, vol. iv, pp. 54, 349). But little is known of this clergyman. Upon the rolls of the Venerable Society he is entered as having been sent out in 1704, after which his career, so far as the Society goes, seems to be a blank, for immediately after his name and date is entered "resigned." According to the above entry by Dominie Falkner, he was still performing religious rites as late as 1712. Another account names him as a chaplain at New York.

us in a thousand ways by forgiving us our offences, trespasses and sin, let not one of the above standing names be blotted out from thy book [on account of having been baptized by a minister of a different faith], but let them be therein written and remain there through Jesus Christ, thy beloved Son, Amen." [416]

FAC-SIMILE OF DOMINIE FALKNER'S ENTRY OF HIS MARRIAGE.

In the marriage record the following personal announcement is perhaps the most interesting:

Under date May 26, 1717. "On Rogate Sunday did Reverend William Vesey, commissary and preacher of the English church in New York, on a license of his Excellency Robert Hunter, at the time Governor of this Province, Me, Justus Falkner, pastor of the Protestant Lutheran congregation, in my house in little Queen street in New York, marry and consecrate in the bonds of holy matrimony with the honerable virgin, Gerritge Hardick, born in the Province of New York, County Albany.

"I leave you not, you bless me then. Amen."

Three children blessed this union:

[416] *Heere, Heere Gott, Barmhertig ende Genadig ende Lanckmaedig ende van groote Genade ende Trouwe, die Ghy bewyst in duysent leeden ende vergeeft misdaad, oventreedinge ende Soude, laat doch niet een van de boven staande naamen uyt u Boek uytgedelgt woordten, maar laat se daarin geschreewen syn en blyven door Jesum Christum, uwen lieven Soon. Amen.*

Anna Catherina, born in New York, July 17, 1718; baptized in the church on July 20; and Sara Justa, born at Loonenburg, May 5, 1720; baptized May 8; married Niclas van Hoesan, December 22, 1738; Benedictus, a son, born April, 1723; baptized at Calverack, April 11th.

In the performance of the arduous duties called for by his widely extended field of labor, the Dominie had but little time for rest or the enjoyment of home life. Forced as he was to be away from wife and babes for weeks and months at a time, his lot was by no means a sinecure, and to make matters worse, so beloved was he that the people, wherever he happened to be, were loth to see him depart for his next station, and would exact promises for a speedy return.

In their attempt to secure his services, the various congregations even went further, and provided glebe houses that should be ready at all times for the pastor and his family. This was the case at Loonenburg, Calverack, and other outlying points.

That notwithstanding his arduous duties, Dominie Falkner still remained in touch with his clerical brethern on the Delaware is shown by correspondence with them, and by entries in the Diary of Pastor Andreas Sandel. The last one reads:

"July 9, 1718. I sent same day by mail a packet to New York, enclosed to Pastor Falkner, to be forwarded by the first vessel bound for England." This letter has reference to Pastor Sandel's journey to Sweden.

Dominie Justus Falkner's married life proved of short duration. We know but little of his movements, except what can be gleaned from his official entries, which show that he continued to cover the whole territory of Eastern New York, Long Island and Staten Island.

The last entry found in his private diary, and copied into the old church register by Pastor Knoll, shows that he was at Phillipsburg early in September, 1723:

"Sept. 4, 1723. Baptized at Phillipsburg, at the upper mill, in the house of David Sturm, Johann Peter, born in the middle of June; *ibidem*, Father Pieter Hentz, mother Maria, Witness Johann Birger."

After this his history becomes a blank, the only documentary notice being a memorandum made by Pastor Knoll in the records of the Lutheran church at Newburgh: "Pastor Justus Falknenier, deceased. Anno 1723."

According to the above record, which is no doubt correct, Justus Falkner died at the early age of 51 years, after having faithfully served the various congregations under his charge for twenty years.

What were the circumstances of his sudden end cannot be told. Whether he died alone among strangers, or amidst his young family, is an unanswerable question. Not even his burial place is know, nor whether he was buried with the rites of the church in consecrated ground, or in some unknown corner.

However, should any record be found to shed some light upon the last hours of this devout shepherd in the fold of Christ, it will no doubt show that he died in the full performance of his duty, true to his ordination vows.

As to his family, it is known that after the father's death the widow with her three young children took up their abode at Loonenburg, where the latter grew up in the Lutheran Church, and were confirmed and married according to its ritual.

One of the last official acts recorded by Dominie Berkenmeyer, prior to his death in 1744, was a baptism of asecond son of one of his church officers,—Benedictus Falkner, a grandson of his immediate predecessor.

Justus Falkner is represented by all accounts as a lovely winning character, a man of excellent gifts, good education, fine mind, devout, of decided Lutheran opinions, active and of great endurance. In fact, he was an ideal pastor, who entered into his office with the full knowledge that without God's grace nothing could be accomplished. As has been shown, his field of labor extended along the Hudson as far north as Albany and landward to Long Island and Raritan in New Jersey.

His services, nominally confined to the Dutch and Germans of the Lutheran faith, were extended to all, irrespective of creed or color, as is proved by the mention of baptisms of both negroes and Indians from the earliest days of his ministry.

Nothing could show the devout and sincere mind of Justus Falkner in bolder relief than the entries of his official acts in the church register, a *votum* being added in every case.

From the documentary evidence come to light of late, and which forms the basis of the majority of these pages, it is shown how the influence of the Pietists of Provincial Pennsylvania spread beyond the bounds of that Province and extended over New York and the Jerseys. No matter what the immediate causes may have been that induced the Falkner brothers to leave their original home in America, how the factor time is apt to set all matters right is evidenced in the history of the elder Falkner and the controversion of the Pastorius slanders.

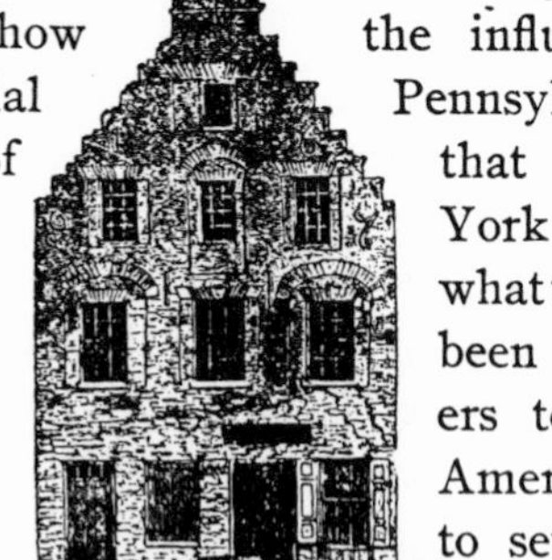

House in New York, built A.D. 1697; demolished 1828.

To the devout and pious Justus Falkner, who first came

to the western world as a Pietist and mystical Theosophist, with the avowed intention there to prepare himself for the coming of the Redeemer, history will ever point as one of the most devout and sincere missionaries and brightest characters in early German-American history.

Although for years almost forgotten by the present generations that now compose the congregations formerly served by him, their very existence at the present day, after the lapse of two centuries, and the fact of their still adhering to the Lutheran faith as based upon the unaltered Augsburg Confession, are his best monuments. They are living memorials, far greater than either shafts of granite or tablets of bronze made by the hands of man.

As a fitting close to this sketch may be quoted the conclusion of the ritual formerly used by the Theosophical Brotherhood of which at one time he was a member,—

"MAY GOD GRANT HIM A BLESSED RESURRECTION."

CONRAD MATTHÄI.

Arms of the Chur-Pfaltz, 1694.

FOR over forty years one of the most familiar figures in and about Germantown was a man of well-knit frame, who went about clad in a garb of coarse, uncolored homespun, while a wide-brimmed hat covered his head with its wealth of long hair and shaggy beard. In front of the hat there was conspicuously displayed a small shell, such as are found on the banks of the romantic Wissahickon. In his hand he always carried a long staff or *alpenstock;* upon his feet he wore a mere, sole or sandal, and in winter protected them with heavy woolen stockings. The whole appearance of this strange character was such as to attract the attention of any stranger who chanced to meet him.

Such was Conrad Matthäi, the last Magister of the Hermits on the Ridge, or, as he was locally called, *der alte Matthäi.* In his later years he was known by sight to every man, women and child in the German Township of Philadelphia County. He was respected by the aged and

Conrad Matthäi, 1678–1748, from an old Etching.

reputable citizen, feared by the frivolous and by the children and superstitiously inclined was avoided as a supernatural being.

After the death of Kelpius in 1708, and upon the refusal of Seelig to assume the responsibilities of the leadership of the Theosophical Community, Conrad Matthäi became recognized as the Magister of the Fraternity on the Wissahickon, and after the disbanding of the communal organization, he was still recognized as the Magister or Magus of such as remained upon the Vicaris tract and vicinity and lived the life of anchorites or hermits.

The hut on the Hermitage estate, pointed out by Phoebe Righter, and the remains of which, enlarged and improved, now serve as a tenant or farm-house, was undoubtedly the one inhabited by Conrad Matthäi during the last forty years of his life.[416]

But little is known of the family or antecedents of this recluse Theosophist, except that he came to the Province in 1704, with others, to reinforce the Community and join the Chapter of Perfection.

According to some accounts he is said to have been a Swiss gentleman, a member of a wealthy and influential family, who had left his native country to join the Mystics on the Wissahickon, and there put to a practical test the occult theories with which he became imbued during his academic career.

Another old record examined by the writer intimates that Conrad Matthäi was a relative of the noted Georg Heinrich Matthäi, who was an instructor at the Harburg (Haarburg?) University in 1695. However, be this as it may, that the subject of our sketch was a student of note and a man of great learning is shown by the deference paid to him, not alone by the various religious enthusiasts

---

416 *Vide* p. 210, *supra.*

who came to these shores, but also by the leaders of the different orthodox denominations within the Province.

Upon frequent occasions his advice and judgment were sought in the various religious movements in which the first half of last century was so fertile.

But little is known of Matthäi during the years immediately succeeding the death of Kelpius, except that the communal system was abolished and that of the Separatists or Anchorites adopted.

The evangelistic and educational features of the old Community, however, were retained by the different hermits, as was the practice of astrology and medicine.

The first definite information of Matthäi is found in the "*Chronicon Ephretense*," where he is mentioned in connection with the arrival, in the fall of 1720, of Conrad Beissel, who had come to America, together with three companions, with the avowed intention of joining the Chapter of Perfection which they thought still flourished here. Finding, upon their arrival, that the Community had been abandoned, after a year's sojourn in the vicinity, Beissel and his companion Stuntz, upon the advice of Matthäi, journeyed to the wilds of Chester County to live there a life of contemplation and solitude. The intercourse between Matthäi and Beissel during the latter's sojourn at Germantown was intimate and close, and tended much to influence the latter's eventful course in after years.

In the year 1725 the population of Germantown was increased by a little party consisting of an old woman and her four stalwart sons. She was the widow of Michael Eckerling of Strasburg, who had been one of the prime movers in combining the Pietistical movement with the secret mystical organizations of the day, and in consequence had suffered great persecution in his native city from both church and state. He was by trade a master cap-maker, and a man of some wealth.[417]

There is no written record as to what interest, if any, Matthäi took in building the large Community house or Monastery, in 1738, on the Wissahickon, some distance up the stream, as a branch of the Ephrata Community; nor is there anything but tradition to show that he ever visited the Mystic Community on the Cocalico.

The Ephrata traditions, however, lead us to believe that the Swiss Magus was not an entire stranger to the camp of the "Solitary" at Ephrata. He certainly took an active interest in the Community affairs, as is shown by the temporary estrangement with Beissel, after the expulsion of the Eckerling brothers in 1745, where Matthäi espoused the cause of the four brothers.

The differences thus engendered, however, did not last, and were healed prior to the old Theosophist's death. The final reconciliation between the two leaders was effected during a pilgrimage from Ephrata to Philadelphia, June 12, 1747, when the two leaders again embraced each other. The following account of this incident appears in the "*Chronicon Ephretense*:"

"On the journey he (Conrad Beissel, Father Friedsam) visited his old friend, Conrad Matthäi, not far from Germantown. He alone was left of a venerable society, which the celebrated Johann Kelpius had founded, which, after his death, however, was again scattered, as has been mentioned. At this visit, when they embraced each other, a difference

---

[417] In the "*Chronicon Ephretense*," p. 41, Israel Eckerling, the oldest of the brothers, and who afterwards became the Prior of the Brotherhood of Zion on the Cocalico, tells us how, upon the advice and council of Conrad Matthäi, he, together with his mother and brothers, in the year 1727 left those regions (Germantown) because those people lived in vanity, and he came to the Conestoga country.

which had existed between their spirits was removed. They had formerly been good friends, but after the Superintendent (Beissel) had permitted himself to be instrumental in the new awakening in Conestoga, a separation of their spirits took place, which was healed again by this visit, as just mentioned. Therefore he wrote a favorable letter to him as soon as he returned home, and likewise exhorted Johannes Wüster, in Philadelphia, who was also his benefactor, not to withdraw his hands from him." [418]

As has been before stated, the recluse Anchorites on the Ridge, according to popular tradition, in addition to their Theosophical speculations and religious studies, engaged in "white magic," such as casting nativities, exorcising spirits and the practice of horoscopy and devination.

Conrad Matthäi, in addition to the above, was also credited with maintaining communication with the unseen spirit-world, and with the ability of detaching at will his own soul or spirit from the body. Of this latter power, wonderful as it may seem, the following well-authenticated account has come down to us:

"In the year 1740 the wife of a ship captain living in Philadelphia, whose husband was on a voyage to Africa, and from whom she had been long without tidings, overwhelmed with anxiety for his safety, upon the advice of a friend, as a last resort journeyed to the glen of the Wissahickon to consult, for council or consolation, "old Father Matthäi." The latter received her kindly and listened to her fears and story. After she was through, he bade her remain and wait where she was for a short time, when he would bring her the intelligence she sought for. He then left her, going into the back room or closet of his cabin,

[418] *Chronicon Ephratense*, translation, p. 204.

which was separated from the main room by a door having a small curtained sash in the upper half.

"Long waited the sailor's wife for the Magician's return; as the time passed slowly by minutes became as hours, and yet no movement was heard or came from the other room. At last her impatience became so great, thinking that the old hermit had perhaps passed out of another door and forgotten her, that she peeped through a corner of the sash which was not covered by the curtain, and there, to her surprise, beheld the hermit lying on a rude wooden pallet, as pale and motionless as if he were dead.

"She then resumed her vigil. Shortly afterwards the door opened, and the old hermit entered, looking pale and wan. He told her that her husband was then in a coffee-house in London, that he was well and would shortly return. Further, for certain reasons, which he told her, the husband had not been able to send her any letter. With her fears thus greatly allayed, she left the cabin of the old recluse and returned to her home in the city.

"When at last, after a lapse of three months, her husband returned to Philadelphia, she learned from him that the cause for his delay and unusual silence had been word for word as was stated to her by the old Hermit on the Wissahickon.

"The curiosity of the woman, now thoroughly aroused, determined upon a visit to Matthäi with her husband. Upon the arrival at the cabin, the moment that the captain saw the old hermit (who was entirely unknown to him) he told his wife that he had seen this very man, upon such a day (it was the very day that the women had made her visit) in a coffee-house in London, and that he came to him telling him how distressed was his wife that he had not written.

"He then told him why he had not written, with the reasons why his return was delayed, but that he was then upon the eve of his departure for home, after which the stranger was lost sight of.

"Another account of this strange occurrence describes the hermit, Conrad Matthäi, a man of retired habits, who spoke but little; in demeanour grave, benevolent and pious, with nothing against his character except that he, in common with his associates, possessed secrets which were accounted not altogether lawful."

How intimate the relations were between the old Theosophist and the various evangelists and missionaries, has been aready told in a previous chapter.

In the latter years of his life the old recluse became too feeble to support himself by his own manual labor. In these days he found a firm friend in Johannes Wüster, the Philadelphia merchant, who lived at Germantown, and who befriended him until his death.

Toward the close of his earthly sojourn, Conrad Matthäi became very friendly with the Moravian Bretheren, and even in his advanced age continued to take a great interest in their efforts to spread the Gospel among all people, and bring about a union of all Christian denominations as well as the education of the children. So great was his interest in the educational problem, that upon the opening of a Moravian boarding-school, in John Bechtel's house, on March 8, 1747, the first to send greetings to the Brethren is old Father Conrad Matthäi, "who," as Bishop Cammerhoff writes, "lives a few miles from here in his hut as a recluse." [419]

A few months later, May 22, 1747, during the Synod

---

[419] Bethlehem Diaries.

held at Germantown, Brother Martin Mack visited Matthäi, at his cabin on the Ridge, accompanied by three Indian converts, who were presented to the old Pietist as an living evidence of the Brethren's success in spreading the Gospel of Christ among all people.[420]

It was, indeed, a picturesque sight wherein the patriarchial anchorite, with his snow-white hair and flowing beard, clad as he was in his rough home-spun pilgrim garb, formed the chief figure. The Moravian Brethren, in direct contrast, with their long hair, smooth-shaven faces and plain brown garb, brought out the figure of the old Pietist in in even bolder prominence, while the three dusky Indians, still partly robed in their semi-barbarous costume, added yet more to the charm, and completed the composition, as it were,—the background of which was formed by the hut of the old recluse, with its surroundings of flowering shrubs and dark foliage.

It was a happy day for the Moravian Brethren to be able to present their "first fruits" before the old Magister, and it afforded the latter no less pleasure to greet these practical evidences of the Moravian missionary efforts.

Conrad Matthäi received the Indian converts very kindly, and exhorted them to remain steadfast in their faith, and he finally dismissed them with his blessing, given with his hands uplifted and his face turned to the Orient.

It is recorded that this interview made a lasting impression upon the three Indian converts.

In the fall of the same year Conrad Matthäi, together with Brother Jaebetz (Rev. Peter Miller), Prior of the Ephrata Community, attended the Pennsylvania Synodal Conference held September 25, 1747.

---

420 These Indians were from Shecomeco and were baptized by Brother Rauch at the Synod held at the house of John de Turck at Olney, February 21, 1742.

This seems to have been the last public occasion on which he was present. During the following winter his health continued to fail, the old man getting feebler and feebler as the months rolled by.

When his helpless condition became known to the Moravian Brethren, he was frequently visited by their evangelists, and upon a report of Brothers John Wade and Ludwig Huebner, who came from Neshaminy for the purpose of visiting him in the summer of 1748, Brother Richard Utley[221] was sent down from Bethlehem to remain with him and minister to his wants.

Brother Jasper Payne and his wife, who were then in charge of the Moravian school at Germantown, also attended to his wants, and occasionally sent some of the children over to his cabin to sing for him, an act which he ever appreciated. As his serious condition became known at Ephrata, a member of the Zionitic Brotherhood was at once dispatched to the Wissahickon to minister to him.

This action upon the part of the Ephrata Community caused more or less friction between the Moravian and Ephrata Brethren, for each party claimed the dying Magister as their own. This peculiar condition was aggravated still more by the fact that the object of their solicitation would neither renounce the one nor acknowledge the other faith.

---

[421] Richard Utley was born in Yorkshire, England, February 22, 1720. He was a weaver by trade, received into the Moravian Church in 1742; came to America with the "*2d Sea Congregation;*" ordained a Deacon by Spangenburg at Philadelphia, August 14, 1746; Pastor at New York (twice), Lancaster, Philadelphia (1749–52), Graceham (twice). In 1766 was sent to North Carolina and served in congregations, was Warden at Salem, and from 1772–75 member of Prov. Helpers Conference. Died October 9, 1775. "He loved to preach much better than to attend to the duties of Warden or a member of the Conference."—J. W. JORDAN.

However, toward the latter part of August, 1748, as Conrad Matthäi felt that his end upon earth was drawing near, he sent a request to Brother Payne at Germantown that the children at the Moravian school be sent over to him. When they arrived he asked them to sing for him some parting hymns,—a custom which was then in vogue among the Germans when one's end was approaching.

The hymn which pleased him most and gave him the greatest comfort was the peculiar Moravian hymn of the period,[322]—

> "Was macht ein Kreuz-luft vögelein
> Wann's 'naus fliegt aus dem Hüttelein?"

After the singing was over, Matthäi turned toward the East, raised up his hands and prayed fervently; then turning once more to the children, he blessed them according to the ritual of the Mystic Brotherhood, after which he dismissed them.

Two days later he departed from his humble recluse hut on the Wissahickon to enter into the glorious palaces of his Redeemer the celestial Bridegroom.

Bishop Cammerhoff, in his diary, notes, in reference to the death of Matthäi, that "at his ending his heart was filled with love and tenderness for the Lamb and His congregation (*Unitas Fratrum*). Though the enemies (the Ephrata Mystic Community) tried their utmost to turn him against the congregation, they did not succeed in diverting him."

After the death of the old Pietist, both parties claimed the body for burial, and the Moravian *einlader* (invitor) went from door to door in Germantown to inform the people that "old Father Matthäi" was dead, and when he was to be buried.

---

[422] Hymn 2251 *Zugabe to the xii Anhang.*

Notwithstanding this somewhat unseemly rivalry between the two opposing orders, in the end a compromise was effected by which both parties officiated at the funeral. This happy result, it is said, was effected by Johannes Wüster, who bore the funeral expenses.

In the main the wishes of the deceased were respected, at least in so far that his grave was dug at the feet of that of his former Magister, Johannes Kelpius, as he considered himself unworthy to repose by his side. This spot, according to Bishop Cammerhoff, was but a short distance from the hut lately inhabited by the dead Mystic.

The interment took place on Thursday, September 1, 1748, in the presence of a large concourse of people, prominent among whom was Dr. Christopher Witt, now the last survivor of the former Community, and Johannes Wüster, the German merchant of Philadelphia. Although the services commenced with an address by Brother Timotheus (Alexander Mack) of the Zionitic Brotherhood of Ephrata, the ceremonies virtually ended in a Moravian burial, the chief feature of which was the reading of a biographical sketch of the deceased, followed by a sermon by Rev. James Greening, who had come up from Philadelphia expressly for that purpose, and, as Bishop Cammerhoff writes, "portrayed to all present the Lamb with His wounds and bloody martyr scene," after which the body was consigned to the mother earth amidst the singing by all present of the hymn, "*Christi blut und gerechtigkeit.*"[423]

[423] This hymn is still in use by the Moravian Church throughout the world. The English translation, hymn 302 in the new Hymnal, reads:

"The Saviour's blood and righteousness
My beauty is, my glorious dress;
Thus well arrayed, I need not fear,
When in His presence I appear."

The *Chronicon Ephretense*, commenting upon the death of the old Mystic, states: "Conrad Matthäi, after he had fulfilled righteousness among men by works of love, came to live a life of faith, whereupon God awakened for him a rich merchant, by the name of Johannes Wüster, who served him with his possessions, and also helped to bury him by the side of Kelpius, although he in his humility had not desired to lie beside him, but only at his feet. May God grant him a blessed resurrection."

Two weeks after the burial of the last of the Hermits who remained on the Ridge, Christopher Sauer, in his paper *Pennsylvanische Berichte*, September 16, 1748, published the following notice:

"*Conrad Matthäi, der alte Einsiedler auf der Ritch, ist den 1sten dieses Monats begraben im 70 Yahr seines Alters.*"

In the MS. minutes of the *Brüder-Synode*, held at Bethlehem from October 12-23 to 16-27, 1748, appears the following interesting entry relating to the death and burial of Conrad Matthäi. On account of its quaintness and as an illustration of the peculiar religious literature in vogue in Pennsylvania at that period, the extract is reproduced *verbatim:*

"*Bei gelegenheit der Kinderanstalt in Germantown allwo geschwister Payns mit ihren gehülfen sind wurde erzählet dass unser lieber Bruder Conrad Matthäi der auf der Ridge zwei meilen von Germantown gewohnet vor 5 wochen recht selig zum lieben Lämmlein gegangen sei.*

"*Zu seiner krankheit haben ihn unsere geschwister von Germantown desgleichen auch bruder Uttly der express dazu von Bethlehem aus abgeschickt worden, fleissig besucht. Und sonderlich sind die Kinder in der Germantown anstalt seines herzens lust und freude gewesen, die ihn auch etwa 2 tage vor seiner heimfarth noch einmal besucht, und ihm auf*

GROUP OF MORAVIAN EVANGELISTS WHO LABORED IN PENNSYLVANIA.

1 Count Ludwig von Zinzendorf.
2 Bishop August G. Spangenberg.
3 Bishop David Nitchmann.
4 Bishop J. C F. Cammerhoff.
5 Bro. John Martin Mack.
6 Bro. Friederich Martin.
7 Bro. Georg Neisser.

FROM THE ORIGINAL PORTRAITS IN THE ARCHIVES OF THE CHURCH AT BETHLEHEM. BY PERMISSION OF THE SESQUI-CENTENNIAL MEMORIAL COMMITTEE, VIDE FOOT-NOTE, P. 7, SUPRA.

besucht, und ihm auf seinem verlangen viel wunden und seiten-hölchens-versel zum abschied gesungen haben.

"*Item,—Sein Seelchen wird sich auch einmal aus seinem Hüttlein schwingen.*

"*Da er dann seine Hände empor gehoben und mit einem hertzlichen gebet die Kinder gesegnet und ein paar tage darauf recht selig ins seiten-hölchen gefahren. Sein hertz ist bis an sein ende voller liebe und zärtlichkeit zum Lämmlein u zu seiner Gemeine geblieben, und alle die feinde die ihr äuserstes an ihn versucht um ihn gegen die Gemeine einzunehmen haben ihn nicht zu stöhren vermocht.*

"*Und da sein Hüttlein nahe bei den alten Baron Kelpio zur ruhe gebracht worden so hat zuerst Alexander Mack dabei eine rede gehalten und hernach Bruder Greening das Lämmlein und seine wunden und blutige Martyrs gestalt allen anwesenden vorgemahlet. Wie dann auch in den zeitungen etwaz davon erzehlet worden.*"

DOCTOR CHRISTOPHER WITT.

Arms of Penn, from the First Provincial Currency, Printed 1723.

DOCTOR Christopher Witt, who died at Germantown toward the close of January, 1765, at the advanced age of ninety years, was, so far as is known, the last survivor of all the Pietists, philosophical students and religious enthusiasts who, during the lifetime of Magister Kelpius, had been connected with the Theosophical Community on the Wissahickon.

It was ordained for him to outlive his fellows, to soothe their sufferings, and in some cases to close the eyes of such as remained in the vicinity, or came to him from afar in their time of sore distress,[424] as in the instance of Isaac van Bebber.[425]

---

[424] *Chronicon Ephretense*, translation p. 18.

[425] This Isaac van Bebber, according to the *Chronicon*, was a young Hollander and an early companion of Beissel; he was a nephew or relative of the Isaac van Bebber at whose house Köster instituted the Lutheran services upon his arrival in 1694.

When finally it came to the time for Christopher Witt to leave this transitory world and rejoin his former companions, his last act was to devise the bulk of his property, together with the house in which he lived, to Christian Warmer, a grandson of the charitable tailor who had done so many acts of kindness to Kelpius and his fellow Pietists during the times of sickness and adversity.

Christopher Witt, or DeWitt as he is sometimes called, was born in Wiltshire, England, in the year 1675; he came to America in the year 1704, and at once joined the Theosophical enthusiasts on the Wissahickon. He was then in his twenty-ninth year, and in addition to being a thorough naturalist and a skillful physician, was well versed in the occult sciences and in practical astronomy.

Christopher Witt

AUTOGRAPH OF DOCTOR CHRISTOPHER WITT.

On account of his varied accomplishments he was perhaps, to the public at large, the most valuable man of the Mystic Community, and from the very outset his services as a physician were called into requisition, not only by the residents of the immediate vicinity, but also from outlying districts, his fame extending even into the adjoining provinces.

Shortly after the death of Kelpius and the partial dismemberment of the Community, Doctor Witt, together with Daniel Geissler, the former *famulus* of the Magister, removed into a small house in Germantown upon the land of Christian Warmer. Their personal wants were carefully attended to by the Warmer family, which then consisted of Christian, the emigrant, Christiana his wife, two sons, George and Christian, and two daughters, Christiana and Elizabeth.

In September of the year 1718, Dr. Witt purchased, for £60, silver currency, from John Doeden and wife, two tracts of land containing in the aggregate 125 acres; 101 of which were located within the inhabited parts of the town, the rest being pasture land in the township. The witnesses to this conveyance were Matthias Zimmermann[426] and Daniel Geissler.

On the 21st of May, 1720, Witt, as "Doctor of Physic and Chirurgene," deeded the whole of this purchase to Christian Warmer, "Taylor," the consideration being the same amount as above. This deed was witnessed by Daniel Geissler, Pieter Keyser, Phillip Christian Zimmermann and Matthis Melan.

Christian Warmer, prior to his death in the spring of 1728, made the following provision in his will for the two Theosophists:

"And as Concerning all that my twenty-five acres of "Land wch I Purchased of Daniel Geissler in Germantown[427] "sd together with all & singular the Messauage building "& appurtinances part in the possession of Doctor Witt, I "Give & Divise the same unto my Daughters Christiana "& Elizabeth their Heirs & assigns for ever, in equal pro- "portions between them to commence on & immediately "after the Determination of my Wifes Estate as afsd and "the term & Estate therein of the afsd Doctor Witt & "Daniel Geissler their lives being also Expired."

That Doctor Witt still kept in close touch with the now scattered members of the former Community is shown by the Ephrata records, and by the different wills upon which he figures as either witness or executor.

---

[426] A son of Magister Zimmermann.

[427] This land was a part of the tract bought from Reynier Jansen the printer, October 20, 1701. "Pennsylvania Magazine," vol. iv, p. 37.

A notable instance of the latter is the case of the widow Zimmermann, who died in Germantown, wife of Magister John Jacob Zimmermann, who originally organized the Community.

Upon this occasion Dr. Witt came into possession of some of the personal belongings of the late Magister, among which were:

"A sondry sort of books, 2 Bibles & some latin Boocks, 33 in number besides the latin bocks."

These were valued at £3-16-0.

"An old Vorginall."[428]

"A little old box, with some brass things, and an old Cheīnter."

History and tradition are both silent as to what became of either the books or the old "brass things," which were no doubt some of the Magister's philosophical or astronomical instruments.

It is known that the two philosophers, Witt and Geissler, continued to live in a house on the Warmer lot until the death of Daniel Geissler, which took place in the summer of 1745. In his will, proved August 10, 1745, he gives and bequeaths "all his moveables or personal property estate, wherewith it hath pleased the Lord to bless his endeavours, to one Maria Barber Schneiderin, widow, in Germantown."

During all these years Geissler attended to matters requiring manual labor, such as the cultivation of the medicinal herbs and plants for the use of the doctor in his profession, thus leaving the latter free to devote himself to his practice and study.

After the death of his faithful companion, Dr. Witt

[428] This was without doubt the first Virginall (a kind of piano) that was brought into the Province.

changed his quarters to the large mansion house[429] which had in the mean time been built by Christian Warmer the younger, and when the latter died in the fall of 1749,[430] the son, like unto the father before him, left an ample provision in his will for the old Theosophist, who was now past three score and ten.

"9thly, I do hereby give and bequeath unto my affection- "ate and loving friend Christopher Witt with the full free "use liberty, and Priviledge of any fruits or garden Erbs "Growing or belonging to any part of my sd lotts, lands "and tenements aforesd. As also the sowing, planting "such trees Quick setts & Erbs as he shall think proper "and shall have occasion of on the same with all necessary "use of ye S. E. end of my Mansion house diet firewood, "attendence & finally all that he may or shall reasonably "require or have occassion for during his natural life. "All which my sd wife children & their Trustees shall "truly & faithfully fulfill & perform as aforesd."

His wife Lydia, together with Dr. Witt, are named as sole executors.

Dr. Witt was a skilled botanist, and upon his removal to Germantown after the death of Kelpius, he started a large garden for his own study and amusement, and to him probably is due the honor of starting the first botanical garden in America. This was about twenty years prior to Bartram's purchase on the Schuylkill for a like purpose.

Dr. Witt was for many years the friend and correspondent of the celebrated Peter Collinson of London, whose letters to some of the leading men in the Province all mention the high esteem and regard in which Dr. Witt was held by

---

429 Tradition seems to point to the house still standing at the south-east corner of Main and High streets as the homestead of the Warmers and of Dr. Witt.

430 September 12, 1749.

that celebrated English naturalist and antiquarian. In later years there was a frequent intercourse between Dr. Witt and John Bartram. The following letter from the latter to Peter Collinson gives an interesting insight into the private life of the learned Theosophist:

"JUNE 11th, 1743.

"FRIEND PETER:

"I have lately been to visit our friend Doctor Witt, where I spent four or five hours very agreeably—sometimes in his garden, where I viewed every kind of plant, I believe that grew therein, which afforded me a convenient opportunity of asking him whether he ever observed any kind of Wild Roses in this country, that was double. He said he could not remember that ever he did. So being satisfied with this amusement, we went into his study, which was furnished with books containing different kinds of learning; as Philosophy, Natural Magic, Divinity, nay, even Mystic Divinity; all of which were the subjects of our discourse within doors, which alternately gave way to Botany, every time we walked in the garden. I could have wished thee the enjoyment of so much diversion, as to have heard our discourse, provided thee had been well swathed from hips to arm-pits. But it happened, a little of our spiritual discourse was interrupted by a material object within doors; for the Doctor had lately purchased of a great travellar in Spain and Italy, a sample of what was imposed upon him for Snake Stones, which took me up a little time beside laughing at him to convince the Doctor that they were nothing but calcined old horse bones.

"Indeed to give the Doctor his due, he is very pleasant, facetious and plaint, and will exchange as many freedoms as most men of his years, with those he respects. His understanding and judgement, thee art not unacquainted with, having had so long and frequent intercourse with him by letters.

"When we are upon the topic of astrology, magic, and mystic divinity, I am apt to be a little troublesome, by inquiring into the foundation and reasonableness of these notions which, thee knows, will not bear to be searched and examined into; though I handle these fancies with more tenderness with him, than I should with many others that are so superstitiously inclined, because I respect the man. He hath a considerable share of good in him.

"The Doctor's famous Lychnis, which thee has dignified so highly, is, I think, unworthy of that character. Our swamps and low grounds are full of them. I had so contemptible an opinion of it, as not to think it worth sending, nor afford it room in my garden; but I suppose, by thy account, your climate agreeth so well, that it is much improved. The other, which I brought from Virginia, grows with me about five feet high, bearing large spikes of different coloured flowers, for three or four months in the year, exceeding beautiful. I have another wild one, finely speckled, and striped with red upon a white ground, and a red eye in the middle, the only one I ever saw.

"Our worthy friend, Colden, wrote to me he had received a new edition of Linnaeus's Characteres Plantarum, lately printed. He advised me to desire Gronovius to send it to me. I should be very glad to see it. The first I saw, was at the Doctor's, and chiefly by it he hath attained to the greatest knowledge in Botany, of any I have discoursed with.

JOHN BARTRAM."

The following interesting references to Doctor Witt are from the Bartram papers now in the collection of the Pennsylvania Historical Society:

PETER COLLINSON TO JOHN BARTRAM.

"LONDON, AUGUST 16th, 1735.

"I am glad to hear that the Medlar grows. It is the large Neapolitan sort, which produces a large fruit. Doctor Witt, at Germantown, wants it much. I sent him some at the same time; but whether he has any luck, I can't tell."

"LONDON, SEPTEMBER 20, 1736.

"But on the other side of the question, I have received from my ingenious friends, J. Breintnall and Doctor Witt, very particular accounts of the power it has over creatures, by charming them into its very jaws."

"LONDON, FEBRUARY 3rd, 1736-7.

"I am pleased to hear thee art acquainted with Dr. Witt, an old correspondent of mine, and has sent me many a valuable, curious plant. But I am afraid the old gentlemen has been too cunning for thee. Those fine Lady's Slippers, which make my mouth water, have slipped beside it. The Doctor says he would have sent them me, but that he was afraid they were spoiled in bringing home, for want of proper care to wet the roots by the way."

"LONDON, DECEMBER 14th, 1737.

"This we call the small mountain Ranunculus, as it really is. I had it formerly sent me, by Dr. Witt, but I should be glad of a few roots more. It is a pretty plant, and keeps a long while in flower."

"LONDON, JANUARY 31st, 1738.

"The pretty white Ranunculus (*Anemone thalictroides, L.*) that Dr. Witt sent to me, some time agone, is a neat, delicate, double flower; but I never knew before, it was a Snake-root. It is described by the celebrated Plukenet, who has most of your country plants. He names it—"Ranunculus nemorosus, Aquilegioe foliis, Virginianus, Asphodeli radice."

"LONDON, APRIL 6th, 1738.

"I have received three sorts of Jaceas from Doctor Witt. He distinguishes them by Early Jacea, Elegant Jacea, and Gigantic Jacea. I wish thee could find them out, to send specimens of them, as they grow in your country."

"London, January 26th, 1738-9.

"There is a small packet for Doctor Witt. Pray, somehow or other, convey it to him. Some fine Melon seed for Thomas Penn; some Burgundy Trefoil (Medicago sativa, L. or Lucerne), for J. Logan; and pray, where there is sufficient, let him have a share of the other seeds."

"London, July 10th, 1739.

"It differs from the great Marsh Martogon, for that will not flower till the middle of August, and another sort, I had formerly from Doctor Witt; but that was a smaller sort, and never had but four or five flowers on a stalk."

"London, July 10th, 1739.

"The pretty Spiroea, that thee sent me a specimen of in the quire before last, that I doubted if it was of your natural growth, I have now a plant in flower, that Doctor Witt sent me, which shows that it is."

"London, July 22nd, 1740.

"Doctor Witts hollow-leafed Lavender, is, no doubt, the Side-saddle flower; but what relation it has to Lavender, I must leave to him. The plant with Tricolor leaves, I amm well assured, is your fine Clinopodium. Our late severe winter has carried all mine off; so pray send me some more seed, and of the Lychnis with Crosswort leaves.

"The doctor did not carefully distinguish, or observe, the fruit he mentions, which I take to be no more than an excrescence raised by insects, like Galls and Oak-apples; which have a pulpy substance in them of a beautiful complexion."

"London, October 20th, 1740.

"I am much obliged to thee for the account of Dr. Witt's rarities. Thee has unravelled the whole mystery."

"London, September 16th, 1741.

"Pray send some Ginseng seed; but roots will be better. I had great expectation I had this rare plant, but don't find it proves so. The young leaves of the Prenanthes, or Doctor Witt's Snake-root, I took for it."

"London, June 16th, 1742.

"I have a Lychnis, from Doctor Witt, different from any yet that I have seen. It seems to be the King of that tribe. Its stalk is near as thick as my little finger (which is but small, for a man). It is now about two feet high, and yet no flowers appear. The stalk is most finely spotted, which is very distinguishing from all the rest that I have seen."

"LONDON, JULY 20th, 1759.

"I am concerned to hear poor Dr. Witt, my old friend, is blind. A well-spent life, I doubt not, will give him consolation and illuminate his darkness. I must conclude, my dear John, against my inclination.

JOHN BARTRAM TO PETER COLLINSON.

"JULY 24th, 1744.

"Our friend, Doctor Witt, is as well as usual."

"MAY 22d, 1761.

"Doctor Witt and Alexander went on purpose and fetched seeds and roots; but both miscarried."

"JULY 19th, 1761.

"I have now a glorious appearance of Carnations from thy seed,—the brightest colours that ever eyes beheld. Now, what with thine, Dr. Witt's and others, I can challenge any garden in America for variety. Poor old man! he was lately in my garden, but could not distinguish a leaf from a flower."

Dr. Witt, it is said, built the first stone house in Germantown (it was next door below Andrew Keyser's house); he was also an ingenious mechanic, and during the long winter, when botanizing was out of question, he constructed the first clocks made in Pennsylvania, if not in America. One of these he made for his own use: it struck the quarters, and was quite a curiosity at that early day. These timepieces were made of brass and steel, they were set on two brackets against the wall, and ran for thirty-six hours, with one weight and an endless chain; being wound by merely pulling the chain, which would raise the weight. The long pendulum, as well as the weight and chain, were exposed, as were also the works behind the dial; the bell on which the hour was struck was placed immediately above the works.

At that time these timepieces were valued at from 15 to 25 pounds currency; they were known as wall clocks, or *Wand-uhren*, and were the precursors of the high-case clocks so common in the early years of the present century, many of which are still preserved as heirlooms.

With his other accomplishments Dr. Witt combined that of an artist and musician. He possessed a large pipe organ, said to have been of his own construction, and the only instrument of the kind in the possession of a private individual in America, He was also a skillful performer on the "virginal," a keyed instrument, of one string, jack and quill to each note, like a spinnet, but in shape resembling an upright piano. Notwithstanding his mechanical and extensive professional labors and scientific researches, he kept up his studies in the occult sciences as well as the Theosophical speculations of the old Brotherhood long after the state of affairs brought around by the growth of the new country had scattered most of his former associates, as well as deprived the Quaker element of its supremacy. He also was an adept in astronomy, having a fine large telescope. His reputation as an astronomer was of a high order, and his deductions were generally accepted as final by the various scientists of the day.

A good illustration of his observations is shown by his description of the "great" comet of 1743, and it is by far the best that we have of that celestial phenomenon.[431] His observation was made through his eight-foot telescope, a few days after the comet's appearance on Christmas night of that year; it then appeared as large as the planet Jupiter. Dr. Witt says:

"His atmosphere or tail is not long, but directing itself to the S. E.; his motion but slow, making to the N. W. He rises about ¾ past 10 in the morning in the E. N. E., and passes our Meridian ¾ after five p. m. in latitude 15.

[431] For a full account of the "great" comet, see "An Ephrata Legend," by the present writer, in *Christian Culture*, Lancaster, Penn., 1891, vol. i, No. 11.

30 N.; and sets ¾ after night in the W. N. W. His latitude with respect to the eliptic is 21 D. 30 m. His longitude from Aries 14 D. 30 m."

The learned Doctor also practised horoscopy, and would as the occasion required, cast nativities according to the position of celestial bodies, and he was wont to use the hazel rod in his divination. These facts, together with his wrinkled features and bent figure in his later years, made him an object of fear and terror to the naturally superstitious Germans of the settlement, whose favorite occupation after dark was the telling and retelling of ghost stories. Whether sitting in front of the fire on the spacious hearth, or on the bench under the stoop in front of the house, spook-stories were always the favorite theme. In many of these legends the *hexen-meister*, as Dr. Witt was universally known among the Germans, figured as the chief actor, The doctor, however, minded not these idle tales and rumors, and willingly went into any of their houses to alleviate their suffering, even if he saw them making three crosses in the air or on the door-jamb as he entered, or knew that while he was ministering to the ailing child, the anxious parent was saying a *Vater Unser* to keep off the Evil One. To make matters worse for the local gossips, on one occasion Dr. Witt returned from Philadelphia accompanied by a slave whom he had purchased there. This man was a mulatto with a sharp, piercing black eye, light skin and curly hair, and was known as Robert. He became the trusty servant and companion of his master, and whenever Dr. Witt went out after dark Robert invariably preceded him with a lantern. It was not long before it would have been hard to say whether master or servant inspired the most fear with the simple-minded Germans; some of whom honestly believed that Robert was really a familiar spirit, sent from the regions below at the request of his master. Robert, however, proved a reliable and trustworthy servant, competent to wait on the table, curry horses, clean knives, boots and shoes, lay a table, shave and dress wigs, and carry a lantern; and in addition to these multitudinous accomplishments, being of a mechanical turn of mind he soon mastered the science of clockmaking.

Doctor Witt accumulated considerable property, and, as before stated, about the middle of the century, after the death of Geissler, took up his abode in the large stone house which had been built by Christian Warmer (2d). The old house, however, was not rented, but was used by the doctor as a workshop or laboratory, and in the course of time became an object of dread to all passers by after dark. The many gruesome tales connected with this old house were only equalled by those told in connection with the old *Hexen-meister* and his *Teufels-bursche.* The mysterious sounds and lights said to have been heard and seen there frequently during the long winter nights, if probed, no doubt would have been found to emanate from Robert's turning-lathe, or the Doctor's brazier, as he was preparing some of the medicaments used in his profession.

When the Doctor was eighty years old his eyesight failed him, and this in a few years resulted in total blindness.

During the years of his affliction he was tenderly cared for by his slave Robert, who not only proved his devoted servant, but acted as his agent.

Before his eyesight had entirely failed him, he sent for three friends in whom he had the fullest confidence, viz., Hugh Neile, Charles Witherholtz and John Knorr,[432] and

[432] John Knorr was a son-in-law of Ludwig Biedermann, one of the leaders of the original Community. His wife was Hannah Ludwig Biedermann, and her mother, Maria Margaretta Beidermann, was a daughter of Magister Zimmermann, who died at Rotterdam.

in their presence he made and executed his last will and testament, November 7, 1761. He could then hardly see to write his name to the document. He appointed Richard Johnson and Christian Warmer (3d) as his executors.

SIGNATURE TO WILL.

But few particulars are known of the end of this old mystic and philosopher, or even the exact date of his death. It appears from some fragmentary documents that it was in the latter part of January, 1765, and that the last offices were performed for him by the third generation of the Warmer family.

His remains,—wrapt in a spotless linen sheet and resting upon the shavings made in planing the boards,[433] in the plain, unvarnished deal coffin, without lining or ornament, made by Robert for his late master,—were buried in the family's private ground, situated on the top of the hill behind the Warmer homestead, and which is fully described in the next chapter. At his request his remains were lowered into the ground just as the winter sun sunk beneath the horizon.

The old magus had outlived all of his former associates and friends. In the three score years that he had passed in

---

[433] This custom has survived until of late years and is still occasionally insisted upon in the burial of decendants from the early Sabbatarians in Pennsylvania. Poplar wood, however, is usually used in place of pine. The superstition about the shavings made in building a coffin is an old one. It was believed that in case that a shaving from a coffin would find its way into any house death would result in the near future. Both shavings and sawdust were therefore always carefully swept up by the cabinet-maker and placed in the coffin before he delivered it. A modern instance of this custom is described by the writer in the *Philadelphia Times* of August 3, 1893.

Germantown, he had witnessed probably greater changes than almost any one, and the tradition may be a true one which tells us that the sincerest mourner at the funeral was the trusty slave Robert. The following obituary appeared in the *Pennsylvania Gazette*, No. 1885, February 7, 1765:

"Last week died at Germantown Dr. Christopher De Wit a Gentleman long and well known throughout this and the neighbouring provinces for his great services and abilities in his profession of a physician."

Although Doctor Witt lived and died in the home of the Warmer family, it appears that he was not without kinship in this country, as he had a nephew, William Yates,[434] living in Germantown. Just how great the intimacy was between these two men is difficult to surmise, as all that is known about the latter is gleamed from a deed of gift to Yates, and the reference to him in Witt's last will.

From the former it appears that when Dr. Witt felt that he was approaching the end of his earthly career, he gave to his relative a stone house and tenement with a lot of ground containing 54¾ perches, fronting on the northeast side of the main street. This gift, for such it was (as the consideration was only a nominal one) was evidently in lieu of all and any claims Yates might eventually make against the estate of his uncle. The conveyance is dated November 2, 1758, and is recorded in Deed Book H, 11, page 186.

It sets forth that, "For and inconsideration of the natural love and affection which the said Christopher Witt hath and doth bear unto and towards his said nephew William Yates and for his the said William Yates better and more comfortable subsistance in this world and for divers other good causes him the said Christopher Witt (as uncle) there-

[434] William Yates was a wheelwright by profession, and was a son of Witt's sister.

unto especially mooving, as in consideration of the sum of Five Shillings lawfull money of Pennsylvania unto him the said Christopher Witt well and duly in hand paid by his said Nephew William Yates, &c."

A tradition that the writer has thus far not been able to verify intimates that the house given by Witt to Yates formerly stood upon the site now known as 5073 Main Street. It is described as having been a quaint little building, and subsequently for a time served as the local post-office.

After De Witt's death, when the will was admitted to probate, February 4th, it was found that after a bequest to "William Yeats, commonly called my relative," of "One English shilling," he manumits his trusty servant Robert (Claymore) absolutely; further giving him the lot on which the old house stood, describing it as "the certain tract of land in the Township of Germantown, on the north side of the lane commonly called Keyser's and bought of Adam Holt." He further gives him "all tools, instruments and utensils belonging or appertaining to the making of Clocks, also the feather bed and bedstead, a bolster-pillow and other furniture; also my great Clock which strikes the quarters, also all household goods belonging to me which shall be found in my old house, where I formerly lived next door below Andrew Keyser's *alias* Pistorius. That is to say 2 chairs, a Black walnut table, Chest of drawers, a press cupboard, with all that is contained in the same. Also all other goods and effects of mine which shall be found in the same old house at the time of my decease."

After thus liberally providing for his trusty servant, he bequeaths £60 cash, then in the hands of one Leonard Frelich, to the Pennsylvania Hospital in Philadelphia, an institution then in its infancy, "the said legacy to be for the use of the poor in said Hospital."[435] After a few minor bequests, he leaves the rest of his estate, including the large house in which he lived, to his friend Christian Warmer (3d), the grandson of the emigrant.[436]

Thus Doctor Christopher Witt, the Rosicrucian Mystic of Germantown, the last of the Kelpius community, lived and died charitable even unto death, not only rewarding his trusty slave with his liberty, and his old benefactors, the Warmer family, with a home and fortune, but leaving a legacy for the alleviation of human misery for ages to come. Comparatively, his bequest to the Hospital will prove a more enduring monument to his worth and memory than perishable stone or corroding brass.

---

[435] This is said to have been one of the first legacies left to the embryo institution. In the Hospital records the estate of Dr. "Wilt" is credited with $160.00.

[436] His personal property was appraised at a total of £314, 5s, od. Among the items we find:

Telescope,	£1-10-0
Maps and Pictures,	1-5-0
Organ,	40-0-0
Virginal,	1-15-0
Belongings to apothecaries and Doctor's way,	60-0-0
Two Clocks,	30-0-0
One Clock,	15-0-0
Clockmaker's tools,	3-0-0

THE ROMANCE OF SPOOK HILL.

ONE OF THE WARNER TOMBS ON SPOOK HILL.[438]

CHRISTIAN WARMER and his wife were not only solicitous for the bodily welfare of the individual members of the Theosophical Community, and tenderly cared for such as were sick or distressed in the early days of the experiment on the Wissahickon, but they went even further, and set apart a piece of their land in Germantown[437] as a burial-place for themselves and such Theosophical Brethern as should die in the vicinity. This cemetery, within the very heart of Germantown, has for some reasons thus far escaped the notice of antiquarians and local historians. It is located upon the high ground within the square bounded by High and Haines Streets, and Morton and Hancock Streets, and

---

[437] A seemingly well-founded tradition indicates that the ground was originally set aside for burial purposes by Dr. Witt, who held title to the same for two years before he conveyed it to Warmer. See page 404 *ibid.*

[438] The name of the *Warmer* family about the middle of last century was Anglicized to *Warner*, *vide* signature of emigrant, page 245, *supra.*

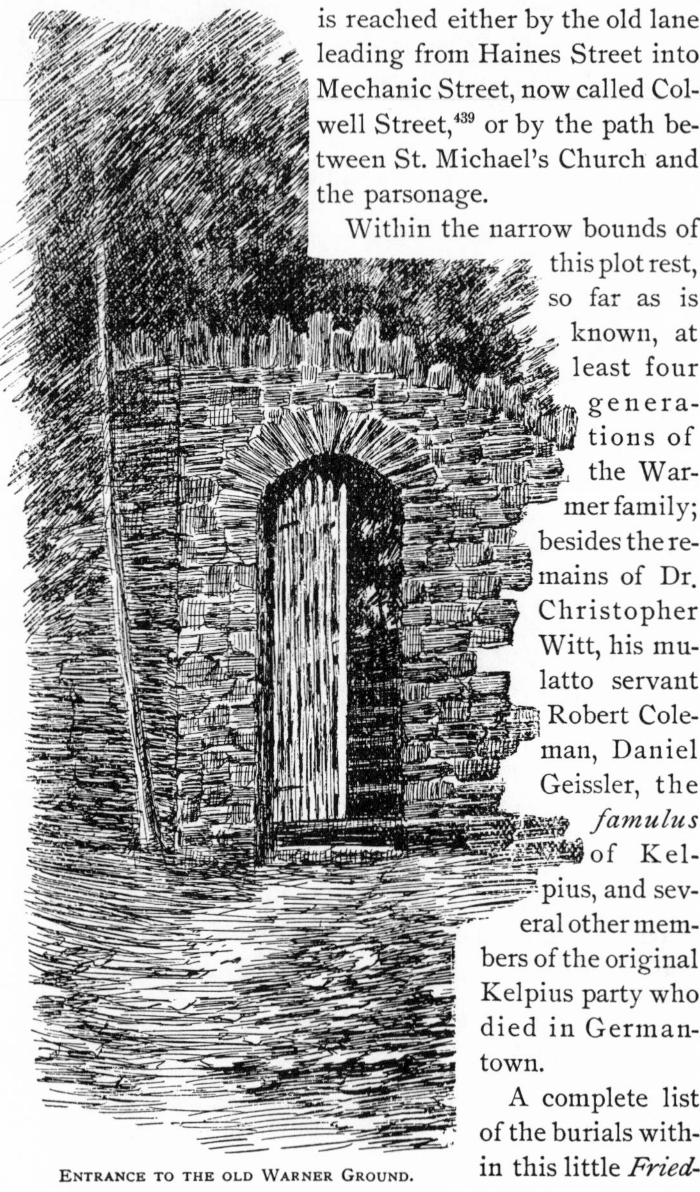

ENTRANCE TO THE OLD WARNER GROUND.

is reached either by the old lane leading from Haines Street into Mechanic Street, now called Colwell Street,[439] or by the path between St. Michael's Church and the parsonage.

Within the narrow bounds of this plot rest, so far as is known, at least four generations of the Warmer family; besides the remains of Dr. Christopher Witt, his mulatto servant Robert Coleman, Daniel Geissler, the *famulus* of Kelpius, and several other members of the original Kelpius party who died in Germantown.

A complete list of the burials within this little *Fried-*

hof was still in existence a few years ago, and not only contained a list of all who rest within its bounds, but also a short synopsis of the ceremonial with which they were committed to the earth.

Unfortunately for our purpose this list cannot now be found. The writer has during the past two years made untiring efforts, without avail, to trace and obtain this document, but although four persons have at different times seen and examined the list, all trace of it now seems to have been lost.

This piece of ground on the hill-top in Germantown was originally forty feet square, stepped out and consecrated according to the mystic ritual. Many are the vicissitudes that have passed over this little plot during the past two centuries. For a number of years it was merely known as a private burial ground, such as was set apart by John Bechtel from his own ground upon the west side of the Main Street opposite Fisher's Lane; in later years for the use of the *Unitas Fratrum* or Moravian Brethren.

From the very day when the first body was interred within this enclosure on the hill, the spot was assumed to be haunted by the credulous German population. This was probably on account of the mystic ceremonies with which the last rites were performed.

As the time passed and additional interments took place, the gossip as to uncanny sights and sounds increased, as did also the belief in their re-occurrence at certain intervals. Many were the strange tales told by the honest Germans as they sat upon their hearth-benches (*ofen-bank*) during the long winter nights, all about this quiet spot, now surrounded by a low stone wall. Brave indeed would even a strong man have been, when crossing the fields after dark, to have cast his eyes toward the haunted spot.

[439] As the order now stands, Colwell Street—Mechanic Street.

An old legend is to the effect that frequently during the *geister-stunde*, or ghostly hour of midnight, shadowy forms were to be seen flitting about in the dim moonlight, clad in outlandish attire, some being robed in light, and others in black garb. Upon such occasions, it is stated that the shrivelled and bent form of old Dr. Witt could be seen slowly toiling up the hill-side behind his house to the ghostly spot where he would join the supernatural visitors, until the clock in the little German church steeple struck the hour of one, when all would vanish except the old Mystic, who would then slowly retrace his steps toward his house, being met at about half the distance by his faithful servant. It was mainly on account of these weird happenings that the spot became known as *der Spook-bühel* or Spook Hill.

After the death of Dr. Witt, in 1765, and his burial within the enclosure, the fear of the uncanny spot increased. Tales were told which have survived even to the present time, how upon the night following the burial of the old Mystic, spectral blue flames were seen dancing around his grave,[440] which it is said continued for weeks.

Another matter which increased the mystery was the nocturnal visits made by the dusky Robert to his late master's grave. The latter, however, ceased after a certain period, when the place was rarely visited by any one, except now and then by a *wunder-doctor* or witch-doctor, who went to gather lichen from the mossy tombstones, or certain plants plucked from a grave, to be of service in incantations for the cure of persons or cattle supposed to have been bewitched, or in some cases for the discovery of hidden treasures.

After the battle of Germantown, October 4, 1777, a

[440] This seems more strange when the season of the year is considered.

number of soldiers, English as well as Hessian, are said to have found their last resting-place within the little cemetery on the hill. For many years afterwards a weird story was current in addition to the many tales connected with this gruesome spot. It was of a spectral horseman, dressed in the uniform of a British officer, mounted upon a grey horse, who upon certain nights was to be seen riding around the enclosure, and motioning as if rallying his men, and after encircling the wall a certain number of times he would vanish into the air.

A few years ago there were yet some aged persons living in the immediate vicinity who declare that not only did they hear of these uncanny doings and sights from their parents and friends, but in days gone by saw them upon different occasions when passing the spot.

Toward the close of the last century and in the early part of the present one, the Warmer estate was gradually divided into lots and sold, and as the adjoining ground changed ownership and the family which was immediately interested in its maintainance left the vicinity, the old graveyard became neglected and overgrown with noxious weeds and brambles, and it almost seemed as if the generations of Warmers, together with the dead Mystics and Theosophists, buried there were left to care for themselves.

While the ground was in this condition, the weird ghost stories connected with it lost nothing by being repeated over and over, but on the contrary multiplied among the naturally superstitious inhabitants, where every well-regulated household had a *spook* or two of its own. Consequently the place was avoided more than ever after nightfall. Eventually it became a mere receptacle for rubbish, and on account of its wretched condition the name by mutual consent was changed to "Mount Misery."

In all the sales and conveyances of the surrounding ground care, however, was taken by some interested parties to preserve the old cemetery, as well as to make a provision for the narrow lane that formed an approach to it.

In the conveyance recorded in Deed Book D 56, page 231, Lydia (Powell) Warmer, widow of Christian Warmer (2d) and her daughter Elizabeth, December 7, 1776, convey to John Bringhurst a part of their land, in which they reserve for "themselves, their heirs and assigns forever one perch or sixteen foot and one-half in breath along one side of said premises, along Jacob Keysers lot or land in his possession, said reserved perch of land or breadth across the said lot of land to be for a road for the use and behoof of the said Lydia Warmer and Elizabeth Warmer and their Heirs and Assigns forever." This is the reservation for the lane leading to the cemetery.

In his will dated September 28, 1793, Jonathan Warner,[441] son of Christopher (who was the godson of Dr. Witt, son of Christian (2d), and great grandson of the emigrant), charges his mother Elizabeth, the widow of Dr. Christopher Warner, who had intermarried with one Leibert, with the special care of "forever hereafter upholding and maintaining the Graveyard and Graveyard wall or fence adjacent to Germantown, commonly known by the name of Warner's Graveyard."

Jonathan Warner, who was also a "Doctor of Physic," died quite young, and was unmarried. He left all his property to his mother, and she and his step-father were appointed his executors.

The writer has been further informed by trustworthy persons, who have lived all their lives within sight of the old ground, that Dr. Christopher Witt had ordained that

---

[441] *Vide* note 438, *supra.*

ST. MICHAEL'S PROTESTANT EPISCOPAL CHURCH.

BUILT UPON THE OLD WARMER GROUND.

the whole top of the hill adjoining the enclosure should be given free, for the purpose of building a meeting-house,[442] to any Christian Protestant denomination that should make demand. It was also stated that this bequest was on record. Diligent search, however, has failed to discover any documentary evidence which would substantiate this tradition.

As the years rolled by and no organization claimed the above privilege the ground became more neglected than ever; a stone-quarry was opened just outside the southeast corner of the walls and encroaching upon its bounds, one angle of the wall fell in and was carted away for building-stone. It now became known as "Vinegar Hill," and was only used for the occasional burial of a negro. It is stated that the last one of that race buried there was a servant in the Leibert household.

But when the little piece of consecrated ground seemed to be in its most neglected condition, with graves sunken, tombstones broken and crumbling wall, a turn was reached in its history. Together with the surrounding property it came into the possession of the Morris family, and eventually of Miss Elizabeth C. Morris.

In the course of events a condition of affairs arose which was destined to redeem this plot of consecrated ground from its neglected and desolate state, and to fulfill the alleged wishes of the old Pietist and philosopher, as expressed in the foregoing tradition. It came about in the following manner:

A few years before the outbreak of the Civil War, a spirit of religious revival arose in the ancient village of Germantown which, at that time incorporated as a part of

---

[442] Wording according to an old deed examined by the Rev. J. K. Murphy, D.D.

the consolidated city,[443] had become the most fashionable suburb of Philadelphia. Then the desire arose among the new residents from the city, as is usually the case under similar circumstances, to form congregations, institute new parishes and build churches.

Among these new congregations was one under the leadership of the Rev. J. Pinckney Hammond, who secured a lot on Coulter Street near Wayne, and proceeded to build a church. Its corner-stone was laid with considerable ceremony December 5, 1858, by Bishops Bowman and Doane, and it was called "the Church of the Holy Cross."

This act upon the part of the new congregation gave rise to a serious complication with the adjoining parish of Calvary, which had erected a church in the vicinity.[444] This trouble led to the abandonment of the location by the new organization, whose services were once more transferred to the Town Hall.

The promotors of the new enterprise in nowise disheartened at once looked about for a new location,—one that would be suitable, and at the same time would not interfere with any existing parish. This coming to the knowledge of Miss Elizabeth C. Morris, she extended an offer of that part of her land adjoining and including the old cemetery to Rev. Mr. Hammond, provided a church were erected in union with the Protestant Episcopal Church, and to be free from pew-rents forever.

When the parties interested went to view the proffered land it was found to be as desolate a spot as could well be imagined. Its surface covered with rubbish and overgrown with rank briars and weeds, it looked anything but a favor-

---

[443] Philadelphia city and county was consolidated in 1854.

[444] Manheim and Pulaski Avenue. The late Rev. Thomas K. Conrad, D.D., was the first rector.

able spot for a church. The ground fronted on High Street, and was on the high ground about two squares east of the main street.[445] The most prominent object upon the church lot, which was to be 150 feet front on High Street, with a depth of 125 feet, was a large spreading mulberry tree (*morus multicalus*), while here and there among the growth of briars was to be seen a leaning or broken tomb-stone, to indicate that the spot was one of sepulture. The name by which this tract was locally known was well chosen: "Mount Misery." The proffered gift, however, was accepted with its provisions by the parties interested, and preparations were made forthwith to erect a neat church.

The first piece of sod was turned on the 18th day of April, 1859; on the 29th of the same month the corner-stone was laid by Bishop Bowman, and so diligently was the work prosecuted that just five months later, on September 29th, St. Michael's Day, the first service was held within the walls, when it was named after the day, "St. Michael's."

In planning the church it so happened that the chancel extended over a part of the old cemetery, and in digging the trench for the foundation, traces of interments were found. Care was taken, however, not to disturb any of the graves more than could possibly be avoided. As a result the remains of the elder Warmer, Geissler and Dr. Witt, members of the original band of Pietists and mystic philosophers, now repose beneath the chancel of the church, with an altar erected over them at which prayers are read daily, anthems sung, responses chanted and the Gospel preached according to established forms of Christian worship, which their Community was so instrumental in establishing within the Province.[446]

---

[445] Now known as both Main Street and Germantown Avenue.

Outside the church a part of the original enclosure can yet be traced by the foundations of the old wall. Within the bounds of the enclosure, to the south of the church, are still to be seen the tombstones of father and son, the third and fourth generations of the Warner family. The inscriptions are as follows:

"Doctor	Memory
Christopher Warner	Doctor
Who departed this life	Jonathan Warner
February 17th 1783	Who departed this life
Aged 39 years & 4 months	December 24, 1793
	Aged 22 yrs & 1 month"

[446] After the consecration of St. Michael's at Germantown, September 29, 1859, it continued under the rectorship of its founder, the Rev. Dr. Hammond, until his resignation of the parish on the 8th of August, 1861, to accept the position of chaplain in the U. S. Army. After an interval of a year, the Rev. Levi Ward Smith was called as rector, he also became chaplain in the army, and was assigned to duty at the Cuyler General Hospital, Germantown. He held both positions until he was prostrated by a nervous disease, and "met his death at midnight, December 23, 1863, aged 43." He was a good, gentle, lovable clergyman, and, strange to say, made an attempt to have a burial vault made at the rear of the chancel of the church, alongside the Warner grave-yard, for the temporary reception of the remains of soldiers who died under his sympathetic ministrations. The ground was too stony to allow the work to proceed. After another year of vacancy, the Rev. Edward Hyde True was called, and entered upon his duties December 9, 1864; he resigned December 31, 1867. The following day (New Year's Day, 1868), the present rector, the Rev. John K. Murphy, D.D., assumed the position, having been elected to the office upon Mr. True's resignation. Mr. Murphy has continued in uninterrupted charge for nearly 28 years. He has had a united and prosperous congregation.

A large lot has been secured to the east of the plot of land laid off by the will of Dr. Witt "for the use of any society of Christians who would build a meeting house upon it," and so the sacred spot of his burial is now more guarded from intrusion than ever. A beautiful and commodius rectory thus protects it on the north, and a large and handsome stone parish building has been constructed to the south of it. It will thus be seen that the grave-yard need never be disturbed as it is completely protected by the group of buildings now surrounding it.

The elder of the two was a grandson of the emigrant, and was named after Dr. Witt; the other was his son.

There are also a few rough unlettered stones, such as it was the custom to place at the head and foot of graves to prevent any interference in the future.

These remains of the old cemetery are overshadowed by the wide-spreading branches of the mulberry tree, before mentioned, which was planted there by Dr. Physic, a well-known Philadelphia physician, during the silkworm excitement half a century ago. The ground not covered by the chancel is now included within the church lawn, and carefully sodded and kept in order. The spot, but a few decades ago so desolate and neglected, is now one of beauty and attraction, and upon the very ground once feared and avoided can now frequently be seen worshippers of the church strolling over the velvety sward or sitting upon the benches under the shadow of the old mulberry, enjoying the beauty and peacefulness of the scene.

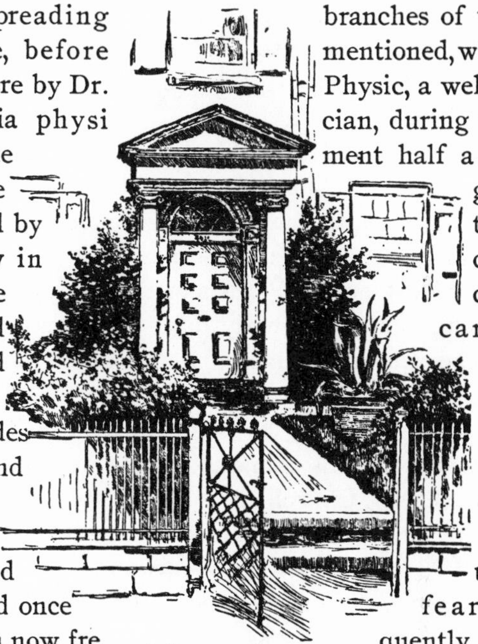

A Colonial Doorway in Germantown.

The lands surrounding the cemetery, which but a few years ago were nothing but worn-out pasture fields, are now crossed by regular streets, lined with ornate mansions and costly improvements; the church and its parsonage being a picturesque feature.

While Kelpius, Seelig and Matthäi rest in the place of their selection, now unmarked; Köster sleeps within the consecrated precincts of Lutheran ground in the Fatherland; the Falkner brothers, in unknown graves in different provinces; and while even the sepulchre of Pastorius remains a matter of conjecture, it was appointed by destiny that at least such as were gathered within this ancient *Friedhof* on the hillside were to have erected over them, after the lapse of two centuries, so glorious a monument as a Christian temple of worship.

It may be argued that this fact was merely accidental, and so it may be. The ways of good providence, however, are inscrutable, and the fact still remains that under the chancel of St. Michael's in Germantown repose the ashes of some of the German Pietists of Provincial Pennsylvania, whose influence in the early days of our province was so widespread, and whose labors were exerted in the interests of piety, their chief aim being once more to establish religious services according to orthodox church forms within the bounds of Penn's domain.

St. Michael's Church is a fitting monument to the memory of these early pioneers. May its career upon old "Spook-Hill" be a long and active one; and may the truths taught within its sacred walls take root and bring forth fruit as plentifully as did the efforts of the old Pietists who flourished here in days gone by, and whose history, tradition and legends have formed the subject of these pages.

APPENDIX.

This picture representing an early meeting of the Quakers, has of late years, been claimed to represent a meeting held at the "Bull and Mouth" in London, at which William Penn and the Duke of York (afterwards James II) were said to have been present. There is no evidence whatever to support this theory, and almost conclusive proof that the picture represents a Quaker Meeting in Holland; for while the costume of two principal figures would seem to show they were Englishmen, they were certainly not of the same nationality as the others present.

From information received from the authorities at the British Museum, the original was a painting by Egbert Hemskirck the younger, (1645-1704) and was engraved for the Dutch market by J. Gole.—It was lettered:

E. HEMSKIRCK PINX. J. GOLE, SCULPSIT.

"DE QUAAKERS VERGADERING."

Subsequent to the year 1727, the well worn plate 21 x 15½ inches was bought by J. Bowles, a print seller of London, who had the Dutch inscription obliterated and re-lettered

E. HEMSKIRCK PINX. I. BOWLES EXC.

THE QUAKERS' MEETING.

LONDON, SOLD BY J. BOWLES AT MERCER'S HALL IN CHEAPSIDE.

The reproduction is from one of the latter impressions in the collection of The Historical Society of Pennsylvania. Prints even from this condition of the plate are extremely scarce.

According to the best European authorities the scene represented is laid in Benjamin Furly's house in the Wynstraat in Rotterdam. The principal portraits are said to be those of William Penn, George Fox and Benjamin Furly, which would indicate one of the meetings mentioned in Fox's Journal, held between July 28 and October 20, 1677. An opinion which is without doubt correct.

THE PIETISTS OF PROVINCIAL PENNSYLVANIA.

BENJAMIN FURLY.

ROYAL ARMS OF HOLLAND, A.D. 1694.

BENJAMIN FURLY, the friend of William Penn and promotor of the first German emigration to America, was a native of Colchester, England, where he was born April 13, 1636.[447] He began life as a merchant there, and became identified with the early Quakers. Subsequent to the year 1660 he immigrated to Amsterdam,[448] but afterwards made Rotterdam his permanent

[447] According to a Dutch account (Unger, in "Rotterdamsch Jaarboekje," 1890, p. 114), he was born at Rotterdam, of English parentage. There is, however, nothing to substantiate the above claim, as the learned writer evidently confuses Benjamin Furly with his son Benjohan.

[448] "Gerhard Croesens Quaker Historie, von deren Ursprung bis auf jüngsthin entstandene Trennung." Berlin, bey Johann Michael Rudiger, 1696, p. 644. The title of the English edition reads, "The General History of the Quakers &c. Being written originally in Latin by Gerard Croese." London, 1696.

Two editions were printed in Latin,—"Gerardi Croesi Historia Quakeriana,"—viz., Theodore Boom, 1695, and Amstelodamie, anno M.DC.IVC. Copies of all editions are now in the library of the writer, also *vide* pp. 43, *et seq. Supra.*

home, where he engaged in the mercantile and shipping business, his first establishment being in the *Scheepmakershaven.*[449]

Although an Englishman by birth, he soon became identified with the land of his adoption, and married "Dorothe Graigne," a Dutch maiden. His eldest child by this marriage was a son Benjohan, born January 6, 1681. Furly, by his honesty and industry, became known as one of the leading merchants of Rotterdam, and removed his residence and warehouse to the *Haaringvliet,*[450] then the chief commercial centre of the city. He, however, did not confine himself exclusively to his commercial life and to the accumulation of wealth, but continued his interest in literary pursuits, and, as Croese intimates,[451] "to thoroughly perfect himself in the various branches of learning," he cultivated the society of the leading critics and scholars of the period, and subsequently became a patron of letters.

His house became the rendezvous of such learned men as Leclerc, Limborch, Algernon Sidney, Edward Clarke and Locke, and his library, with its wealth of manuscripts and rare imprints, was one of more than local reputation, being frequently quoted and consulted by *littèrateurs* from different parts of Europe, two notable instances of which were the

---

[449] From the records at Rotterdam it appears that down to 1672 he lived in the *Scheepmakershaven;* from 1672 to 1693 on the north side of the Wynstraat; 1693-1709 on the Wynhaven, whence in 1709 he removed to the large house wherein he died on the Haaringvliet, and which is still standing. Present number 48.

[450] The "Haaringvliet" is one of the numerous basins or canals that form the harbor of Rotterdam.

[451] "Quaker Historia," p. 645.

visits of Ludolph Küster and Zacharias von Uffenbach, accounts of which have been preserved. Benjamin Furly also took an active interest in the religious questions of the day, taking the side of the Separatists, as opposed to the established churches, and his home in Rotterdam upon frequent occasions was the scene of devotional meetings at which George Fox, Keith, William Penn and others were prominent participators.

At an early age he became convinced of the Quaker doctrine, and became one of the most active champions of that Society upon the Continent. He was a prolific author, writing with equal facility in English, German, Dutch and French.

His zeal in the doctrine he had embraced is attested by the publication of his numerous controversial writings, together with those of Fox and Penn, which were translated by him and printed at his expense.

Furly afterwards became the chief agent of William Penn on the Continent for the sale of his newly acquired lands in America. His wife having died in 1691, he married,[452] on December 10, 1693, Susanna Huis, the widow of one Jacobus van der Lijt.[453]

Benjamin Furly died March, 1714, in the seventy-eighth year of his age, and was buried, as befitted a man of his standing and wealth, in a tomb (No. 175) in the centre aisle of the St. Laurentius or Groote Kerk, formerly the cathedral church of Rotterdam.[454] Four children are known

---

[452] Benjamin Furly was married both times at the *Stadhuis* or town hall of Rotterdam. The banns for both marriages were, however, read in the *Groote Kirk* by permission of the clergy prior to the ceremony.—*Church Records of the Gemeente*, Rotterdam.

[453] "Archief der Gemeente," Rotterdam.

[454] "Rotterdamsch Jaarboekje," vol. ii, p. 114.

to have survived their father,—Benjohan, John, Arent and a daughter Dorothy; all, presumably, issues by the first marriage.

It has been questioned whether Benjamin Furly became a Quaker before or after his settlement in Holland. We know that he was a man of marked and peculiar religious views, and that from his first arrival in Holland he was in sympathy with the so-called Separatists; and from the fact that members of his immediate family in England were among the early followers of George Fox, it is probable that he was convinced prior to his immigration to Holland.

According to a Dutch account, it would appear, however, that he did not join the Society of Friends until after his residence in Rotterdam. If this be true, it must have been prior to the years 1659–60, as in those years he, together with John Stubs, assisted in the compilation of George Fox's "Battle-door for Teachers & Professors to learn Singular & Plural: You to Many, and Thou to One: Singular One, Thou; Plural Many, You."

A Battle-Door
FOR
TEACHERS & PROFESSORS
TO LEARN
Singular & Plural,
You to *Many*, and *Thou* to *One*: Singular *One*, *Thou*
Plural *Many*, *You*

Wherein is ſhewed forth by Grammar, or Scripture Examples, how ſeveral Nations and People have made a diſtinction between *Singular* and *Plural*. And firſt, In the former part of this Book, Called *The Engliſh Battle Door*, may be ſeen how ſeveral People have ſpoken *Singular* and *Plural*; As the *Apharſathkites*, the *Tarpelites*, the *Apharſites*, the *Archevites*, the *Babylonians*, the *Suſanchites*, the *Dehavites*, the *Elamites*, the *Temanites*, the *Naomites*, the *Shuites*, the *Buzites*, the *Moabites*, the *Hivites*, the *Edomites*, the *Philiſtines*, the *Amalekites*, the *Sodomites*, the *Hittites*, the *Midianites*, &c.

Alſo, In this Book is ſet forth Examples of the *Singular* and *Plural* about *Thou*, and *You*, in ſeveral Languages, divided into diſtinct *Battle Doors*, or Formes, or Examples; *Engliſh*, *Latine*, *Italian*, *Greek*, *Hebrew Caldee*, *Syriack*, *Arabick*, *Perſiack*, *Ethiopick*, *Samaritan*, *Coptick*, or *Egyptick*, *Armenian*, *Saxon*, *Welch*, *Mence*, *Corniſh*, *French*, *Spaniſh*, *Portugal*, *High-Dutch*, *Low-Dutch*, *Daniſh*, *Bohemian*, *Slavonian* And how Emperors and others have uſed the Singular word to *One*, and how the word *You* came firſt from the Pope.

Likewiſe ſome Examples, in the *Polonian*, *Lithuanian*, *Iriſh* and *Eaſt-Indian*, together with the Singular and Plural words, *thou* and *you*, in *Sweediſh*, *Turkiſh*, *Muſcovian*, and *Curlandian*, tongues.

the latter part of this Book are contained ſeverall bad unſavoury Words, gathered forth of certain School-Books, which have been taught Boyes in *England*, which is a Rod and a Whip to the School-Maſters in *England* and elſewhere who teach ſuch Books

George. Fox. John Stubs. Benjamin Furley

LONDON, Printed for *Robert Wilſon*, and are to be ſold at his Shop at the Signe of the *Black-Spread-Eagle* and *Wind mil* in *Martins le Grand*, 1660.

Fac-simile of the Title Page of George Fox's "Battle-Door."

It was a folio of fifty-seven sheets, printed in thirty languages, of which, among others, his grandson says that the Chaldee, Syriac, Welsh, and French portions were written by Furly.[455] Croese, in his "Historia Quakeriana," distinctly states that "Benjamin Furly had this clever and ingenious work printed at great expense, and that Fox, although he knew of these thirty tongues but a single one, yet poses as the author." George Fox, in his journal, mentions that this work was finished in 1661, and that Benjamin Furly took great pains in compiling it.

During the next fifteen years Benjamin Furly published a number of controversial works in the interest of the Quakers, prominent among which may be named the following:

"De Eere des Werelds ontdekt, en om desselfs onnuttigheids ende onprofijtelyksheid wille verworpen, Ende de Eere, die van God alleen komt, bevestigt, en un't werk gestelt. Ofte Eenige Redenen, waarom het Volk Gods, Quakers genaamt, verzaken het gewoonlyke Eerbewys, ende de Groetingen des Werelds . . . . Door een Vriend der Waarheid, dewelke geen Aannemer der Persoonen is. B. F(urly) Genaams en een Quaker . . . Rotterdam by Henricus Goddaeus . . . 1662."

"Die Sache Christ und seines Volks." (German.) (The Cause of Christ and His People Justified.) By W. Ames. The large preface is by B. Furly. 4to, 1662.

"The Light upon the Candlestick." By W. Ames. The English translation is by Furly. 4to, 1663.

"The World's Honor detected &c. By a Friend to Truth who is no respecter or regarder of persons, called a Quaker." B. F[urly]. 4to, 1663.

---

455 "Original Letters," etc. Preface, p. 79.

"John Philley's Arraignment of Cristendome." Printed and published by B. Furly. 4to, 1664.

"Eine Beschirmunge d'unschuldigen," etc. (Dutch.) By Wm. Caton, with a postscript by Benjamin Furly. 4to, 1664.

"Copye van eenen Brief: geschreven aen seeckeren Vriend, over syn Ghevoel en Oordeel, Dat alle de gene, die niet en gebruycken de uytterlycke Instellingen van Doop ende Avondmael, Kerck-gang &c. niet en zyn geleyd door den Geest Gods, maer door eenen Dwael-geest . . . Door B. F(urly) Gedruckt voor den Autheur, in't Jaer 1666."

"A Recantation by Benjamin Furly. Given in Rott[erdam] in 1669." (This is in relation to the hat controversy.)

"Anthoniette Bourignon ontdeckt, door B. Furly, ende haeren Geest geopenbaert uyt haere Druckten," etc. (Dutch) 4to, 1671.[456]

"The Universal Free Grace of the Gospel asserted," etc. By George Keith. (Part by B. Furly.) 4to, 1671.

"A Letter to George Whitehead, about the Hat Controversy." 8vo, 1673.

"Forderung der Christenheit für Gericht, den wederlegger wederlegt door B. Furly."[457] n. d.

"Copye van een Missive uyt London, geschrievan door William Penn. Aen Burgermeesteren en Raadt der Stad Embden. En haar in de Latynsche en Duytsche Talen in Geschrifte toegesonden (in d. 24 Dec. 1674). En nu tot Opmerkinge van alle menschen, sonderling de Machten der Aarde, en de Predikers, door den Druckgemeen gemaakt Ten eynde by haar eens soude mogen werden overwogen het schadelyke gevolg van die Gronden diemen leyt tot vervolginge van andere menschen, om de saken van

---

456 A second edition is noted in the "Bibliotheca Furliana," p. 84. No. 932.

457 Title from "Bibliotheca Furliana."

den Gods-dienst, enz Rotterdam, Pieter van Wynbrugge . . . 1675."[458] 12 blz.

"Met een voorrede van den vertaler, Benjamin Furly, gedagt Rotterd. 18, Febr. 1675."

In the Archives of Rotterdam there is preserved a document written in Hollandese, in which Furly, together with Symon Jansz Vettekeücken, makes the following appeal to the burgomasters and regents of Rotterdam for the protection of the Quakers who were then holding meetings in that city. This interesting document, in the handwriting of Benjamin Furly, is dated July 8, 1675, and was photographed by the writer during the past summer,—1894.

TRANSLATION.

"*To the Burgomasters and Regents of the City of Rotterdam:*

"The people of God, mockingly called Quakers, who have taken up their residence in this City, cannot refrain from making known, with christian respect, unto you, as Magistrates of this City, that now twice, to wit;—yesterday, within and without their regular meeting place, where they come together to wait in silence upon the Lord, they have been treated and handled with violence and annoyance by divers sort of men, not only young but also of greater age, which is so publicly known that the thrown-in window-panes and the broken doors and benches are clear witnesses thereof. All the which they make known unto you not so much for anxiety for their persons and goods, as they well know that the same God is living yet, and shall live unto eternity, who hath set limits to the sea and hath said hitherto shalt thou come but no further, and who can prevent the

Psalm 62, 2.

Job 38. 11.

[458] A missive by William Penn. Translation, with a large preface and conclusion, by Benjamin Furly. 4to, 1675.

raging of the people when it pleases him: but
Psalm 2. 1, 4. to avoid thereby the blame, such things having befallen them, of not having made known the same to you,
for your discretion, and above all for the mani-
Matt: 6. 2, 12. festation of God in your consciences which dictates to every one to do unto others as he would have
others to do unto him, because with what meas-
Eccles: 10, 8, 9. ure he metes, it shall be measured to him again. In the name of all signed by us

"BENJAMIN FFURLY
"SYMON JANSZ VETTEKEÜCKEN

"At Rotterdam the 8th day of the Month which one calles July, 1675."

When, two years later, Penn, accompanied by Robert Barclay, George Fox, Keith and others[459] made his celebrated tour through Germany and Holland, it was this same Benjamin Furly who met them upon their landing.

George Fox records that the party was becalmed when a league from the shore, and that William Penn and Robert Barclay, understanding that Benjamin Furly was to come from Rotterdam to the Briel to meet them, got two of the sailors to lower a small boat and row them ashore; but before they could reach it, the gates were closed, and there being no house without the gates, they were forced to lie in a fisher's boat all night. As soon as the gates were opened in the morning they entered and found Benjamin Furly, who brought them to Briel, where the Friends received them with "great gladness."[460]

---

[459] The party, in addition to the three named, consisted of John Furly, a brother of Benjamin Furly, of Rotterdam, G. Watts, William Tallcoat, Isabella Yeomans and Elizabeth Keith.—*Journal of William Penn.*

[460] Penn in his Journal mentions Aaron Sonneman, S. Johnson and [Symon Jansz?] Vettekeücken as being among the number, *vide* "Penna. Mag.," vol. ii, p. 249.

The party arrived at Rotterdam on the same day, Saturday, July 28, 1677. The next day—First day (Sunday)—two religious meetings were held at the house of Furly, who them lived in the Wynstraat, the latter and John Claus acting as interpreters. The next fortnight was spent in visits to various towns in Holland. On the 7th of August the company divided up into two parties, when Keith, Barclay and Penn left the others at Amsterdam and set out towards Germany, where, as Fox states in his journal, "they traveled many hundred miles, and had good service for the Lord," Benjamin Furly going with them and acting as interpreter for the party, and upon that occasion was largely instrumental in influencing the Germans in favor of Penn. It is further a matter of record that Furly remained with Penn and Keith during their entire stay on the Continent. Towards the close of this memorable pilgrimage, four tracts of an exhortative character were written by Penn,[461] designed for distribution among the Separatists in Germany and Holland. These tracts were revised and translated by Benjamin Furly, and printed at his expense after Penn's departure. The German titles are as follows:

Het CHRISTENRIJK
TEN
OORDEEL
gedagvaart.

Een tedere beſoekinge in de Liefde Gods, aan alle die gene die een begeerte hebben om God te kennen en hem in Waarheyd en Opregtigheyd aan te bidden; van wat *Secte*, of ſoort van *Godsdienſt* de ſelve zouden mogen weſen

Een Miſſive aan alle die gene, die, onder de belyders der Chriſtelijkheyd, afgeſondert zijn van de ſichtbare *Secten*, en *uyterlijke* Gemeenten.

EN

Een Miſſive aan al die gene, die gevoelig zijn van den dag hárer beſoekinge

Alles in d' Engelſe Tale geſchreven door

WILLIAM PENN.

En daar uyt overgeſet.

Tot ROTTERDAM
Gedrukt voor JAN PIETERSZ GROENWOUT, Boekverkooper, wonende op het Spuy 1678

FAC-SIMILE OF THE DUTCH TITLE-PAGE OF PENN'S TRACTS, ORIGINAL IN THE "ARCHIEF DER GEMEENTE," ROTTERDAM.

---

[461] "Penn. Mag.," vol. ii, p. 276.

"Forderung der Christenheit für Gericht." (A Call to Christendom, etc.)

"Eine Freundliche heimsuchung in der Liebe Gottes." (A Tender Visitation in the Love of God.)

"An alle diejenigen so unter den Bekennern der Christenheit," etc. (To all Professors of Christianity, etc.)

"An Alle diejenigen welche empfinden," etc. (Tender Counsel, etc.)

The above were also published collectively in Dutch under the general title, "Het Christenrijk Ten Oordeel Gedagvaart," etc. Rotterdam, 1678. 4to.

Two of the above tracts—"A Call to Christendom," and "Tender Counsel"—were printed separately at the time in English.[462]

It was about this time that the friendship between John Locke, who had been introduced to Furly by Edward Clarke, of Chipley,[463] ripened into intimacy, and the correspondence which ensued lasted until the death of Locke. Algernon Sidney and the Earl of Shaftesbury were also frequent visitors at the Furly homestead, and the former, at his death, bequeathed to Furly a large silver goblet, which is still in possession of his descendants.[464] When the grant to William Penn was consummated, and there became a likelihood of a large German and Dutch immigration to Pennsylvania, Penn submitted to Benjamin Furly the drafts of several instruments which he proposed to make the basis for the laws and government of his Province. Furly's comments on these papers, in his handwriting, entitled,—

Goblet Bequeathed by Algernon Sidney to Benjamin Furly.

"FOR THE SECURITY OF FORREIGNERS WHO MAY INCLINE TO PURCHASE LAND IN PENNSYLVANIA, BUT MAY DY BEFORE THEY THEMSELVES COME THEIR TO INHABIT."

These papers are among the "Penn Manuscripts" in the collection of the Historical Society of Pennsylvania. In them he suggests the protection of the interests of the German and foreign settlers who it was expected would immigrate to Pennsylvania, and makes a number of criticisms on the laws which Penn proposed, suggesting in some instances the usages followed in Holland.

This interesting document, never before published, is reproduced in its entirety at the end of this paper, as originally published in the "Pennsylvania Magazine of Biography and History," vol. xix, pp. 277–305, and it deserves the careful consideration of every student of Pennsylvania-German history,[465] for it will be noted that Benjamin Furly

---

462 Whiting's "Catalogue of Friend's Books," London, 1708, pp. 119, 120.

463 Edward Clarke, Esq., of Chipley, near Taunton, was one of the burgesses for that borough in seven Parliaments, from the first of King William, which met in 1690, to the third held by Queen Anne, which was dissolved in 1710.

464 A drawing of this cup forms the frontispiece to the second edition of "Original Letters of John Locke, Algernon Sidney and Lord Shaftesbury," London, 1847.

465 Fredk. D. Stone, Litt. D., the learned librarian of the Historical Society of Pennsylvania, in commenting upon these suggestions, states: "The following paper, in the handwriting of Benjamin Furly, is among the "Penn Papers" in possession of the Historical Society of Pennsylvania. It is endorsed "B. F. Abridgm^t out of Holland and Germany. Laws of Gov^t Pense." It contains a series of criticisms called forth by a comparison of the "Frame of Government Signed by Penn April 25 1682, together with The Laws Agreed upon in England May 5, 1682," and a paper called "The Fundamentall Constitutions of Pennsylvania," a copy of which is also among the "Penn Papers." This last is a form of government that Penn, after considerable deliberation, had decided upon as a suitable one for the government of his province, but which was abandoned for what we know as the "Frame of Government." This action does not

was not alone concerned about the religious and civil liberty of the prospective immigrants, but of their personal rights as well. This is instanced in the clause granting immunity from arrest and fine to such persons as choose to labor upon the First day of the week,[466] —a suggestion that was made in the interest of the Sabbatarian movement which was then attracting considerable attention in both England and Holland.

FAC-SIMILE OF ANTI-SLAVERY CLAUSE IN FURLY'S SUGGESTIONS TO PENN.

Then, again, his suggestions and advice to Penn as to the course to pursue in regard to a possible attempt to introduce negro slavery into the Province[467] is of great interest, as the first public pro-

appear to have been approved of by Furly, and hence his criticisms. As Furly's comments were made upon the "Frame of Government" as finally published, it cannot be claimed that Penn was influenced by Furly in drafting his "Frame," unless it was through a correspondence of an earlier date. There is, however, little doubt that the 21st section of the "Frame of Government," included in the act of settlement passed at Philadelphia, March 1, 1683, which provides for the protection of the estates of aliens, was the result of Furly's suggestion, and a further examination of that instrument, with Furly's criticisms, might indicate an influence in other sections. The paper is interesting as showing how widely and earnestly Penn sought assistance in drafting the fundamental laws for his province, and the attention that was given to the subject."

[466] XIX.—The 26th Law enjoyning all to abstain from Labour on ye first day may prove a vile snare to ye conscience of many in this day, who do not look upon that day as of any other then human institution, & may

test against negro slavery in America was made at Germantown in 1688 by some of the German pioneers who came to Pennsylvania under his auspices and bounty.

Subsequent to the grant Benjamin Furly became Penn's most active and useful agent on the Continent for the sale of his lands.

Pastorious in his autobiographical memoir in the "Beehive"[468] states: "Upon my return to Frankfort in 1682, I was glad to enjoy the company of my former acquaintances and Christian friends, assembled together in the house called the Saalhof, viz.: Dr. Spener, Dr. Schutz, Notarius Fenda, Jacobus Van de Walle, Maximilian Lerfner, Eleonora von Merlau, Maria Juliana Bauer, etc., who sometimes made mention of William Penn of Pennsylvania, and showed me letters from Benjamin Furly, also a printed relation concerning said province," etc.

How great a factor Furly was in bringing about the extended German immigration is a matter of history.[469] It was he who negotiated the first land purchase of the Cre-

---

be pressed in spirit (whether right or wrong is not the question) sometimes to work upon that day, to testify agt that superstitious conceit that it is of divine institution, & is the Christian sabbath.

Onely thus far there may a service be in Setting Servants at liberty from the oppressions of grinding, covetos masters &c—that it be declared that no master shall compell his servant to labor on that day because its fit y^t ye very body of man & beast should have some rest from their continuall labor.

[467] XXIII.—Let no blacks be brought in directly. And if any come out of Virginia, Maryld. ~~or elsewhere~~ in families that have formerly bought them else where Let them be declared (as in ye west jersey constitutions) free at 8 years end.

[468] Francis Daniel Pastorious his Hive, Beestock, Melliotrophium Alvear or Rusca Apium. Begun Anno Domini or in the year of Christian Acc't 1676. M.S. Folio.

[469] "Penna. Mag.," vol. ii, pp. 237–282.

felders,[470] and the deeds were dated and delivered by him. It was also through his efforts that passage to America on the "Concord," Captain William Jeffries, was procured for the thirteen pioneer families, consisting of thirty-three German emigrants, who were met and welcomed upon their arrival by both Penn and Pastorius.[471]

To encourage further immigration of Germans and Hollanders to Pennsylvania, Furly had printed in English, soon after it appeared, a German and Dutch translation of "Some Account of the Province of Pennsylvania in America," published in London, 1681.

Een kort Bericht
Van de Provintie ofte Landſchap
PENN-SYLVANIA
genaemt, leggende in
AMERICA;
Nu onlangs onder het groote Zegel van Engeland
gegeven aan
WILLIAM PENN, &c.
MITSGADERS
Van de Privilegien, ende Macht om
het ſelve wel te Regeeren.
Uyt het Engels overgeſet na de Copye tot Londen gedrukt by *Benjamin Clark*. Boekverkooper in George Yard Lombardſtreet. 1681
Waer by nu gevoegt is de Notificatie van s' Konings Placcaet/ in date van den 2 April 1681, waer inne de tegenwoordige Inwoonders van PENN-SYLVANIA, belast word WILLEM PENN en zijn Erfgenamen, als volkomene Eygenaars en Gouverneurs, te gehoorsamen.
Als mede,
De Copye van een Brief by den ſelven W.P. geſchreven aan zekere Regeeringe Anno 1675. tegens de Vervolginge en voor de Vryheyt van Conſcientie, aan alle &c.

Tot ROTTERDAM,
Gedrukt by PIETER VAN WYNBRUGGE, Boek-Drukker in de Leeuweſtraat, in de Wereld Vol-Druk. *Anno* 1681.

FAC-SIMILE OF THE DUTCH TITLE-PAGE. FROM THE ORIGINAL IN CARTER BROWN LIBRARY, THROUGH COURTESY OF JOHN NICHOLAS BROWN.

Three years later this was followed by

"Beschreibung der in America neu-erfunden Provinz Pensylvania." 4to, 32 pp. Hamburg, 1684.

---

[470] *Ibid*, vol. ii, p. 280.

[471] When Francis Daniel Pastorius came to Rotterdam prior to his departure for Pennsylvania in 1683, he took lodgings at the house of Mariecke Vettekeuken, the widow of Symon Jansz, the signer of the protest on page 439. It is stated that it was at this house where the final arrangements were consummated between Pastorius and Furly relative to the settlement of the Frankford Company's tract near Philadelphia, *vide* "Penna. Mag.," vol. ii, p. 250.

A translation into French was published at the Hague in the same year.[472]

A religious work was also published about the same time in Dutch and German. It was entitled

"Die alte Wahrheit erhöhet." B. Furly & W. Penn. 4to. n. d. [Evidently 1684.]

"De Oude waarheid ontdeckt door Verscheide Vrienden der Waarheid." Rotterdam. 1684.

The landed interest of Benjamin Furly in Pennsylvania originally consisted of five thousand acres of land, obtained from William Penn, shortly before his departure for America, under Deeds of Lease and Release, dated at Rotterdam, 11th and 12th of August, 1682.

From letters and documents in the Lawrence collection of the Historical Society of Pennsylvania it appears that in later years there was a well-grounded cause for dissatisfaction on the part of Furly as to Penn's agents in Pennsylvania, notwithstanding Penn's personal efforts in his favor. For this reason Furly gave to Reynier Jants (Jansen), to whom he had previously sold some land,[474] a power of attorney to act for him in Pennsylvania upon his arrival.

Eine
NACHRICHT
wegen der Landschaft
PENNSILVANIA
in
AMERICA.
Welche
Jüngstens unter dem Grossen Siegel
in
ENGELLAND
an
William Penn., &c.
Sambt den Freyheiten und der Macht / so zu behöriger
guten Regierung derselben nötig /
ubergeben worden
und
Zum Unterricht derer / so etwan bereits bewogen / oder noch
möchten bewogen werden / hinb sich selbsten darhin
zu begeben / oder einige Bediente und Gesinde
an diesen Ort zu senden / hiermit
kund gethan wird.
Aus dem in London gedrucktem und aldar bey Benjamin Clark
Buchhändlern in George-Yard Lombard-street befindlichem
Englischen übergesetzet.
Nebenst beygefügtem ehemaligem im 1675. Jahr gedrucktem
Schreiben des oberwehnten Will. Penns.

In Amsterdam / gedruckt bey Christoff Cunraden.
Im Jahr 1681.

FAC-SIMILE OF GERMAN TITLE-PAGE.[473]

---

[472] An English version of this rare work was printed in the "Penna. Mag.," vol. vi, p. 321.

This document was subsequently revoked in favor of a similar one granted to the brothers Daniel and Justus Falkner, prior to their departure for America in 1700.

William Penn's personal interest in the protection of Benjamin Furly's claims is shown by his letter of instruction to James Logan prior to his departure from Pennsylvania in 1701, wherein he commands him to prepare a warrant for four thousand acres of land for Benjamin Furly. It appears in the record of a session of the Commissioners held at Philadelphia the 12th of 11th month, 1701.[475]

Subsequent action of the Commissioners appears as follows, the 16th of 12th month, 1701:

"Signed a Warrant of Resurvey and Survey of 5000 acres to Ben. Furly, Ordered 12th Ult."

Two days later, 18th of 12th month, 1701, it was resolved:

"Daniel and Justus Falkner's, attorneys to Benja. Furly, claim the Common proportion of Lib'ty Land in Right of his Purchase of 5000 acres, Mentioned pa. 59, But that being none of the First hundred purchasers it cannot be now granted, Yet they insisting on it as his certain Right, 'tis Ordered that they have Liberty to pitch upon Some Convenient Tract of a Sufficient Number of acres within the Liberties, which shall be reserved, and in Case the said Benjamin, in 18 Months, make good his Claim from the Proprietary, it may be granted; Ordered also in their Request a New Warrant for the said Benjamin's Lott already Survey'd to him."

---

[473] "Prefatory note to the German edition.—The translator to the indulgent reader.—How difficult, I will not say almost impossible, it is to render the actual meaning and certain expressions which appear in the old Laws and usages of a foreign Land, and its language into High German, so as to translate them intelligently, has been fully experienced in the present instance.

"Therefore I have here, not to be incommodious, conceived the plan to add in several instances the English words, with a short explanation, in the hope that the indulgent reader will not chide me, but rather accept them in the same spirit as by me intended."

[474] Deed July 17, 1685. Acknowledged before a notary in Holland. Minute-Book "H," "Pennsylvania Archives," Second Series, vol. xix, p. 598.

[475] "Pennsylvania Archives," Second Series, vol. xix, p. 219.

WILLIAM PENN.

PORTRAIT BY GODFREY VON KNELLER.

1st and 2d 12th, month, 1702,—

"Ordered a Patent to Benj. Furly on 1000 Acres in Bucks, and Patents on 2900 Acres More in Philadelphia County."

5th and 6th, 2d month, 1703,—

"Dan'l and Justus Falkner Producing D. Powell's return of a Warrant for 50 a's Lib. Land Surveyed to Benj. Furly. Ordered a Patent thereupon when examined in the Office together with an High Street Lott of 132 foot as it fell in the Draught."

8th month, 22d, 1705,—

"Dan'l Falkner, by Order of Benjamin Furly, Informs that by the said Benjamin's Letter he finds the Prop'ry had Promised him 2 lotts in the City Philad'a, for his 2 sons, Jno. and Arent Furly, and gave him an Expectation that he had wrote to the Sec'ry about it, y'rfore, by his Petition, Requests the said lotts, but the Sec'ry nor any Other Person haveing Rec'd any Orders about them 'tis referred till Such Orders arrive."

11th month, 20th, 1708,—

"There haveing been a tract of 1000 a's Surv'd To Benj'n Furly in the Welch tract, which has been granted since to D. Lloyd, and Is. Norris, in behalf of Thomas Lloyd's Estate, Jno. Henry Sproegle, to whom Dan'l Falkener, as attorney To said Benjamin, by Virtue of a power, dat. 23d Apr., 1700, recorded in Philad'a, Book D., 2, Vol. 5, pa. 17, &c., Granted his right to all the said Land, as also grant'd 1000 acres more in Bucks, and 50 a's more untaken up, of the whole 5000 a's, by Deed dat. 30, 6 mo., 1708, req'ts a warrant to take up the s'd 1000 acres. Granted."

A number of letters from Furly, addressed to Justus and Daniel Falkner, have also been found among the Lawrence papers before mentioned;[476] the latter was for a time the mercantile correspondent of Furly in America, and of the sons Benjohan and John after their father's death.

In some of these letters Furly expresses his unbounded confidence in the integrity of the two Falkner brothers, in others he characterizes a prominent person in Pennsylvania

[476] Thomas Lawrence was elected mayor of the city of Philadelphia by the Common Council, October 1, 1728.

as a forger and embezzler, and charges him with defrauding him out of his lands in Pennsylvania.

With the exception of a tract of land sold to Jacobus Van de Walle, the deed for which is recorded in Deed Book E, 2, pp. 80–82, it does not appear that Furly ever derived any profit from his lands within the Province, as for some reason the claim became a matter of litigation, which ended in an almost total loss to him, notwithstanding the strenuous efforts made by his attorneys, Daniel and Justus Falkner, to maintain his claim, as has been shown in previous pages of this work.[477]

He appears even to have had some trouble with his mercantile correspondents in Philadelphia, as is shown by the letter of attorney, recorded in Deed Book E, 2, p. 277, under date of 12th, 5th mo., 1694:

"Know all men by these presents, That I, Benjamin Furly of Rotterdam in the province of Holland Merch't, have made Constituted & Appointed and by these prs'ts doe make Constitute and app't Thos. Lloyd of Philadelphia in the Province of Pennsylvania, Gentleman, Samuel Carpenter & John Delavall of ye same place Mch't my true & Lawfull Attorneys, giving them or either of them jointly or severally full power & authority for & in my name to aske & demand of ye heirs Executors or Adm'rs of James Claypool late of ye same place Mch't all such debts, dues, sum or Sums of Money as were due unto me the S^d^ Benjamin Furly at the time of the decease of the S'd James Claypool for any goods or merchandize by him Sold for My aco't, an acco of Sales to demand the same, to examine & debate or approve & acquiece in all goods that may be yet unsold to receive & of the same to dispose for my use the moneys received for what was sold to receive acquittances in due forme of Law to give for all sums of money or goods which they shall receive. And further all other Acts Deeds & things to doe w'ch I myself if I were there personally ye . . . or could doe in the Premisis. Promising by these p'sents to approve, ratify & confirm all w^t^soever my said Attorney or Attorneys shall lawfully doe or cause to be done in the premisis.

"In witness whereof I have hereunto sett my hand & Seal this 16th 8br in Rotterdam Anno Domini 1693.

"Signed, Sealed & Delivered
in the p'sence of us
"PETER SOUMANS, BENJAMIN FFURLY."
"JOSEPH LACY.

But little has thus far been written or published of the private life and character of Benjamin Furly, who was so important a factor in organizing the German immigration to Pennsylvania, and in procuring for the immigrants the necessary transportation,[478] except that he was an eccentric person of peculiar religious views. His correspondence, however, with Locke, Sidney, Lord Shaftesbury and others, whose letters to him were privately printed some fifty years ago,[479] shows that Benjamin Furly was a man whose literary attainments were of no mean order, and that he was upon intimate terms with many of the leading scholars and states-

---

[477] Among the list of purchasers known as the "Old Rights" appear the following parcels of land in the name of Benjamin Furly:

"No. 775, Furley, Benjamin, return, 1900 acres.

"No. 776, Furlow Benjamin, return, 1000 acres.

"No. 779, Furly, Benjamin, warrant, 1000 acres, 19th 10 mo., 1684.

"No. 777, Furly, Benjamin, warrant, 6th 9th mo., 1685.

"No. 778, Furly, Benjamin, war't resur'y, on all his lands, 16th 12 mo. 1701.

"No. 780, Furly Benjamin, 2 returns, 967 and 501 acres, see 11 Philad'a W, 23 December, 1735 and 5th March, 1735-6.

"No. 781, Furley, Benjamin, warrant, 1000 acres, 19th 10th mo. 1684.

"No. 782, Furlow, Benjamin, return, 1000 acres, 3d 12th Mon., 1684.

"No. 783, Furlow, Benjamin, resurvey, 1000 acres.

"No. 784, Furlow, Benjamin, warrant, city lott, 3d 12 mo., 1684.

"No. 785, Furlow, Benjamin, return, 1048 acres, 25th 4 mo., 1703.

"No. 786, Furlow, Benjamin, return, 1900 acres, 18th 12 mo., 1702.

"No. 858, Furlow, Benjamin, return, 50 acres, L. Land, 22d 1 mo., 1703.

"No. 859, Furlow, Benjamin, return, Res., 1000 acres, 16th 12 mo., 1703.

"No. 860, Furlow, Benjamin, return, 1900 acres, 18th 12 mo., 1703.

"No. 861, Furlow, Benjamin, warrant, 50 acres L. L., 26th 11 mo., 1702.

"No. 862, Furlow, Benjamin, return, 50 acres L. L., 5th 2 mo., 1703."—"Pennsylvania Archives, Third Series, vol. ii, p. 704, *et seq.*

[478] A notable instance of his liberality is shown in the case of Kelpius and his band of German Pietists, who left Rotterdam in 1693. *Vide* Croese, "Historia Quakeriana," pp. 539 *et seq.;* also pp. 44-46, *supra.*

[479] "Original Letters of John Locke, Algernon Sidney and Lord Shaftesbury," London, 1847.

men of the period who labored incessantly to establish civil and religious liberty in Europe.

It further appears that Locke spent much of his time at Furly's house, and as he was particularly fond of children, one of his chief amusements while there was playing with the young folks.[480]

Although usually classed among the leading Quakers of that period on the Continent, and notwithstanding his purse and pen were at their disposal and used in their interests, it appears that his connection with them was not one of uninterrupted harmony. Croese,[481] states that "Benjamin Furly was an English Merchant, first at Amsterdam, then at Rotterdam, who, together with his merchandize, had addicted himself to the study of learning, and in his favor of these men [Quakers] wrote several little Tracts in Divers Languages. But yet refrained himself from exercising the office of a Teacher or Minister amongst them, alledging this reason for it, that he could safely enough be taught at all times, but could scarce be a Teacher himself without danger. Altho' as time and age teach Men many things, this same man afterwards found fault with and went off from many things in the doctrine and Manners of the Quakers." Just what these differences between Furly and the Quakers were, and when they took place, is unknown to the writer. Joseph Smith, in his catalogue, classes him among such as were disunited, and returned, but are believed to have again left the Society.

In later years he is credited with being the author of the following works:

"Ene Wonderlike voorseggiinge tot Rome," etc. (Dutch.) Folio, 1689.

---

480 "Original Letters," etc., Preface, p. 74.

481 English edition, Book III, p. 208.

"Copie Van een oude prophetie," etc. (Dutch.) Folio, 1689.

"Anwysinge tot de ware Kirke Gods, met Annotatien door." B. Furly (1690).

"A Prophecy of St. Thomas the Martyr" (from MSS. of Algernon Sidney). 1709.

"Discernement des Ténèbres d'avec la Lumière." (French.) 8vo, 1710.

"Éclair de Lumière decendent," etc. (French.) 8vo, 1711.

"The Approaching Judgments of God upon the Roman Empire," etc. Translated out of high Dutch by B. Furly. 8vo, 1711.

"Spiegel der Leevaren, om zig te kennen, of zy ware Herders der Zielen zyn of niet, uyt het Frans vertaalt door." B. Furly 1713. 8vo.

"The divine Remedy for all Evils, both Soule and body." Written in French by Moses Caron and Englished by B. Furly. 4to.[482]

It can matter but little whether or not Benjamin Furly lived continuously and died within the fold of the Society of Friends,[483] but it cannot be denied that to him more than any other person is due the credit of materializing the dream of Penn, so far as the German element is concerned, for he not only encouraged them with advice and counsel, but with more substantial means in the shape of concessions of land, transportation and loans of money.

The only trustworthy personal description of Benjamin Furly and his peculiarities that has come down to us is the interesting account given in the Memoirs of Zacharias von

---

[482] "Bibliotheca Furliana," p. 324, No. 33.

[483] From the fact of his burial within the walls of the chief orthodox church at Rotterdam, it would appear that he had renounced Quakerism prior to his death.

Uffenbach,[484] who visited Rotterdam in the year 1710; he had been a classmate, at Halle, of Justus Falkner, one of the early German Pietists in Pennsylvania, and later was an attorney for Furly.[485] He writes:—

"On the morning of November 21, we went *Op-Te Haaring Vliet*, to visit Benjamin Furly, an English Merchant, who was the chief of the Quakers in Holland, and posesses a curious stock of Books, mainly *suspectæ fidei.* He lives in a very fine house, and is a man of about seventy years of age, and of peculiar actions. [Sonderbarem wesen.]

"We were ushered into his *comptoir* as it was called, but this appeared more like a library or Museum than a mercantile counting house, as the walls were shelved and covered with books, to the number of at least four thousand. They were mostly on theological subjects, of the *suspectæ fidei* order, and appear to be well suited to Mr. Benjamin Furly's taste, who is a paradoxial and peculiar man, who soon gave us to understand that he adhered to no special religion.

"Unfortunately we were not permitted to examine any of his books except the original manuscript of the 'Libri Inquisitionis Tolonsanæ,'[486] edited by Limborch,[487] and this work only after earnest and repeated solicitation.

---

[484] Zacharias Conrad von Uffenbach, born at Frankfort, February 22, 1683. From his youth he was known as a lover and collector of books. He first attended the University at Strasburg, later at Halle, where he graduated, after which he made a tour through Northern Europe, Holland, and England in search of rare imprints and manuscripts. He thus accumulated one of the most valuable private libaries in Germany, which contained many works on early American history.

His Memoirs were published at Ulm, in 1753, and contain many notices of books and persons not to be found elsewhere. A partial printed catalogue of this library may be seen at the Philadelphia Library: "Bibliotheca Uffenbachiana," etc.

[485] *Vide supra.*

"It proved to be a *Codex membranaceus in folio constans foliis* 203, and was neatly and plainly written.

"This was indeed a great curiosity, especially as it was found in the possession of a non-Catholic. This was further instanced by the actions of the former Bishop of Utrecht, who upon that account doubted its authenticity, and sent a clerical to compare Limborch's edition with this original. Mr. Furly would not permit this examination until the above clerical assured him that if he found the two works to agree, he would so certify to the fact officially over his hand and seal, which was done, and it is now pasted on the cover of the volume.

"Mr. Furly complained that Limborch failed to mention that he had obtained the original Codex from him.

---

[486] The Latin title of this work is given in the catalogue of the "Bibliotheca Furliana." Translated it reads as follows: "Book of Maxims; beautifully written on parchment, and bound between two wooden leaves; the autograph itself is written; and everywhere it is subscribed in the hand of the clerks of the Inquisition; beginning only with the year of Christ, 1607, [and going] as far as 1622; and by undoubted indications it is agreed to be the original manuscript, derived from the archives of the Inquisition of Toulouse. The Maxims themselves, as far as can be gathered from the resemblance of the handwriting, are written in the hand of Peter of Clav . . . down to the eighth discourse, which begins fol. 97. The remainder of the book, down to the end, is in the hand of William Julian; James Marquette has written beneath the Maxims almost throughout; [it is] the rarest book of all rarest ones, and of the highest possible price."

The original manuscript was bought in by John Furly at the sale of his father's library, and afterward sold to Archbishop Secker, who presented it to the British Museum, where it now remains. It was translated into English and published by Samuel Chandler, London, 1731. A copy of this translation can be seen at the Ridgway branch of the Philadelphia Library.

[487] Philippus Limborch was a learned divine, born at Amsterdam, 1633. He embraced the tenets of the "Remonstrants," and first appeared as a public preacher at Haarlem in 1655. He was an able annotator and an esteemed writer, as is shown by the tributes paid him by Locke and Tillotson. He died in 1711.

"This," continues Uffenbach, "seemed the more strange to me as it would have added to the value of Limborch's edition if he had made mention where the original of this curious work could be seen, as the Catholics, in time, would throw doubt upon the facts, as it was a thorn in their eyes and a bitter conviction of their spiritual tyranny. As we began to touch upon this subject, Furly complained that the same spiritual tyranny was also still in vogue among the Protestant denominations.

"When I reminded him that in Holland religious liberty prevailed, he denied emphatically that this assumption was true, and he became quite excited over the procedure of the local magistrates against the so-called English New-prophets.

"He admitted that he not only harbored their tenets and had printed their writings with a preface of his own, but had defended them as well before the Magistrates, and endeavored to shield and protect them, yet, notwithstanding all his efforts, these innocent people had been expelled from the country.

"He related all that had happened to these people, here as well as at the Hague. This he did not only in a general way, but he read to us, word for word, a long relation of the facts, that he had just written to Herr Gronovium. This lasted for over two hours.

"I thought that I should die from impatience, and although I repeatedly referred to the subject of his books, and begged him to show us some of the rarest and most curious of the collection, the man was so excited that he failed to notice my request.

"Thus he continued to complain, over and over again, how badly these people were treated, especially Herr Facio, whom he characterized not only as a devout man, endowed with many gifts of the Spirit, but also as a learned man and an excellent mathematician.

A SCENE IN OLD ROTTERDAM.

NEGATIVE BY J. F. SACHSE,
AUGUST, 1895.

"He declared that they were pious and innocent persons; against whom no accusations could be truly brought, except that their prophecy of a personal return of Christ at a specified time had not been fulfilled.

"He stated that the clericals had used the following quotations of Scripture, viz.: Deuteronomy xviii, v, 21, 22, against them, and had attempted to convict them as false prophets and deceivers.

"We were astounded that this man, a merchant, should be so well versed in Latin, Hebrew, &c., the more so as he formerly had no means at his disposal, and had only acquired them here of late. We complained that on account of his extended discourse we had failed to obtain an insight to his literary treasures, but even this hint failed and proved of no avail.

"As we were leaving, the honest patriarch led us into a kind of a Cabinet, that gave us an unsurpassed view of the river Mass. One of the most conspicuous objects on the walls of this room was a large framed map of Pennsylvania."

At the subsequent sale of Furly's effects this map was described as follows:

"Enn seer nette Landkaard van Pensylvania met alle den Rivieren, Bayed &c. Konstig met die Pen op Parkement getrokken, en fraai ofgesezt, in een Swarte Lyst."

According to the memorandum by Benjohan Furly it was bought at the sale for four florins by Fritsch & Bohm the Dutch printers.

"In his personal appearance," continues Uffenbach, "Benjamin Furly is, as we had pictured him to be, an old, tall, lean, serious man who, although it was already cold and chilly, went about in a thin, threadbare gray coat; around his head he wore a band of black velvet, as he stated for the purpose of keeping his hairs from coming in his face when writing."

After the death of Benjamin Furly, his great library was catalogued and sold at auction October 22, 1714. The following is the title of the catalogue:

"Bibliotheca Furliana sive Catalogus Librorum, Honoratiss. & Doctriss. Viri Benjamin Furly, inter quos excellunt Bibliorum Editiones Mystici, Libri proprii cujuscumque Sectæ Christianæ, & Manuscriptii Membranei. Auctio fiet die 22 Octobris 1714, in Ædibus Defuncti in Platea Vulgo dicta. Haringvliet. Roterodami, Apud Fritsch et Bohm. 8vo, 1714."[488]

Benjamin Furly's two elder sons succeeded their father after his death as merchants and shippers at Rotterdam, and also for a time pressed claims for lands in Pennsylvania.[489] Benjohan, the eldest son, married Martha Wright,[490] a young woman from London, who died in 1713. She was buried September 18th; a few weeks later, October 9th, her babe was laid by her side. Twenty-five years afterwards, August 7, 1738, Benjohan Furly was buried in the family vault in the St. Laurentian Kerk, beside his wife, child and parents. Of John Furly nothing is known, except that he became a leading merchant of Rotterdam and London, and left a family.

Arent Furly, the youngest son, who was a great favorite of Locke and Lord Shaftesbury, entered the military service of England, and went with Charles, Earl of Peterborough, to the West Indies in 1702–03, and in 1705, as his secretary, to Spain, where his patron was General and Commander-in-Chief of Her Majesty's forces. Several of the orders dated

---

[488] Benjohan Furly's priced and named copy of this catalogue is now in the British Museum. It is catalogued No. 11901, A11.

[489] "Pennsylvania Archives," Second Series, vol. xix.

[490] From the fact that this marriage was also consummated at the *Stadthuis* it would appear that Benjohan was also either a Quaker or Separatist.

in the camp before Barcelona in 1705 are countersigned by Arent Furly. According to a letter from Lord Shaftesbury to Benjamin Furly, he died during this expedition, early in the year 1712.[491] He was unmarried.

Benjamin Furly's daughter Dorothy, born July, 1710, married Thomas Forster, of Walthamstow, England, and it was his grandson, Thomas Ignatius Maria Forster, who published the volume of letters of Locke, Sidney and Shaftesbury so frequently quoted in this sketch.

There are but few of the hundreds of American tourists that annually visit the Groote Kerk in Rotterdam, and wander through its broad aisles, who know that in the centre aisle in the nave rest the remains of Benjamin Furly and his kin, the man who was so instrumental in bringing about the first German immigration to America and in securing for the immigrants equal rights and privileges.

[491] "Original Letters," etc., p. 205

MAGISTER JOHANN JACOB ZIMMERMANN.

ARMS OF WÜRTEMBERG, A.D. 1689.

MAGISTER JOHANN Jacob Zimmermann, whose name figures so frequently upon the preceding pages, and who was one of the chief instigators of the Theosophical experiment on the Wissahickon, was a native of the Duchy of Würtemberg, born in the year 1644, in the little hamlet of Vaihingen on the Entz. From early childhood he evinced a remarkable talent for learning, and at the age of seventeen he was taken into the Ducal service.[492] He was subsequently sent to the university at Tübingen, where he graduated in 1664 with the title of *Magister der Philosophie.* He was at once appointed instructor of mental arithmetic (*Wiederholungslehrer*).

Subsequently he was admitted into the ministry, became a Lutheran clergyman and in 1671 was appointed Diaconus of the church at Bietigheim, a town adjacent to his birth-

[492] Fischlein, *Memoria Theologorum Wirtenbergensium. Ulmae, 1710. Supplementa ad Mem. Theol. Wirt. pp. 230.*

place. Here he served until 1684, when he was deposed for his outspoken views upon the coming millennium.

Zimmermann, after leaving Würtemberg, was called to the chair of mathematics at Heidelberg University, which he filled for the next five years. Upon becoming involved still deeper in his mystical speculations, he, in 1689, lost his professorship and went to Hamburg, where he became "corrector" or proof-reader for Brandt, the Hamburg publisher, who then printed many of the Mystical and Theosophical works of that period which were not strictly orthodox, and known as "*Suspecta Fidei*." It was here that Zimmermann came into personal contact with such men as Horbius, Spener, Furly and others of like convictions, and where the plan was perfected for putting to a practical test, in the Western World, some of the theoretical speculations of the Theosophists.

Heretofore but little has been known of the history of this noted philosopher, except that he was the leader of the band of Pietists that started for America, and that he died just prior to their embarkation at Rotterdam.

But he deserves a prominent place in the religious history of Pennsylvania, for it was mainly upon his astrological deductions and calculations respecting the near approach of the millennium that the organization of the emigrants was consummated.

Now, after the lapse of two centuries, it has become possible to present a sketch of this eminent philosopher and scientist; a result which has been brought about only by a long and persistent search after material extending over both continents, a search pursued with great difficulty and much expenditure.

The first direct clue to Zimmermann was found in a fragmentary title of one of his books printed at Hamburg shortly before his death. From this the long search was kept up through Germany until Bietigheim was reached, where on account of missing records little or no information was to be had.

When almost ready to give up further enquiry an active co-worker was found in Stuttgart,[493] who introduced the writer to Professor D. Th. Schott, the Royal *Bibliothekar* in that capital. This librarian instituted a search for traces of Zimmermann, and found, among the musty archives of the Royal Free Library, four scientific works of his, the titles of which were photographed and placed at the disposal of the writer.

A further search by Professor Schott among long-forgotten legal proceedings stored within the Royal Archives at Stuttgart, brought to light once more the charges under which the Magister was tried and convicted.

From these data it appears that Magister Zimmermann, in addition to being an erudite theologian, was one of the best astronomers and mathematicians of the day, and that he received acknowledgment as such from the Royal Society of England. He was also a prolific writer upon theosophical as well as astronomical and mathematical subjects, both under his own name and the pseudonyms of *Ambrossii Sehmanni* and *Johannis Matthaeus.* He was also something of a poet and hymnologist.

From the old records in the archives at Stuttgart it appears that while Zimmermann was officiating at Bietigheim he was stricken with a dangerous fever. His physician was the celebrated Ludwig Brunnquell, who was also a great admirer of Jacob Boehme. The acquaintance thus commenced between patient and doctor ripened into friend-

---

[493] Otto Schaettle, Esq.

ship, and ended in the physician convincing his charge of the correctness of Boehme's speculations.

Zimmermann, who during this time actively pursued his study of the heavens from his observatory, which tradition states was upon the old church tower at Bietigheim, now combined Boehme's speculations with his astronomy, and in 1684 issued the unique work wherein he prophesies amelioration of the times prior to the year 1694. These deductions were based upon the appearance of the comet of 1680. The title of this book, which was to have so peculiar an effect upon social and religious affairs in Pennsylvania was:

"*Mundus Copernizans; linguâ vernaculâ. Muthmassige Zeit-Bestimmung bevorstehende Gerichten Gottes uber das Europaeische Babel und hierauf erfolgenden Anfang dess Reichs CHRISTI auf Erden. Unter den nahmen AMROSII Sehmann de Caminicz, Anno 1684. 8vo.*"

In this work he desires written information from the Consistory upon the four following general questions:

"(1) The downfall of Babylon in Europe.

"(2) The millennium of the pious, and universal conversion of Jews, Turks and Gentiles.

"(3) True prophets existing even now.

"(4) Certain doubts concerning the Augsburg Confession and Apology."

The answer of the Consistorium not being to his liking, he publicly denounced the Established Church as a Babel. This gave rise to considerable disturbance, which was increased still more by another book from Zimmerman, viz.,

"*Bey nahe gantz aufgedechter Anti-Christ oder unvorgreiffi Redencken über die frage: Ob die Evangelische Kirche mit recht Babel und Anti-Christisch zu schelten von welche auszugehen seye? Nach Grund der Heil. Schrifft aufgesetzt, mit Beantwortung anderer dieser Materia verwandten Nebenfragen. Anno 1685, 4to.*"

The Consistorium at once ordered Zimmermann's books to be refuted, which was done by Schellenbaur and Häberlein. Zimmermann, nothing daunted, followed with another work:

"*Orthodoxia Theosophiae Bohmianae contra Holsbusium Defensa, oder Christliche Untersuchungen der Holtzhausischen Anmerckungen über und wieder J. Böhmens Aurorant.*" *Franckfurt und Leipzig, Anno 1691.*

This work was issued under the name of Johannes Matthäi. In the appendix he sarcastically scores Erasmus Franciscus for his "Counter-Ray to the Aurora" and "Arrows of Calumny of Ishmael and Simeus Shivered."

One of the most curious charges brought against Zimmermann was that he sought to elevate Jacob Böehme over the Apostles. This was founded upon the fact that he had written under Boehme's portrait the following epigram:

"Waan Petrus Juden fischt,
Der Weber wirbt die Heyden.
Beginnt der Schuster jetzt
Sie beiderseits zu weiden.
Weil Er die Heil'ge Schrifft
Mit der Natur verfasst,
Doch ist Er eine last
Die Amasias hassti"

[If Peter fishes Jews, the weaver enlists Gentiles. Now the cobbler commences to feed them both, because he combines Holy Writ with nature, and becomes a power which Ananias detests.]

After Zimmermann had become so thoroughly imbued with the teachings of Jacob Boehme, he at various times gave utterance, in the pulpit, to expressions defamatory of the Established Church of which he was a Presbyter. As he professed to be able, by aid of his astronomical observa-

The old church at Bietigheim, Würtemberg, from the tower of which Magister Zimmermann made his astronomical observations, and which led to the establishment of the "Woman in the Wilderness" on the Wissahickon.

tions, to foretell the exact time of the millenium, he became the leader of that class of mystic philosophers and their followers who then believed the great catastrophe to be impending.

When this period passed without confirming his calculations, he still continued in his denunciations of the ecclesiastical establishment. After repeated admonitions he was summoned to appear before the Ducal Consistorium; was tried, convicted of heresy, and ordered to leave the Duchy within a certain time.

This the deposed clergyman did with a bad grace, and it appears that he indulged in prophesying all sorts of dire disasters for his native country and its rulers as a chastisement for the fancied injustice done him.

He also issued a brochure in which he charged that he was persecuted solely on account of a notice of him written by Breckling and published by Gottfried Arnold. The Duchy being invaded and devastated by the French about this time, Zimmermann boldly claimed that this terrible misfortune was nothing more nor less that the fulfillment of his predictions of a Divine retribution, and that still greater calamities were in store for the land of his birth unless he should be reinstated.

The publication of these pamphlets and the fact of his adherents in Würtemberg giving them credence, induced the authorities to set forth a counter-statement or apology, printed partly in Latin and partly in German, with the facts of the case from the government standpoint. This curious document reads as follows:

"CAROLUS" *Wirtenbergische, Unschuld Act: Ulm, 1708, 4to.*" *Page 50, article v.*

"Proceedings of the Ducal Government of Würtemberg *versus* Magister Johann Jacob Zimmermann:

"(Section 1).—Even as it was the duty of the government of Würtemberg to censure and proceed against M. Ludwig Brunnquell, so must the same proceedings be enacted against M. Joh. Jac. Zimmermann if the facts are as mentioned in Breckling's catalogue, which were embodied by Arnold in the preface to his notable work, viz.:

"'M. Joh. Jac. Zimmermann, a profoundly learned astrologer, magician, cabbalist and preacher, expelled from the Würtemberg Domain (shortly before its devastation by the French) hath written under the name of Ambrose Sehmann of Caminicz,[494] many profound and learned writings of the truths of philosophy, astrology and of comets, as well as of chronology and the computation of time; and because he, in these deductions, agreed with Jacob Boehme, he was discharged from his position at Bietigheim. He afterwards boldly defended his position against Hincklemann and Holtzhausen.'

"(Section 2).—That this Magister Zimmermann has far excelled many others in the astrological sciences is willingly conceded. But of what service he was to the church is a vital question, as he, by virtue of his sacred office, introduced his theories of astrology, magic and cabbalism into his teachings.

"Then again the charge boldly made and published in large type, that his dismissal, in a measure, was one of the great national sins which called forth such terrible retribution as the subsequent devastation by the French of several cities and large tracts of the country, is both blasphemous and malicious.

"The fallacy of his prognostications, too, as to the time of divine judgment, published under an assumed name, has been publicly proven and established by the late Dr. Haber-

---

[494] Evidently old Comines in Belgium.

lin in his published work. The extraordinary zeal with which Zimmermann endeavored to elevate Jacob Boehme's writings and impart to them divine inspiration is well known. With what amount of justice he has sought to maintain his position against Hincklemann and Holtzhausen, all who are competent may judge for themselves.

"(Section 3).—That his removal from the diaconate at Bietigheim was due to the Breckling report as quoted by Arnold, and wherein he is said to have sanctioned the computation of time in accordance with the writings of Boehme; or that any one should charge the forcible removal of Zimmermann from office, and his banishment, merely to the above allegation, which is in itself meager, is entirely erroneous. The true facts of the case are in short as follows:

"M. Zimmermann was a great admirer of Ludwig Brunnquell, and was by the latter seduced into all manner of superstitution, as is clearly shown from the passage in Arnold which states that 'Zimmermann was awakened by Brunnquell.'

"Therefore, the Lutheran Church must have been an abomination to the man: he regarded her as anti-Christian, and used to call her nothing but Babel. He opposed our symbolical books, with which he found great fault, although when entering upon his ministry, he subscribed to them as perfectly consonant with the Word of God.

"He became greatly interested in the writings of Jacob Boehme, sought curious divine mysteries therein, praised them highly, both orally and in writing, strove to popularize them with the people, and circulated the books among them. He did not confine to himself these teachings wherein he deviated from our doctrine, but promulgated them wherever opportunity offered, and courted the favor of such as gave him an audience. But herein he, for the most part, acted covertly, for he feared the light.

"Therefore he used a pseudonym for his writings; first that of Ambrose Sehmann, and afterwards that of Johannes Mattheus[495] (without knowing, perhaps, that the Haarlem Anabaptist prophet, who confused the minds of the people about A.D. 1534, bore the same name). He could not conceal his mystic speculations, and some of his heresy soon appeared in his sermons. Hence he was closely watched, and several times amicably admonished, and when it was ascertained that he was the author of the alleged computation of time, by promulgating which he violated in various ways the fundamental laws of this Duchy, he was summoned in regular manner, and sufficient time granted him to prepare a defence.

"Whereupon he defended himself, and even ventured to vindicate his erroneous views, rejecting what was adduced against him from the Word of God, and the doctrine based thereon; and persisted in scattering his pernicious seed, nor did he desist therefrom in despite of all commands, and the pains that were taken to set him aright. All was in vain. Therefore, finally, a prominent minister of State, who had heretofore been his special patron, now no longer interested himself in his behalf, but suffered him to be degraded from his position.

"Though he seemed quite happy after his dismissal, he nevertheless acted after the manner of common people, complaining greatly of the dire persecution he was forced to endure. He maligned the Ducal Consistory, and talked much concerning divine judgments which would overtake the country upon his account. As an illustration he would

---

[495] A copy of E. Francisci's answer to Johannes Mattheus is in British Museum, No. 3907, A5.

quote the misfortunes and death of his former Superior. His allegations, however, consisted partly in a demonstrable falsehood, and partly in the fallacy of a non-cause as a cause (*fallaciâ non causae ut causae*). Yet he was so audacious as to maliciously circumvent people in high life, both in and out of the country, partly by himself, partly through some adherents.

"(Section 4).—It would therefore have been a fallacy not to get rid of such a man: for with what disposition he served our church may easily be inferred. He could neither serve a congregation of our confession with a good conscience, nor could such a communion retain him as their teacher, for he held our doctrine and confession despicable and our church as anti-Christ.

"Should a man who desires to lead the people from the Lutheran doctrine still desire to be called a Lutheran presbyter?

"Should he want to be considered an 'Anti-Christian servant of Babel?' Moreover, should a Christian congregation continue a teacher in office among them who is unwilling to adhere to their confession, which is founded upon the Word of God?

"Shall she be united with one who, as a shepherd, declareth the Church to be a congregation of Babel?

"Let it only be considered what has been written (I will not say by our theologians), but in order that Arnold may have less chance to take exception to what has been written by Herr von Puffendorff, the Christian statesman, and endorsed by Seckendorff.

"It will possibly be better in such cases to judge in consideration of the above circumstances, briefly touched upon, whether M. Zimmermann of Würtemberg was treated justly or unjustly by being discharged from his sacred office.

"The following is a partial list of Zimmermann's writings:

"*Theoriae Secondorum Mobilium Perfectae,*" etc. Tübingae, 1664. 4to.

"*Amphitheatrum Orbis Stellarum.*" Tübingen, 1669. 4to.

"*Differentia Latioudinum,*" etc. Tübingen, 1669. 4to.

"*Calendaria, in annos complures.*" Stuttgart, 1675. 4to.

"*Provromus biceps convo-ellipticae,*" etc. Stuttgart, 1679. 4to.[496]

"*Substructio Tabularum Theoricarum,*" etc. Stuttgart, 1679. 4to.[497]

"*Cometoscopia,*" etc. Tübingen, 1681. 4to.

"*Cometolgia,*" etc. Tübingen, 1682. 4to.

"*Portendens gravia X agiulane future Cometes,*" etc. Stuttgart, 1682. 8vo.[498]

"*Mundus Copernizans,*" etc. Ambrosii Sehman, 1684. 8vo.

"*Beynahe gantz aufgedeckter Anti-Christ,*" etc. 1685. 4to.

"*Jovis per umbrosa,*" etc. Norimbergia, 1686. 4to.

"*Philalethae Exercitatio,*" etc. Hamburg, 1689. 4to.

"*Scriptura Sacra Copernizans*" etc. Francof., 1690; Hamburg, 1704. 4to.

"*Orthodoxia Theosophiae Böhmianae,*" etc. Frankfurt and Leipzig, 1691.

"*Logistica Astronomica Logarithmica,*" etc. Hamburg, 1691. 8vo.

"*Theoria sacra Telluris—Biblische Betrachtung des Erdreichs—Von T. Burnett in Latein herausgyeben in Hoch-Deutsche übersitzt*" (2 ed), 1703.[499]

---

[496] Copy in British Museum, No. 532, f. 31 (2)

[497] Copy in British Museum, No. 532, f. 31, (1)

[498] Copy in British Museum, 532, E 43.

[499] Copy in British Museum, 4374, c.

"*Coniglobium nocturnale Stelligerum*," etc. Tub., 1704; Hamb., 1704; German, Tub., 1706 and 1729. 8vo.[500]

According to the certified copy of the old church record of Beitigheim, the Zimmermann pair had six children:

(1) A daughter (stillborn) December 14, 1671.

(2) A son, Johann Jakob, born January 10, 1673. Died, February 25, 1697.

(3) Maria Margaretha, baptized October 10, 1675.

(4) Phillip Christian, baptized February 18, 1678.

(5) Matthäus, baptized June 25, 1680.

(6) Jakob Christoph, baptized May 14, 1683.

The four living children accompanied the mother to Pennsylvania, where shortly after their arrival the daughter Maria Margaret married Ludwig Christian Biedermann, a candidate of theology, one of the original members of the Chapter of Perfection, who was the first of the Theosophical party to break his vows of celibacy. The three sons all settled in the vicinity of Germantown and survived their mother, as is shown from the will of the widow Zimmermann, probated July 29, 1723.

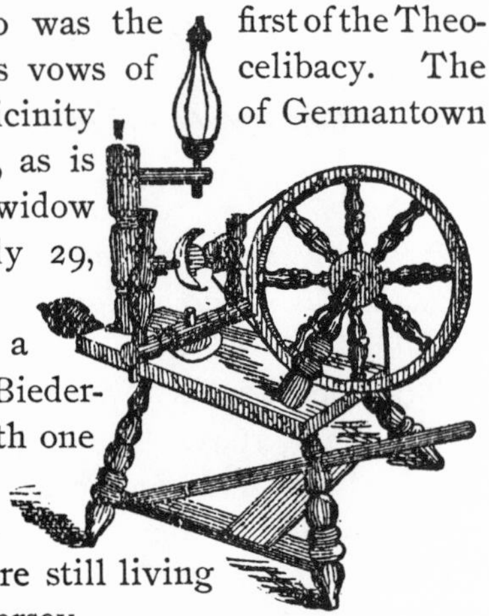

Ludwig Biedermann left a daughter, Hannah Ludwig Biedermann, who intermarried with one John George Knorr and settled in Bristol Township. Decendants of this couple are still living in Pennsylvania and New Jersey.

---

[500] Copy in British Museum, No. 531, f. 25.

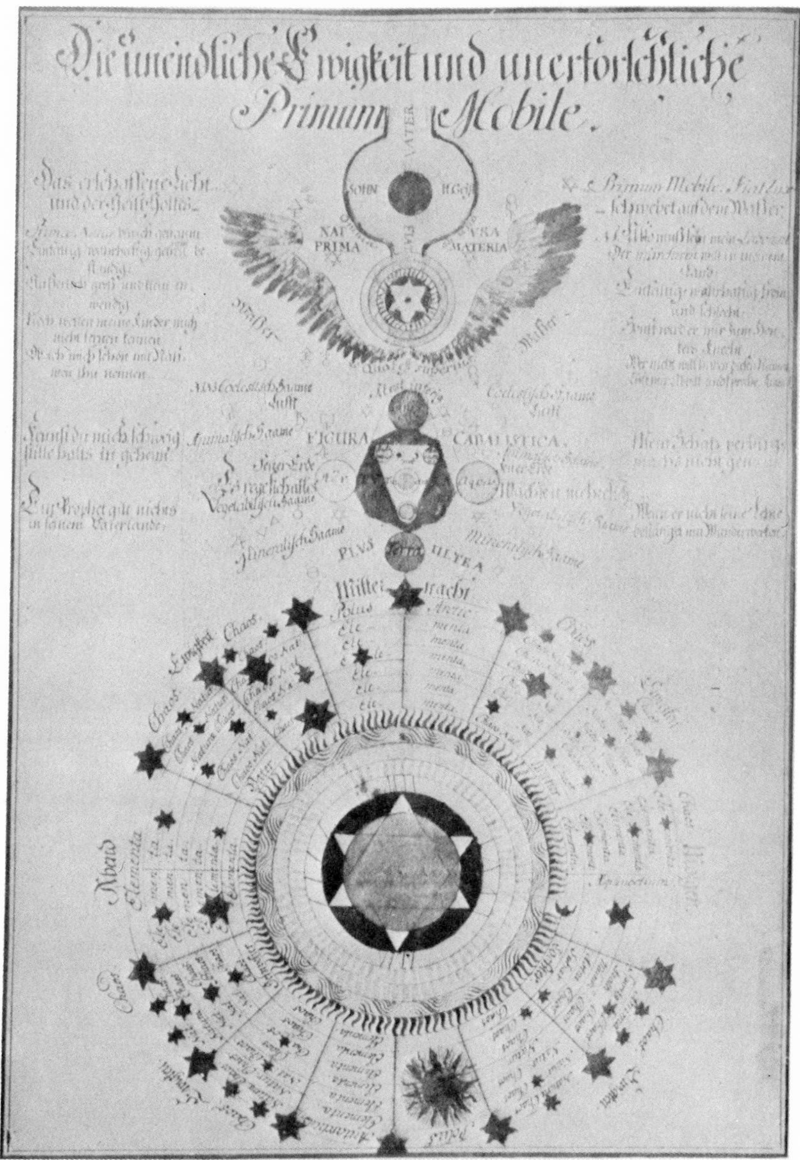

A PAGE OF ROSICRUCIAN THEOSOPHY.

FAC-SIMILE (REDUCED) OF ORIGINAL MANUSCRIPT,
IN POSSESSION OF THE WRITER.

DOMINIE ANDREAS RUDMANN.

SIGNATURE AND SEAL OF AXEL OXENSTIERN.

DOMINIE ANDREAS RUDMANN, who will always rank as one of the most active and devout clergymen in the early church history of Pennsylvania and the adjoining provinces where he preached to the Swedes, Dutch, English, German and Welsh, was a native of Gevalia, in the province of Gestrickland, one of the eastern divisions of Sweden. He was born in the year 1668, and after receiving a liberal education was sent to the University of Upsal, where he attracted the attention of Prof. Jesper Svedberg,[501] and became a scholar in the latter's Homiletic Seminary.

When finally King Charles XI consented to give heed to the repeated petitions of the Swedish Lutherans on the Delaware, the subject was laid before the Consistorium at Upsal by Archbishop Olof Swebilius, February 18, 1696. In the discussions that followed, Andreas Rudmann's name was the first that was presented, his cause being championed by no less a personage than his former tutor, Dr. Svedberg.

After his selection the young clergyman was summoned

[501] Page 93, *ibid.*

before that august body, and as the matter was an entire surprise to him, he asked for time to consider the proposition. After a lapse of several days he again appeared before the Consistorium, and stated his willingness to accept the call to the western wilderness; with the proviso that the royal promise be extended to him, "that provided God spared his life he should be recalled in a few years and advanced to some charge of honor and profit in his native land."

This was granted him without hesitation by the King. Strange as it may seem, Pastor Rudmann, devout and sincere as he was, by making this apparently reasonable request, unwittingly established a precedent which was taken advantage of, and followed by every succeeding Swedish missionary who came to America. The effect of this was eventually to make the American mission a mere stepping-block for clergymen who were ambitious for subsequent home preferment, and it was just this unfortunate circumstance which in the course of time alienated the Swedish Lutheran Church in America from the faith, and landed both church and congregations within the Protestant Episcopal fold.

However, it is not intended that the above statement of facts should in any manner be taken as a reproach to Rudmann, for it is not the intention of the writer to reflect in the least upon that devout missionary. The circumstance is merely mentioned as a historical fact not generally known —one that has thus far escaped most of the writers of early church history, whose effect upon the religious situation in Pennsylvania during the provincial period was of more than ordinary importance, and which has extended even down to the present day.

After Pastor Rudmann had accepted the call, he was

asked to select two clergymen as his assistants. Upon his refusal to do this, Dr. Svedberg proposed Eric Tobias Biörck of Westmanland, who was then living with him as tutor to his children, while the King named Jonas Auren from Wermeland.

The King thereupon presented Rudmann with 500, and the other two with 400 guilders, wherewith to discharge their debts and prepare for the voyage. Moreover, the King issued an order to send with them, securely packed for the use of the congregations in America, the following books:

"30 folio Bibles, 10 printed by Vankis and 20 by Keiser.

"6 books of Homilies (*Postillen*); 2 Cabinets of Treasure; 2 of Moeller's; 2 of Luther's.

"150 Manuals.

"100 religious treatises of different kinds, among which were 12 by Kellingius, and a number of '*Paradies Gärtlein.*'

"100 Swedish hymn books.

"Ecclesiastical Acts (*Agenden*).

"2 Church Regulations.

"100 Catechisms (*Swebilius*).

"300 Smaller Catechisms.

"400 A. B. C. books, bound in strong wooden covers.

"500 copies of Campanius' Indian Catechism."

The last, a special contribution from the King, were by his orders handsomely bound, and intended for the Indian missions of the Lutheran Church in America.

Before the clergymen started, the King granted them a personal audience, and appropriated three thousand guilders toward their expenses and passage. In dismissing them, he gave them his hand and said:

"Go now in the name of the Lord to the place whither I send you. God be with you, and prosper your undertaking. If any adversity or opposition befall you, return home, and I will remember you."

From Sweden the trio went to England, where they remained until the following February (1697), when they embarked on the ship "Jeffreys," Captain James Cooper. It was not until June 24, that they dropped anchor at the Bohemia Landing on the Chesapeake.

More or less mention has already been made in the course of this work of the labors of Dominie Rudmann, setting forth some of his labors and trials down to the time of his return to the Delaware from New York in 1703.[502]

During his absence in the adjoining province the religious situation had changed somewhat in Pennsylvania. Rudmann prior to his departure for New York, had installed Sandel as *Pastor loci* at Wicacoa. Biörck was still at Christiana, while Auren was serving the churches in New Jersey.

The newly organized Society for the Propagation of the Gospel in Foreign parts at London, had in the meantime supplied clergymen for most of the embryo parishes in Pennsylvania and the adjoining provinces; a condition which virtually left Rudmann without any charge.

He, however, by direction of George Keith, began at once to minister to the outlying English and Welsh congregations in connection with the indomitable Evan Evans, as well as supplying his place at Christ Church when the latter was absent.[503]

---

502 Page 347, *et seq.*

503 "October 5, 1704, Mr. Andrew Rudmann, late Swedish Minister, by the direction of Mr. George Keith serves there (Oxford) now in hopes of encouragement from the Honorable Society . . . At Germantown in the same County the people are numerous, they want both Church and Minister."—EVAN EVANS.—M. S. records of the Church General, Archives of S. P. G., London.

It was mainly on account of these services among the Welsh at Radnor and Oxford that the Swedish Lutheran clergyman became particularly obnoxious to the Quakers, and various were the plans made by the dominant party to rid the Province of such an active missionary, who had been so signally successful in leading the Welsh residents from Quakerism back to the church of their fathers, and who was now recognized as in the employ of the Propagation Society of London.

The first open breech occurred when the Quaker authorities again attempted to prevent both pastor and laymen from crossing the Schuylkill on Sundays to attend public worship. Orders were given to prevent the clergymen from being ferried over the river. This led to much dissension between the parties, and ended by the Churchmen, who knew from their previous experience[504] the uselessness of appealing to the Council, obtaining a boat of their own to ferry themselves and parishioners across the river as occasion demanded.

This action at once caused a protest from the Quakers, and culminated in an "Information" being lodged against Pastors Rudmann and Sandel. This was presented to the Provincial Council, May 4, 1704,[505] by Benjamin Chambers[506] proprietor of the ferry:

---

504 Page 264, *supra*.

505 "Minutes of the Provincial Council, Colonial Records," vol. ii, page 137.

506 Benjamin Chambers was one of the passengers with Penn on the "Welcome" and a man of powerful physique. As early as 1683 he was appointed to keep order among the public houses in the growing city; after serving a term as High Sheriff, was licensed to operate a ferry below that of Philip England before mentioned. Tradition tells us that this privilege was granted him with special reference to the trouble with the Swedes. The King's road to Darby, etc., was afterwards laid out so as to pass over this ferry, and it is still known by the name of Chambers' successor: "Gray's Ferry."

"Benja. Chambers presented an Information to ye Board, upon an apprehension of another ferry boat, being intended to be sett up on his ferry Landing place, by two swedes ministers, setting forth y^t^ he had been at very great charge & Trouble in erecting ye sd ferry for ye Publick Good, that by his Diligence & Expenses he had cut through ye Rocks, made long Causeys through ye mudd, & for ye accomodation of ye Countrey, at whose instance he had first sett it up; he had made such conveniences as ye like had never been known before in these parts, and therefore requested that his merits might be considered, & no other persons suffered to enter upon his Labours by oppression, to bereave him of that small benefit wch thought reasonable should accrue to him, & was far short of what those who endeavoured to take part with him imagined."

In the minutes of Council, held on May 27,[507] following, we find:—

"The case of Andrew Rudman & Andrew Sandel, Clerks, & their answers to ye Informations exhibited to this board, by Benjamin Chambers, relating to ye Scuylkill ferry, was read. Ordered thereupon, that notice be given to both ye sd parties, to appear at this Board next Council day."

A month later, June 23, 1704:[508]

"Andrew Rudman, ye Swedish Minister, & Benja. Chambers, appearing according to ye Ordr of ye last Council before ye Board, & their several applications being again read, B. Chambers, in answer to ye Swedes, offer'd a long Paper, wch proving too tedious, & ordered to be changed in ye Direction. It was referr'd to ye afternoon, & ye Council adjourned to four of ye Clock."

In the afternoon session of the Council:[509]

"The Paper of Benja. Chambers, in answer to the Swedes ministers offered in the morning, was read, & both Parties called in & heard, & the Consideration of it was deferred, & the Council adjourned to 8 in the morning."

Here all record of the case stops. What the final disposition of the matter was does not appear, as the minutes of the succeeding meetings are silent upon the subject.

---

[507] *Ibid* page 147.
[508] *Ibid* page 149.
[509] *Ibid* page 150.

When Dominie Rudmann, who was physically frail, first took charge of the Oxford and Radnor congregations, he walked to and from the city, stopping at the houses by the wayside, no matter of what nationality the inmates—whether English, Welsh, Swedish or German—catechising in some, reasoning in others, and often administering consolation in the hour of sorrow; while in some cases, where the occupants were too strongly imbued with Quakerism to heed his discourse, he would meet with a rebuff strong enough to cause him to obey the scriptural injunction—"To shake the dust from off his feet and pass on."

On these lonely pilgrimages he would frequently, when his strength was exhausted, sink down, faint and weary on a rock or stump of a tree, pray for both bodily and spiritual strength, and after thus refreshing himself again start upon his journey, singing a few verses of the good old rhythmical prayer of the Fatherland:

> "Liebster Jesu, gnadensonne,
> Meines herzens zuversicht,"

to cheer him on his way while toiling wearily through the forest, over hill and dale, to his distant charges.

He was frequently overtaken upon these journeys by the sudden storms so common in our country, with no protection but such as was afforded by the trees of the forest which happened to be near the road-side.

When he realized that his frail constitution would no longer sustain such exposure and fatigue, he tried to hire a horse in Philadelphia, but soon found that his slender means would not bear so great an outlay. Consequently there was no other remedy, when the weather permitted, but to continue his ministrations on foot.

It was not until Dominie Rudmann had thus served the congregations for three years that he was notified by Mr.

Chamberlain that he had been granted a gratuity by the Society in London. This amounted to a total of £62 sterling, from which he paid Mr. Club 15 pounds Pennsylvania currency for his services at Radnor, and £5, 7 shillings, to remove an old debt for ceiling Oxford church. He also bought a horse so that he could supply his distant charges with more certainty.

During Mr. Evans' absence in England, while he was in charge of Christ Church, a misunderstanding arose between the two ministers in relation to a bill of exchange, which induced Pastor Rudmann to resign the care of Oxford to Mr. Club, the Welsh schoolmaster at Christ Church. This he reported to the Society in a letter dated August 26, 1708, which proved his last communication thereto. He succumbed to his zeal on September 17, 1708, as foreshadowed in his letter:

"I am a sickly man, and now for seven weeks together in consumption, I have buried lately one of my daughters, and most that come to see me give me up for a dead man, which I do believe also. If I should die this time, what a miserable family I should leave behind me—a helpless widow, and two poor small children who cannot procure a farthing."[510]

On the day following his death, Dominie Rudmann, according to an old record, was attended to his last resting place in Wicacoa church by a long procession of mourners—Swedes, Hollanders, Englishmen and Germans—where his colleague and fellow-laborer Biörck tendered him the last service and buried him in front of the altar of the church which he had built. He delivered a funeral sermon in English on the text selected by Rudmann himself; Psalm 73: 24.

---

[510] Pennsylvania Records S. P. G., London.

All nationalities present followed with blessings the faithful laborer who had understood how to give in abundance to so many.

Dominie Rudmann had lived in America eleven years, and in the world not quite forty years, and left behind him his wife, who was one of the Mattson family, and two daughters, Gertrude and Anna Catherina Rudmann. His tomb bears the following inscription:

"MORS MIHI VITA IN COELO QUIES EST.

"This marble covers the remains of the Rev. Andreas Rudmann. Being sent hither from Sweden, he first founded and built this church; was, a constant faithful preacher, eleven years, in this country where he advanced true piety by sound doctrine and good example. He died 17, September 1708, aged 40 years."

Since the year 1840 the stone over his grave, together with other tombs within the church and chancel, have been hidden from view by the flooring then put into the church. The arrangement of the pews was also changed, the wide aisle up the centre being replaced by the two side aisles. The baptismal font, the two gilt cherubim and the tablet in front of the organ-loft are really all that remain at the present day of the original church, except the walls.

AUTOGRAPH OF GUSTAVUS ADOLPHUS.

Shortly after Pastor Rudmann's death, the old trouble between the Quakers and the Swedish Lutherans broke out anew, when it appears that forbearance upon the part of the Swedish Lutherans ceased to be a virtue. Sandel who, it seems, was a muscular Christian, attempted to take the law into his own hands, as is shown by the minutes of Council, August 11, 1709:[511]

"A Petition & Complaint from Benjamin Chambers to the Board, was read, setting forth, that pursuant to his Covenants, formerly entered into with this Govmt., at ye first erecting of his ferry over Skuylkill River, being employed in Repairing ye long Causey leading to the ferry on this side the said River, he was attacked by Andrew Sandal, minister of the Swedish Church in the County of Philadia., & by Violence drove from his work thereon; Whereupon, 'Tis Ordered, that the said minister, Andrew Sandal, attend this board the 16th Instant, about Eleven in the forenoon, to render an acct. of the said act, and the reason of his Interrupting a person employed in the Queen's High Way, in the necessary repairs thereof."

At the next meeting of Council, five days later, August 16, 1709, the accused clergyman appeared in his own behalf:[512]

"Andrew Sandal, the Swedish minister, according to order, appeared and the Petition and Complaint of B. Chambers being read to him, he desired a Copy of it, and that he might have time to answer it, being now new to him, for that he had not notice to appear at the board till last night.

"Ordered, that he have time till the first Council day next week."

In obedience to this order Pastor Sandel again appeared before Council, August 23, 1709,[513] with the following result:

"Pursuant to an Order of the 16th Instant, the Swedish minister, A. Sandel, appeared by an address to this Board in writing, gave his answer to the Petition & Complaint exhibited against him by B. Chambers,

---

511 "Colonial Records," vol. ii, pp. 477-8.

512 *Ibid* page 478.

513 *Ibid* page 484-5.

which being read, it appeared that the said minister, claimed a right to erect a fferry there on this side of Schuylkill, because the road & Causeway leading to the ferry is laid out thro' his land; & further Charged B. Chambers with a violation of his contract, with making spoil of the timber on the Land which he had taken of the owners thereof on this side of the River, with Divers other allegations in his own defence.

"But the Govr. and Council taking into Consideration, that Roads when once laid out for the Publick Service according to Law, are no longer the property of any particular person, but belong wholly to the Publick, & the Road leading from Philadia. to the said ferry, being generally called the Queen's Road, is therefore wholly under the Cognizance of this Board; and further, considering that all ferries upon such Publick Roads are a Privilege of the Proprietor, only by Virtue of the Royal Grant to him & his heirs. It is therefore unanimously ye opinion of the Govr. and Council, that neither the said minister, Andrew Sandel, nor any other person claiming a Right or Interest in the Land through which the said Road is laid out, has any better right to ye Road or ye adjoyning ferry than any other of the Queen's Subjects has or can claim to the same, and that no person under any pretence whatsoever; shall be allowed to erect a Publick ferry over the River Skuylkill, or any other water in such Roads as aforesaid, but by special Grant of the Proprietor & this Board. Adjourned."

Thus end the official records of this controversy, which stands out in such bold contrast to the "Great Law" promulgated by William Penn at Chester on the 7th day of 10th Month, called December, 1682, and which was intended to assure religious liberty to every resident of the Province.

INDEX.

C.

J.

K.

L.

M.

Q.

R.

S.

T.

U.

V.

W.